Training

for

E C D L

Editor

John Brennan

Blackrock Education Centre
2003

© Blackrock Education Centre

ISBN   0 9540287 3 2

Published by
Blackrock Education Centre, Kill Avenue, Dún Laoghaire, Co. Dublin, Ireland.

Tel. (+353 1) 2 302 709   Fax. (+353 1) 2 365 044
E-mail. ecdlsales@blackrock-edu.ie   Web. www.ecdlmanual.org   *and*   www.blackrock-edu.ie

First published   2003
Reprinted with minor changes   2003

""European Computer Driving Licence" and ECDL and Stars device are registered trade marks of The European Computer Driving Licence Foundation Limited in Ireland and other countries. Blackrock Education Centre is an independent entity from The European Computer Driving Licence Foundation Limited, and not affiliated with The European Computer Driving Licence Foundation Limited in any manner. Training for ECDL, Syllabus 4 may be used in assisting students to prepare for the ECDL Version 4.0 Syllabus Examination. Neither The European Computer Driving Licence Foundation Limited nor Blackrock Education Centre warrants that the use of this Training for ECDL, Syllabus 4 will ensure passing the ECDL Version 4.0 Syllabus Examination. Use of the ECDL-F Approved Courseware Logo on this product signifies that it has been independently reviewed and approved by ECDL-F as complying with the following standards:

Acceptable coverage of all courseware content related to the ECDL Syllabus Version 4.0.

This courseware material has not been reviewed for technical accuracy and does not guarantee that the end user will pass the ECDL Version 4.0 Syllabus Examination. Any and all assessment items and/or performance based exercises contained in this Training for ECDL, Syllabus 4 relate solely to this Training for ECDL, Syllabus 4 and do not constitute or imply certification by The European Driving Licence Foundation in respect of any ECDL examination. For details on sitting ECDL examinations in your country please contact your country's National ECDL/ICDL designated Licensee or visit The European Computer Driving Licence Foundation Limited web site at http://www.ecdl.com.

Candidates using this courseware material should have a valid ECDL/ICDL Skills Card. Without such a Skills Card, no ECDL/ICDL Examinations can be taken and no ECDL/ICDL certificate, nor any other form of recognition, can be given to the candidate.

ECDL/ICDL Skills Cards may be obtained from any Approved ECDL/ICDL Test Centre or from your country's National ECDL/ICDL designated Licensee.

References to the European Computer Driving Licence (ECDL) include the International Computer Driving Licence (ICDL). ECDL Syllabus Version 4.0 is published as the official syllabus for use within the European Computer Driving Licence (ECDL) and International Computer Driving Licence (ICDL) certification programme."Microsoft® Windows®, Microsoft® Office, Microsoft® Word®, Microsoft® Access®, Microsoft® Excel®, Microsoft® PowerPoint®, Microsoft® Internet Explorer® and Microsoft® Outlook® are either registered trademarks or trademarks of the Microsoft Corporation. The use of WinZip and the WinZip trademark is with the kind permission of WinZip Computing Incorporated.

Other products mentioned in this manual may be registered trademarks or trademarks of their respective companies or corporations.

The companies, organisations, products, the related people, their positions, names, addresses and other details used for instructional purposes in this manual and its related support materials on the manual's support website **www.ecdlmanual.org** are fictitious. No association with any real company, organisations, products or people are intended nor should any be inferred.

Blackrock Education Centre

Director/Stiurthóir: Séamus Cannon / Séamus Ó Canainn
Walter Cullinane (Chairperson), Deirdre Keyes (Vice Chairperson), Betty Behan, Valerie Burke, Mary Crosbie,
Phil Caulfield, Dóirín Creamer, Patrick Fox, Kieran Griffin, Joseph Keane, Jean Hughes, James Malseed,
Thérèse McPhillips, Matt Reville, Donal Ryan, Cora Uí Chuinn.

Blackrock Learning

This manual is produced by Blackrock Learning,
a division of Blackrock Education Centre.
Project Management for this production by John Brennan and Siobhán Cluskey.

Credits

Text
Paula Kelly, Denise O'Connor

Editorial Consultant
Kristin Jensen

Layout
Annette Bolger

Line Drawings
Helen Mac Mahon

Cover Design
Generation Graphics

Original Design
Tom Mac Mahon

Website
Emmet Caulfield
Thomas Holmes

Blackrock Education Centre is an accredited ECDL Test Centre

Contents

About This Book

The Manual

'Training for ECDL Syllabus 4' offers a practical, step-by-step guide for any person who wishes to use the Microsoft Office 2000 suite, Outlook Express and Internet Explorer on Windows 2000 PCs. It has been designed primarily as a study aid for students of the European Computer Driving Licence (the International Computer Driving Licence – ICDL – outside Europe).

The manual has been approved by the ECDL Foundation as suitable for use with the new ECDL/ICDL Syllabus, Version 4.

Design

Every use has been made of the expertise we have gained from working closely with ECDL over many years. Additionally, the knowledge and skills of our substantial pool of trainers hugely influenced the content and layout of the material.

We use plain English, not computer jargon. We take you point by point through detailed explanations and action sequences. We pay particular attention to relating what you see on the pages of the manual to what you see on the computer screen. Where necessary, we include small amounts of additional information to enhance your understanding of very important topics.

You will also find that the A4 size of the manual, the side-by-side layout of graphics and text, and the spiral binding all combine to make it an ideal *desk-top friendly* training manual.

Exercises and Web Support

Throughout each module, there are carefully placed exercises which you can use to practice and reinforce the new skills and concepts. Any files you need may be downloaded directly from our support website **www.ecdlmanual.org** free of charge.

You will also find extra exercise materials there. Practical exercises, self-check tests and answers, have been developed for each module. These are also available on our support site without obligation.

A new feature of our web support is the development of interactive material for Module 7. Users of this manual can send e-mails and receive responses, download sample files, complete a sample on-line form, handle media files, review different types of links, manipulate on-line text, and review web page frames all on-line at **www.ecdlmanual.org/syllabus4**. Access to these particular resources is described in the relevant section of Module 7 of this manual.

This manual was produced – writing, design and layout – using only the Microsoft Office suite of programs and the skills described in the manual. The screen shots were captured using a small utility program and most were inserted directly onto the page.

The Editor

Foreword

Blackrock Education Centre provides support services to teachers and to partners in education under the auspices of the Department of Education and Science in Ireland. It is one of a network of thirty Centres dispersed throughout the country. For many years the Education Centre has provided training for teachers in the use of Information and Communications Technology. While introductory courses were always popular, we frequently experienced difficulties in progressing beyond the basics. There was a large gap between the introductory course and what was being offered at university, with little in between that was both comprehensive and practical. There was a need for a training programme that measured progressive development of competency across a range of skills.

The European Computer Driving Licence (ECDL) provides a very good framework for such a training programme. Blackrock Education Centre put a pilot programme in place in 1997 and subsequently opened it up to larger numbers. The initial response was very encouraging and interest has grown over the years. The demand for I.T. training in Ireland increased dramatically with the Schools IT2000 – the national I.T. programme launched by the Department of Education and Science – and since then, the Blackrock initiative has been supported by the National Centre for Technology in Education.

The key attractions of ECDL/ICDL are the focus on practical competency and the flexible syllabus, independent of platform or software. These enabled us to tailor our training while maintaining standards that are recognised internationally. It is the experience of Blackrock Education Centre that completing the ECDL/ICDL programme gives the user confidence in using the computer, a significant level of practical skill and an excellent preparation for further study.

In the Information Age, all of us are required to engage in continuous lifelong learning. We have been aware that many of the schools we work with want to offer a programme to parents and to other members of the community. Increased access to learning opportunities, through libraries and other community institutions, is more and more the norm. Our training programme has encouraged this development and many schools have themselves become accredited ECDL/ICDL test centres offering local training. In addition, *Training for ECDL*, our first manual, has come to be used extensively in the commercial and corporate training sectors, both in Ireland and abroad.

We are pleased to note how many users of our training manuals comment on their continued usefulness as reference materials after they have completed their courses. We believe this reflects well on all who work on our development projects who deserve great credit in maintaining high standards. Particular thanks are due to Director Séamus Ó Canainn, to John Brennan, Project Manager, to Paula Kelly and Denise O'Connor, the authors and to Siobhán Cluskey, the Executive Director of Blackrock Learning. These training materials are a testament to the thoroughness with which they have addressed the requirements of lifelong learning in the Information Age.

Walter Cullinane
Chairperson

Blackrock Education Centre
June 2003

ECDL

The European Computer Driving Licence
(ICDL outside Europe)

The European Computer Driving Licence is a means of indicating that you have acquired the basic skills to use a computer in a wide variety of applications, just as your standard Driving Licence indicates that you have acquired the skills necessary to drive a car on public roads.

As with learning to drive a car, a variety of skills has to be learnt before the licence is issued. Also, it is important that these skills be acquired by actually using the computer: one does not expect to have a vehicle Driving Licence issued just by reading all about it and answering questions in a written examination.

The ECDL concept originated in Finland in 1988 and has spread all over Europe since then, with headquarters now established in Dublin. In each country, ECDL operates under the auspices of and in association with the national computer society. In Ireland, this is the Information Society Commission.

The success of ECDL throughout Europe has been due to the well thought out and structured modular approach which allows training establishments to provide flexible training in basic computer skills with varying degrees of emphasis according to the candidates' needs, while at the same time maintaining uniformly high standards.

ECDL has now spread beyond European borders and attracted the attention of trainers and training establishments in many parts of the world. It is now known inter-nationally as ICDL – the International Computer Driving Licence.

At present, there are seven modules in the ECDL syllabus. On first registering for an ECDL test, candidates are assigned a unique ECDL Skills Card by an ECDL authorised test centre. The card is used by the test centre to maintain the candidate's record of success with the various tests. The modules can be studied and tested in any order. Individual modules can be completed at different training centres or even in different countries.

ECDL approved computer based tests are used by some test centres to assess candidates. These tests vary in duration. There is also an official paper based test. These tests are of 45 minutes duration each. All tests, except the paper based Module 1 test are hands-on tests at the computer. The paper based Module 1 test is the only written test. Candidates are required to pass all seven assessments within three years of their first successful test. On completion of all seven tests, the Skills Card is returned to the national ECDL office which then issues the ECDL certificate.

The issue of the certificate – the European Computer Driving Licence – is administered in Ireland by ECDL Ireland/ICS Skills, which controls accreditation and provides tester training on a national level. It also monitors very closely the standards under which ECDL/ICDL training and testing are carried out at the hundreds of accredited training centres throughout the country.

Training and training materials for the ECDL/ICDL are the responsibility of the individual training establishment. Blackrock Education Centre has over twenty years' experience in Information Technology training and has been closely associated with ECDL/ICS Skills Ireland from the beginning, organising and administering one of the first ECDL/ICDL pilot projects in this country.

Before You Begin

BYB

Before You Begin

Section 1   The Computer Workplace

1.1   Introduction

The Microsoft Office Suite of Applications – Word, Access, Excel, PowerPoint, Outlook and Explorer – share many common features. Opening an application, its appearance on the computer screen and the way in which you work with it are similar across the whole suite.

This chapter describes a number of the most common features, which are important for the effective use of the computer. It also explains how to use them. These features and skills are important elements of the course.

This chapter is best studied with two purposes in mind. The first is for you to gain an overview of the common elements and skills that are required throughout the course. The second is that in being aware of them before you study the other modules, you will be better prepared to understand and use the skills required for each module as you come to it.

1.2   Where You Work

The first thing you see when the computer has finished starting up is the **Desktop** screen. It is referred to as the desktop because you will be using it as you would the top of a real office desk.

You will place new or previously created work here as you would place a writing pad, a sheet of paper or a calculator on top of your real desk. You will do this electronically, of course, on the computer.

Items on the desktop are represented by small pictures, or **icons**, with their names underneath.

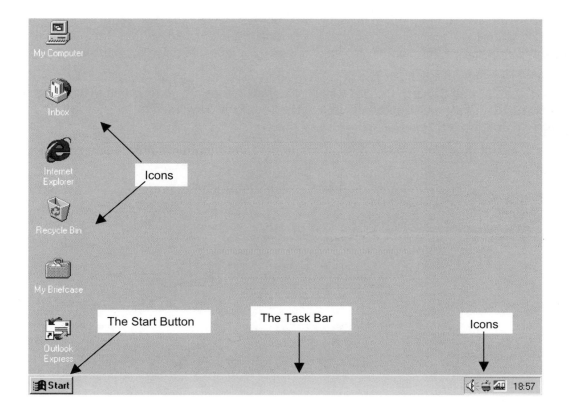

1.3   The Taskbar

The **taskbar** is a bar (or strip) that appears along the bottom of the **Desktop**. It is usually visible no matter what program you are using, although it can be hidden if you want to make more space available for your work.

The taskbar contains a number of icons in the form of **buttons**. A button is an icon that you can click on to perform a specific action. Some buttons are always on the taskbar while others appear on it from time to time, depending on the work in progress.

Think of the items on the taskbar as if they were drawers in a real desk where things can be put away when they are not being used. The taskbar in the illustration below shows some examples.

- The **Start** button is permanently in position at the left of the taskbar.

- The **Microsoft Word** button represents a document, named **BYB jb** here.

- The **Calculator** button represents a calculator on which you can make calculations.

- The **Printers** button represents a folder that contains information about printers.

When a button has a **pressed in** appearance like the **Calculator** button above, it indicates that the Calculator is the **active** item, one that is currently displayed and that you are working on at the moment. The other items may or may not be visible on the desktop but the buttons on the taskbar remind you of their presence.

Clicking a button on the taskbar makes the object it represents the active item. If it had been hidden, it will now be displayed.

1.4   The Keyboard

The computer **keyboard** is similar to the standard typewriter keyboard. Most computer keyboards, however, have an additional numeric keypad to the right of the usual keys. There is also an extra row of keys at the top, called **Function** keys, which are used by some programs or applications.

In addition, there are some extra keys that are frequently used in computer work. For example, the **arrow** keys can control the cursor on the screen. The **Tab** key can move from box to box when forms have to be filled in. The most commonly used of the extra keys are the **Ctrl** (Control), **Alt** (Alternative), **Backspace**, **Delete** and the **Enter** keys.

Familiarity with basic keyboard skills – simple typing – will be an advantage if you are going to use the computer a lot.

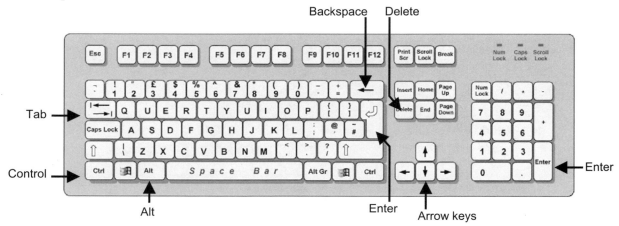

1.5   The Mouse

The **mouse** is the principal means of controlling the computer. It is a small box that you move around on a pad called a **mouse mat**.

The usual mouse has two buttons, on the left and right.

As you move the mouse on the mat, a **cursor** (or **pointer**), usually in the shape of a small arrow, moves on the screen in tandem with the mouse. Move the mouse to the right and the cursor moves to the right, and so on.

The **cursor**
or **pointer**

When the pointer is placed in a particular position – over an icon, for example – pressing a button causes the computer to perform an action related to the icon.

Using the mouse may appear deceptively simple at first. Learning how to use it properly takes practice, however, and is crucial for confident and easy use of the computer.

Three actions are performed with the mouse – **pointing**, **clicking** and **dragging**.

1   When you **point** to an object on the desktop, move the mouse until the tip of the pointer rests on, or inside, the object.

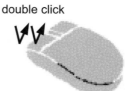

Practise: Point to the **Start** button.

2   To **click** on a object, first point to it. Then quickly **press and release** the left mouse button. (Unless otherwise stated, it is usually the left-hand button that is clicked. **Left-click** and **Right-click** are often used to describe which button to use.)

single click

- A **single click** selects an object or performs an action.

   Practise: Click on the **Recycle Bin** icon. The icon darkens, or is highlighted. This shows that you have selected it.

- A **double click** means clicking twice in rapid succession. This performs a different action, such as opening a folder or starting a program or application.

   double click

   Practise: Double click on the **Recycle Bin**. A window opens to display the contents of the bin. (If the bin has nothing in it, the window will be empty.)

3   To **drag** means to move an object on the desktop with the mouse.

   Practise: Place the tip of the **pointer** on an icon e.g. the recycle bin, on the desktop. Hold down the left mouse button and move/drag the mouse. An outline of the icon moves with the mouse.

   Release the button to 'drop' the icon in its new position. (It may spring back to its original position, however, depending on how your computer has been set up.)

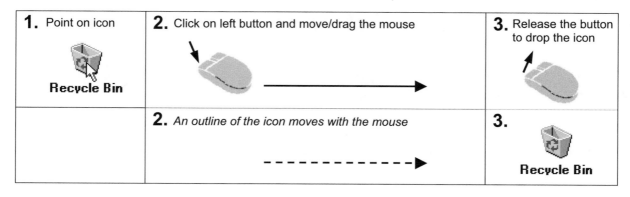

1. Point on icon Recycle Bin	**2.** Click on left button and move/drag the mouse	**3.** Release the button to drop the icon
	2. *An outline of the icon moves with the mouse*	**3.** Recycle Bin

1.6   Pointers

The **pointer** (or **mouse pointer** or **cursor**) can have different shapes that are used for different purposes. The shapes appear automatically, depending on the action being performed. They give the user a visual indication of their purpose.

Some of the more common pointers are described here.

- The **arrow pointer** is probably the most common. It is used to select objects, to click buttons and to choose options in menus and on toolbars.

- The **busy** pointer (or **hourglass**) appears when the computer is engaged in an activity that will take a few moments to complete. You should wait until the action is completed and the pointer resumes its original shape.

- The **help** pointer (or **question mark**) appears when you click the **Help** icon on the toolbar. When you point to an object or menu with this pointer, a pop-up explanation is displayed.

- The mouse pointer on a **text** document is called the I-beam. Its tall, thin shape enables it to be placed between letters in the text.

- The **flashing vertical line** you see on a text page is *not* a mouse pointer. It is the **insertion point** at which the next thing you type or insert will appear. *(Do not confuse it with the mouse pointer above.)*

- Click with the **mouse pointer** to place the Insertion Point where you want to type, make corrections or insert text. (Then move the mouse pointer away to avoid confusion.)

Flashing
Insertion Point

Once upon a|

Mouse Pointer

When you are using an application such as a word processor, the action you are engaged in or the function you choose determines which mouse pointer appears. Some other pointers and their functions are described below.

- The **crosshair** pointer is used as a drawing tool or to select a specific area of a graphic.

- The **resize** pointer can be vertical, horizontal or diagonal, depending on where you place it. It appears when you select shapes or graphics to be resized.

- The **move** pointer is used to move graphics from one position to another on the desktop or on a page.

- This pointer appears when you are trying some option that is not available. It may appear momentarily when, for example, you are dragging an object from one location to another and the object cannot be 'dropped' until you reach the new location.

1.7   Office 2000 Pointers

The **I-beam** pointer in Office 2000 is associated with the way the text will be aligned on the page. (Aligning text is described in Module 3, Section 3.2.2.) The alignment icons appear beside or under the I-beam to indicate how the text will be aligned.

Left aligns the text

Centre aligns the text

Left aligns the text
and applies a left indent

Right aligns the text

You can place text anywhere in the document by double clicking the position and then typing the text. This process is known as **Click and Type**. Click and Type automatically applies the alignment and/or indentation. To disable Click and Type:

- Select **Options** in the **Tools** menu.

- Click the **Edit** tab in the window that appears.

- Click to remove the tick from the **Enable click and type box**.

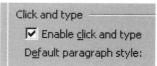

1.8   Windows

Windows are used to let the user 'see' what is stored in the computer. A window is a panel that appears on the desktop. It gives the user a picture of what is essentially an invisible electronic item.

A window enables the user to relate the (invisible) electronic files in the computer to objects in the real world. The files are represented by **icons**.

The illustration shows the **Control Panel** window of the computer. By clicking on the icons, the user has access to a variety of settings which can then be adjusted as required.)

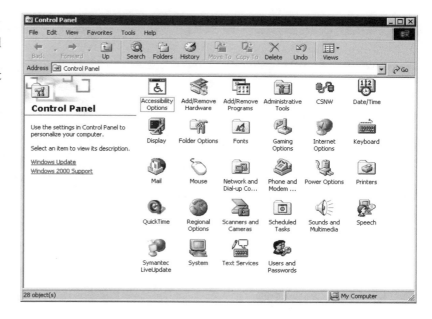

Important: Do *not* open or make any changes to control panels until you have learned how to use them.

When you are using the computer, various windows appear on the desktop from time to time. Many windows are similar to that in the illustration, serving to show the contents of a folder or disk, for example.

A special window – called a **dialogue box** – allows you to make choices, such as how many copies of a document are to be printed. Other dialogue boxes present information for your attention and require you to click an **OK** button before you can continue.

Working with windows is described in detail in Module 2, Section 2.

Section 2   Opening an Application

2.1   Introduction

Before you begin your work you must open the application, such as a word processor, that you will need to produce the work. You can open an application in a number of ways.

The two most usual ways to open an application are:

- Using the **Start** button on the left of the taskbar at the bottom of the desktop.

- Using the **Office Toolbar**, if it is displayed on the desktop.

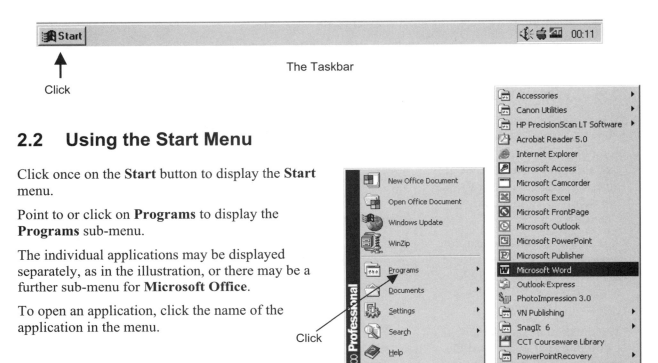

The Taskbar

Click

2.2   Using the Start Menu

Click once on the **Start** button to display the **Start** menu.

Point to or click on **Programs** to display the **Programs** sub-menu.

The individual applications may be displayed separately, as in the illustration, or there may be a further sub-menu for **Microsoft Office**.

To open an application, click the name of the application in the menu.

Click

Sub-Menu

2.3   Using the Office Toolbar

The **Office Toolbar** is a special small toolbar that usually appears at the top of the screen. (It may not be visible on some computers.)

There are usually buttons for the four Office applications: Word, Excel, PowerPoint and Access. Other buttons may also be present.

To open an Office application, click once on its icon on the toolbar.

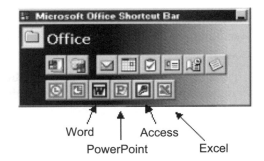

Word

Access

PowerPoint

Excel

Section 3   Selecting

3.1   Selecting Text

From time to time you will want to change the look of your document. You may want to make a particular piece of text larger than the rest, colour it, underline it and so on.

The first step in making changes to a piece of text or an image is to **select** it. It must be selected so that the Application knows what you want to apply the changes to.

When text is selected, a black colour appears over it to **highlight** it, just as you would use a highlighter on text on a sheet of paper.

From time to time you will **want to change** the look of your document.

Highlighted Text

Text can be selected in many different ways, depending on your requirements. These are described in Module 3, Section 2.

3.2   Selecting Graphics

A **graphic** or **image** is an **object**, as distinct from a piece of text. Text continues down the page line after line until it fills the page. An object can be placed on the page independently of text or other objects and can be moved about at will. The graphics (illustrations) used in this manual are objects.

To select an object, click once inside the object. When an object is selected, it is not highlighted in the same way as text. Instead, a series of square dots, called **handles**, appear around it as in the illustration.

The size of an object can be changed, as can the way text flows around it. See the section on **Graphics** in Module 3, Section 4.2, for detailed information.

A Selected Graphic

3.3   Selecting in Tables

A **table** presents information in rows and columns. The table appears on the page as a **grid**.

The columns are identified across the top by letters of the alphabet. The rows are numbered down the left-hand side. The individual boxes in the grid are called **cells**.

To select a number of cells, drag through them from side to side, from top to bottom or diagonally. The selected cells are **highlighted** as with text.

A whole column can be selected by clicking the letter at the top of the column. A row can be selected by clicking the number of the row on the left.

To select the whole table, click **Select Table** in the **Table** menu.

Tables are described in detail in Module 3, Section 4.1.

Munster Office Returns				
	A	B	C	D	E
1	Munster Office First Quarterly Report				
2					
3					
4			September	October	Novembe
5					
6					
7		Telephones	116	79	56
8		Answer Mach.	47	50	35
9		Calculators	9	38	17
10		Shredders	297	225	120
11		Laminators	79	56	34
12		Binding Mach.	83	88	38
13		Mini Recorders	57	69	7
14		Transcribers	57	69	36
15			745	674	343
16					
17					

Section 4 Copy, Cut and Paste

4.1 Copying and Cutting

Copy, **cut** and **paste** are common to most applications and are listed in the **Edit** menu.

Before you can copy or cut an item, it must first be **selected**.

When a piece of text or an object is **copied**, the original stays in position in the document and the copy is stored in a part of the computer's memory called the **Clipboard**.

When a piece of text or an object is **cut**, a copy is stored on the Clipboard but the original is deleted.

The Clipboard is normally invisible to the user so when you copy a piece of text, for example, nothing appears to happen.

The Clipboard can only hold one item at a time. When you copy or cut something, anything previously on the Clipboard is discarded and is no longer available.

Edit	View	Insert	Format	Too
Undo Typing			Ctrl+Z	
Repeat Typing			Ctrl+Y	
Cut			Ctrl+X	
Copy			Ctrl+C	
Paste			Ctrl+V	
Paste Special...				

4.2 Pasting

A copy of what is on the Clipboard can be **pasted** into another part of the same document or into a different document.

It can also be pasted into a document in a different application.

If required, copies can be pasted repeatedly – to place a row of graphics across a page, for example.

The illustration on the right shows part of a spreadsheet copied and pasted into a Word document.

Munster Office Returns

	A	B	C	D	E
1	Munster Office First Quarterly Report				
2					
3					
4			September	October	Novembe
5					
6					
7		Telephones	116	79	56
8		Answer Mach.	47	50	35
9		Calculators	9	38	17
10		Shredders	297	225	120
11		Laminators	79	56	34
12		Binding Mach.	83	88	38
13		Mini Recorders	57	69	7
14		Transcribers	57	69	36
15			745	674	343
16					
17					

Spreadsheet

Word →

	September
Telephones	116
Answer Mach.	47
Calculators	9
Shredders	297
Laminators	79
Binding Mach.	83
Mini Recorders	57
Transcribers	57
	745

4.3 Toolbar Buttons

Cut, Copy and Paste buttons are also available on many toolbars.

Cut, copy and paste are described in detail in Module 3, Section 2.4.

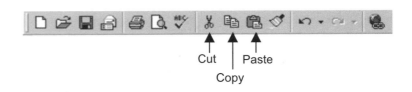

Cut | Paste

Copy

Section 5   Toolbars

5.1   Tools for Work

A **toolbar** is a strip, or **bar**, that (usually) stretches across the top of the desktop. It contains buttons and icons for menus, commands and tools needed by the user to work on a document.

Some commands and tools, such as **Save** and **Print**, are common to most applications. Others are specific to certain applications or parts of applications. A word processor will need commands for use with text, while a database or spreadsheet program will need to deal with numbers, for example.

When there are many commands, tools and buttons available, they will not all fit on a single toolbar, so several toolbars may be necessary. Toolbars occupy space on the desktop, so only those needed for the purpose in hand are usually displayed.

5.2   The Menu Bar

The most commonly used toolbar in applications is the **Menu Bar**. It contains a number of menus which, in turn, contain lists of commands for use with the application. Some menus, such as the **File** and **Edit** menus, are common to almost all applications. Most of the other menus are specific to the particular application. The **Word** Menu Bar is shown here.

| File Edit View Insert Format Tools Table Window Help |

Click on a menu name to display the menu. Click on an item in the menu to perform an action. The action may be to save a document, for example, or to open a window that gives access to other options or choices.

Many of the commands in the menus can be duplicated at the keyboard. These **keyboard shortcuts**, if available, are shown at the right of the menu item. Pressing the **Ctrl** key and the letter **S**, for example, **saves** the current document.

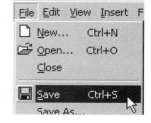

5.3   Office 2000 Menu Bars

It is important to note that menus in Office 2000 differ from the menus in earlier versions of Office in that only the more frequently used items are displayed at first.

To display the full menu, click the chevron symbol.

The additional items are then displayed against a lighter background.

Note also that many buttons may not be displayed on the toolbars (see following sections) at first. When Office 2000 detects the user accessing these 'hidden' buttons, it automatically places them on the toolbar for future use.

Chevrons

5.4   Other Toolbars

A toolbar with commonly used items in an application is called its **Standard Toolbar**. The **Word Standard toolbar** is illustrated here. Commonly used word processing functions are accessed by clicking the appropriate button on the toolbar.

Clicking a button allows the user to open a new document, save, copy, paste, print, and much more. Clicking the **ABC** button, for example, checks the spelling of the current document.

The **zoom** tool is used to alter the size of the document as it appears in the window. Click the arrow to display a menu. Then click on the magnification you want to use, or type your own preferred size in the box.

Note that the size of the document as displayed on the screen is independent of the size that will be printed by the printer.

Another example of a toolbar is the **Formatting toolbar**. It has menus and buttons for some of the most frequently used tools needed to change the appearance of text.

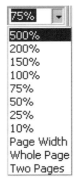

Selecting text and clicking a button on this bar allows you to change the font type, its size, make it bold, make it italic, align it on the page and much more.

5.5   Displaying Toolbars

Most applications do not display all their toolbars. This leaves the maximum amount of workspace available for the document you are working on.

A list of available toolbars can be displayed in a **sub-menu** of the **View** menu. This allows you to display an additional toolbar or remove one that is currently displayed.

When there is a **tick** beside a toolbar name in the menu, the toolbar is currently displayed in the application window.

To **remove** a toolbar from the window, click the name in the menu again. The tick is removed and the toolbar is hidden.

To display the **Drawing** toolbar in Word, for example, do the following:

- Select **Toolbars** in the **View** menu.

- Click **Drawing** in the **Toolbar** menu.
  The Drawing toolbar appears at the bottom of the Word window.

You can create your own toolbars, customise the ones already there, and place your own buttons on a toolbar. Instructions are given in the **Help** system (see Section 7 in this module).

5.6 Moving Toolbars

Toolbars normally appear at the top of the application window but they may be placed elsewhere according to personal preferences.

To move a toolbar, click on a blank space on the toolbar and drag it to its new position.

If there is no blank space, drag the **slider handle**, the ribbed area at the left of the toolbar.

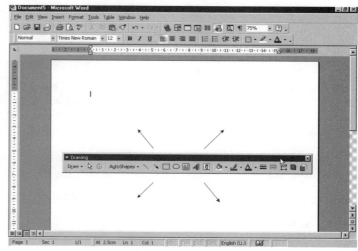

To return a toolbar to its normal place, drag it back to its original position.

5.7 Hidden Buttons

Chevron symbols (») on toolbars in Office 2000 indicate that there are hidden buttons.

To display the buttons, click the chevrons.

Alternatively, move the toolbars to a new position on the desktop to view the wider range of buttons.

If a toolbar is obscured by another, use the **slider handle** to reposition either one.

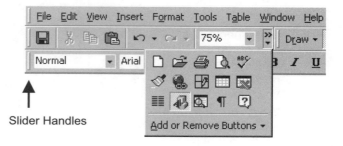

Slider Handles

5.8 Adding Buttons

Buttons may be added to, or removed from, an Office 2000 toolbar. To add a superscript button, for example, do the following.

- Display the toolbar you want to modify, if it is not already displayed.

- In the **View** menu, select **Toolbars** and then **Customise** in the sub-menu.

- Click the **Commands** tab and select **Format** in the **Categories** panel.

- Scroll to find **Superscript** in the **Commands** panel and click on it to select it.

- Drag **Superscript** onto the toolbar.
    (The mouse pointer changes to a toolbar pointer during this process.)

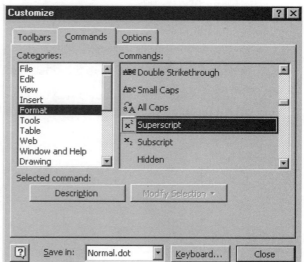

To remove a button, drag it off the toolbar until an **X** appears in the mouse pointer. Then release the mouse button.

Section 6   Saving

6.1   Saving a Document

It is very important to save a permanent copy of your document. If you don't, it will no longer exist when you turn off the computer and all your hard work will have been wasted! You can save your document on the computer's hard disk, on a floppy disk, on a zip disk or other media.

The procedure for saving a document for the first time is different from saving changes to it afterwards. The first time you save a document, the computer needs to know certain details.

To save a document for the **first time**, do the following.

- Click **Save** in the **File** menu.
  Alternatively, click the **Save** button on the toolbar.

  The **Save As** window opens.

- Type a name for the document in the **File Name** box.

  Use a name that will easily identify the document for you later.

  What you type will replace anything that is already in the box.

- Make sure that the folder or disk where you want to save the document appears in the **Save in** box.

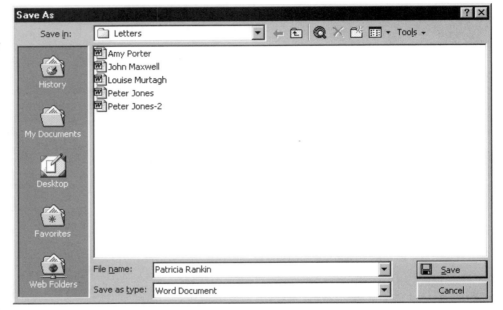

- Click the **Save** button to save the document.

When you save a document, the name you have given it appears in the Title Bar at the top of the screen. (An unsaved file usually has a name such as 'Document 1'.)

See Module 2, Section 3.3 for detailed instructions on how to save your work.

6.2   Saving Changes to a Document

As you work on a document, you should save your work from time to time as you proceed. If the computer 'crashes' or if there's a power failure, you will lose any unsaved work. When you save regularly, only the work done since the last save will be lost and any inconvenience will be minimised.

There are two methods you can use:

Save Button

- Click the **Save** button on the toolbar.

- Click **Save** in the **File** menu.

As the computer already has the information you typed in when you first saved the document, the **Save As** window does not appear again and your work is saved with the minimum of disruption.

> Use **Auto Recover** to save files automatically after a set time interval, e.g. every 10 minutes. Then only work done since the last Auto Recovery save will be lost if there is a major problem. See Module 2, Section 3.3.10.

6.3   Good Saving Practice

Save soon and save often. It is good practice to name and save a document from the earliest stage of its creation. Do not wait until you have finished the document before saving it. If a problem should occur before the document is saved, you may lose your work.

On beginning a new document in Word, for example, you should name and save it immediately.

As you continue to work on the document, you should click the **Save** icon on the toolbar at regular intervals. *Alternatively*, select **Save** in the **File** menu. In the event of serious mishap, this will ensure that only the most recent work is lost. Previously saved work will not be affected.

Section 7   The Help System

7.1   On-line Help

While you are using the computer, there are comprehensive **Help** systems available on the screen to assist you with problems that may arise in the course of your work.

System help assists you with using the computer. It is available in the **Start** menu.

Application help assists you with using an application. It is available in the **Help** menu on the **Menu Bar** in each application.

In both cases there are different types of help available, depending on the task. Step-by-step instructions are also available for procedures with which you may not be familiar.

As both System help and Application help are similar and are used in the same way, the following examples apply to both.

System Help

7.2   Using Help

The **Help** systems can be used for general information as well as for specific queries.

- To use the **System** help, select **Help** in the **Start** menu.
  To use **Application** help, select **Contents and Index** in the **Help** menu.
  The Help window opens.

- Check that the **Contents** tab at the top of the window is clicked.
  A list of **books** is displayed according to topic.

- Double click a book to 'open' it and display further books or topics.
  When you open the book with the information you are looking for, a list of subject headings is displayed with **question mark** buttons on the left.

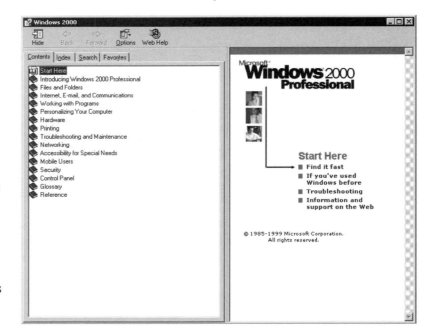

A **question mark** button means that this is the actual help topic itself.

- Click a question mark to display detailed help or instructions on the topic.

  The detailed information relating to your topic is presented in the right-hand pane.

  The other Help topics are in a new window (see right). The Help topics remain listed in the left-hand pane for easy reference. Minimise the window to hide it temporarily if you want to refer to it again later. This saves the trouble of searching for it afresh.

- To print out the help, select **Print Topic** in the Help window **Options** menu.

- Click **Help Topics** to return to the main **Help** window.

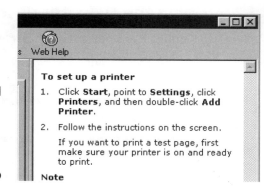

7.3 Searching for Help by Topic

The **index** is probably the most convenient way of finding help if you know what you are looking for.

Click the **Index** tab in the main Help window for help on a specific topic. The index gives a wider choice of topics than are listed under the **Contents** tab.

To search for help on a subject or topic, type a word or words in the box at the top of the window. As you type, a list – or index – of related topics appears in the box underneath. You may have to scroll to see them all if the list is very long.

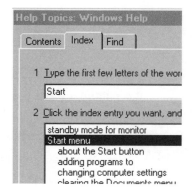

Double click the appropriate index entry to display a Help window as before. Alternatively, click the topic to select it. Then click the **Display** button at the bottom of the window.

Click the **Find** tab to look for specific words or phrases. Use this option if you can't find the topic you are looking for under the **Contents** or **Index** tabs.

Type the word in the top box. Some related words are shown underneath to help you narrow your search. The Help system is searched for occurrences of the word you typed in.

Click on a topic and then click the **Display** button to display it.

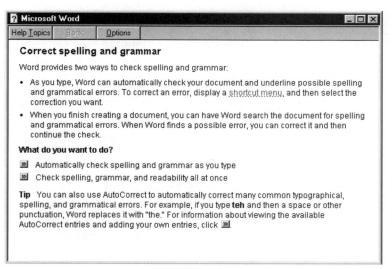

A Word Help Window

7.4   Using the Help Windows

The Help window has the usual **minimise**, **maximise** and **close** buttons as well as its own buttons.

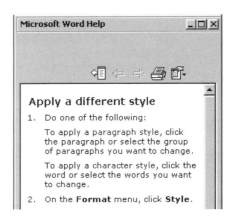

- Click the **Toggle** button to hide or replace the tabs window.

- Click the **Back** button to move back to the previous topic you looked at.

- Click the **Help Topics** button to return to the **Contents** window.

- Click the **Options** button to display menu options that toggle the display of tabs, navigate through pages, to print the information and so on.

Note that topics that have related or additional information in other areas of the Help file will have links (blue underlined words) that simply have to be clicked to bring you to the new information.

7.5   ScreenTips

ScreenTips displays information about different objects on the screen. Use ScreenTips to find information about toolbar buttons or menu commands, for example. ScreenTips can also be used to provide information about objects in the various windows that appear from time to time.

To see a ScreenTip for a menu command, toolbar button or screen region, do the following.

- Select **What's This?** in the **Help** menu.
  The cursor changes to an arrow with a question mark.

- Click the item about which you want information.
  A **Help** box which describes the selected element appears.

- To **close** the Help box, click anywhere else on the screen.

ScreenTips are useful when you are asked to select preferences or make decisions in a window called a **dialogue box**. (A dialogue box is a window in which you can select preferences or enter information, such as the Save As window.)

- Click the **Question Mark** button at the top right of the title bar of the window.

- The cursor changes to an arrow with a question mark.

- Click the part of the window or the object for which you want help.
  A **Help** box appears, as before.

- If there is no Question Mark button in the window, click the item for which you want help and then press the **Shift** + **F1** keys on the keyboard instead.

7.6   The Office Assistant

One of the items in the Help menu is the **Office Assistant**. It appears in Word as **Microsoft Word Help**, in Excel as **Microsoft Excel Help**, and so on. The Office Assistant can answer your questions, offer tips and provide help for a task that you may want to carry out.

To use the Office Assistant, do the following:

Office Assistant
Button

- Click the **Office Assistant** button on the toolbar or press the **F1** key on the keyboard.

  Alternatively, select **Microsoft** (*Name*) **Help** in the **Help** menu.

  The Assistant appears as a small window with a paper clip 'character'.

  A **speech bubble** contains a box where you can type a question or key words for help on a specific topic.

- Click **Search** when you have typed your request.

  A list of relevant topics appears. Click the one you require.

- A **Tips** option in the speech bubble box provides hints on using some of the features of the application or details of keyboard shortcuts.

  A tip is also available when a yellow **light bulb** appears in the Assistant. Click the light bulb to see the tip.

- Click the **Close** button to close the speech bubble or tips box at any time.

  Note that this doesn't close the Office Assistant itself, just the speech bubble.

- If the Assistant is still on the screen, the speech bubble can be reopened at any time by double clicking the Assistant **title bar**.

- The Office Assistant sometimes gives **Suggested Help** automatically. It senses what you are doing and appears when it thinks you might like some assistance, whether you do or not.

  The help it offers is relevant to the specific task you are performing.

- To close the Office Assistant, click the **Close** button as usual.

Close Button

In Office 2000, a 'lightbulb' may appear on the screen when you are performing a task.

Click the lightbulb to display help related to the task.

7.7   Wizards

Wizard is a term used to describe a set of instructions that lead you through the steps of performing a task. The wizard asks you various questions about the available options. When you make your choices, the wizard then performs the task for you.

Wizards are usually available for complex tasks that involve many steps, such as creating a table or performing a Mail Merge.
(See Tables in Module 3, Section 4.1 and Mail Merge in Module 3, Section 5.)

The advantage of using a wizard is that it simplifies a complex procedure – you just follow the steps. Automating the task also saves time. The disadvantage of using a wizard is that you may have less control over the final result, as your choice of options may be limited.

We shall see some examples of using wizards later in the course.

Section 8   Settings

8.1   Default Settings

When the computer is switched on, it presents its information and screen displays in a certain manner. The colour scheme of the desktop, the arrangement of the icons, the size of the display font, the behaviour of the mouse and much more are all preset. These preset values for the different features are referred to as the **default** settings, or **defaults**.

Defaults are used by the computer when the user does not specify any other values. Individual users, however, can change the defaults to suit individual preferences or for specific purposes.

The original defaults remain available at all times and can be restored by either cancelling the new settings or choosing the default options, as explained below.

8.2   Application Display Settings

An application usually display a document in a number of ways.

Different displays, or **Views**, allow the user to work on the document in the most convenient way for a particular purpose. The different **Page Views** available in Word are shown here.

Click **View** in the **Menu Bar** to display a list of views with small buttons on the left. The button for the view currently displayed has a 'pressed in' appearance. Word views are described in detail in Module 3, Section 1.2.

The **View** menu also allows the user to display or hide the **Ruler**. When a tick appears beside **Ruler** in the menu, it is currently displayed. To hide the ruler, click it in the menu again. The ruler is hidden and the tick removed.

Toolbars are listed in a sub-menu of the **View** menu. Toolbars can be displayed or hidden in the same way as the ruler. Most toolbars appear at the top of the application window when they are displayed. An exception is the **Drawing** toolbar, which appears at the bottom. (See Section 5 of this module for more information on toolbars.)

Selecting **Header and Footer** in the **View** menu displays the Header and Footer toolbar in the centre of the window. Any text on the page is 'grayed out' and the (small) header area at the top of the page is displayed for you to work in. Click the button on the toolbar to change to the footer. When you return to the main page, any text in the header and footer is grayed out as it is no longer available to work on. Headers and footers are described in detail in Module 3, Section 3.3.3.

A special window in which choices may be made is called a **dialogue box**, as mentioned before.

- Select **Zoom** in the **View** menu to display the Zoom window.
  The **Zoom** window gives a greater choice of options than the **Magnification** menu on the toolbar.

A document's magnification on the screen can be selected, or you may type in a specific magnification of your own.

- Click the desired magnification in the **Zoom to** panel.
  Alternatively, type your own requirement in the box lower down. (You can also click the small arrows in the right of the box to enter a size.)

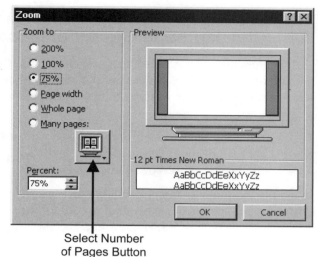

A button just above the **Percent** box allows you to select the number of pages that are displayed on the screen at the same time.

Select Number
of Pages Button

A preview of the display is shown in the **Preview** panel on the right.

The various display options allow the user to use the settings that are most convenient for his or her way of working. The many rulers, toolbars and other aids take up valuable document space on the desktop, however, and leave you with less space for your actual work. A larger monitor is one way of solving this problem. This is why you will invariably find large monitors in design and publishing establishments.

To increase the amount of space available on the screen for your document, especially if you are using the usual 15" or 17" monitor, select **Full Screen** in the **View** menu.

This hides the rulers and toolbars, etc., and enlarges the document window to full screen size.

A mini window then appears on the screen so that you can restore the usual display when required. The mini window can be dragged to any convenient part of the screen. Click **Close Full Screen** to restore the original display.

8.3   Application Default Settings

When you use an application to open a new document all the document settings, such as font, text size, page layout and so on appear with preset values. These are the application **default** settings.

These default settings can be changed if they are not convenient. The way in which they are changed, however, varies from one application to the next.

The default font size for a new document in Word is **10 point**, for example. If you find this too small, you can make **12 point** the default.

Select **Font** in the **Format** menu, set the font size to 12 point and click the **Default** button at the bottom of the window. Click **Yes** to confirm this in the following window. Now every time you open a new document, the font size will be set to 12 point.

Select the Font Size in the
Font Window

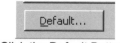

Click the Default Button

Section 9   Checking Spelling

9.1   Checking Spelling Automatically

Many computer users think of the **spell check function** as only being useful (and available) for word processing. In the Office Suite, it is available in all the applications. You can use it to check a single word, a selected section of text or the whole document.

Word automatically checks your spelling as you type. Zig-zag red lines appear under unrecognised words. A word is not recognised if it is incorrectly spelled or if it does not appear in the Word dictionary.

As you type, zig-zag red lines appear under unrecognised words.

Automatic Spell Check

In the illustration, **zig-zag** is not in the dictionary, **appaer** is not spelled correctly and **unrecognised**, although correctly spelled, is questioned because the dictionary used is an American English one, which spells the word with 'z' rather than 's'.

As you type you can make corrections to marked words – and the red markers disappear – or you can choose to ignore them. The zig-zag markers are shown on the screen only. They do not appear if you print out the document.

9.2   Checking Spelling Manually

Click the **Spelling and Grammar** button on the toolbar – indicated by the pointer in the illustration – to check spelling manually. Normally, the whole document is checked. If you only want to check a piece of text or even a single word, select it first.

When an unrecognised word is found, the Spelling and Grammar window opens.

The suspect word appears in red with its context in the upper **Not in Dictionary** box. There will usually be a list of suggestions in the lower box, with the first, most likely, suggestion highlighted.

Buttons on the right allow the user to make changes, ignore the word or add it to the dictionary. This is described in detail in Module 3, Section 6.1.1.

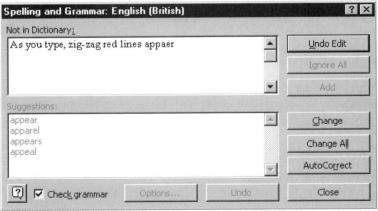

9.3   Checking Your Work

Using the spell check facility to correct spelling mistakes does *not* guarantee that the document is free of errors. 'I want to meet her' will not be questioned, for example, even though you meant to write 'I want to meet here'. You must still read through your work to make a final check.

Section 10   Closing Down

10.1 Closing a Document or Application

There are a number of steps to be followed when you have finished your work and want to close the document, the application, the computer or all of them.

First, you should save your work unless you have no further use for it.

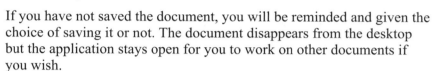

To close a document, click the document **Close** button. Alternatively, select **Close** in the **File** menu.

If you have not saved the document, you will be reminded and given the choice of saving it or not. The document disappears from the desktop but the application stays open for you to work on other documents if you wish.

To close an application, click the application **Close** button (see below). Alternatively, select **Exit** in the **File** menu.

If you have not saved your work, you will be reminded and given the choice of saving it or not. The application disappears from the screen but the computer is still operational and the desktop appears.

Notice that there are **two sets of buttons** at the top right-hand corner of the application window when a document is open in Office 97. The upper buttons control the application while the lower set controls the document. Don't close down the application when you only want to close the document! Office 2000 may have only one row of buttons or just a single button on the lower row.

It is not necessary to close a document or application when you want to use or open another one. Several documents and applications can be open at the same time and you can switch between them as needed.

To temporarily hide a document or application, click the **Minimise** button to reduce it to an icon on the **taskbar**. Click its icon on the taskbar when you want to see it or use it again.

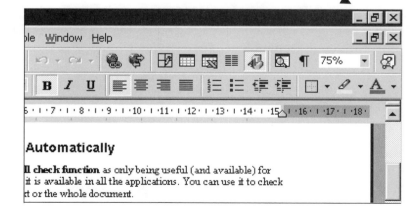

Working with more than one window is described in Module 2, Section 2.2.4.

Working with more than one document is described in Module 3, Section 1.1.7.

Module 1

Basic Concepts
of
Information Technology

1

Module 1

Basic Concepts
of
Information Technology

Introduction

Syllabus Goals for Module 1

Basic Concepts of Information Technology (IT) requires the candidate to have an understanding of some of the main concepts of IT at a general level. The candidate is required to understand the make-up of a personal computer in terms of hardware and software and to understand some of the concepts of Information Technology (IT), such as data storage and memory. The candidate shall also understand how information networks are used within computing and be aware of the uses of computer-based software applications in everyday life. The candidate shall appreciate health and safety issues as well as some environmental factors involved in using computers. The candidate shall be aware of some of the important security and legal issues associated with using computers.

Basic Concepts

Computers are information processing machines. No matter how small or how large and no matter how simple or sophisticated they are, they perform three basic functions. They accept information, they process it according to predefined instructions and they produce results based on their work.

Knowing how your computer does these things will make it easier to interact with the machine and to use it productively. This module sets out to explain the basic concepts associated with the computer and its operation and it deals with issues that relate to information processing.

Computers and Society

Computers are not just machines sitting on office desks. Computer control is a matter of everyday life, from the operation of traffic lights to setting the video recorder, from playing music on your CD player to paying your bills and withdrawing money from the bank by inserting a plastic card in the automatic teller machine (ATM).

We tend to take familiar technology for granted. Take, for example, the hundred-year-old system of communication now in every home in the land. Invented long before the computer, it is now controlled by it and sometimes described as the largest computer network in the world – the humble telephone.

Knowing how computers are used and how they affect our lives will help you to put the computer in context as you work your way through the various modules of the ECDL.

Legal Restraints

Computers make it possible to access information from all over the world and to send and receive messages with an ease and facility that is astonishing. With this new technology, however, there are accompanying legal considerations. These range from knowing how to position your computer to avoid stress and health problems, to being aware of your rights in connection with personal information about you that is stored on computers by businesses and government departments.

The programs that make the use of computers possible, such as word processors, drawing programs, games and so on, are also subject to various legal constraints, as are their users and the owners of the computers on which they are used. It is important to be aware of them.

Section 1   General Concepts

1.1   Hardware, Software and Information Technology (1.1.1.1)

There are two principal components of computer use in the field of **Information Technology**.
They are **hardware** and **software**.

- **Hardware** refers to the physical parts of the computer such as the screen, system box, keyboard or cables which come in the large heavy box or boxes when you buy a computer. The word 'hardware' can describe the complete computer, a part of it, the printer, or any other such items. The hardware, however, can do nothing without software.

- **Software** refers to the sets of instructions, or programs, which tell the computer (the hardware) to do something and how to do it. Software can be loaded into a computer from, for example, a CD or a floppy disk. Word processors, graphics programs, encyclopedias and computer games are examples of software frequently used on the computer. Without software, the computer would be like a TV set without any TV programs.

- **Information Technology** is a term commonly used to describe the use of computers and computer-related equipment to produce, store, manipulate, print, receive and transmit information in electronic form, whether it is text, pictures, sound, video or other data. The ease with which large amounts of information can be processed electronically and the speed and convenience with which it can be routed from place to place or even around the world has given rise to the phrase **the Information Superhighway**.

1.2   Types of Computers (1.1.2.1)

Different types of computers are used for different purposes. The principal categories are listed here.

1.2.1   Mainframe Computers

These room-sized computers are used by major organisations such as banks, supermarket chains and government departments. They can handle vast amounts of information at high speed and they have correspondingly large storage capacities. The cost of installing, running and maintaining such computers runs into hundreds of thousands of euro or more.

Mainframe computers are usually connected to a large number of terminals – screens and keyboards – such as you may see in banks and in travel agents' offices. Some terminals are known as 'dumb' terminals. They cannot operate on their own as all the processing is carried out by the mainframe. Other terminals, while still relying on the mainframe, have a certain amount of processing power themselves that can be used locally by the user. These are known as 'intelligent' terminals.

1.2.2   Personal Computers

The personal computer is commonly known as a **PC**. When first introduced, PCs allowed a complete, self-contained computer to be placed on an office desk. PCs are manufactured under different brand names throughout the world. They are also referred to as **IBM-compatible** computers. This indicates that although brand names may differ, they can run the same programs and applications as similar computers made by **IBM**, the American company whose PCs became the business standard.

PCs are also distinguished from **Macintosh** computers, which use a completely different operating system and are made by **Apple**.

Computers can be connected together, or **networked**, to share programs and information between users. Bodies like universities, government departments and businesses use networks to share information and manage their data. Since the PC has become a universal office and home machine, prices have dropped from thousands of euro to just hundreds for a basic machine. The desktop PC is now the most widely used small computer. Modern PCs can facilitate many tasks, from composing simple letters to video editing.

1.2.3 Laptop Computers

These are small, portable, briefcase-sized computers that can be carried around and used, as the name suggests, on your lap. They are characterised by small screens and small keyboards. Some laptops can be connected, either directly or through a **docking station** – a connecting device – to a standard monitor and keyboard. In this way, the disadvantages of working with a small screen and keyboard for extended periods may be overcome. Because of high manufacturing costs laptop computers are usually much more expensive than desktop computers of similar capacity. Modern laptops can do all the jobs a desktop computer can do. They are commonly used where there is a need for portability; people such as sales representatives, journalists, photographers and university lecturers use them.

1.2.4 Palmtop Computers

Palmtop computers are small, hand-held computers. The very small size of the screen and keyboard has obvious limitations but they are becoming increasingly popular for people on the move to take notes and keep appointments or telephone numbers. They are usually used in conjunction with a desktop or laptop machine. Palmtops can offer some of the functionality of a laptop, such as word processing, e-mail and spreadsheets, in a much-reduced size. Files can be transferred from palmtops to desktop or laptop machines for further editing or storage. Prices for these computers are generally high when compared with laptop and desktop machines.

1.2.5 Personal Digital Assistant (PDA)

These are a fully functional computer that can be held in one hand and can hold downloaded e-mail and play music. With developments in palmtop computers, PDAs and mobile telephones, the dividing line between them all is becoming fainter and a multipurpose small computer may soon emerge.

1.2.6 Computers in Networks

Networked computers are computers that are linked together. In a business with many PCs, it becomes necessary for work done on one computer to be available to other workers in the business. The PCs may be physically connected by cables or by infrared or radio waves and files and documents can then be sent from one PC to another.

Each networked PC is a self-contained 'normal' computer that can be used independently. It has its own processor and hard disk. Documents and files can be prepared and stored on the hard disk as with non-networked computers or stored centrally on a more powerful computer called a **server**.

Most networked computers make use of a server (see below). The server is typically used to store common files. A list of customers' names and addresses stored on the server, for example, may be added to or edited by anyone on the network. The updated list is then instantly available to all the other computers on the network.

1.2.7 Network Computers

A network computer is a low-cost computer or **workstation** on a network. It is constructed with only essential equipment, devoid of CD-ROM players, disk drives and expansion slots that are typically on a powerful multimedia PC. It is designed to be managed and maintained centrally by a **server** where files are stored and all processing is done. All software and data files are stored on the server and distributed to the network computer as required. Generally these computers are less powerful than a PC and are referred to as **dumb terminals.**

MODULE 1

1.3   The Main Parts of a Personal Computer (1.1.3.1)

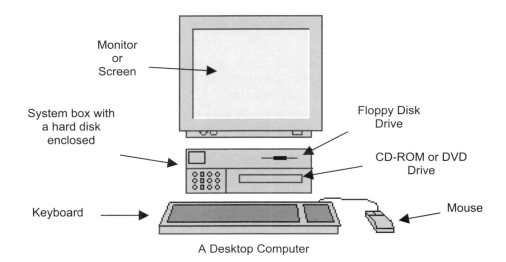

A Desktop Computer

- The **Systems box** houses the **power supply**, **hard disk, floppy disk drives** and the **CD-ROM** drive. These are all connected to the **motherboard** where an array of microchips such as the **CPU** and **RAM** store and process data. Special plugs called ports are attached to electronic cards that fit into slots in the motherboard. The **peripheral** devices listed here are connected to these ports.

- **The hard disk** is the main data storage area used by a computer. Hard disks are used to store the data that makes a computer work. Data can be retrieved much faster than from CD-ROMs or floppy disks.

- **The floppy disk drive** appears as a slot on the front of the systems box. Special floppy disks that hold small amounts of data can be put into this disk drive so that the computer can read the data that they hold.

- **The CD-ROM or DVD drive** opens out from the systems box to accept compact discs. These discs hold substantially more data than floppy disks.

- The **keyboard** and **mouse** enable the user to input data into the computer.

- The **monitor** is a display unit (also known as a **VDU – visual display unit**) like a TV screen. It displays the task that is being preformed by the computer.

The system box may be either horizontal (known as a **desktop** case), as in the illustration, or vertical (a **tower** case).

Other items – printers, scanners, modems and so on – which can be added on to the basic computer for different purposes are known as **peripheral devices** or, more commonly, **peripherals.** These are covered in detail in Section 2.3 in this module.

1.4   Computer Performance (1.1.4.1)

1.4.1   Central Processing Unit

The central processing unit (CPU) is the brain of the computer and it is located on the motherboard. It is also called the **microprocessor**. The CPU is a microchip that contains millions of electronic components. It interprets and executes instructions and performs calculations. It is governed by a clock, in much the same way the playing of a piece of music is governed by a metronome or an orchestra by its conductor. Along with the processor and other components, the clock speed determines how fast the computer carries out the instructions it receives. In general terms, the faster the clock speed, the more efficient the computer. The clock speed of current computers may be as high as 2GHz (billions of cycles per second) or more. Older computers may have much lower clock speeds.

A common PC microprocessor is the **Pentium** but there are several other types made by different manufacturers.

1.4.2 Memory

When the computer is switched on, the programs you use are loaded into **RAM** (random access memory) from the hard disk. Any work you do is also held in RAM until you choose to save it or not. The computer uses RAM because anything contained in RAM is instantly available to it. It does not have to look for the information on the hard disk.

RAM can only store data when the computer is switched on. Everything in RAM vanishes when the power is switched off.

The amount of memory (RAM) installed on the computer may affect the speed at which it operates. The system software takes up an appreciable part of the available memory. Thus, if there is not enough RAM available for what the user wants to do, the computer uses some space on the hard disk as **temporary** or **virtual memory**. It takes much longer to access data in virtual memory on the hard disk than it does to access data in RAM, which slows the computer down.

1.4.3 Hard Disk

The speed at which the hard disk can save and access information has an effect on the overall speed of the computer when it is using the hard disk. This is connected with the speed at which the disk rotates, commonly 5,000 to 10,000 rpm. As a general rule the faster the speed of rotation, the faster the computer can save or gain access to the data.

To illustrate the speed difference between the hard disk and other media, it takes the computer perhaps 10 times longer to access data from a CD-ROM than from a hard disk and even longer to access data from a floppy disk.

1.4.4 Bus Speed

A further factor in the speed of a computer is the speed at which data is sent from one part of the system in the CPU box to another. The System Bus transfers this data like a bus moving passengers between a railway station and an airport. (It is usually the slowest part of your journey.) System Bus speeds are typically 100Mhz or more, much slower than the CPU (1000Mhz or more) which has to 'wait' for data.

1.4.5 Graphics Acceleration

As well as performing all the calculations for the user's work in progress, the CPU also has to calculate and display information graphically on the monitor, so it has a double task. By using a graphics acceleration card, which has its own processor and memory for the display, the CPU is relieved of a large part of its workload. The overall apparent speed of the computer as seen by the user is thus increased, according to the type of graphics card and the amount of memory on it.

1.4.6 Number of Applications Being Used

The more tasks that are being worked on at any one time that are held in RAM, the more the CPU is put under pressure. The number of applications open and the volume of work being executed can affect the performance of a computer.

Section 2   Hardware

2.1   The Central Processing Unit (1.2.1.1)

The three main parts of a CPU are the **arithmetic logic unit** (**ALU**), the **immediate access memory** and the **control unit**.

- The **ALU** carries out arithmetical, comparative and logical processes (the processing).

- The **immediate access memory** is where the data used by the ALU is stored.

- The **control unit** ensures that the program instructions are followed in the correct sequence.

The speed of the CPU is measured in megahertz (MHz) or for more powerful systems, gigahertz (GHz).

2.2   Memory (1.2.2.1)

Random access memory is the main working memory of the computer. RAM is measured in megabytes, so a computer could be said to have 128Mb of RAM. RAM is empty when the computer is first switched on. The system software, such as Windows, is loaded into it so that the computer can carry out all the functions that make it work. If you are using a word processor program to produce a document, the word processor program is first loaded into RAM and the document you are preparing is also stored in RAM as you work on it. Should the computer be switched off before your document is saved or should there be a power cut, everything in RAM is lost and you will have to start all over again when the power is restored.

Read only memory (**ROM**) is also stored on 'memory chips' but data is burnt into it permanently when it is manufactured and cannot be altered afterwards. The information and instructions are there before you turn the computer on and still there when the power is off. Unlike RAM, the computer cannot place data in ROM. It can only read from it, thus giving it its name.

Typically this kind of memory is used to store the instructions that the computer needs to start up so that it can run a self-check and detect attached equipment. It must be available immediately when the computer is switched on. Only small amounts of data are stored in ROM compared with the large amounts in RAM.

2.2.1 How Computer Memory is Measured (1.2.2.2)

The computer must be able to 'remember' the information with which it is working. The information is 'remembered' by being stored, either temporarily or permanently. All information processed by the computer is handled and stored in digital form using **binary code**. This code only uses two digits, 0 and 1. In our daily work, we normally use a number system that has ten digits, 0 to 9, the **decimal system**. Here is how you and a computer count from 0 to 10.

You:	0	1	2	3	4	5	6	7	8	9	10
Computer:	0	1	10	11	100	101	110	111	1000	1001	1010

A single digit, **0** or **1**, is called a **bit**. Bits are grouped together, typically in sets of eight, to make **bytes**. Computer memory is measured in bytes – in the same way as the length of a newspaper article is measured in words – as follows:

1 Bit	1 Byte	1 Kilobyte (Kb)	1 Megabyte (Mb)	1 Gigabyte (Gb)	1 Terabyte (Tb)
A single digit: 0 or 1	8 Bits Can represent (e.g.) the letter 'A'	1,024 Bytes (One thousand)	1,048,576 Bytes (One million)	1,073,741,824 Bytes (One thousand million)	1,099,511,627,776 Bytes (One trillion)

Thus, bits combine to make bytes. A number of bytes together describe a **character** (or number) and so on. The entire document is a **file.** A set of **data**, such as information about pupils in a school, consists of files. Files vary in size as documents of one, two or ten pages have varying memory requirements.

2.3   Input Devices (1.2.3.1)

The computer is programmed to work on information (data) that is entered by the user. Various devices enable the user to enter data. Any device that is connected to a computer is referred to as a **peripheral**.

2.3.1 Mouse

The mouse is a small hand-held device. It is mouse-shaped and connected to the computer by a cable (the mouse's tail). As the mouse is moved on the mouse mat, it transmits information to the computer, which moves a cursor in sympathy on the screen. The standard PC mouse has two buttons. When the mouse button is clicked over an item it can activate a program, select a particular function and so on.

2.3.2 Keyboard

A keyboard has character keys with the same arrangement as a typewriter. The standard keyboard is known as a **Qwerty** keyboard (from the first five letters on the top row of letter keys). Most keyboards have a numeric keypad on the right-hand side as well as extra keys that may be used for other purposes.

2.3.3 Trackball

This is essentially a mouse turned upside down. The user rotates a ball that is mounted on a small box to move the cursor about the screen. The trackball saves the space normally taken up by the mouse and the mouse mat. Usually there are buttons beside the trackball which duplicate the functions of the mouse buttons.

2.3.4 Scanner

There are various types of scanners, each designed to do a specific job. Regardless of the job they have been designed to do, they all have one thing in common – they read data from an outside source and transfer it to the computer for processing.

- **Bar-code reader**s scan barcodes of the type that are visible on grocery items. The computer is pre-programmed to recognise the various codes represented by the bars and transfers them into numeric information such as prices and so on.

- **Desktop** or flatbed scanners look like a very small photocopier. This device scans images such as graphics, pictures or text and converts them into digital information that can be understood by a computer. The images and text can be manipulated with the computer and printed or stored for later use.

- **OCR scanners** (optical character recognition) are used to recognise printed or written text characters by a computer. It uses a photoscanning technology that scans text character by character. It is commonly used to process cheques and credit card slips and sort the mail. Optical character recognition can be used to scan documents that can then be converted to speech.

2.3.5 Touchpad

A touchpad is a touch-sensitive device, an inch or two square, that replaces the mouse on a typical laptop computer. When a fingertip is moved over the surface the result is similar to using a mouse or trackball. Touchpads are common on laptop computers but may also be seen on some keyboards as an alternative to the mouse.

2.3.6 Light Pen

A light pen looks like a conventional writing pen but it transmits electronic information to the computer. It can be used to move the cursor and select objects on a display screen by directly pointing to them.

2.3.7 Joystick

A joystick is a hand lever that can be moved in various directions to control movement on the screen. Most joysticks include a number of buttons that can be pressed to perform various actions. Joysticks are commonly used for playing games on the computer or to control computer-operated machines.

2.3.8 Digital Camera

This is a camera that does not need film as images are digitised and saved onto a special memory card. These images can then be transferred to a computer for editing and printing.

2.3.9 Microphone

As well as allowing sound to be recorded on the computer, a microphone can also be used to allow speech to control computer function when the appropriate software is installed. Speech can be digitised, converted into text and placed in a word processing program.

2.3.10 Graphics Pad and Tablet

A graphic tablet is a two-part pointing and detection device. It is comprised of a flat rectangular base or tablet and a special pen. As the pen is moved over the flat base it records the strokes made by the pen and replicates them onto the screen just as a mouse would. It is very popular for work such as picture drawings that demand a more comfortable and responsive feel than a mouse. There are many specialist peripheral devices manufactured to input information into computers, all far too numerous to mention here. There are, however, a range of devices that help people with special needs.

2.4 Output Devices (1.2.4.1)

The computer can output information in various ways using different pieces of peripheral equipment.

2.4.1 The Monitor

This is also known as a **video display unit** (**VDU**). It is a screen similar to a television screen but with a much sharper picture. It displays the work being done by the CPU – and by the user – in graphical form so that the user can **monitor** what is happening. Remember that early computers were not equipped with monitors. Information was typed on a keyboard and output on punched tape.

The standard computer monitor uses a **cathode ray tube (CRT)** similar to that used in a television set but capable of displaying a much sharper and clearer picture. CRT monitors are large and heavy. They take up a large amount of space on the desk.

Monitor size is measured diagonally between opposite corners of the screen. Common sizes are 15" and 17". Larger sizes, usually 19" to 21", are used for large graphics and full-page layout work where one or more pages can be shown full-size on the screen.

The monitor's **resolution** is the number of dots or **pixels** that can be displayed on the screen. For many years, the usual display was 640 pixels across the screen and 480 pixels from top to bottom. This is known as VGA (video graphics array) resolution.

The present standard is 800 x 600 pixels, or SVGA (super VGA). A higher resolution of 1024 x 768 pixels, or XVGA (extended VGA), is also available. Resolutions higher than XVGA are also available for specialist purposes.

A monitor with higher resolution will display more of a document than one with a lower resolution on the same size screen but the print will appear smaller. A monitor that can display different resolutions is called a **multiscan** (or **multisync**) monitor.

The quality of the colour displayed by a monitor depends on the construction of the monitor itself as well as the electronic circuitry in the computer. It is common to describe colour quality by the number of colours that can be displayed.

Early computer monitors could only display four or sixteen colours, but 256 colours gradually became a standard used in software. Computers and their monitors are now able to display thousands or even millions of colours, giving photographic quality to the display.

Liquid crystal displays (LCD) are commonly used in laptop computers where CRT displays are impractical. LCD displays for desktop computers are small and light. They take up little space on the desk, being only four or five centimetres deep. Their widespread introduction to the market as flat screens has been slowed down by their cost.

Light emitting diodes (LED) displays are small light sources commonly used to indicate the equipment is switched on. There is usually one on the front of the monitor and the CPU box. LEDs are also used to indicate a level of activity – on modems, for example – where they flash within a series to show levels of activity.

2.4.2 Printer

A printer allows documents produced on the computer to be printed on paper or other material. Such documents are often referred to as **printouts** or **hard copy**. **Inkjet** and **laser** printers are the most widely used.

There are many different kinds of printers. They are generally used to print on paper but transparencies or other media may also be used.

- **Daisy wheel:** The characters are raised on a piece of metal or plastic which strike a ribbon placed between them and the paper, thus imprinting the shape of the character on the paper. Being an impact printer, it is possible to produce carbon copies. Daisy wheel printers are generally slow and noisy.

  The Daisy wheel mechanism is now used only in electric typewriters.

- **Dot matrix** printers are also impact printers. They use a print head with pins that produce dots on the page by striking through an inked ribbon. The greater the number of pins and the greater the number of times they strike a particular area, the better the quality of the print but the slower the printing speed. Carbon copies can also be produced with these printers. Dot matrix printers produce a characteristic whining noise.

  They are now used only where small printouts are needed, such as in ticket machines or at supermarket checkouts.

- **Inkjet** printers work by shooting minute jets of ink directly onto the paper. They use different coloured inks to produce high-quality colour images. Most inkjet printers use separate black ink for ordinary text.

  Inkjet printers are inexpensive but running costs are high, with cartridges having to be replaced after a few hundred copies. When a printer uses a single cartridge containing all the colours, the whole cartridge has to be replaced when one of them runs out. Some printers use separate cartridges for the different colours, up to six in some cases, but then several cartridges have to be replaced on a regular basis. For maximum print quality, special paper has to be used, adding to the expense.

Carbon copies cannot be produced by inkjet printers as there is no mechanical striking action involved. Inkjet printers are quiet in use but are slower than laser printers.

- **Laser** printers work in the same way as photocopiers. Instead of a lens, they use a laser to place an electrical charge in the shape of the text and/or graphics to be printed on a rotating drum. The charged area of the drum attracts fine black powder (toner) to itself and the powder is pressed onto the paper as the drum rotates. The paper is then heated to seal the image onto the paper.

  Laser printers produce high-quality images, usually only in black and white (or greyscale) because of cost. Colour laser printers typically cost two or three times as much as an equivalent black and white model.

  An office-quality laser printer is much more expensive than a small inkjet printer but it is of more robust construction and it is designed for heavy use. It is also much faster than an inkjet printer and running costs are lower, as a toner cartridge typically produces 5000 or more pages before having to be replaced.

  As with inkjet printers, carbon copies cannot be produced. Laser printers are very quiet in use.

2.4.3 Plotters

A plotter is a special type of printer used principally by architects, engineers and scientists in conjunction with **computer aided design (CAD)** and **mapping software**. The machine uses actual pens to draw directly on the paper. Plotters can select pens and colours, as directed by the computer, to produce complex technical drawings.

2.4.4 Speakers

Multimedia applications have made the use of loudspeakers or headphones with computers essential. Loudspeakers are standard equipment in modern computers used in the home. In education, headphones are often more appropriate in the classroom because the user will not disturb other students. Small loudspeakers are usually supplied but the computer can be connected to an external amplifier and larger loudspeakers, if required. Modern flat-screen monitors are being supplied with speakers built into the side panels.

2.4.5 Speech Synthesiser

When installed on the computer, software can produce sound that resembles human speech. This can be used to assist people with disabilities or it may be used in areas where verbal feedback may be preferable to visual. The computer can read out documents and can also 'speak' to the user to confirm commands.

2.5   Input and Output Devices (1.2.5.1)

Some devices can be classified as both input and output devices. These include touch screens, modems and specialised equipment such as musical instruments with midi capabilities. These instruments can be connected to a computer via the sound card and the input manipulated with special software. The results can be transferred to CD or stored on the computer's hard disk for further editing or playback.

2.5.1 Touch Screen

A touch screen is both an input and output device. It enables the computer to be controlled by a finger directly touching the screen. No mouse or other device is needed. Touch-sensitive screens are used in information booths for public access where a mouse or other device would be impracticable.

2.5.2 Modem

This piece of hardware allows a computer to connect to telephone lines so that the user can send and receive data.

2.5.3 Removable Media

Data can be input from or output to floppy disks, tape, data cartridges, compact disks and other removable media for transfer to remote computers for back-up storage, for transfer of information and for other purposes.

2.6   Storage Devices (1.2.6.1)

The programs you use and the work you produce must be stored before the computer is switched off so that they are available for future use. The next time you turn on the computer they can be loaded into RAM again and you can continue with your work. This kind of mechanical storage is often referred to as **secondary memory.** Common examples include the following:

- **Hard disk.** The hard disk is located within the computer system box. It is usually composed of several metal (hard) magnetically coated disks encased in a sealed metal box. The capacity of a typical hard disk is 40Gb or more. Larger sizes are readily available. Extra hard disk units can be added to the computer, either internally or externally. External hard disks are separate to the system box and are attached to it by special cables.

- **Floppy disks** are small, portable versions of the hard disk that use a plastic (floppy) magnetically coated disk in a compact plastic case $3\frac{1}{2}$ inches square. A floppy disk has a nominal capacity of 1.4Mb. They are commonly used to transfer files from one computer to another, particularly when the computers are not linked in any way. A variation of the floppy disk, the Super Disk or Smart Disk, has a nominal capacity of 120Mb but needs a special drive unit.

- **Compact discs.** While floppy and hard disks are magnetic, a compact disc is an optical disc that uses a laser to read the information. It can store very large amounts of data, typically 650Mb. CD-R (compact disc recordable) is a write once, read many times compact disc (CD) format that allows one-time recording on a disc. CD-RW (compact disc rewriteable) is a compact disc format that allows repeated recording on a disc. CD-ROM is a pre-recorded compact disc that cannot be recorded on.

  Compact discs are most suitable for storing large files and for programs that mix text, graphics and audio, i.e. **multimedia**, such as illustrated encyclopedias, interactive games, computer-based training programs and so on.

- **Zip drives** and similar units are small, portable versions of the hard disk that use **cartridges**. The cartridges are slightly larger than floppy disks but they have a much larger storage capacity. 100Mb, 250Mb or 750Mb capacities are available.

- **DVD** (digital versatile disc) is a high-capacity development of the CD-ROM that can store gigabytes of information. While the CD was originally designed for recorded music, DVD has had many uses from the beginning. It may replace the standard videocassette, for example, as it can store an entire feature film with very high picture quality. Like CD-ROM, DVD discs cannot be recorded on by the user but DVD-R, a recordable version, is now becoming popular with home users.

- **Data cartridges** are designed to fit purpose-designed drives. They are usually used to back up large amounts of data and are available for all computer systems. They provide higher storage capacities and have greater durability and reliability than floppy disks.

MODULE 1

> A **disk drive** – often called a drive – is a unit that makes use of a disk.
>
> - A floppy drive uses floppy disks.
> - A hard drive uses a hard disk (usually only one).
> - A zip drive or similar uses cartridges.
> - CD-ROM and DVD drives use CD-ROM or DVD discs.

The illustration shows how different drives are represented on the computer screen.

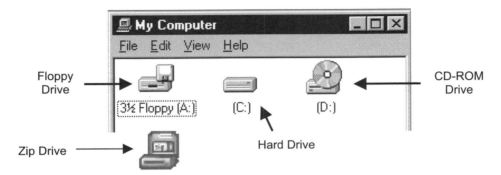

2.6.1 Speed, Cost and Capacity

Here is a guide that illustrates the speed, cost and capacity of storage media. This is only a guide as circumstances may vary between hardware platforms.

Drive	Access speed	Sample Cost	Capacity
Hard disk	150 Mb per second	350 units	40 – 80 Gb
Floppy disk	0.06Mb per second	1 unit	1.44 Mb
Compact discs R	3.3 Mb per second (at 32x)	2 units	650 Mb
Compact discs RW		8 units	650 Mb
DVD	4.8 Mb per second (at 32x)	20 units; 34 units	100 Mb; 250 Mb
Zip disks	1.4 Mb per second	17 units; 30 units	100 Mb; 250 Mb
Data cartridges	7Mb per second	68 units	20 Gb

Based on 1 unit = .75c per floppy disk

2.6.2 Formatting (1.2.6.2)

The surface of a disk is magnetic and before formatting this surface is a confusion of magnetic signals. When formatting is complete this confusion has been ordered into tracks and sectors that accept data.

Therefore, in order to prepare floppy disks for use they must be formatted to suit the type of computer they will be used in. So as to save a computer user's time, most disk manufacturers sell pre-formatted disks. When purchasing these disks it is important to read the label to ensure that the disks are formatted to suit the computer in which they are going to be used. It is also possible to format a hard disk but only a qualified technician should do this task.

Section 3   Software

3.1   Types of Software (1.3.1.1)

A computer program is a set of instructions written in a format that a computer understands. It directs the computer to operate in a particular fashion and to carry out tasks. Thousands of software programs are available from a wide variety of sources, from computer shops to supermarkets, to programs that can be downloaded from the Internet. Some common examples of software are described here.

3.1.1   System Software

System software is software that operates the computer. It is generally supplied pre-installed on the hard disk when you purchase a new computer. When you use the computer for the first time you may need to enter certain information, for example your name and the area you live in. Other 'set-up' information may also be required about Internet connections and certain peripheral devices that are connected to the computer.

3.1.2   Application Software

This is a set of instructions written by a person called a programmer that tells a computer how to do a pre-defined task such as word processing or a game. All software that is not system software is regarded as application software. Application software written for one type of computer will not work on another. As a result, it is important to check the system requirements when purchasing new application software.

One of the most popular application software is Microsoft Office. This is recognised as an integrated suite of programs because it is supplied with a number of programs that work together.

3.1.3   Upgrading Software

Each year computers are becoming more powerful and as a result they can increasingly perform more demanding tasks. This necessitates constant upgrading of both system and application software. Newer versions ensure that the software is taking full advantage of the computer's power. As new **upgrades** of software become available they are referred to as versions. The numbering or naming of versions varies from company to company. Usually the first issue of a software title is Version 1 with minor upgrades being referred to as version 1.1,1.2 and so on.

Microsoft Office has evolved to harness the power of both hardware and system software developments. Microsoft Office and Windows have developed different versions in the following sequence:

Windows 95	Office 95
Windows 98	Office 97
Windows 2000	Office 2000
Windows XP	Office XP

3.2   Operating System Software (1.3.2.1)

This is a program that holds all the instructions that make the computer work, e.g. the start-up procedure, monitor display and the use of hard or floppy disks and so on for storing data.

The operating system manages other programs such as word processors, games and Internet browsers. It accepts instructions from them, passes them to the CPU, arranges the display on the monitor, takes the results from the CPU and sends them to be stored on the hard disk or to the printer for printing. It is permanently stored in the computer and is automatically started when the computer is switched on. Without an operating system, the computer would be like a car without an engine.

Two common examples of system software are the Mac OS (Macintosh) and Microsoft Windows (PC). Examples of other operating systems are MS-DOS, UNIX, OS/2 and Linux. Various versions of Windows (95, 98, NT, 2000, XP) are the most commonly used operating systems on PCs today.

3.3   Applications Software (1.3.3.1)

Applications software is all the other software that runs on a computer. This is the software most users recognise as the **applications** with which they do their work. The Microsoft Office suite of programs, which you are learning to use as part of this course, is an example of applications software. The suite is made up of the following applications:

Software type	Product name	Function of software
Word Processor	Word	Used to prepare documents such as reports and letters.
Spreadsheet	Excel	This software allows the user to manipulate numbers and perform mathematical functions.
Database	Access	Used to keep track of information.
Presentation tools	PowerPoint	Used to make slide shows for presentations.
Desktop publishing	Microsoft Publisher	This software is designed to prepare newsletters, magazines, etc.
Internet browsing	Internet Explorer	Used to surf the Internet.

There is a considerable range of application software available to address different needs within organisations and businesses. Personnel management systems are available to record and track employee profiles, entitlements, salary, assignments and so on. Management information systems in a customer services division of a company would typically record a customer needs profile, product support record, levels of access permitted to on-line information, contact details and other relevant information. There are also applications such as customer relationship management systems that generate, maintain and update customer contact information. Additionally, there are telesales management systems that can monitor connections made, call durations, compile response rates of prospective clients and perform many more functions. Accounting software can maintain financial records, produce cash flow statements, balance sheets, maintain ledgers, and depending on their sophistication, prepare quarterly reports, tax returns, forecasts and so on.

3.4   Graphical User Interface (1.3.4.1)

A **graphical user interface (GUI)** uses pictures, or **icons,** that are familiar to users of Windows or Mac OS to represent objects or information on the monitor. The GUI, introduced by Apple Computer in the early 1980s, is now universally used. The icons can be clicked and manipulated with the mouse to make the computer perform actions or carry out instructions. Users can relate the work they are doing to the real-life objects and concepts, thus making the computer easier to use.

My Computer

My Documents

Internet Explorer

3.5   Systems Development (1.3.5.1)

Systems development involves the design, development and implementation of computer operations to replace or update some process within a business or an organisation. A manual payroll system, for example, could be replaced by a computerised version. There are many stages in the development of such a system, ranging from identifying the organisation's requirements to the implementation of the new system and staff training.

In organisations such as banks, insurance companies and multinational corporations, system design teams are comprised of analysts, programmers and engineers collaborating to develop the hardware and software facilities required to meet the organisation's needs.

The steps involved in the development of a system are much the same as for any design project. The diagram illustrates the possible steps in developing a computer system.

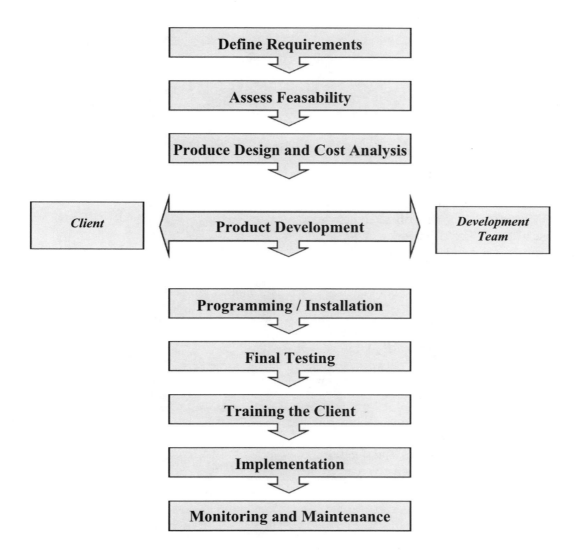

Section 4   Information Networks

4.1   LAN, WAN (1.4.1.1)

In a **local area network** (**LAN**), a number of computers are **networked** – linked together – by means of cables or wireless communication devices within a limited area, often in the same building or group of nearby buildings. Company offices are often networked in this way.

In a **server/client** network, a computer called a **server** stores common data which it 'serves' to the other computers, called **clients**. The client computers store data on the server, which is then available to the other clients' machines.

For example, a single copy of a file that is held on a network server can be used by everyone on the network who has permission to use it. Any updates or changes made by one user are immediately available to the others.

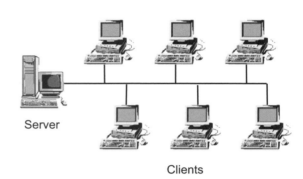

Server

Clients

The **P2P** is an acronym for a particular network arrangement. It stands for "**peer-to-peer**", where each computer is a server in itself. Unlike client/server networks, where the server is central to the management of the network, P2P networks do not use a server. These networks are ideal where security is not an issue, for example in a home network.

In a **wide area network** (**WAN**) computers, as well as computer networks, are linked together over a large distance.

The WAN operates in the same way as a local area network but on a much larger scale. Many organisations operate wide area networks to link their offices in different parts of the country or even in different parts of the world.

Worldwide coverage is provided largely by satellite communications. Data is transmitted across the world using satellite technology. The satellite transmits the data, which can then be received in a distant location without the need for extensive land lines or undersea cables.

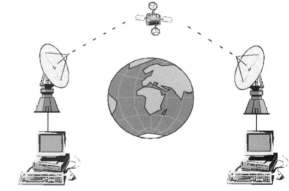

Satellite Communication

4.1.1 Group Working (1.4.1.2)

The development of networks has meant that people who are working on aspects of a common task can use their own computer or terminal but they can also share documents, files and resources with other workers over a network. Workers can communicate by means of a LAN or telecommunications network. Resources can be efficiently shared as information can be sent to all members of the group at once. Documents can be produced collaboratively. The same word processing file, for example, can be accessed and edited as necessary by different people in different locations.

Peripherals such as printers and scanners can also be shared, thus reducing operating costs.

4.2   Intranet, Extranet (1.4.2.1)

4.2.1   Intranet

An **intranet** is a group of computers within an organisation configured to communicate with each other. This arrangement allows internal communication and sharing of information within the organisation. A website constructed for a company intranet looks and acts just like any other site, but special software protects it from unauthorised access.

4.2.2   Extranet (1.4.2.2)

An **extranet** is an extension to an organisation's intranet. It allows external access to different parts of a company's intranet, for example. Typically customers may have access to on-line ordering or account enquiries. Normally you can only gain access to an extranet if you have a valid username and password. The username and password you enter will determine your level of access and the parts of the extranet you can view.

4.3   The Internet (1.4.3.1 and 1.4.3.2)

The **Internet** is a worldwide network of computers and computer networks that are linked by telecommunications networks. Any computer that has the appropriate software, hardware and a telecommunication connection can access it. The computer on your desk can be – and probably is – one of them. A computer with an Internet connection gives the user access to large amounts of information on practically every subject imaginable and on a scale that was not possible before the invention of the Internet. Here is a list of the requirements for a very basic connection to the Internet.

A computer	Any computer can be used to connect to the Internet. The special communication language that is used on the Internet allows all types of computers to communicate with each other.
A modem	This is a special piece of computer hardware that converts computer signals so that they can be transmitted down telephone cables.
A browser	This is a piece of software, such as Netscape Communicator or Microsoft Internet Explorer, that allows the computer to interpret the signals that come from the Internet.
An Internet service provider account (ISP)	This is a company, typically a telecommunications company, that connects your computer to the Internet.
A telephone line	A standard telephone line.

4.3.1   History of the Internet

- The first transfer of data between two remote computers took place in the USA just over 30 years ago. This was the beginning of what is now known as the Internet. Only text could be transmitted at that time and a high degree of computer skill was needed to use the system. As a result, it was mainly used as a research tool by universities and other large organisations.

- The development of hypertext in the 1990s brought with it a simplified way of using the Internet. By just clicking a word on the screen, the user could connect to the remote computer that the word represented.

- Later, methods of transmitting graphics, sound and video over the Internet were developed. This 'multimedia' branch of the Internet is now referred to as the **World Wide Web** (**WWW**). It has become synonymous with the Internet for many people.

- The introduction of the World Wide Web facilitated greater access to the Internet by ordinary people.

Governments, universities, and individuals all over the world publish information on the Internet. Other, less reputable organisations also publish information there as well.

4.4   The Telephone Network in Computing

4.4.1   Use of Telephone Network in Computing (1.4.4.1)

The telephone system we are all familiar with is called the **public switched telephone network (PSTN)** or **public switched data network (PSDN).** It was originally designed for transmitting voice as analogue signals across cables in a continuously varying electrical signal, but now it is also used for the transmission of data.

Throughout the final years of the twentieth century, the rate at which data could be transmitted over telecommunication networks was an important research issue. Several solutions were discovered, most of them centred on compression of the data. Here are two of the most significant developments that have been made:

- The **integrated services digital network** (**ISDN**) was designed for the transmission of digital signals, the kind that computers use. While these signals are transferred down ordinary telephone lines, special technology installed at either end of the line assists in faster transfer rates. ISDN is much faster than PSDN although it still supplies information at a rate far below the capacity that a computer can deal with. The basic transfer rate of information across an ISDN line is 64Kbps (kilobytes per second). 128Kbps is available but often at extra cost. Additional ISDN lines can be combined to give increased speed.

- The **asymetric digital subscriber line (ADSL)** is a high-speed data communications technology that allows the use of existing analogue telephone lines for fast access to the Internet. The connection is permanently live so there is never a need to dial up your connection. It is faster than ISDN with speeds in excess of 512Kbps. Data is received more quickly than it is transmitted.

4.4.2   Transfer Rate (1.4.4.2)

Inside a computer, data travels around as a digital signal with the electrical current turning over usually between +6 Volts for the binary digit 1 and –6 Volts for the binary digit 0. Digital waveform is represented graphically, as in the diagram here.

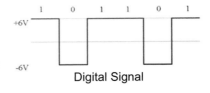

Digital Signal

With a telephone line, the signal is analogue, a continuously varying electrical signal that produces a waveform like the one in this graphic.

Analogue Signal

The process of imposing a digital signal on an analogue wave is called **modulation** and the piece of equipment that does this is called a modulator/demodulator or **modem**. Before the introduction of ISDN or ADSL, in order to transmit digital computer information over normal analogue telephone lines, the data had to be converted from its digital format to analogue format by a modem. At the other end of the line, another modem converted from analogue back to digital for the receiving computer.

The maximum processing speed that can be achieved by modems is about 56Kbps. This is sometimes referred to as the **baud rate**. 1 baud = 1 binary bit per second. 1 Kilobaud = 1000 bits per second.

This connection speed is only a tiny fraction of the speed that the computer itself is capable of, so the transfer of data via a modem is very slow compared with the transfer of data within the computer. Noise and interference on the telephone lines slow the signal further and the claimed maximum speed is rarely achieved consistently.

It is worth noting that equipment referred to as ISDN modems are not really modems. Because ISDN lines carry digital signals there is no need for the signal to be converted. The piece of equipment that is between the ISDN line connection box and the computer is more properly referred to as a 'terminal adaptor'.

MODULE 1

Section 5   The Use of IT in Everyday Life

5.1   Computers at Work (1.5.1.1)

Whether at the checkout in the supermarket or withdrawing money from an ATM machine, computer technology has become an integral part of our lives. For some work, computers are more appropriate than people. They are ideal for tasks that are repetitive or monotonous or those that require accuracy, speed and calculation. Manufacturing industries employ computers to control machines for automation of assembly line processes, thus saving on large wage bills. In areas where it is dangerous for people to work, such as marine oil, space exploration or the chemical industry, computer controlled **robots** can be programmed to do many tasks that would otherwise have to be done by humans.

People are more appropriate, however, for tasks which are one-off or different each time, as well as for tasks that require a personal touch or where feelings need to be considered, e.g. medical diagnosis, some banking operations and aspects of education. Essentially, when and where tasks cannot be broken down into a series of pre-written instructions, people are superior to computers.

5.1.1   Computers in Business (1.5.1.2)

In business there are many different types of activity, each requiring different systems to meet varying needs. Here are some examples:

- Industries use computers for stock control, accounting and payrolling.

- Airlines use Internet technologies to allow passengers to plan their journeys and pre-book flights. From the time the passenger logs on to the airline's website the whole system, from queries to booking flights, may be automated.

- Insurance companies use computers to process claims. This technology allows more than 95% of claims to be adjudicated automatically, thus freeing valuable human resources previously dedicated to manual claims processing.

- Banks employ high-security Internet tools to allow customers to carry out banking transactions on-line 24 hours per day; this service is very convenient for customers. This is a very good example of how the Internet has changed the way business is done and the way institutions such as banks have had to modify their methods of working to facilitate greater demands for access from the public.

5.1.2   Computers in Government (1.5.1.3)

One of the first times a computer was used for a large-scale project was the 1890 census of The United States of America. Herman Hollerith, an engineer, had developed a machine that was the first electromechanical computer and it was used to process the very large volume of data generated by the census. Today, the largest user of computers is governments. As well as processing census data, government agencies use computer systems to carry out a wide range of tasks such as those listed below.

- Public records may be kept on a large computer system that can be accessed by authorised government employees.

- Census information may be analysed by computers. This can assist the various state agencies when they are making decisions.

- Cars are registered on vehicle registration computers, thus allowing authorised people to find out who owns a car.

- Many countries have self-assessment income tax systems that allow taxpayers to fill in their tax returns on-line.

- The introduction of electronic voting means that the results of an election or a referendum can be processed more quickly than in countries where there is manual vote counting.

5.1.3 Computers in Healthcare (1.5.1.4)

It is difficult to think of a profession that has not benefited from the invention of the computer. Of particular note has been in the delivery of healthcare. When a patient goes to hospital with a suspected ailment, computer technology may be used to assist in diagnosis, monitoring, and administering the healthcare programme. Medical establishments and hospitals have sophisticated computer-controlled monitoring and life-support systems. Computer technology and **robotics** have become so sophisticated that surgeons with specialist medical equipment can operate on a patient who is located many miles away. It is not only in the administration and treatment of illness that hospitals use computer technology – they employ scheduling and tracking systems to monitor ambulance movement, blood collection, patient transfers and so on.

5.1.4 Computers in Education (1.5.1.5)

In education, computers are used in universities, colleges and schools for training, teaching and research as well as for administration. There would be separate requirements for administration and classroom use. In a typical school situation you might expect to find:

- **Networked** or **stand-alone** computers with multimedia facilities, i.e. with CD-ROM and sound cards, printers, modems, scanners, graphics tablets and specialised keyboards for children who have special needs.

- **Software** for administration that would include word processing, an administration database, accounts packages, timetabling software, Internet tools and so on.

- For **classroom use,** you would expect to find multimedia authoring, Internet and e-mail applications, computer-based instruction/training programs, word processing, spreadsheets, desktop publishing programs, and presentation and graphics packages.

One of the great breakthroughs in education and training was the development of distance learning. The introduction of computer technology has added a tremendous advantage to distance learning programmes. Today, students can avail of classes conducted on the Internet or use a range of computer-based training (CBT) resources to study their chosen courses. Using specially designed software, many teachers now set and correct homework or project work over the Internet.

5.1.5 Teleworking (1.5.1.6)

With the development of better telecommunications and better security software, many people can and do work from home. This is called **teleworking** and it is fast becoming a popular option with many organisations. Here are some advantages of teleworking:

- Some tasks are easier to focus on away from the bustle of the office.

- A parent can be at home for their children and plan their work around the family schedule.

- Many employers allow teleworkers to nominate their own working hours and have agreed schedules and timeframes for the completion of projects.

- Commuting is reduced or eliminated altogether as employees do not have expensive travel bills and waste valuable time commuting. This can allow them to have a wider choice of areas in which to live.

- Companies that avail of teleworking for their employees make a considerable savings on overheads such as office space, heating, parking, canteens and so on.

There are some disadvantages to teleworking, which are:

- There are very few opportunities for employees to meet and develop work communities. There is little chance to meet new people through their work and new employees tend to feel isolated.

- It is very difficult to generate a culture of teamwork with teleworking groups.

- As the employee is working from home it is difficult to establish boundaries with family, friends and work.

- Most modern homes are small and space is limited. The teleworker must dedicate a certain amount of this space, thus giving the family less living space.

- In some areas people running a business from home or using space for office use have to pay local taxes.

5.2   The Electronic World

5.2.1 Electronic Mail (1.5.2.1)

E-mail, as it is commonly known, is a method of sending and receiving mail messages over the Internet. In order to use e-mail, you must have Internet access. It is possible to get Internet and e-mail access free, the only cost being the telephone charges. E-mail has revolutionised communication between individuals, businesses and organisations.

- It allows fast, low-cost communication around the world. An e-mail message or document can usually be sent to any destination in the world for the cost of a local call.

- You can send and receive messages or documents in electronic form, edit them and forward them to someone else.

- You can correspond with friends easily and quickly.

- An e-mail message can be sent to a number of people simultaneously.

- You can request and receive information by e-mail.

- E-mail speeds communication. As writing conventions are very informal, a reply can be sent to a message by typing a few words and clicking a button on the screen.

E-mail has a writing convention that is generally friendlier and more informal in use than traditional written communication.

5.2.2 E-commerce (1.5.2.2 and 1.5.2.3)

E-commerce is the use of technology for conducting business over the Internet. It is sometimes referred to as **B2B** (business to business). As more and more people realise the convenience of doing business on-line, the number of people involved in the e-commerce business is expanding constantly. Shopping, airline bookings and holiday arrangements are a few examples of services that are available over the Internet. As people's lifestyles change and they have less time to queue for services, they are using the Internet more than ever to avail of a range of services from grocery shopping to holiday bookings.

With the onset of secure lines, personal details such as credit card details can be communicated across the Internet safely. Most reputable companies selling on the Internet offer a very efficient sale and return guarantee. If goods are unsatisfactory or not functioning as advertised, the customer can contact the company and arrange for the immediate replacement of the item or a refund of the cost. Usually this does not affect the customer's statutory rights but this depends on local laws.

The Internet never sleeps. One of the great advantages of the Internet is that goods and services can be purchased online 24 hours a day. Many businesspeople with a product or service to sell have been very imaginative in taking advantage of the facilities offered by the Internet. Food chains can offer on-line ordering and once the food is ordered on-line it is delivered directly to the purchaser's door. Another fast-growing business is on-line shopping, where the customer can choose a range of goods from an on-line store ecnd have them delivered by courier or post.

One of the fastest-growing industries on the Internet is the music business, whether in the form of downloadable **MP3** files, CDs or good old-fashioned sheet music. Today, there is very little that cannot be purchased on the Internet. The customer has an opportunity to view a wide range of products and, most importantly, compare the prices.

There are disadvantages to shopping on-line though, which include:

- Lack of human contact.

- Delay between purchase and receiving the goods.

- The vendor's word has to be taken in relation to quality.

- As the technology advances, so does the possibility of computer fraud and there can be a risk associated with insecure payments.

Section 6   Health and Safety and the Environment

6.1   Ergonomics (1.6.1.1)

Ergonomics is the study of the interaction of people with equipment and machines. The main concern of ergonomics is that people can work with machines safely and efficiently. Stress-related illness can result from improper working conditions and practices. To avoid these and other problems and create a good working environment, simple precautions should be taken in the computer work environment.

Some of these include:

- Making sure the work area is comfortable and that adequate temperature is maintained.
- Avoiding visual fatigue, making sure that there is adequate lighting.
- Positioning the monitor so that it is not affected by glare.
- Using an adjustable chair that conforms to current health standards.
- Ensuring that the mouse and keyboard are positioned so that they do not cause discomfort.
- Fitting a monitor filter to eliminate glare and eye strain.
- Keeping pathways clear of cables.
- Ensuring that there is adequate ventilation.
- Taking regular breaks.
- Complying with local fire and safety regulations.
- Examining plugs, sockets and leads for defects and have any necessary repairs carried out by qualified personnel.

You should refer to your local health and safety authority for more detailed recommendations and any legal requirements with which you need to comply.

6.2   Health Issues (1.6.2.1)

As well as taking care that the physical working environment conforms to regulations, employers and employees need to be aware that computer systems need to be logical and easy to use. All users should be instructed in the use of all hardware and software.

The guidelines illustrated here are based on common sense and simply reflect good work practice. Continuous use of a computer in a poor, unsafe working environment can lead to health problems. Among the most frequently recorded problems is **repetitive strain injury** (RSI). This can be a serious and very painful condition that is easier to prevent than to cure. Doing the same task repetitively can cause RSI. Continuous use of an incorrectly placed keyboard or mouse can cause RSI. Using a monitor in poor lighting conditions can contribute to eyestrain. Poor seating or bad posture can contribute to back problems.

6.3   Precautions (1.6.3.1)

The illustrations here are given as examples of good arrangements for the computer operator. Please note that these recommendations are only general guidelines; always follow the manufacturer's guidelines and local health authority recommendations.

- Be in a position to look down, not up, at the monitor.

- Place the monitor on the desk rather than on top of the CPU box for the correct viewing level and to avoid neck strain.

- Set the monitor back on the desk to avoid eyestrain.

- Position the monitor to avoid glare from lighting or from windows behind.

- Fit windows with adjustable blinds to remove any reflections from the screen.

- Use a document holder beside the screen and at the same level to minimise head and eye movements.

- Use the mouse on a mouse mat so that it will move smoothly.

- Use a chair with adjustable height and backrest facilities.

- A footrest should be provided if required by the users.

- Under desk knee and thigh clearances should be adequate for different users.

- The elbow angle should be between $70°$ and $90°$.

- Have the keyboard and mouse at the correct level for the individual user.

- Use a desk lamp to provide local illumination where necessary.

- Ensure cables are safely secured.

- Supply adequate power points and do not overload existing power points.

- Ensure that there is appropriate ventilation arrangements.

MODULE 1

6.4   The Environment (1.6.4.1)

With the creation of digital documents one would imagine that the demand for paper would be reduced. This is not the case. The international demand for paper is higher than ever. This is putting unsustainable demands on the world's forests for supplies of wood to manufacture paper. The solution to this problem is to recycle or use paper that has been made from wood harvested in managed forests.

As computer equipment including printer cartridges expire or become obsolete, they have to be disposed of. Inappropriate disposal is contributing to the build-up of non-biodegradable waste. One of the ways computer users can help the environment is by using recycled printer cartridges and to consider upgrading instead of replacing their computers.

Computers consume energy in the form of electricity. Most computer equipment is supplied with hardware that can be configured to allow for energy-efficient running. It is important that computer users are aware of these features and learn to adjust the settings in order to minimise power consumption. This logo is shown on energy-efficient computer products. Ensuring awareness of such facilities and developments makes people more aware and more favourably disposed towards environmentally friendly use of computers.

6.4.1   Electronic Documents (1.6.4.2)

A digital document is one that can be stored digitally and read from a screen. Many people do not like to read from computer monitors. Instead they like to print documents and read them off-line. Developments in monitor design and the proliferation of laptops with flicker free screens have overcome some of the discomforts associated with reading digital documents.

Section 7   Security

7.1   Information Security (1.7.1.1)

Security involves not only the physical security of the computer equipment but also the security of the data contained on the hard disk, floppy disks and other storage media. After a computer malfunction or a fire, hardware is easily replaced but data may be damaged and rendered completely useless. It is well documented that companies can go out of business after a complete data loss.

There are many risks associated with the storage of computer data so it is essential that organisations and their employees are proactive in protecting important information. This is best achieved by introducing an information security policy. This policy might include recommendations such as:

- Well-documented company procedures for backing up data.

- Employees being aware of their responsibilities when working with sensitive data.

- Procedures for reporting and dealing with security incidents.

- Regular staff seminars designed to highlight changes in security procedures.

- The appointment of a person solely responsible for data security.

7.1.1 Privacy Issues (1.7.1.2)

When a person's data is entered into a computer system it is the responsibility of the computer owner to ensure that the data is kept confidential. This confidentiality is covered by data protection legislation and is dealt with in more detail in Section 8.2.

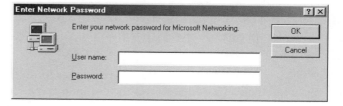

A Typical Log-On Window

Data in any organisation should be available only to those who have and need **access rights** to ensure the privacy of people whose details are kept in databases. These rights must be linked to a system of security clearance controlled by someone in authority. In order to control access rights, all computers or networks must be configured so that users are required to enter a **username.** This is a special word or group of characters that uniquely identifies the user. As well as a username a unique **password** should also be entered. A password is similar to an ATM PIN number but is made up of characters and numbers.

This system of usernames and passwords protects data from being accessed by unauthorised people. As many computer systems are now accessible over the Internet, the need for security is self-evident.

7.1.2 Back-ups (1.7.1.3)

Information on a computer is stored electronically. Because of this, there is always a possibility that it can be lost due to a malfunction in the system or through human error. So as to avoid total loss of data, it is important to have copies of all important files stored on disks or other removable media. These copies are called **back-ups**.

Back-ups can be made in several ways. Copies can be made to floppy disks, zip disks, tape cassettes or external hard disks. The data from some files may also be kept as hard copy. These back-ups should be kept in a safe and secure place – for example, locked away in fireproof containers or off the premises in a remote location.

7.1.3 Security of Personal Equipment (1.7.1.4)

The security risks attached to small IT equipment such as mobile telephones or laptop computers must be realised and steps taken to ensure their security and safety. If a mobile telephone, PDA or laptop computer is lost or stolen a considerable amount of private data is put at risk. All of these pieces of equipment are supplied with security tools and it is very important that the people responsible for them use these features.

In the event of a mobile telephone being stolen or lost, the owner should contact their service provider and advise them of the situation. This will ensure that the telephone will not be used to make calls, but it does not stop someone from using the data that has been stored on the **SIM card**.

Unfortunately when a PDA or laptop is lost or stolen, the owner has no control over what happens to the data, yet some precautions can be taken:

- All data should be backed up regularly, as outlined above.

- Sensitive data should not be kept unprotected. The files should be password protected.

- The laptop or PDA should be configured so it will not start without a username and password.

Apart from the inconvenience of losing a mobile phone, PDA or laptop the loss of important contact details, files, e-mails or confidential information may lead to a breach in client confidentiality or contravene data protection legislation.

7.2 Computer Viruses (1.7.2.1)

Viruses are software programs written with the intention of causing inconvenience and disruption. They can cause serious damage to files or to the whole operating system and even to networks by corrupting their data or operating system software. Unless precautions are taken, a computer user may be unaware that there is a virus on the computer until its effects become apparent, and often at that stage the damage has been done.

Viruses can be spread from one computer to another by files on floppy disks or on other media that are shared. They can also be spread across a network or via e-mail and the Internet.

Many viruses are specific to a particular kind of file, such as a word processing file. When an 'infected' file is opened on the computer, the virus attaches itself to other similar files and so the virus spreads within the computer. If an infected file is sent to a different computer, the virus can infect that computer too and so the process continues.

Other viruses, called **worms**, can operate independently and spontaneously and do not depend on file transfer to infect computers. A **Trojan horse** virus can be innocently downloaded as a music or graphic file and when clicked on the damage starts. Each computer virus is designed to have a particular effect on a computer. Here is the profile of a typical virus.

Name	Bugbear
Discovered	September 2002
Risk	Medium
Method of distribution	E-mail and networks
Trigger mechanism	Opening or previewing an infected message in an e-mail program can start an infection.
Result	When the virus is let loose it will attempt to immobilise security products, including many forms of anti-virus and firewall protection. It will also attempt to install a 'backdoor trojan' that can capture what the user types, including passwords and sensitive data.

7.2.1 Prevention is Better than Cure (1.7.2.2)

It is important to guard against viruses by installing software that checks for viruses before they enter the system. Anti-virus software is available from software vendors. It can detect and remove viruses found on the computer and it can automatically check floppy disks and e-mail attachments for viruses. As new viruses appear all the time, after virus protection software has been installed it is important to keep it up-to-date by investing in regular upgrades. If your virus protection detects a virus it cannot handle it will advise you of the situation and make recommendations for dealing with the rouge file.

If up-to-date anti-virus software is not installed on your computer, you should take certain precautions:

- Do not use the Internet unless you have to.

- Avoid using floppy disks from unreliable or unknown sources.

- Use only reputable registered software.

- Never open an e-mail attachment.

- Keep regular back-ups of your data to minimise any disruption caused by virus infection.

7.2.2 Viruses on the Net (1.7.2.3)

The Internet is rapidly becoming the primary source of virus infection. As more people spend more time using the Internet, they need to become aware of how easy it is to become infected. Here are some simple precautions that should prevent your PC from contacting a virus from the Internet:

- When purchasing virus software be certain that it can automatically scan e-mails when they are being received or sent.

- When setting up the virus software make sure you install and configure all the various features that are supplied with the product.

- Take care when downloading files from websites. Make sure that you scan them with current virus software.

- Be aware that having the latest version of the virus software does not guarantee protection.

- Sometimes viruses are distributed by e-mail. These can arrive in the form of special offers or good news, friendly greetings, advice and so on. Never open a suspect e-mail or attachment.

- Check out your virus software vendor's website for news bulletins on virus infection.

- Listen to the news on radio and TV, as large virus outbreaks are often reported.

Section 8   Copyright and Law

8.1   Copyright (1.8.1.1)

Copyright is defined as a group of legal rights that protect creative works from being reproduced, performed or disseminated without permission. Commercial software is covered by copyright similar to printed media such as books. You are obliged to look after your software and not allow others to copy it. You should purchase and register your own software for your own use.

- Program or application disks should be copied only for the purposes of back-up and safe-keeping as specified in the licence agreement. If the original disks are damaged or become corrupted, the back-up copies can be used to reinstall the software.

- Sharing or lending program disks may be in breach of licensing agreements.

- Transferring or copying software over a network should only be carried out under the terms of the software license agreement. **Single user** or **stand-alone** copies of software should not be used on networks.

- **Software piracy**, the illegal duplication, distribution, sale and use of software, is a criminal offence.

- Copyright legislation may also apply to shareware and freeware (see below).

The Internet allows access to a vast library of information in various formats. Material downloaded from the Internet is the property of the person or organisation that put it there. Whether in paper or digital format, all graphics, text, audio and video files on the Internet are protected by copyright and the owner's permission must be sought if the material is to be used for any purpose other than that intended.

8.1.1   Disks and Copyright (1.8.1.2)

Material stored on removable media such as CDs, zip disks or diskettes must be checked for copyright before it is distributed. Commercial software produced on these media are likely to require your commitment to a licensing agreement.

8.1.2   Product ID and Shareware (1.8.1.3)

Most commercial software is distributed with a **product ID number**. This unique number usually identifies the product item and distinguishes it from other versions of the same product that are licensed to users. Telephoning the manufacturer and quoting the number can check its authenticity. It is important to note that the product ID number may be required to update or run a program. It is common practice amongst software developers to provide access to an application's product ID number through the Help function. Typically, with Microsoft Office applications, clicking on the word **Help** on the application's Menu bar and selecting the **About** menu item on the drop-down list will present you with a window containing the number.

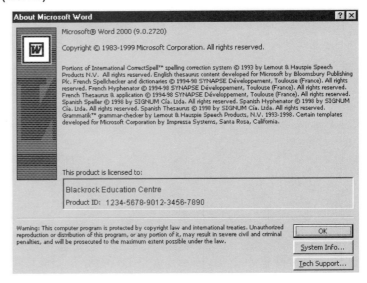

8.1.3 Shareware

Many computer programmers and hobbyists write software programs and allow them to be distributed freely as **shareware**. Distribution may be via the Internet or on the CDs distributed with magazines. Shareware is copyrighted software that allows you a try-it-out period before you make the purchase. Payment for shareware is based on an honour system. If you wish to continue using the software after the trial period, you are required to send a payment, usually nominal, to the author.

To encourage payment, many shareware programs will only function for a limited period or some functions may be disabled. Paid-up users may get additions and free updates. The quality of shareware is variable but some programs, such as early versions of the popular image-editing program Paint Shop Pro®, are of professional standard. Current versions of this program are no longer shareware.

8.1.4 Freeware

Freeware is similar to shareware. It is also distributed freely, but no payment is expected. Some authors may ask for feedback or for a reciprocal action ('Do something nice for someone', or 'Send me a postcard.') As with shareware, freeware comes in an 'as is' condition. Some developers may freely distribute the first version of their product so that they can benefit from users' reactions in the development of the program. Freeware authors often retain all the rights to their software under copyright legislation. Copying and distributing further copies of the material may not be allowed.

8.1.5 Public Domain Software

This is software in which ownership has been relinquished to the public at large. It is freely available, can be copied and/or modified and no payment is involved.

8.1.6 End User Agreement

When you purchase a software package, you are not paying for ownership but for the right – a **licence** – to use the product. It is important to read the **licensing agreement** displayed on the carton or in the accompanying documentation. It is also common practice among software companies to display the agreement on screen at some stage when the software is being installed on the computer. No matter where the licence agreement is displayed, you are legally obliged to adhere to it if you use the software.

Most copies of software are **single-user** copies. This means that the purchaser may only use the software on one computer. A **site licence** can be purchased if the software is to be installed on a number of computers. Only one copy of the software is supplied but the site licence legally entitles the purchaser to install it on a specified number of computers. The cost of a site licence is generally much lower than the cost of buying individual copies of the software for each machine.

8.2   Data Protection Legislation (1.8.2.1)

Personal data is legitimately held by a number of institutions and agencies. People's detailed financial records may be held by a bank or financial lending institution with which they conduct business. Such records could include a person's monthly income, mortgage repayment details, schedules of loan repayments, overdraft requirements, credit rating, savings and investments and so on. Local authorities may have details on services to which an individual is entitled that could include payment records of local taxes and charges, dog licences, applications for planning permission, planning objections and appeals. Some of this information may indeed be stored for public access. Sensitive medical records will be held by various agencies from health boards, general hospitals, local area clinics and general practioners.

In each of the cases cited, it is important to govern access to the information and the use to which the information is put. Data protection legislation exists to ensure appropriate levels of privacy are safeguarded and the information is used only in an appropriate manner.

In the Republic of Ireland, a Data Protection Act was passed on 13th July 1988 and came into force on 13th April 1989. The following is an extract from *IRELAND The Data Protection Act, 1988, A Summary from the Data Protection Commissioner.*

> 'The Act gives a right to every individual, irrespective of nationality or residence, to establish the existence of personal data, to access any such data relating to him, and to have inaccurate data rectified or erased. It requires data controllers to make sure that the data they keep are collected fairly, are accurate and up-to-date, are kept for lawful purposes, and are not used or disclosed in any manner incompatible with those purposes. It also requires both data controllers and data processors to protect the data they keep, and imposes on them a special duty of care in relation to the individuals about whom they keep such data.'
>
> *The Data Protection Commissioner, Dublin*

Similar legislation has been passed by other governments. You should contact the appropriate authority regarding the legislation that applies in your own country.

It is essential that any data relating to individuals that you store or to which you have access on a computer be adequately protected. There are certain legal obligations relating to this in many countries.

The following points illustrate the importance of protecting privacy and of knowing the procedures that may be in place governing your work with such information. They are taken in part from the *Guidelines for Data Controllers* issued by the Data Protection Commissioner for the Republic of Ireland.

- **Use of Data:** '...the data...shall be kept only for one or more specified and lawful purposes...'

- **Not Excessive:** '...the data...shall be adequate, relevant and not excessive in relation to that purpose or purposes...'

- **Retention of Data:** '...the data...shall not be kept for longer than is necessary for that purpose or purposes...'

- **Disclosing Information:** '...the data...shall not be used or disclosed in any manner incompatible with that purpose or purposes...'

- **Security:** '...appropriate security measures shall be taken against unauthorised access to, or alteration, disclosure or destruction of, the data and against their accidental loss or destruction...'

- **Right of Personal Access:** 'Every individual about whom a data controller keeps personal information has a number of rights under the Act, in addition to the Right of Access. These include the right to have any inaccurate information rectified or erased, to have personal data taken off a direct mailing list, and the right to complain to the Data Protection Commissioner.'

Module 2

Using the Computer
and
Managing Files

2

MODULE 2

Module 2

Using the Computer
and
Managing Files

MODULE 2

Introduction

Syllabus Goals for Module 2

Using the Computer and Managing Files requires the candidate to demonstrate knowledge and competence in using the common functions of a personal computer and its operating system. The candidate shall be able to adjust main settings, use the built-in help features and deal with a non-responding application. He or she shall be able to operate effectively within the desktop environment and work with desktop icons and windows. The candidate shall be able to manage and organise files and directories/folders, know how to duplicate, move and delete files and directories/folders and compress and extract files. The candidate shall also understand what a computer virus is and be able to use virus-scanning software. The candidate shall demonstrate the ability to use simple editing tools and print management facilities available within the operating system.

The Computer

This module begins with instructions about how you turn on the computer. From this starting point you will progress through descriptions of the various ways of working with the computer. You will learn how to manage and manipulate what you see on the screen. The purpose of this module is not just to assist you in getting around but to provide you with the skills to be in control, to know where you are going and what you are doing when you interact with the computer.

In computer terms, this module will provide you with the operational skills and knowledge to work effectively with the Windows operating system.

Files and Filing

In a traditional office, all your work is produced on paper and can be seen, stored, filed and retrieved relatively easily. The computer can be thought of as storing files in exactly the same way as traditional office filing systems, but it does this electronically.

But where are all your documents? How are they stored? Will you be able to find them again the next time you switch on the computer? The work you have produced with the computer and the information you have stored in it may also be retrieved. When you need it again, the computer locates the stored information that you wish to use and places it on the screen for viewing.

It is important to understand where and how the computer stores the information so that you can access it with the same ease and facility you have with paper files. In this module you will learn to relate electronic files to 'real world' files so that you can organise and use them efficiently.

Section 1   The Computer Environment

1.1   Getting Started

1.1.1   Starting the Computer (2.1.1.1)

Most computers have two switches, one on the computer
'box' and another on the monitor. There may be another
switch for the loudspeakers, if any. Each of these switches
must be in the 'on' position, usually indicated by a
coloured light.

The switches and lights on your computer may be in
positions different to those in the illustration. When you
turn the computer on, various items appear briefly on the
screen while the computer is starting up.

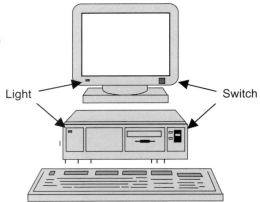

Do not use the mouse or keyboard until you see the
Welcome to Windows screen, as this may interrupt the
start-up process.

In a network environment a message may appear on the screen. You may be asked to press a
combination of keys, such as **Ctrl+Alt+Delete**, to login. You may also need to supply a user name
and password. Your instructor will tell you what to do at this point. Alternatively, if you are working
on your computer at home, the desktop should be the next screen that you will see.

The Windows desktop will appear, a sample of which is shown below. The desktop is covered in
detail in Section 2 of this module.

1.1.2 The Start Menu

The **Start** button, located at the bottom left of the Windows screen, is the focal point of the Windows environment. Using the Start button you can access everything that your Windows environment has available, such as programs, hardware, documents and so on.

Click the **Start** button once with the left mouse button to display the **Start** menu.

A **menu** is a list of **commands** for the computer. You can choose from a menu by moving the **pointer** over an item on it or by clicking an item with the mouse.

When you select a menu item, the computer performs an action. Typically it will move you to a sub-menu.

A small arrowhead to the right of a menu item indicates there is an associated sub-menu. When you move the cursor over it, as illustrated here, the sub-menu appears.

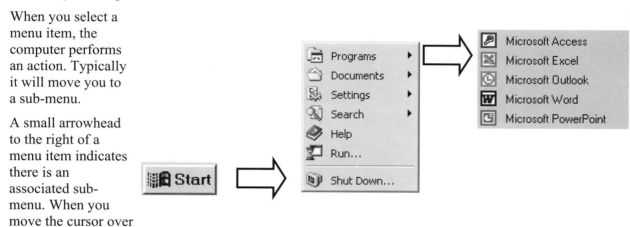

Moving or clicking the pointer over the menu item **Programs** displays the **Programs** menu, a list of the programs on the computer. Programs are commonly referred to as **applications**. The words are interchangeable. Menu items in the sub-menu may have further sub-menus associated with them. Click on the item you require to open it.

The principal items in the **Start** menu are described in this table.

Menu Item	Function
Programs	Displays a list of the programs installed on the computer.
Documents	Displays a list of the documents you have recently used.
Settings	Displays sub-menus from which you can alter various computer and printer settings.
Search	Opens a program to help you find documents, files, folders, shared computers or mail messages.
Help	Displays a Help screen to assist you in using the computer.
Run	Manually starts a program when you type in a command.
Shut down	Shuts down, restarts or allows you to 'log off' the computer.

1.1.3 Shutting Down (2.1.1.2)

When you have finished using the computer you must follow a special **Shut Down** procedure.

If you switch off the computer without going through the Shut Down procedure there will be problems the next time you switch it on. You will also lose any work that was not saved prior to switching off.

If the computer is connected to a network, you may have to disconnect from the network before shutting down. To shut down the computer, do the following:

- Click the **Start** button.

- Select **Shut Down**.

- Check that **Shut down** is selected in the window that appears.

- Confirm by clicking the **OK** button.

You will be prompted to save any work you have been doing that you have not already saved.

The computer then takes a few moments to prepare itself to be switched off. When you see the message '**It is now safe to switch off your computer**' you can switch it off.

Some computers will automatically switch off and the message is not displayed. In most instances, the monitor and loudspeakers must be switched off separately.

1.1.4 Switching On Again

If you want to switch on the computer again after switching it off, you should wait for *at least ten seconds* before doing so. This allows all the electrical circuits in the computer to discharge completely before you switch it on again. Switching on too soon may cause problems.

Remember to wait for the desktop screen to appear before using the keyboard or mouse.

1.1.5 Restarting the Computer (2.1.1.3)

There may be times when you want to restart the computer to reset any of the default settings or you may feel that there is a problem with the computer that could be corrected by simply restarting. When you **restart** your computer it is momentarily switched off and restarted again.

- Wait for the Windows desktop to appear.

- Click the Start button.

- Select Shut Down.

- Click on the arrow and select Restart.

- Click OK to restart the computer.

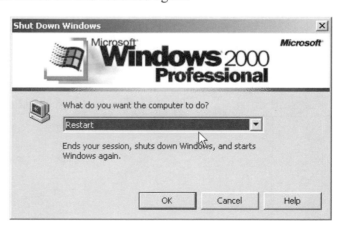

1.1.6 Shutting Down a Non-Responding Application (2.1.1.4)

Occasionally a problem may arise where the computer appears to 'freeze' or ceases to respond to the mouse or to the keyboard. In this case it is necessary to force the computer to end the task it is engaged in.

Using the **Task Manager** you can force the computer to end a task that appears to have a serious problem. For example:

- Press **Ctrl+Alt+Delete**.
  The **Windows Security** window is displayed.

- Click the **Task Manager** button.
  The **Windows Task Manager** window is displayed.

- Click on the **Task** name for the non-responding application.

- Click **End Task**.

Section 2   The Desktop

2.1   Working with the Desktop

The computer **desktop** is a screen with a number of **icons** arranged vertically on the left and a bar, called the **taskbar**, along the bottom. The work you do on the computer will be done on top of this desktop in much the same way as you would do work on a normal desk.

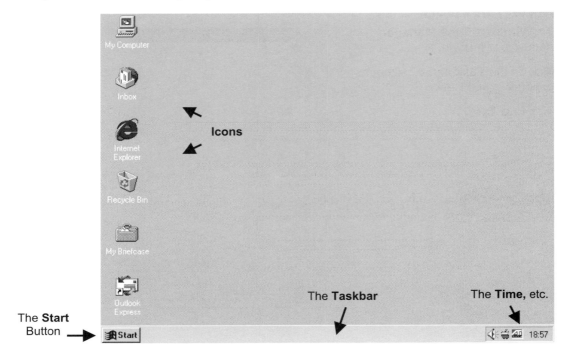

The **Start** button appears on the left-hand side of the **taskbar**. As discussed in **Section 1**, you can use the **Start** button to access programs, games, documents and so on.

2.1.1   Working with Icons (2.2.1.1)

Each icon on the desktop represents a program, function, folder or document that you can open and work with. By double clicking a desktop icon, the function it performs is activated.

Some of the icons common to the desktop are listed below.

       Opens a window which displays the contents of your computer.

       An application icon, such as the **Word** icon here, can be used to start the program.

Opens the Recycle Bin which lists any files and folders that you have previously deleted. See Section 3.6 in this module for more details on using the Recycle Bin.

A folder icon, such as **My Documents**, can be clicked to open and view the folder contents.

A document icon, such as the **Facsimilie.doc** example here, can be used to open the file within the application in which it was created, such as Word, Excel, etc.

A printer icon can be used to open a window to display the status for the printer, whether or not it is the default printer, or to access the list of documents it may have lined up for printing.

2.1.2 Selecting and Moving Icons (2.2.1.2)

The icons on the desktop are usually arranged in a vertical line down the left side of the screen but the user can change the arrangement to suit his or her individual preferences.

- To **select** a desktop icon, simply click on the icon. The icon will be highlighted and a fine border will appear around the outside of the icon's name.

- To **move** an icon, click on it once to select it and hold down the mouse button and move (drag) the icon to another location on the desktop.

2.1.2.1 Arranging Icons

In addition to moving individual icons on the desktop, you can also **arrange** them in a more specific way.

- Right click anywhere on a blank area of the desktop. A **menu** is displayed. Select **Arrange Icons** to display a sub-menu.

- Click on the different options and observe the effect as the icons are arranged by **Name**, by **Type** and so on.

- When there is a tick by **Auto Arrange** at the bottom of the menu, the computer will arrange the icons automatically. With **Auto Arrange** ticked it is not possible to drag icons to other positions on the desktop.

  Notice that it is always brought back to the vertical arrangement at the left of the screen.

2.1.3 Opening an Icon from the Desktop (2.2.1.3)

You can start an application or open a file or folder using desktop icons.

- Double click the icon representing the application or file/folder you wish to open.

2.1.4 Creating a Desktop Shortcut Using the Menu Options (2.2.1.4)

As an alternative to using menus to open an application, you can create your own **desktop shortcuts** for direct access to regularly used applications.

In this example we will create a desktop shortcut to the application **Notepad**, a simple word processing program, using the following steps:

- Click on **Start**, then **Programs** and select the **Accessories** option in the sub-menu.

- Point at the **Notepad** option and right click.

- Select **Create Shortcut** in the pop-up menu.
  A new shortcut will appear below the **Notepad** menu item.

- Point at the new shortcut, left click, hold and drag the new shortcut onto the desktop.
  The menu disappears and the new shortcut is left on the desktop.

2.2   Working with Windows

When you double click a folder icon, a panel opens on the desktop in which the contents of the folder – represented by icons – are displayed. This panel is called a **Window** – it is a 'window' through which we can see into the folder.

2.2.1   Parts of a Window (2.2.2.1)

The illustration below shows the open **Control Panel** folder on a computer. The main part of the window displays the contents of the folder. Around the window there are various features you can use to manage and use the window effectively.

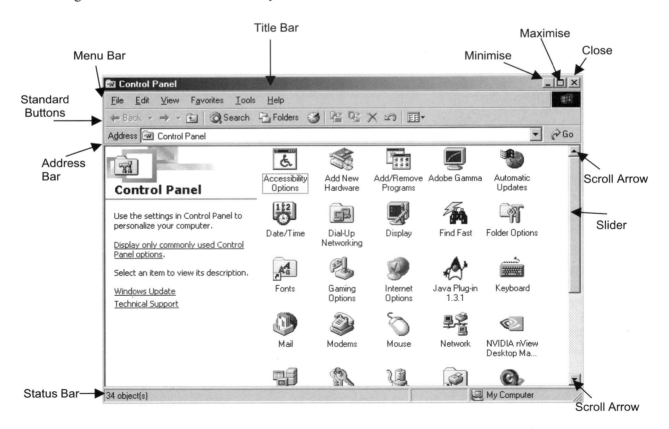

The **Title bar** displays the name of the window on the left. On the right of the Title bar are three buttons for changing the size of the window and for closing it. Please see Section 2.2.3.2 in this module for more information.

The **Standard Buttons** bar displays a series of buttons that can be used to perform different tasks within the current window. If you are in the window of a sub-folder, for example, clicking **Back** returns you to the previously opened window.

The **Address bar** displays the current location – the folder that is open or the location on a drive for a particular file. You can also use the **Address bar** to access the web.

The **Menu** bar contains a number of menus that provide various options. Click on a menu name to display the menu itself. Click on an item in the menu to perform that particular action.

The **scroll arrows** appear when a window is too small to display all of its contents (as in the illustration). Click on a scroll arrow to move the contents of the window up or down or from side to side so that you can see more. Hold down the mouse button on a scroll arrow for continuous movement.

The **slider** indicates what part of the window is presently displayed. If the slider is at the top of the window pane, you are viewing the top portion of the folders window. The slider can be dragged to move quickly to another part of the window.

The **Status bar** at the bottom of the window shows how many objects are in the folder altogether.

A panel at the left of the window displays an icon for the folder that is open, such as **Control Panel** in the illustration. You will also see the folder name in the Address box.

When an object in the window is selected, information about it is displayed in the panel on the left.

Should you open another folder within the current folder, the **Up** button enables you to go back up to the previous folder. You can also use the **Back** and **Forward** buttons to move through the various folder levels you have already viewed.

2.2.2 Viewing Windows

The contents of a window can be displayed and arranged to suit your personal preferences. To arrange icons within a window, do the following:

- Click the **View** menu to display a list of options.

  The tick beside **Status bar** indicates that the Status bar is currently displayed (at the bottom of the window).

  The bullet (large dot) beside **Large Icons** indicates that the contents of the window are currently displayed as large icons.

- Click **Toolbars** to display the sub-menu of toolbar items. Select an item you want displayed.

- Click **List** to display the contents of the window in list format, arranged – with small icons – alphabetically in columns.

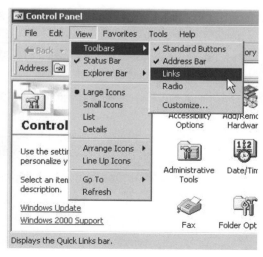

- Click **Small Icons** to display the contents of the window with small icons, which is useful if you have a large number of items to view.

- Click **Details** to view the contents of the window in a list format, with details such as the name, type and size of files listed beside the icons.

- Point to **Arrange Icons** to display a sub-menu with further options.

2.2.3 Manipulating Windows (2.2.2.2)

You can manipulate open windows to suit your own working requirements. It is particularly useful when you are working between two or more windows to be able to move a window, change its size, minimise it or close it.

2.2.3.1 Moving a Window

To reposition a window on the desktop:

- Place the tip of the pointer in the Title bar, hold down the mouse button and drag. When you release the mouse button the window assumes its new position.

2.2.3.2 Resizing Windows

You can change the size of a window to suit your work. If you have several windows open at once, you may want to have the principal one large enough to work in and the others smaller so that, while you can still see their contents, all of them remain visible on the desktop.

To change the size of a window:

- Move the pointer over the bottom right-hand corner of the window.

- When the pointer changes to a double-ended arrow, as in the illustration, click and drag diagonally to change the dimension of the window's frame. When you release the mouse button the window assumes its new extended or reduced shape.

- You can drag the sides of the window in the same way to change the width or depth of a window.

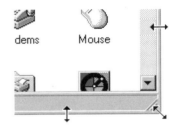

2.2.3.3 Window Buttons

When a window is too small to display all of its contents you can enlarge or **maximise** it to fill the whole desktop area. This is useful where scrolling would be too tedious.

- Click the **Maximise** button at the right of the Title bar to enlarge the window to full screen size.

- When a window is maximised, the **Maximise** button becomes the **Restore** button.

- Click the **Restore** button to return the window to its previous size.

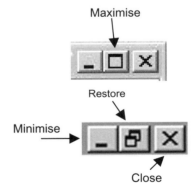

If you want to temporarily remove a window from the desktop you can reduce or **minimise** it. The window closes, disappears off the desktop and a button representing it appears on the taskbar.

- Click the **Minimise** button to temporarily close a window and reduce it to a button on the taskbar.

- To open a minimised window again, click its button on the taskbar.

- To close a window completely, click the **Close** button.

2.2.4 Switching Between Open Windows (2.2.2.3)

It is common to have several windows open on the desktop at once but you can only work with one window at a time.

The window you are working with is called the **active** window. The Title bar of the active window is in colour (usually blue) while the Title bar of an inactive window is grey.

The **My Computer** window is the active window in the illustration. It is in front of the other windows and obscures them.

- Click on a window to bring it to the front. It is then the active window.

- If you want to see the contents of two or more windows at once, move them so that they do not obscure each other or resize them so that you can see the parts that you want to work with.

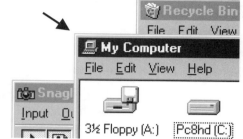

The taskbar always displays a button for any window that is currently open. You may also click on a button in the taskbar to make that window active.

Taskbar Buttons

2.2.5 The Application Window

When you open an **application** it appears on the desktop in its own window, which normally covers the whole desktop area.

A **blank document** – a 'sheet of paper' in the case of a word processor, for example – usually appears in the window when it opens.

The appearance of the window varies, depending on whether or not a document is displayed.

A selection of **menus**, **buttons** and other **tools** appears around the window.

Only some tools are displayed on the screen at any one time although many more may be available. The more toolbars that are displayed, for example, the less screen space that is available for your work. The hidden tools may be accessed as required, using the display options in the **View** menu.

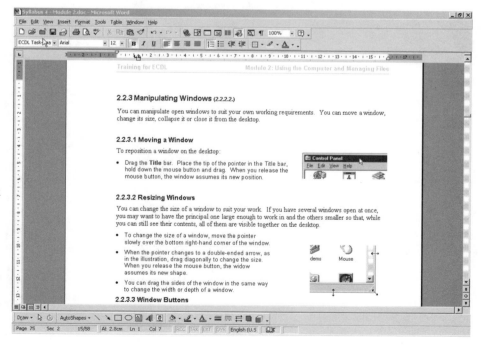

If there is no open document in the
application window, a blank grey area
appears where the document would
normally appear.

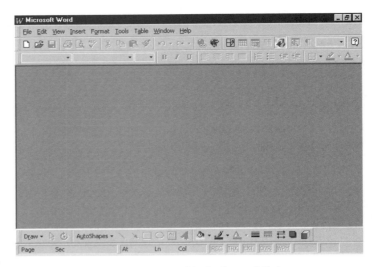

Notice that most of the tools are **greyed
out**, as in the illustration on the right.
This means that they are not available
for use – you cannot use tools when
there is nothing to use them on!

The document in the illustration on the
previous page does not quite fill the
window but it can be **enlarged** or
reduced as required.

No Document – Tools Greyed Out

Using the **Zoom** button on the Standard
toolbar, you can change the percentage
display for a document. The smaller the
percentage, the more the page can be seen but the print will be smaller. The larger the percentage, the
more print can be seen but not as much of the page.

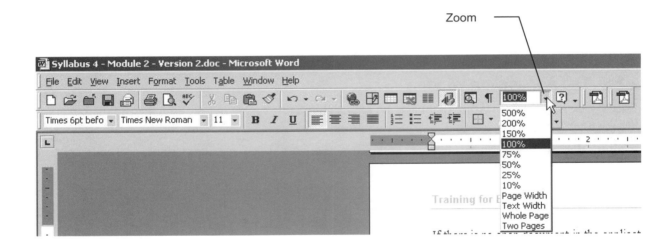

Section 3   Managing Files and Folders

3.1   Introduction

A **file** is an organised collection of information. The word 'file' is also used to describe information that is stored, used or accessed by someone using a computer. Files stored in the office filing cabinet are used by the office staff. The work you prepare on the computer, such as Word documents, are files. The applications that you use to prepare your work are themselves stored in the computer as files. The instructions the computer needs in order to operate are also files.

A **folder** in the computer is an electronic container in which files can be stored. Folders are used to store files in an organised way. A folder may contain both files and other folders, just as a folder in the office filing cabinet may have letters and other folders inside it.

3.1.1 Storage Devices (2.3.1.2)

Files and folders must be saved on a **storage device** so that you can access them again in the future. Typically, files and folders can be stored on a diskette, the hard disk of a computer, a CD-ROM, a zip disk or a network drive. For more information on storage devices, please refer to Section 2.6 in Module 1.

3.1.2 The Directory Structure (2.3.1.1)

The **folders** on the computer's hard disk are also referred to as **directories**. Folders are stored and organised on the computer's hard disk into different levels – somewhat like the levels in a family tree.

The first level is the hard disk (C:) itself – one big folder that contains everything else. For this reason it is referred to as the **root** directory.

When you make a folder or save a file directly on **C:** you are placing it in the root directory – on the first level.

When another folder or file is **inside** a folder on the root directory, it is on the second level. An item inside a second-level folder is on the third level, and so on.

We can see these levels using **Windows Explorer**, an application in the **Programs** menu. See Section 3.2.4 in this module for more details on using Windows Explorer.

The directories **Webshare**, **Winbbs**, **wincake** and **Windows** all branch out from C:, which means that they are *in* the root directory.

The directories **All Users** and **Application Data** branch off to the right – to the next level – from the **Windows** directory. This means that they are *in* the Windows directory.

The **All Users** directory contains two other directories (on the next level), **Desktop** and **Start Menu**, and so on.

The route from C: to a folder or file is called the **directory path**. It is a way of describing exactly where the folder or file is located on the hard disk.

The path from **C:** to the **Start Menu** folder, for example, is written as follows (a backward slash separates the levels): **C:\Windows\All Users\Start Menu**

3.1.3 Icons

Files and folders are represented on the desktop by **icons**. Icons are small pictures that identify the type of object, file, document or folder that is stored in the computer.

File Icons

ECDL Training.doc Training Course.ppt Budget.xls

Folder Icons

Tours Practice Program Files

3.2   Working with Folders/Directories

As you have already learned, a **folder** in the computer is an electronic container in which files can be stored. Folders are also known as **directories**. You can create your own folders where you wish to save files relating to a particular subject or topic. Always use sensible names for your folders. Relate the name to the contents, i.e. the **Letters** folder should contain letters, the **Finance** folder should contain financial documents and so on.

In the following sequences we will create folders in three different ways. The first method will place a new folder called **Office** on the local hard disk (C:) using My Computer. The second sequence will describe creating a folder called **Income Tax** on the local hard drive but using Windows Explorer. The last procedure will demonstrate the creation of a new folder, **Myself**, from within an application. Lastly, we will create a shortcut on the desktop to a file named **My Details** stored within the **Myself** folder.

3.2.1   Creating a Folder Using My Computer (2.3.2.2)

Clicking the **My Computer** icon on the desktop opens a window that displays the disk drives on your computer and some folders. You can use My Computer to make a folder anywhere on the computer, for example on one of the disks. Double click **My Computer** to open its window.

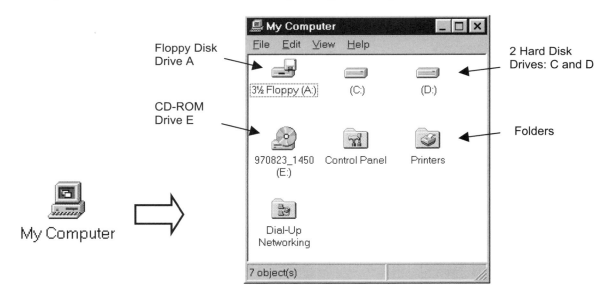

To make a folder on the hard disk (C:), double click the (C:) icon. A window opens in which the contents of the disk are displayed. (The contents of your window may be different.)

This bar displays the name of the window. In this case it is the local disk (C:), the C: Drive window.

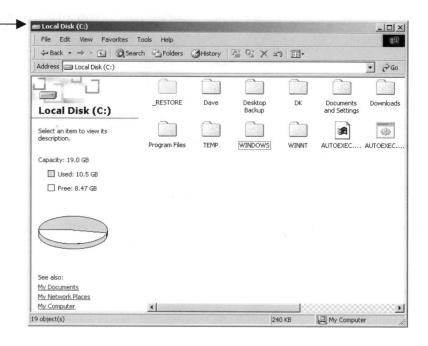

Create a new folder called **Office** on the hard disk (C:). The process is similar to making a folder on the desktop, as described already.

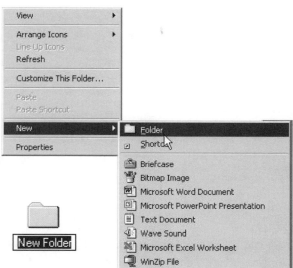

- Right click in a blank area of the local disk window.

- Point to **New** in the menu that appears.

- Click **Folder** in the next menu, the **New** menu.

  A new folder icon appears in the window.

  The words **New Folder** are highlighted, which means that you can type a new name over them if you wish.

- Type **Office** as the name for the folder.

- Press **Enter** or click on the desktop when you are finished.

3.2.2 Creating a Sub-Folder Using My Computer (2.3.2.2)

Now let's create a new folder within the **Office** folder called **Training**. The **Training** folder is known as a **sub-folder**.

- Double click the **Office** folder to open the window for this folder.

- Right click in a blank area of the **Office** window.

- Point to **New** in the menu that appears.

- Click **Folder** in the next menu, the **New** menu.

- Type **Training** as the name for the folder.

- Press **Enter** or click on the desktop when you are finished.

- Close the window on completion.

3.2.3 Navigating to a File or Folder on a Drive Using My Computer (2.3.2.1)

You can navigate through your folders and sub-folders on a particular drive until you find the file or folder you wish to work with.

Once the **My Computer** window is open, simply double click on any folder to open a window that displays its contents. You can then open a sub-folder by again double clicking the folder name.

To practise navigating through different folders:

- Double click the **My Computer** icon on the desktop.

- Double click the **Local Drive (C:)** icon.

- Double click the **Office** folder to open a window displaying its contents.

- Double click the **Training** folder to open its window.

You can use some of the buttons on the **Standard Buttons** toolbar to navigate within the My Computer window.

Use the **Back** button to move back one window at a time through higher-level folders on the directory path you have already accessed. Use the arrow next to the Back button to view the history of windows you have opened.

Use the **Forward** button to move forward one window at a time. Use the arrow next to the Forward button to view the history of windows you have opened.

Use the **Up** button to move back up to the parent folder for the folder you currently have open.

Use the **Views** arrow to select how you wish to view the contents of the window – large icons, small icons, a list or the full details.

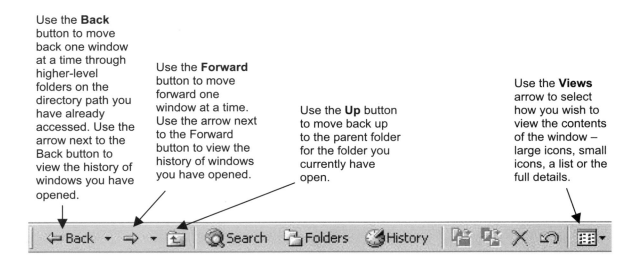

You can also use the **Address** box to view the hierarchical listing for the folder you are currently working in. You can navigate to another folder or drive from this list.

Click on the arrow to navigate between other folders or drives on your computer

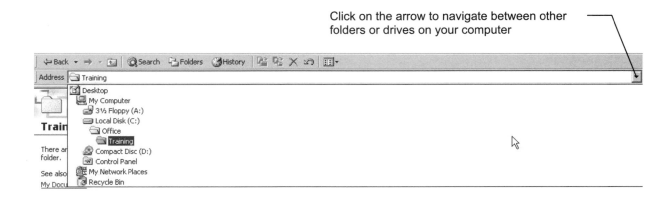

3.2.4 Windows Explorer

Windows Explorer is a program that gives you a more comprehensive view of the computer's contents than My Computer. You should become familiar with it.

To open Windows Explorer:

- Click **Start**.

- Point to or click **Programs** to display the Programs menu.

- Point to or click **Accessories** to display the Accessories menu.

- Click **Windows Explorer**.

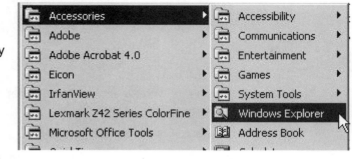

The illustration below shows a set of folders in the **Windows Explorer** window, some of which have been opened to show other folders inside (branching out to the right).

Notice the + and – signs in the small boxes.

When a folder is preceded by a plus (+) it indicates that there are more items inside it.

- Click the plus box (**+**) to display the contents of the folder.

- Click the minus (**–**) box to close an open folder.

Notice the lines that join the folders vertically and horizontally. These help the user to navigate the structure of the hard disk, like a family tree.

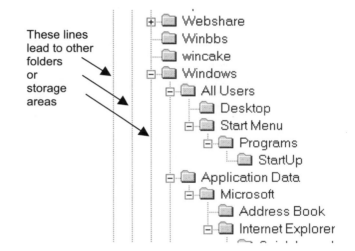

Double click a folder to display its contents in the right-hand part of the window. It is then possible to see any files or other folders it contains and to make new folders there, if required. You can use all the same navigation methods in the Explorer window as you did for the My Computer window. Please refer to Section 3.2.2 in this module for more information.

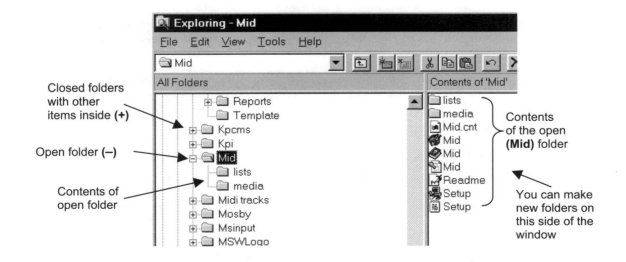

3.2.5 Creating a Folder Using Windows Explorer (2.3.2.2)

To make a folder named **Income Tax** on the **hard disk**, follow these steps.

- Open **Windows Explorer** as described above. Check that the contents of the local disk (drive **C:**) are displayed. (Your computer may be different from the illustration.)

- Click with the right mouse button in the right (Contents) side of the window.

- Click **New** in the menu that appears.

- Click **Folder** in the **New** menu.

  A new folder appears with the words **New Folder** highlighted. This indicates that you may type your own title to replace **New Folder**.

- Type **Income Tax**. It will replace **New Folder.**

- Press **Enter** or click on the desktop when you are finished.

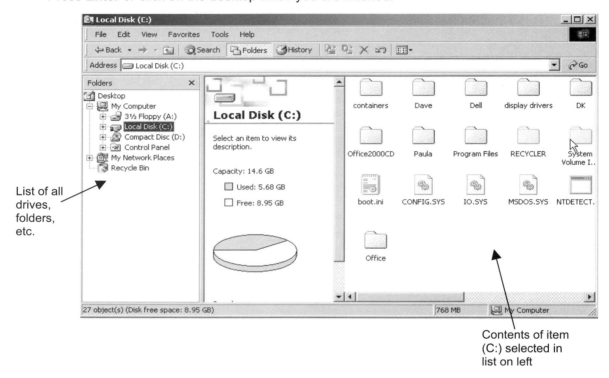

List of all drives, folders, etc.

Contents of item (C:) selected in list on left

3.2.6 Making a Folder from within a Program (2.3.2.2)

You may sometimes need to make a new folder while you are working on a project within an application. In this section we shall open the **Notepad** application, a simple word-editing program. We shall type a few words and save the file in a folder that we will create on the local drive.

Proceed as follows:

- Click the **Start** button and go via **Programs** and **Accessories**.

- Click on **Notepad** to open it.

- Type a piece of text, such as your name and address.

This document must now be saved as **My Details**.

It will be placed in a folder named **Myself**, which we need to create.

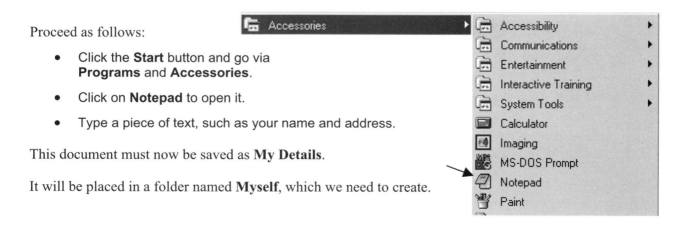

To create the **Myself** folder, follow these steps.

- Select **Save** in the **File** menu.

  The **Save As** window opens.

- The folder in the **Save in** box (**Desktop** in the illustrations) is very often *not* where we want to save the document.

- Click in the **Save in** box to display a menu to help you select where you want to save the file.

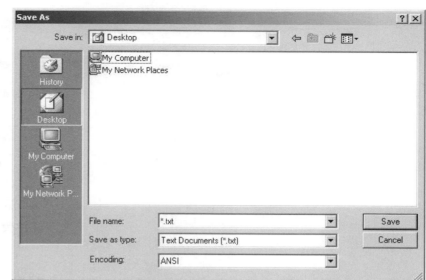

- Click the local disk **(C:)** icon in the menu that appears.

- The **Local Disk C:** icon now appears in the **Save in** window.

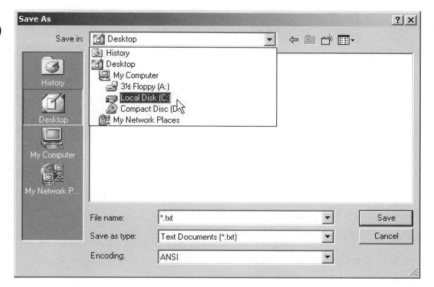

- Click the **Create New Folder** button to the right of the **Save in** box.

  A new folder icon appears.

MODULE 2

- Type the name of the folder, **Myself**, to replace New Folder name and then press **Enter**.

- Double click on the new folder, **Myself**, to open it.

- The **Myself** folder icon now appears in the **Save in** box.

- Type **My Details** in the **File name** box.

- Click the **Save** button.

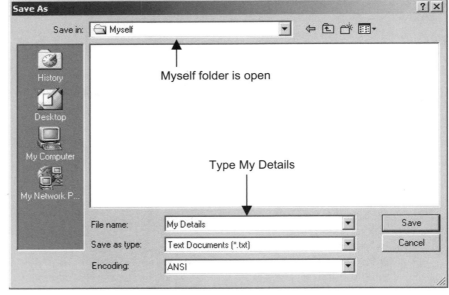

- The file **My Details** is now saved in a new folder named **Myself** on the local hard disk.

- Close **Notepad** if you do not want to prepare any more documents.

3.2.7 Displaying Folder Properties (2.3.2.3)

Using Windows Explorer, My Computer or the folder icon itself you can open a window that displays the folder properties, such as the folder name, its size and location and what it contains.

To display the properties for a folder:

- Right click on the folder name either in the My Computer window or within Windows Explorer.

- Click **Properties**.
  The Properties window opens.

- View the details on the **General** tab.

- Click **OK** to close the window.

3.2.8 Creating a Shortcut to a File (2.2.1.4)

Shortcuts bypass the multiple selections you need to make should a file or folder be located in a sub-directory. To create a desktop shortcut to the file **My Details** stored in the **Myself** sub-directory you would use the following sequence:

- Right click on an empty area of the desktop.

- Click **New** on the pop-up menu, followed by **Shortcut**.
  The Create Shortcut window opens.

- Click the **Browse** button and the Browse for Folder window appears.

- Click the **+** symbol next to the Local Disk (C:).

- Locate the **Myself** folder and click the **+** symbol to expand and see the folder contents.

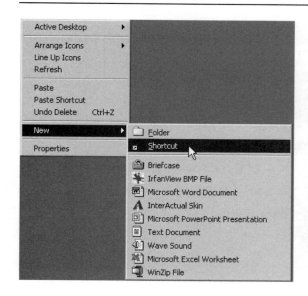

- Click on the **My Details.txt** file to select the target for the shortcut.

- Click **OK** to return to the Create Shortcut window. The location of the file is displayed in the Browse box.

- Click **Next** to continue.

- In the **Select Title** screen, enter an appropriate name for the shortcut and click the **Finish** button to complete the procedure.

You can also create a shortcut to a folder or sub-folder using this process.

This ECDL Foundation approved courseware product incorporates learning reinforcement exercises. These exercises are included to help the candidate in their training for the ECDL. The exercises included in this courseware product are not ECDL certification tests and should not be construed in any way as ECDL certification tests. For information about authorised ECDL test centres in different national territories please refer to the ECDL Foundation website at www.ecdl.com.

Exercise 3A

1   Open the Local Disk C: window using My Computer.

2   Right click on the folder you created earlier named **Office**. View the **properties** for this folder.

3   Close the **Properties** window.

4   Now view the properties for the newly created folder named **Myself**.

3.2.9 Creating a Folder on the Desktop

In addition to creating a folder using My Computer or Windows Explorer, you can also create a folder directly onto the desktop. Use the following steps to create a folder on the desktop called **Training**.

- Right click on an empty area of the desktop.

- Click **New** on the pop-up menu, followed by **Folder**.
  A folder named **New Folder** appears on the desktop.

- Type **Training** to rename the new folder and then press **Enter**.

- Double click the **Training** folder icon to open a window to display the folder's contents (it should currently be empty).

- Close the Training folder window.

Exercise 3B

In this exercise you will create a sub-folder within the newly created **Training** folder.

1   Open the **Training** folder on the desktop by double clicking the **Training** folder icon.

2   Right mouse click in the **Training** folder window to display the pop-up menu.

3   Choose **New** and then **Folder**. A new **folder** will appear in the Training folder window.

4   Type **Letters** as the name of the new folder and press **Enter**.

5   Now create another new folder in the **Training** folder window, this time calling the new folder **Memos**.

6   Close the **Training** folder window.

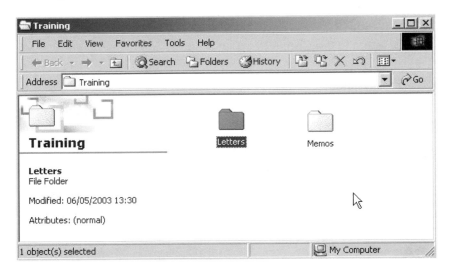

3.3   Saving Files

The work you prepare on the computer, such as documents, spreadsheets and so on, are stored as files. The files that you create should be saved in an organised manner so that they are easier to find and manage. Always use sensible names for your files relating to the contents. For example, **Letter of Acceptance to Sam Smith** is more meaningful than simply **Letter to Sam Smith**.

3.3.1 Saving a Document or File

Any work you produce on the computer must be saved or it will cease to exist when the computer is switched off. You normally save your work on the computer's hard disk. The hard disk is the central storage area of the computer and is generally the safest and most reliable place for your work. You can also save your work on a floppy disk, on a zip disk or other media.

The words **document** and **file** are used interchangeably. A **file** is any kind of work you produce on the computer, whether it is a one-page letter or a database with thousands of records. You might prefer to reserve **document** for something that can be printed out – but remember that a document is also a file.

The procedure for saving a document or file for the first time is different from saving changes to it afterwards. The first time you save a file (or document) the computer needs to know two important pieces of information:

- What is the name of the file?

- Where do you want to save the file?

In the following parts of this section we shall prepare a document, give it a name and save it in a particular location. Begin by completing Exercise 3C.

This ECDL Foundation approved courseware product incorporates learning reinforcement exercises. These exercises are included to help the candidate in their training for the ECDL. The exercises included in this courseware product are not ECDL certification tests and should not be construed in any way as ECDL certification tests. For information about authorised ECDL test centres in different national territories please refer to the ECDL Foundation website at www.ecdl.com.

Exercise 3C

Use the skills you have learned above to do the following.

1   Open the **My Computer** window.

2   Make three folders on the local drive, **Letters**, **Bank** and **Business**.

3   Make three other folders, **National Bank**, **Equity Bank** and **Bahamas Bank** inside the **Bank** folder.

4   Prepare a short letter in **Microsoft Word**, addressed to the **Equity Bank**. (A few words will do.)

How to save the letter is described step by step in the following sections.

3.3.2 Giving a File a Name

To save a document or file for the **first time**, begin by using **one** of the following.

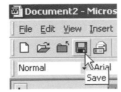

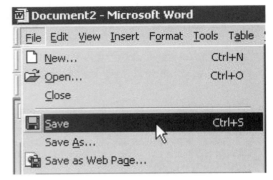

- Click the **Save** button (the one with the floppy disk icon) on the toolbar.

- Select **Save** in the **File** menu.

- Use the keyboard shortcut.

  (Hold down the **Ctrl** key while
  you press the letter **S** on the keyboard.)

Whichever method you use, the Save As window opens.

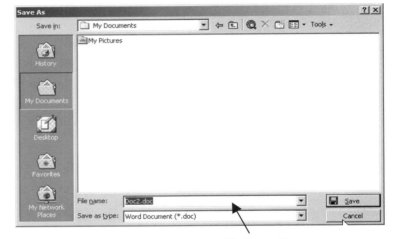

- The appliciation may have already inserted a name in the **File name** box.

  This is rarely suitable and it is already **highlighted** so that you can change it by overtyping a new name on the active text.

  (You do *not* have to click in the box first.)

- For this exercise type **Equity Letter**.

  Whatever you type will replace the text that may be in the box.

  (If you do click in the box first, you will have to delete what is there before you start typing.)

The File Name Box

- Click the **Save** button to complete the saving process.

3.3.3 Where are Files Saved?

If you click the Save button after you have typed in the file name, the computer saves the file for you... but where? If you do not know where the computer saves your file, you will have trouble finding it again when you want to reopen it.

There are two areas where the computer might save your file, in a folder called My Documents or in whatever folder that was last used to save files in, unless you choose the location you desire.

The first area – the My Documents folder – is intended as an 'easy' option for beginners. The computer is set to save everything in it unless instructed to do otherwise.

The second area where the computer might save your file is the folder used the last time a file was saved. This may have been the My Documents folder, but it may just as well have been any other folder on the local drive – whatever was chosen by the last user.

To save your work in an organised way you should set up folders for the principal subject areas of your work. For this exercise, we have already set up the various bank folders.

NOTE

Saving everything in the **My Documents** folder is equivalent to saving all your work and documents in a single drawer in your office desk instead of using the filing cabinet. It may suffice while you only have a few documents, but it will become chaotic very quickly as your work accumulates.

3.3.4 Finding Where to Save

The area where *the computer* is set to save your file is shown in the **Save in** box at the top of the **Save As** window (**My Documents** in the illustration).

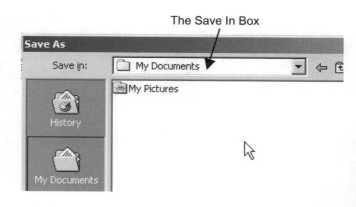

The Save In Box

To save in another location, you must first find the area or folder in which you want the file to be saved.

- Click once in the **Save in** box to display a menu of possible locations.

- Among other icons listed in the menu are those for the **Desktop**, the **Floppy** disk drive (A:) and the **Local Disk** (C:).
    - To save on the **desktop**, click the Desktop icon.
    - To save on a **Floppy** disk, click the Floppy icon (A:).
    - To save on the **Local Disk**, click the Local Disk icon (C:).

The location you select will appear in the **Save in** box.

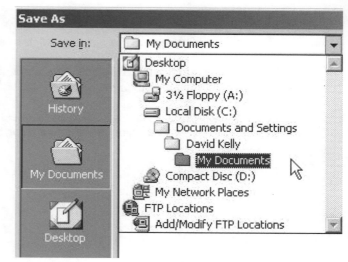

- As the **Bank** folder is on the local disk, click the **Local Disk** icon.

    The **Local Disk** icon now appears in the **Save in** box.

    The contents of the disk appear in the main part of the window underneath.

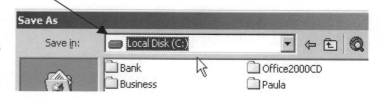

- Scroll through the folders on the local disk, if necessary, to find the **Bank** folder.

- Double click the **Bank** folder to open it.

    The **Bank** folder icon now appears in the **Save in** box with its contents displayed in the main part of the window underneath.

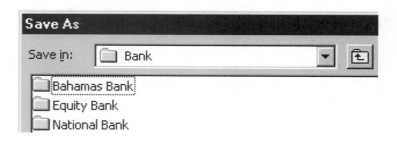

- Double click the **Equity Bank** folder.

  The **Equity Bank** folder now appears in the **Save in** box with its contents (if any) displayed in the window.

  This is where we want to save the **Equity Letter**.

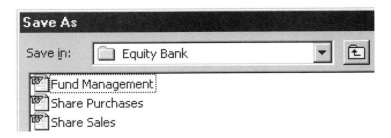

A panel at the left of the window has a number of large buttons.
Click a button to display related information in the main part of the window.

- The **History** button lists the most recently used files and folders.

- File details, such as size, when last modified and so on are also displayed.

- **My Documents** is the folder in which the computer saves your work unless you decide to save it elsewhere.

- The **Desktop** button displays what is on the desktop. You may find this more convenient than clicking in the **Look in** or **Save in** box at the top of the window.

- The **My Network Places** icon identifies the places on the network to which you can save.

3.3.5 Pressing the Save Button

Before you press the **Save** button, you should ask yourself these two questions:

- Have I given my file a name?

- Is the location where I want to save my file shown in the Save in box?

If the answer to both these questions is **Yes**, you can click the **Save** button at the bottom right of the **Save As** window.

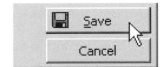

Your file is then saved with the name **you** have given it (**Equity Letter**) and in the location of **your** choice (the **Equity Bank** folder).

3.3.6 Saving Again

When you save a document for the **first** time you have to give it a name and tell the computer where you want to save it, as described above.

As you work on a document you need to **save** it at regular intervals. To save the document **again** after you have added to it or made other changes, use one of the same methods as before.

- Click the **Save button**.

- Select **Save** in the **File** menu.

- Use the **keyboard shortcut** (Ctrl + S).

The **Save As** window does not appear this time. You have already given the document a name and told the computer where it is to be saved, so it does not need to ask you for this information again.

If the document or file is very large, however, you may see a **Progress bar** on the screen telling you that it is being saved. You will then have to wait a moment or two for the computer to finish saving before you can continue using the application.

3.3.7 Using Save As

Save As is also used when you want to save a **copy** of a document or file under a different **name**, in a different **location** or in another **format**.

For example, a previously saved letter to the **Equity Bank** may need only a few changes for a letter you wish to send to the **Bahamas Bank**.

- Open the letter called Equity Letter.

- Make the appropriate text changes.

- Select Save As in the File menu. The Save As window opens.

- Change the name in the File name box to Bahamas Bank Letter.

- Click the Up One Level button on the toolbar to view the contents of the Bank folder.

- Double click the Bahamas Bank folder to open it as the location for where we want to save.

- Click Save.

A new copy of the document is saved with the name **Bahamas Bank Letter** and the new name appears on the **Title** bar.

The original **Equity Letter** document remains unchanged where it was originally saved.

3.3.8 Saving in Different Formats

When you send a document or file to another person they may not be able to use it if they are not using the same kind of computer and software that you used in its preparation. You should check the version of the application the recipient has in advance. Then, if possible, you can save your work in a format they can use, such as an earlier version of Word.

- Go through the **Save** process as before until the **Save As** window appears.

- Click in the **Save as type** box to display a list of available formats.

  (The list on your computer may differ from those in the illustration.)

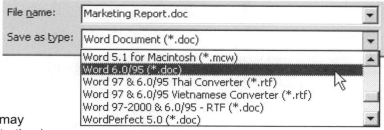

Word **Save As Type** Options

- **Word** options are shown here.

  For alternative word processing save options, select the word processor and/or version your recipient uses, if it appears in the list. For example, for someone with Microsoft Office 95, using Word 6.0, select **Word 6.0/95**. Select the appropriate **Word Perfect** option for a Word Perfect user.

Some other options are described here.

- **Rich text format** (RTF) can be used by most word processors. It preserves common formatting options such as text size, bold, italic and so on but will not be able to reproduce some more advanced formatting.

- **Text only** saves the file as plain text. Any formatting in the original document is discarded but the recipient will at least have access to the text that can then be inserted into other documents and reformatted if necessary. This format can be used by most word processor applications.

- Select **Template** (Document, Presentation, etc.) to save a document in a format that preserves its formatting features for further use. Word templates are described in detail in Module 3.

3.3.9 Saving for the World Wide Web

Documents intended for publication on the **World Wide Web** – on the **Internet** – have to be saved in a special format. The computer language used for documents on the Web is called HTML (see Module 7 for more information) Microsoft Office allows you to save simple documents in this format and they can then be made available to other people on a website.

Documents may be saved in HTML format in two ways.

Using the **File** menu:

- Select **Save as Web Page** in the **File** menu.

  You are asked to give the file a name and say where it is to be saved.

  You are also advised to save the document first as a Word file, as some formatting may be lost in the conversion process.

Using **Save As**:

- Select **Save As** in the **File** menu.

  The **Save As** window opens.

- Select **Web Page (*.htm; *.html)** in the **Save as type** box.

  You are asked to give the file a name, etc., as above.

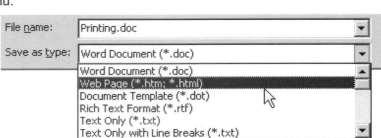

3.3.10 Saving Options

Various options for saving your work are available to suit individual preferences and management options.

- Select **Options** in the **Tools** menu.

  The Options window opens.

- Click the **Save** tab to display the **Save options**.

Select an option you require by clicking in the appropriate tick box. To turn off an option, click in the tick box to remove the tick.

Some of the options available in Word are described here. Similar options are available in the other Office applications.

Always create backup copy saves a second copy of your work every time you save. If the original copy is damaged, your work is not lost.

Allow fast saves speeds up the saving process. Instead of saving the whole document every time you save, the program only saves the additions or changes you made since you last saved and adds them to the previously saved version. This causes the size of the file to increase every time you save.

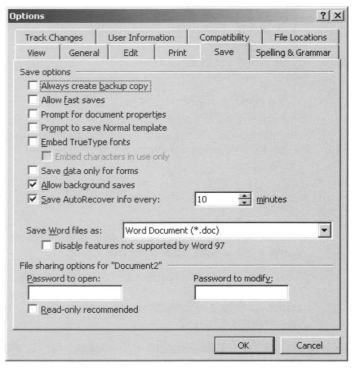

Allow background saves enables you to continue using the computer while your work is being saved. For most users this will be of little significance but more memory is needed to allow background saving. Switching this off will make more memory available to the work in hand.

Save AutoRecover info every automatically saves your work at intervals, as specified in the box. In the event of a computer crash, a power cut or an application freezing, only work done since the last AutoRecover save is lost.

3.3.11 Opening a Saved Document or File

To open a saved document or file, do *one* of the following.

Open Button

- Open the application, such as Word.

- Click the **Open button** on the toolbar.

- Select **Open** in the **File** menu.

- Use the **keyboard shortcut**.

  Hold down the **Ctrl** key while you press the letter **O** on the keyboard.

  The **Open** window appears, similar to the **Save as** window.

- Find the file you want to open.

- When the file is displayed in the

The Open Window

main part of the **Open** window, double click it to open it.

Alternatively, click it once to select it and then click the **Open** button on the bottom right-hand corner of the window.

3.4   Working with Files

The name of a file is in two parts; the **name** itself and the **extension**. They are separated by a dot (full stop) with no spaces. An extension is a set of three letters that identify the file type.

3.4.1   Recognising Common File Types (2.3.3.1)

The **File Name** is the name you give the file when you save it. The extension is usually added automatically when you save a file by the application you are using to create the file. Therefore, in most instances you do not have to type in the file extension.

Each application has its own extension. The extension for a PowerPoint file is **.ppt**, the extension for an Excel file is **.xls** and the extension for an Access database file is **.mdb**, for example. The extension **.doc** in the illustration means that this is a Microsoft Word file – a document.

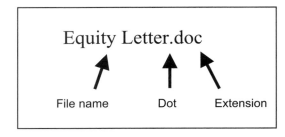

File Name and Extension

When you double click a file icon the computer uses the extension to identify the application it needs to open the file. Thus, **.doc** files are opened by Microsoft Word, **.ppt** files are opened by PowerPoint and so on.

Note that extensions, while always present, may not always be displayed by some computers.

Files are displayed graphically within folders or on the desktop. Each program or application has a unique icon for its files. You can identify the file type by its icon.

Note the sample application icons and their related file extensions below:

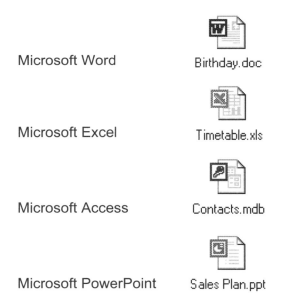

Microsoft Word   Birthday.doc

Microsoft Excel   Timetable.xls

Microsoft Access   Contacts.mdb

Microsoft PowerPoint   Sales Plan.ppt

In addition to the standard file extension for Office programs, there are also many other file extensions. The table below provides a sample of some additional file types and their extensions.

Image Files	**.bmp** (a bitmap format) **.jpg** (a jpeg file interchange format) **.gif** (a graphics interchange format) **.wmf** (a metafile)	
Audio (Sound) Files	**.wav** **.mp3**	
Video Files	**.mpeg (or mpg)** .avi	
Compressed Files (see Section 3.8 on compressing files)	**.zip**	
Temporary Files	**.tmp**	

3.4.2 Maintaining File Extensions (2.3.3.5)

It is important to remember that file extensions help to identify the application with which files were created. It is important that you do not interfere with file extensions that are added automatically. Changing the file extension can confuse the computer as it will not be able to identify which application the file is associated with. When renaming files, for example, you can change the file name but do
not make changes to the file extension.

3.4.3 Counting Files in a Folder (2.3.3.2)

You may wish to keep track of the number of files or sub-folders within a particular folder or on a specific disk or CD. Using the **Properties** window you can display the details of the number of files and folders for a given folder/disk. Access the information using the following procedure:

- Right click on the folder or disk you wish to check, either in Windows Explorer or in the My Computer window.

- Click **Properties**.
  The Properties window opens (see next page).

- The **Contains** line provides details of the number of files within the folder/disk and the number of sub-folders.

- The **Size** and **Size on Disk** lines tell you how much space the folder/disk is using.

- Click **OK** to close the window.

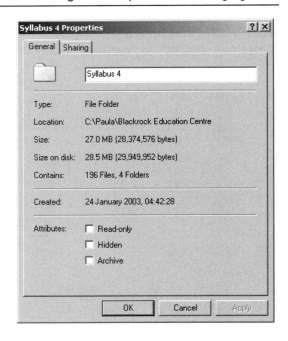

Using a search facility, you can find out exactly how many files of a particular type are contained within a given folder or disk. Please see Section 3.7 on searching for more information.

NOTE

Using Windows Explorer you can click on the name of a folder or disk in the left-hand pane and view the number of **objects** it holds on the Status bar. This number does not distinguish between files and folders, nor does it give details of the contents of sub-folders. However, it is a useful way of quickly seeing the total number of items within a given folder/disk.

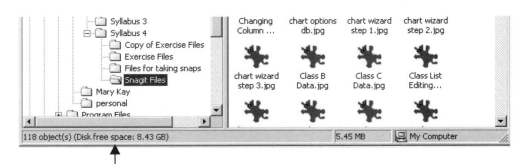

The Status bar displays the number of objects in the **Snagit Files** folder

Exercise 3D

1   Use the My Computer window to view all available drives for your computer.

2   Open the **Local Disk C:** drive.

3   Right click on the folder named **Office**.

4   Choose Properties.

5   View the **General** tab settings.

6   Click **OK** to close the window.

7   View the properties for the **Bank** folder you previously created.

8   Close the **Properties** window on completion.

9   Close the **My Computer** window.

3.4.4 Changing the Status of a File (2.3.3.3)

Most of the files that you create yourself have a status known as "**read-write**". This means that you, or in fact another user, can open the file, read its content, make changes (*write* in it) and then resave it. However, there may be times when you want to make a file "**read-only**" so that the contents of the file can be viewed but not changed.

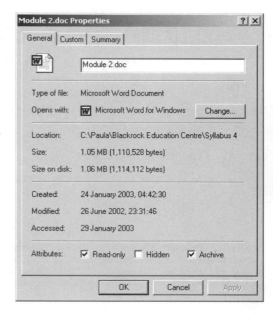

To make a file read-only within the My Computer window or Windows Explorer do the following:

- Right click on the file you wish to make read-only.

- Choose **Properties**.

- Check the **Read-only** box (you can uncheck this box if you want to change the file back to read-write).

- Click **OK** to continue.

3.4.5 Sorting Files (2.3.3.4)

You can sort the contents of a folder or disk into different sequences, such as alphabetically by the file name, the file type (based on the file extensions), by the size of the file or by the date the file was created/modified.

To sort files in either the My Computer window or using Windows Explorer:

- Use the **View** button on the Menu bar to select a view that most suits the sort you are about to perform. For example, if you want to sort by each file's size, it would be a good idea to use the **Details** view so that you can see the size of each file.

- Choose **Arrange Icons** in the **View** menu.

- Select an appropriate sort option from the sub-menu that is displayed.

3.4.6 Renaming Files (2.3.3.6)

You can give a file a new name when using the My Computer window or Windows Explorer. Be careful when renaming files, as files should have unique names. Two files with the same name will cause problems and you may lose data. Remember the importance of file extensions, too. When renaming, make sure that you use the same file extension as the original file name unless there is a very specific reason why you want to change it. Change file names using these sequences:

- Click on the file you wish to rename.

- Right click on the file and choose **Rename**.

Or

- Choose **Rename** from the **File** menu.

- The file name is highlighted.

- Type the new file name and extension.

- Press **Enter** to rename the file.

3.4.7　Renaming a Folder (2.3.3.6)

To rename a folder in the My Computer window or Windows Explorer:

- Click on the folder you wish to rename.

- Right click on the file and choose **Rename**.

Or

- Choose **Rename** from the **File** menu. The file name is highlighted.

- Type the new folder name.

- Press **Enter** to rename the folder.

Exercise 3E

1　　　Rename the folder named **Myself,** naming it **My Work** instead.

3.5　Duplicating and Moving Files

3.5.1　Selecting (2.3.4.1)

Before you can work with a file or folder on the desktop or in a window you must select it first. This tells the computer that this object (file or folder) is the one with which you now want to do something. When an item is selected, its icon changes colour or is **highlighted**.

You can select a single object or several objects at once.

- To select a single object, click on it once.

- To select several objects anywhere in a window or on the desktop, hold down the **Ctrl** key while you click on them in turn.

- To select several files or folders that are beside each other, you can **lasso** them to save time.

- Hold down the mouse button, click in a blank space and drag to make a rectangular lasso over the icons. Note that the lasso does not have to enclose the objects; anything it touches will be selected.

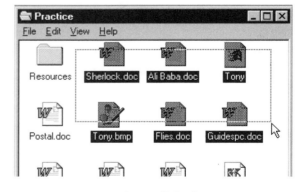

Lasso Selection

- To select all the files and folders in a window, click **Select All** in the **Edit** menu or use the keyboard shortcut, **Ctrl + A**.

When more than one file or folder has been selected they can all be copied, moved or deleted together. Dragging any one of the selected items moves them all.

- To deselect a group of items, click in a blank space on the window pane.

3.5.2 Copying Files and Folders (2.3.4.2)

From time to time you may need to make a copy of a file or folder. For example, you may want to copy an entire folder to back it up. If you copy a folder the entire contents of that folder and any sub-folders it contains are copied to the new location.

To copy a file/folder using the My Computer window or Windows Explorer:

- Click on the file or folder you wish to copy.

- Right click on the file/folder. A menu appears.

- Click Copy in the menu.
  Using My Computer, open the folder or disk representing the destination for the file/folder. Right click in the window and then choose **Paste**. A copy of the file/folder should now be displayed.

  Or

  Using Windows Explorer, click on the disk or folder where the copied file/folder is to be displayed. Right click on the selected object and choose **Paste** in the menu that appears. A copy of the file/folder should now be displayed.

NOTE

When a file/folder is **copied**, the original remains where it is and a **copy** is placed in the new location. This means that there are now two copies of the file/folder available.

3.5.3 Moving Files and Folders (2.3.4.3)

In addition to copying files/folder you can also **move** them. If you move a folder the entire contents of that folder and any sub-folders it contains are moved to the new location.

To move a file/folder using the My Computer window or Windows Explorer:

- Click on the file or folder you wish to copy.

- Right click on the file/folder. A menu appears.

- Click **Move** in the menu.
  Using My Computer, open the folder or disk representing the destination for the file/folder. Right click in the window and then choose **Paste**. The file/folder should now be displayed in the destination location only.

  Or

  Using Windows Explorer, click on the disk or folder where the file/folder is to be displayed. Right click on the selected object and choose **Paste** in the menu that appears.

Exercise 3F

1   Open the **My Computer** window.

2   Open the Local Disk C:.

3   Open the folder named **Bank**.

4   Right click on the **Equity Bank** folder and choose **Copy**.

5   Use the **Up** button on the toolbar to return to the **Local Disk C:**.

6   Open the folder named **Letters**.

7   Right click in the **Letters** window and choose **Paste**. A copy of the **Equity Bank** folder should appear.

8   Open the **Equity Bank** folder and view its contents.

9   Use the **Up** button to return to the **Local Disk C:**.

10   Open the **Bank** folder. Notice that the **Equity Bank** folder is still a sub-folder within the **Bank** folder.

11   Right click on the **Bahamas Bank** folder and choose **Cut**.

12   Use the **Up** button on the toolbar to return to the **Local Disk C:**.

13   Open the folder named **Letters**.

14   Right click in the **Letters** window and choose **Paste**. The **Bahamas Bank** folder should appear.

15   Open the **Bahamas Bank** folder and view its contents.

16   Use the **Up** button to return to the **Local Disk C:**.

17   Open the **Bank** folder. Notice that the **Bahamas Bank** folder is no longer available, as it has been moved.

3.5.4 Moving with Drag and Drop (2.3.4.3)

Another method of moving a file or folder is **drag and drop**. This involves using the mouse to drag the item to its new location (see Before You Begin, Section 1.5).

Here you will drag the folder **My Work** from the local disk window to the **desktop**.

- Use **Windows Explorer** to locate the **My Work** folder that is to be moved.

- Click on the **My Work** folder icon *and keep the mouse button pressed down*.

- Keeping the left mouse button pressed, move the mouse so that the folder moves out of the window onto the desktop.

- Release the mouse button. The file appears on the desktop.

3.5.5 Back-ups (2.3.4.4)

Whilst outside of the scope for this syllabus, at this point it is appropriate to mention the importance of backing up your work onto a removeable storage device in the event that anything should happen to the work in its original storage location or to the computer itself. For example, imagine that you have a folder on your local hard disk (drive **C:**) called **Thesis** that contains a large number of documents relating to a thesis you are working on. If something serious happens to your computer, for example if it was infected by a virus, the contents of the **Thesis** folder could be damaged. Think of the amount of work you would lose if you didn't have another copy of that folder stored separately on another device, such as a **zip disk** or **CD-ROM**.

Back-ups can be made either via Windows 2000 or in the case of some software programs, such as accounting applications, they have their own back-up routines. Seek help in establishing the best way to back up the work on your computer.

3.6   Deleting and Restoring Files/Folders

3.6.1   Deleting (2.3.5.1)

If a file or folder is no longer required, it can be removed from the computer. There are two methods you can use but don't use these procedures with files you are not familiar with:

- **Drag and drop** can be used to move a file from an open folder to the Recycle Bin.

  To delete, drag an item from the My Computer window or Windows Explorer onto the **Recycle Bin**.

Or

- Using Windows Explorer or My Computer, select the file or folder and press the **Delete** key.

- The **Confirm File Delete** window appears. Click **Yes** to delete the file/folder or **No** to cancel the deleting procedure.

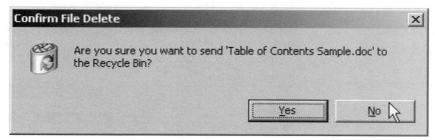

NOTE

Deleting: Deleted files and the contents of folders are not actually removed from the computer immediately – they are placed in the **Recycle Bin** and remain there until it is emptied. This gives you one last chance to retrieve the files/folders.

Note that files deleted from a floppy disk are discarded immediately and cannot be retrieved.

3.6.2   Retrieving and Restoring (2.3.5.2)

If you change your mind about something that you have deleted or dragged to the Recycle Bin, you can restore it if the Recycle Bin has not been emptied.

3.6.2.1 Restoring All Items from the Recycle Bin

- Double click the **Recycle Bin** icon to open it.

- Click on the **Restore All** button in the left panel of the Recycle Bin window.

  The files and folders contained within the Recycle Bin will be restored back to their original locations.

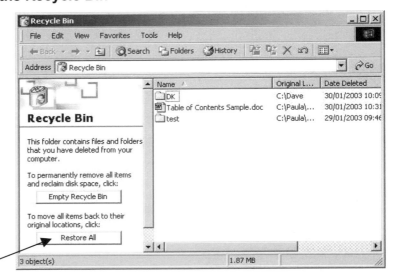

Click here to restore all files/folders

3.6.2.2 Restoring Individual Items from the Recycle Bin

Often you will find that you want to restore only individual items from the Recycle Bin rather than its entire contents.

To restore individual files/folders from the Recycle Bin do the following:

- Double click the **Recycle Bin** icon to open it.

- Click on the file or folder you wish to restore.

- Click on the **Restore** button in the left panel of the Recycle Bin window.

Or

- Choose **Restore** from the **File** menu.

  The file or folder you selected will be restored back to its original location.

Click here to restore the selected item

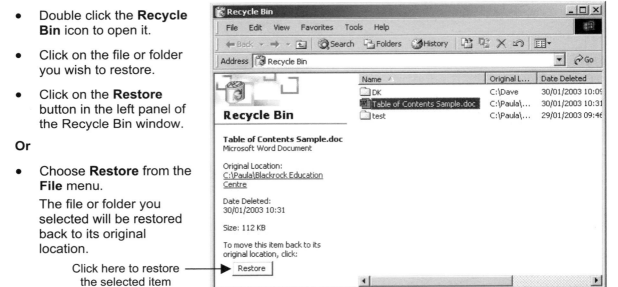

3.6.3 Emptying the Recycle Bin (2.3.5.3)

Items placed in the Recycle Bin remain there until it is emptied. To empty the Recycle Bin it is advised that you open it first to see exactly what it contains before you give the instruction for it to be emptied.

- Double click the **Recycle Bin** icon to open it.

- View the contents of the Recycle Bin to ensure you want ALL items to be permanently removed.

- Click the **Empty Recycle Bin** button in the left-hand panel or choose **Empty Recycle Bin** in the **File** menu.

  The Confirm Multiple File Delete window appears.

- Click **Yes** to delete all items in the Recycle Bin window.

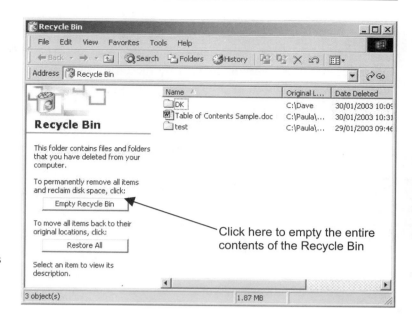

Click here to empty the entire contents of the Recycle Bin

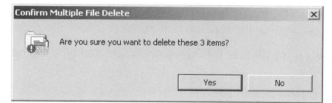

3.6.4 Deleting and Security

Even when you empty the Recycle Bin, the data is **still** not removed from the computer although it is lost to the normal user. What the computer does is to change its hard disk contents list and now marks the area where the data is stored as 'empty'.

The data remains in the 'empty' area until the computer is looking for space on the hard disk to store new data. If it decides that the 'empty' area is suitable, it will replace the old data with the new. It is only then that the old data is erased.

> Imagine having an old music tape that you are no longer interested in. You mentally mark it as being blank – available for taping new material when the occasion presents itself. It is only when you tape new music over the old that the original is erased. Even then some of the old music may remain, depending on the amount of new music you record.

Special recovery programs and utilities may be used to retrieve data even when the Recycle Bin has been emptied. These may be able to rescue important data that has been accidentally deleted or that has been made unavailable because of a major computer breakdown. They can also be used by police and security services to recover information that may help them in their investigations.

For security-sensitive work, programs are available that wipe the 'blank' areas of the hard disk by recording random material over all 'deleted' data, thus ensuring that the information no longer exists.

3.7   Searching

It is sometimes easy to forget where you saved a document or folder in your computer. The **Search** tool helps you to use various search criteria to find 'lost' files or folders. On other occasions you may know where files/folders are stored but you want to view only files of a particular type or files that contain specific text.

3.7.1 Locating a File or Folder by Name (2.3.6.1)

To search for a specific file or folder you need to know its name. For example, imagine that you have a folder containing several hundred exercise files and you want to copy one of those files, named **All About Sydney.doc**, onto a disk to give to another user. Rather than scanning through the documents yourself, you could search for the file to find it.

You can use the Search tool in such windows as My Computer or Windows Explorer. For the purpose of these examples, we will work with Windows Explorer.

- Open Windows Explorer.

- Click on the drive or folder you wish to search in.

- Click on the **Search** button on the toolbar. The Search panel appears on the left-hand side of the window. You can click the **Search** button again to turn the Search panel off, if you so wish.

- Click in the **Search for files or folders named** box and type the name of the file/folder you are searching for.

- Click the **Search Now** button to perform the search.

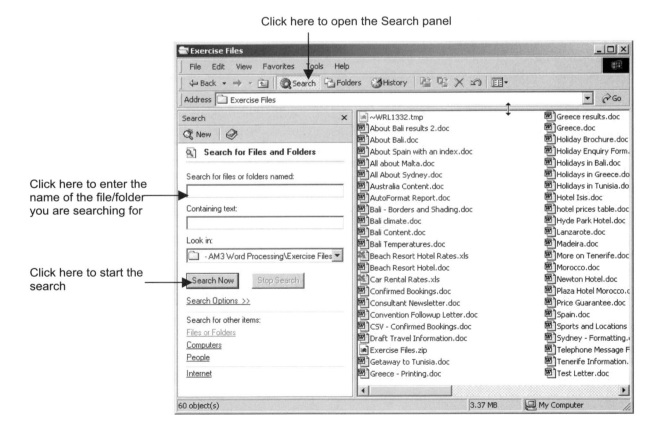

3.7.1.1 Search Results

When you click the **Search Now** button, Windows looks for files containing **any** of the words you have entered for the file name or folder. You may find that several files have been located in the search that are similarly named to the file/folder you want to use.

If you want to perform an entirely new search, click the **New** button on the Search panel and begin your search again.

Once the search results are displayed you can open any of the documents simply by double clicking on their file name icon. You can also copy, move, delete or rename the file using the **Edit** option on the Menu bar.

Click the **Back** button to return to the original folder/drive contents

The Search Results panel shows the name of files/folders that match your search criteria

Click the **New** button to clear the current search information so that you can enter new search criteria

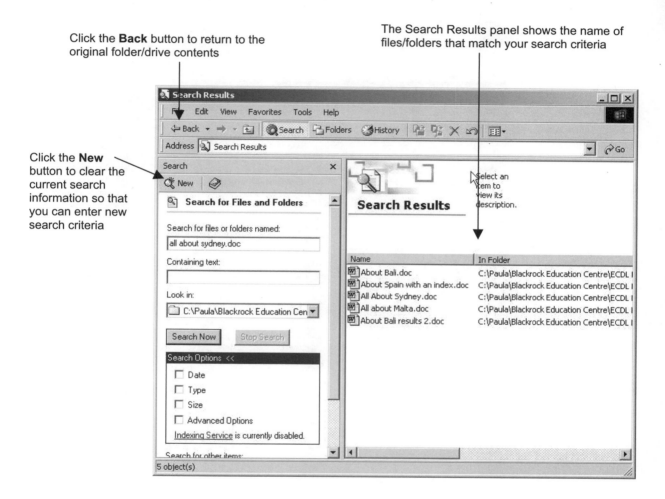

3.7.2 Searching By File Content (2.3.6.2)

A very useful search facility is the ability to search for files containing certain text. For example, imagine that you need to locate all files relating to or mentioning **ECDL**. The files will probably all have very different names. By searching the content of the file and not the file name, you would be able to display all relevant files. For example:

- Open Windows Explorer.

- Click on the drive or folder you wish to search in.

- Click on the **Search** button on the toolbar. The Search panel appears on the left-hand side of the window.

- Click in the **Containing text** box and type the word or phrase you are searching for within each file, in this instance **ECDL**.

- Click the **Search Now** button to perform the search.

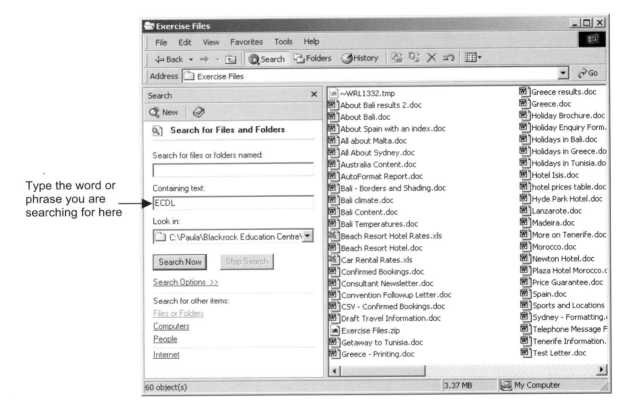

3.7.3 Look In Details

The **Look in** box in the Search panel displays the name of the current drive or folder you have selected to search in. However, you can open the **Look in** box to display a list of available drives and select a new drive to search in or you can use the **Browse** option to select another folder or sub-folder.

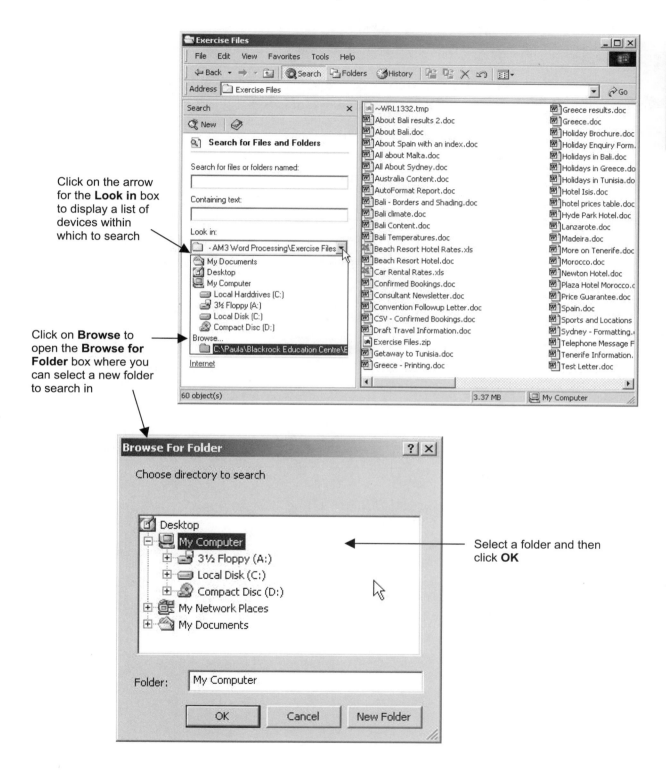

Click on the arrow for the **Look in** box to display a list of devices within which to search

Click on **Browse** to open the **Browse for Folder** box where you can select a new folder to search in

Select a folder and then click **OK**

3.7.4 Search by Date (2.3.6.2)

When searching for files you can specify a **date range** for files that were created, modified or last accessed on or between particular dates as follows:

- Open Windows Explorer.

- Click on the drive or folder you wish to search in.

- Click on the **Search** button on the toolbar. The Search panel appears on the left-hand side of the window.

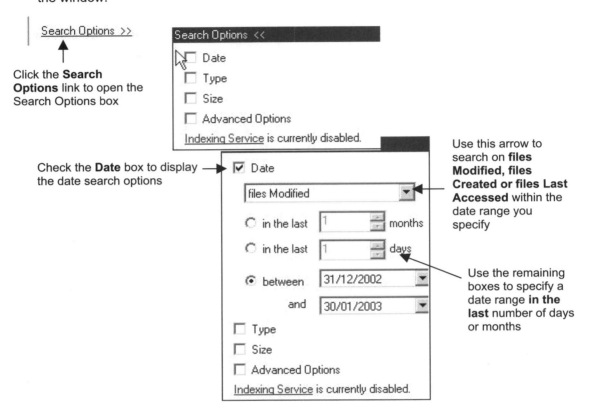

Click the **Search Options** link to open the Search Options box

Check the **Date** box to display the date search options

Use this arrow to search on **files Modified, files Created or files Last Accessed** within the date range you specify

Use the remaining boxes to specify a date range **in the last** number of days or months

- Click the **Search Now** button to perform the search.

3.7.5 Search by Size (2.3.6.2)

You can search for files of a particular size. For example, you may want to find files that are **at least** or **at most** a particular size in **kilobytes**.

- Open Windows Explorer.

- Click on the drive or folder you wish to search in.

- Click on the **Search** button on the toolbar. The Search panel appears on the left-hand side of the window.

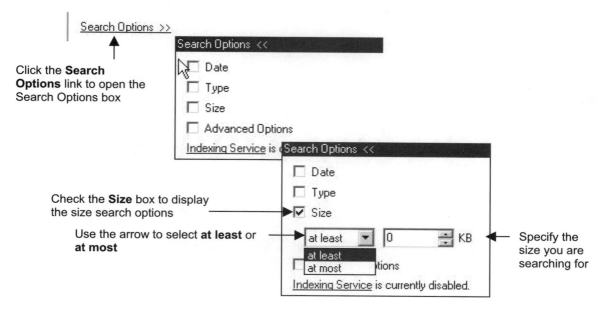

Click the **Search Options** link to open the Search Options box

Check the **Size** box to display the size search options

Use the arrow to select **at least** or **at most**

Specify the size you are searching for

- Click the **Search Now** button to perform the search.

3.7.6 Searching by Type

In addition to the date and size searches, you can also search for files of a particular **type**, such as all **Microsoft Excel Worksheets**, all **Microsoft Word documents**, etc.

- Open Windows Explorer.

- Click on the drive or folder you wish to search in.

- Click on the **Search** button on the toolbar. The Search panel appears on the left-hand side of the window.

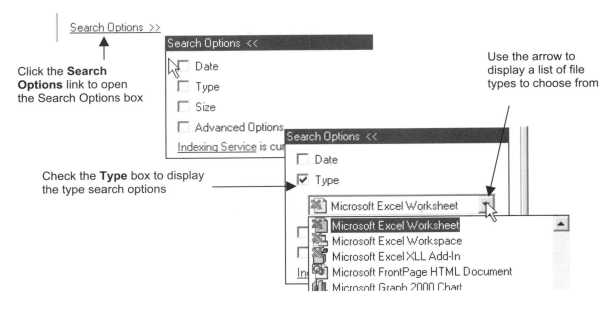

Click the **Search Options** link to open the Search Options box

Check the **Type** box to display the type search options

Use the arrow to display a list of file types to choose from

- Click the **Search Now** button to perform the search.

3.7.7 Advanced Search Options

The Advanced Options feature in the Search Options box provides three additional search criteria items that apply to **any** of the searches you perform.

- Click the **Search Options** link to open the Search Options box.

- Check the **Advanced Options** box.

  Check the **Search Subfolders** if you want to search within any sub-folders for the drive or folder you have selected. This option is checked by default.

  Check the **Case sensitive** box to match files using exactly the same uppercase or lowercase letters as the file/folder name you have entered in the other search boxes.

  Check the **Search slow files** if you want to include files that are stored on removable storage devices, such as back-up tapes. These media can be slow to search through and you may not want them included.

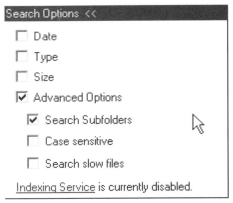

3.7.8 Wildcard Searches (2.3.6.2)

A wildcard character is a keyboard character such as an asterisk (*) or a question mark (?) that you can use to represent one or more real characters when you are searching for files or folders. Wildcard characters are often used in place of one or more characters when you don't know what the real character is or you don't want to type the entire name.

Asterisk (*)

You can use the asterisk as a substitute for zero or more characters. If you're looking for a file that you know starts with **hot** but you can't remember the rest of the file name, type the following:

hot*

When searching for files all files that begin with **hot** including **Hotel.doc**, **Hot.doc**, and **Horticulture.xls** will be found. To narrow the search to a specific type of file, for example type:

hot*.doc

In this case, all files that begin with **hot** but have the file extension **.doc** will be found, such as **Hotel.doc** and **Hot.doc**.

Question Mark (?)

You can use the question mark as a substitute for a single character in a name. For example, if you typed **hot?.doc**, files such as **Hot1.doc** and **Hots.doc** would be located but not **Hotel.doc**.

In Windows 2000, the wildcard search is *implied* when using the **Search** option, in so much as if you search for a file named **hot.doc**, the search results return any file containing the word **hot** in the file name. Files of a particular *type* are handled in the search options rather than using ***.doc**, ***.xls**, etc.

3.7.9 Viewing a List of Recently Used Files (2.3.6.3)

Using the **Start** menu you can view a list of the fifteen most recently used files. This is a convenient way of opening a file that you know you have recently worked on.

- Click on the **Start** button.

- Select **Documents**.

- Open a file from the list by clicking on its file name.

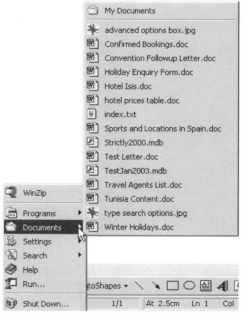

3.8   Compressing Files

3.8.1 What File Compression Means (2.3.7.1)

It is possible to reduce the size of some files so that they take up less space on the computer or can be transferred across a network, including the Internet, more efficiently. The process for doing this is referred to as **compression**. It is important to note that not all files can be compressed equally. Text files may be compressed by up to 90%. Programme files, such as .exe and .dll, typically achieve a 50% rate of compression. Files that are already in a compressed format, such as .jpeg or .gif files which are common picture and graphic file formats, will not normally compress further except by very small amounts.

Imagine that you need to send a large file to a colleague. Should the original file be too large to fit on a standard floppy disk, compressing it might enable you to do so. Your colleague will then need to **extract** the original file from the compressed file you created to work on it.

Whilst there are many different compression programs available, for the purposes of this manual we will be using the **WinZip© Version 8.1** program. Should you wish to use WinZip for file compression it must be installed on your computer. For more information regarding WinZip and how to order or install it, you can access their website: **www.winzip.com**.

3.8.2 Compressing a Single File

You can compress individual files, selected files or all the files within a folder. To compress a single file:

- Using Windows Explorer or My Computer, click on the file you wish to compress.

- Right click on the file to display the shortcut menu.

- Select **WinZip**.

- Select the item on the menu that adds the file to a zip file with the same name as the original file. The extension will be **.zip**. In this example we have used a file named **Book Orders.xls**.

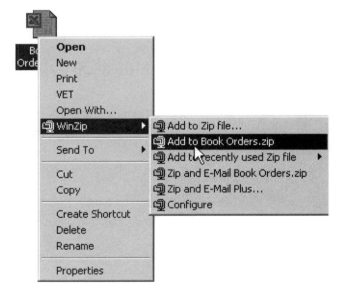

book orders.xls

book orders.zip

NOTE

You can compress multiple files into one compressed file by selecting a group of files. Remember you can use the **Ctrl** key with the mouse to select nonadjacent files in a folder.

3.8.3 Compressing a Folder (2.3.7.2)

You can compress the entire contents of a folder into one compressed file. When the compressed file is **extracted**, all of the files originally contained in the folder will be available to you.

To compress the entire contents of a folder, proceed as follows:

- Using Windows Explorer or My Computer, click on the folder you wish to compress.

- Right click on the folder to display the shortcut menu.

- Select **WinZip**.

- Select the item on the menu that adds the folder to a zip file with the same name as the original folder but with the extension **.zip**.

- The resulting compressed file will be placed in the **parent folder** of the folder you are compressing.

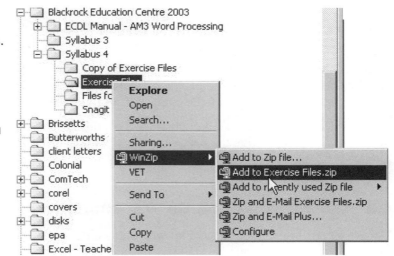

3.8.4 Extracting a Compressed File (2.3.7.3)

A compressed file cannot be used in the way that other types of files can be used in programs such as Word, Excel, etc. Instead, you need to **extract** the original files from the compressed file so that these documents can be used in the usual way.

To extract files from a compressed file:

- Place the compressed file into the folder where the extract files are to be located.

- Right click on the compressed file.

- Select **WinZip** from the Shortcut menu.

- Choose **Extract to here**.

- The files will be extracted from the compressed file but you may need to press **F5** to refresh the contents of the folder before you can see the extracted files.

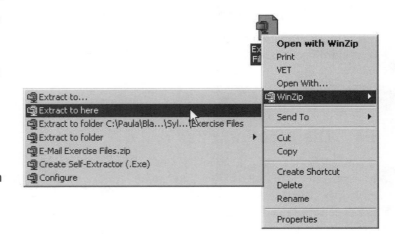

Section 4   Viruses

4.1   What is a Virus and What Can It Do? (2.4.1.1)

A **virus** is a software program written with the intention of causing inconvenience and disruption or even serious damage to data on a computer. This can involve destroying anything from individual files to whole operating systems and networks. Unless precautions are taken, a computer user may be unaware that there is a virus on the computer until its effects become appararent.

Many viruses are specific to a particular kind of file, such as a word processing document. When an 'infected' file is opened on the computer, the virus attaches itself to other similar files and so the virus spreads.

4.2   How a Virus Can Be Transmitted (2.4.1.2)

Viruses can be transmitted to a computer by attaching to files that are sent to that computer. For example, you may be sent an e-mail that has an 'infected' attachment. Upon opening the attachment the virus will activate, often without you knowing, and start infecting your computer/files. A virus can even infect your own e-mail address book so that it can send out an e-mail to every address in your address book with the same virus attached. If an infected file is sent to a different computer, the virus can infect that computer too if it does not have the appropriate virus-scanning software.

In addition to being sent by e-mail, viruses can be downloaded automatically to your computer when you are working on the Internet or can be transmitted via a diskette or CD.

4.3   Using Virus-Scanning Software (2.4.1.3)

It is important to guard against viruses by installing software that checks for viruses before they attack your computer. Anti-virus software is available from software vendors. It can detect and remove viruses found on the computer and it can automatically check diskettes, CD drives and e-mail attachments.

4.4   Disinfecting Files (2.4.1.4)

If your virus-scanning software detects a virus you will be immediately informed. You will then be prompted to permit the software to 'disinfect' any files to which the virus has become attached. The anti-virus software then 'cleans' the infected files and gives you a status report telling you which files have been fixed and whether or not there are any other outstanding problems. If a file cannot be fixed you should contact the anti-virus software vendor for advice.

MODULE 2

4.5   Scanning Drives, Folders and Files for Viruses (2.4.2.1)

If you have up-to-date, correctly installed virus software on your computer, the virus program will automatically sense if there is a virus on your computer or in the computer's memory. You will then be alerted that the virus exists and then usually informed that the virus has been successfully removed. However, there may be times when you wish to scan a particular drive, folder or file for viruses. For example, you may have received a diskette from a colleague containing some Word documents. It would be strongly recommended that you scan the diskette for possible viruses before you start working with any of the documents it contains.

As there are many different virus-scanning software programs available, you will need to become familiar with how to scan for viruses using your own particular virus program. However, some generic steps for scanning for viruses are detailed below:

- Open the virus-scanning software program. This is usually located under the **Programs** section on the Start menu.

- Your virus software will most probably have a **Scan** button on the toolbar. Click this button to display a window containing the scanning options. An example of such a window is displayed here.

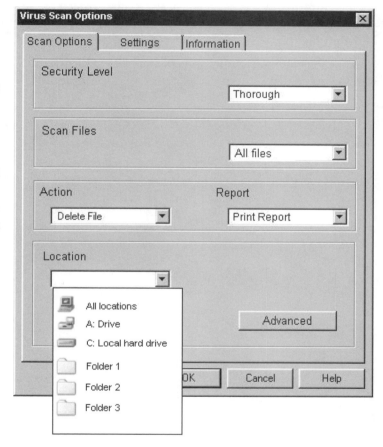

- Select what you want to scan, for example a drive, folder or file. In our example this selection could be made using the **Location** box.

- If you have selected a drive or folder to scan, you can usually specify what type of files you wish to scan within the drive or folder. Typically you would scan document, system, mail files and so on. In our example we have selected **All files**. Other options may, for example, be **All program files** or **All data files**.

- You may be able to select a **security level** for the type of scan you wish to perform. In our example we have selected **Thorough**.

- Select what action you wish to be performed if an infected file is found. Options may vary from changing the infected file's name, isolating it or deleting it altogether. In our location we have selected **Delete File** in the **Action** box.

- You may also be able to specify where the details of the virus scanning process appears. For example, you may want to print the report of the scan or simply display it on the screen. Typically a virus report shows you how many files were scanned, what their names were, the details of any infected files and the result of the action, such as **successfully deleted** or **not successfully deleted**.

Exercise 4A

1   Open your virus-scanning program.

2   Practice scanning your local disk **(C:)** for any viruses. Scan only data files if this option is easily available to you.

3   Close the virus program on completion.

4.6   Updating Your Virus-scanning Software (2.4.2.2)

Once you have purchased a virus-scanning program it is important to keep it up-to-date by installing updated information on a regular basis, as new viruses are being created and transmitted all the time. If you detect a virus you should inform the provider or sender of the infected file, who may be unaware of the problem.

Updates for your anti-virus software can usually be downloaded from the software vendor's website or sent to you on disk.

Section 5   Diskettes

Floppy disks are small, portable versions of the hard disk which use a magnetised plastic (floppy) disk in a compact plastic case 3.5 inches square. A floppy disk has a nominal capacity of 1.4Mb. They are commonly used to transfer files from one computer to another, particularly when computers are not linked in any way (such as in the case of a **network**). A variation of the floppy disk, the **Super Disk** or **Smart Disk**, has a nominal capacity of 120Mb but needs a special drive unit attached to the computer.

Another form of removable storage is that of a **zip disk**. Zip drives and similar units are small, portable versions of the hard disk that use **cartridges** for storage. The cartridges are slightly larger than a floppy disk but they have a much larger storage capacity, 100Mb, 250Mb or 750Mb, according to type.

5.1   Formatting

Before a floppy disk or zip disk can be used for the first time, it must be **formatted** to suit the computer's operating system. There is a procedure to prepare disks for use with particular types of computers. The two common format options for disks are IBM-compatible and Macintosh.

Disks can be purchased preformatted. If you buy unformatted disks you need to format them before they can be used.

5.1.1   Formatting a Floppy Disk (2.1.2.4)

- Double click the **My Computer** icon to open the My Computer window.

- Click the **3½ Floppy (A:)** icon once to select it.

- Click **Format** in the **File** menu.

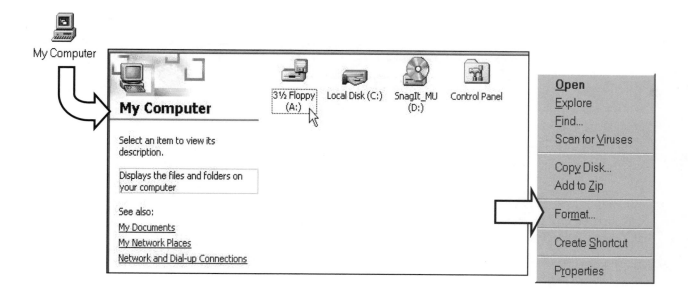

- The **Format** window appears, a sample of which is shown on the following page.

- Use the **Capacity** box to specify the amount of data that can be stored on the diskette – either 1.44Mb or 720Kb.

- The **File system** box should display **FAT**, which stands for **file allocation table** and is the default option.

- The **Allocation unit size** is set to **Default allocation size**.

- The **Volume label** box provides a suggestion for the name that will appear whenever you use the diskette you are about to format. You can enter a different name if you so wish, such as **Word Processing Documents**, **Training Files** and so on.

- In the **Format options** box you can:

  - Check the **Quick Format** box if you wish to reformat the disk by cleaning off files on an already formatted disk but without checking for any **bad sectors**, which can cause problems in certain instances. Only use this option if you have used the diskette previously and you know that it is not damaged.

  - The **Enable Compression** option is usually greyed out as it can only be used when formatting with the **NFTS** file system (and not **FAT**, which is the more frequently used system). By enabling compression you can request that all files and folders are compressed when stored on the formatted disk. For the purpose of this syllabus we are not concerned with this option here.

- Click the **Start** button in the window to format the disk. A warning will appear. Click **OK** to continue.

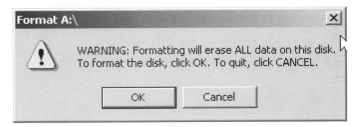

During the formatting process the disk is divided into a large number of electronic areas – called **sectors** – in which the computer can store data.

In the formatting process, all data (if any) previously stored on the disk is erased. Be sure that you do not need any existing data if you are reformatting a used floppy disk.

When the formatting process has been successfully completed an information box appears. Click **OK** to end the formatting procedure and then click **Close** to shut the **Format A:** window.

> **Warning**
> Do not format your hard disk – all the system and other files will be deleted and the computer will be unusable.

5.1.2 Floppy Disk Care

Floppy disks should be looked after properly or data can be lost and/or corrupted. Proper care will help to prevent problems. Remember the following when handling floppy disks.

- Keep disks away from things that have magnets or magnetic fields, such as radios, TV sets, loudspeakers, mobile phones and so on.

- Keep disks away from sources of extreme temperatures, moisture or dust.

- Do not touch the magnetic disk contained inside the plastic casing.

- Before inserting a disk into the drive, check it for damage.

- Always keep disks in a box designed for disk storage.

- Always make sure that the disk drive is completely inactive before inserting or ejecting a floppy disk.

5.1.3 Security

Use the **security tab** to prevent data being accidentally erased from a disk. The tab is a small plastic slider on the underside of the disk, beside one of the two small square holes in the corners.

When the tab is closed – when you **cannot** see through the hole – you can use the disk normally.

When the slider is open – when you **can** see through the hole – the disk is locked and data on the disk cannot be altered by the computer, nor can you save on the disk. The disk is now **write protected**.

Security Tab (closed)   This hole is always open

> **Warning**:
> Floppy disks are easily corrupted and may fail at any moment for no apparent reason. Never work with or store important data on floppy disks **only**. Always save on the hard disk first.

5.1.4 Formatting a Zip Disk (2.1.2.4)

When you purchase a zip disk it is usually preformatted, ready for you to use. However, if you have a used zip disk, you may wish to **format** it so that it returns to its original blank state, ready for any new information you wish to save on it.

To format a zip disk proceed as follows:

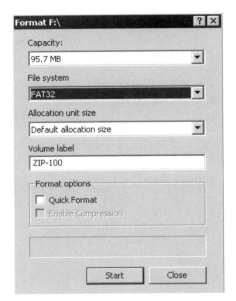

Removable
Disk (F:)

- Double click the **My Computer** icon to open the My Computer window.

- Click the **Removable Disk** icon to select the drive (in our picture the removable disk is known as the **F:** drive).

- Right click on the **Removable Disk** icon to display the pop-up menu.

- Select **Format**. The Format window will be displayed.

- Check the **Quick Format** box in the **Format options** section. The Quick Format erases any files on the disk, reformats the disk but does not check for any errors (such as bad sectors) on the existing disk.

- Click **Start** to proceed. The **Warning** box will appear.

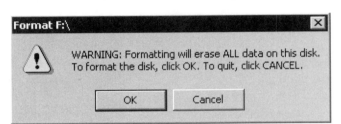

- Click **OK** to continue. The formatting process will begin. On completion, the following box will appear.

- Click **OK** to accept the **Format Complete** message.

- Close the **Formatting** window to return to the **My Computer** window.

- Close the **My Computer** window to return to the desktop.

Section 6   Installing/Uninstalling Software

Using **Add/Remove Programs** you will be helped through the steps necessary to add a new program or to change or remove an existing program.

6.1   Installing a Software Application (2.1.2.5)

To install software using the **Add/Remove Programs** facility do the following:

Add/Remove
Programs

- Click on the **Start** menu and select **Settings**.

- Click on the **Control Panel** sub-option.
  The Control Panel window will open.

- Double click the **Add/Remove Programs** icon.
  The **Add/Remove Programs** window will open.

- Click on the **Add New Programs** icon in the left panel of the window.

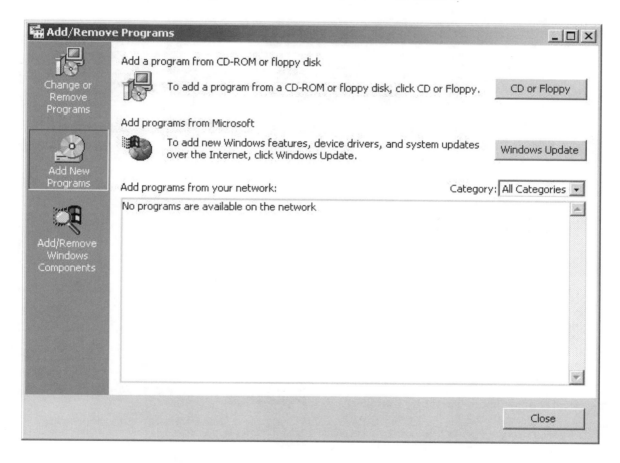

- To add a new program from the CD-ROM drive or the floppy drive, click the **CD or Floppy** button. A special utility known as a **wizard** will help you through the installation process, prompting you with questions at each step.

- When the software has successfully been installed, click the **Close** button to close the **Add/Remove Programs** window.

- Close the **Control Panel** window on completion.

6.2   Uninstalling a Software Application (2.1.2.5)

If you wish to remove an application from your computer it is important that you **uninstall** the application rather than simply deleting the folder in which you think the application resides. The reason why uninstalling is so important is that Windows adds files to many different folders during the installation of a software application. As you will not know where these files have been 'scattered', you should uninstall so that all of the related files are appropriately removed.

To uninstall a software application:

- Click on the **Start** menu and select **Settings**.

- Click on the **Control Panel** sub-option.
  The Control Panel window will open.

Add/Remove
Programs

- Double click the **Add/Remove Programs** icon.
  The **Add/Remove Programs** window will open.

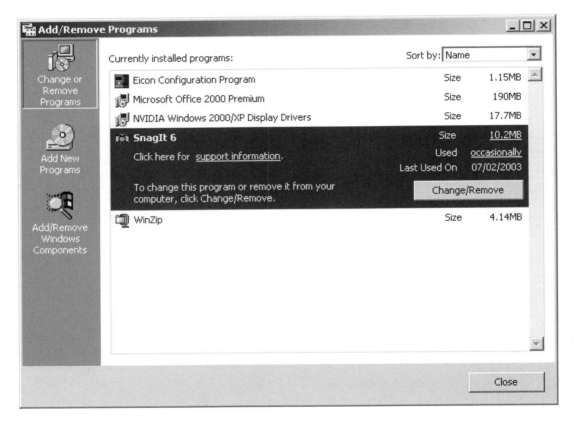

- Click on the **Change or Remove Programs** icon in the left panel of the window if it is not automatically selected.

- From the list of **Currently installed programs** click on the program you wish to remove. In the example above the program named **SnagIt 6** has been selected.

- Click on the **Change/Remove** button.

- An **Uninstall** window will be displayed. Click **Yes** to proceed.

- When the program has been successfully removed, close all of the windows relating to the **Add/Remove Programs** procedure as well as the **Control Panel** window.

Section 7   Information and Settings

7.1   System Information (2.1.2.1)

Information about your computer type is readily available.

Proceed as follows.

- Select **Settings** in the **Start** menu.

- Select **Control Panel** in the sub-menu.

  The Control Panel window opens. It contains a large number of controls, represented by icons,

  with which you can adjust various computer settings and set defaults.

- Scroll through the Control Panel window if necessary to find the **System** icon.

- Double click on the **System** icon to open the **System Properties** window.

System

- A row of tabs across the top of the **System Properties** window gives access to system information under different headings.

- Click the **General** tab if it is not clicked already.

- Details of the version of the Windows System used by the computer appear at the top of the window.

- In the illustration, it is **Windows 2000** and the version number is **1234**.

- Underneath are details of the registered user and the registration number.

- The type of processor in the computer is given in the lower part of the window.

  The processor here is a **x86 Family 6 Model 8 Stepping 10**.

- The amount of RAM in the computer is shown underneath the processor information – here **523,744Kb**.

Click the other tabs to display more specialised information – it is probably of interest to expert users only!

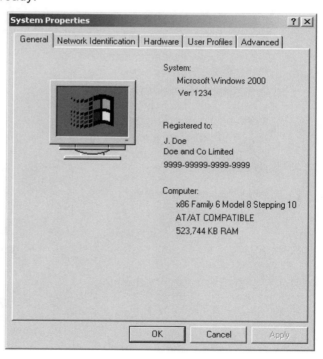

NOTE

You can also access the System Properties window from the desktop. Simply right click on the **My Computer** icon on the desktop to display the Shortcut menu. Select **Properties** from the menu.

7.2 Changing the Desktop Display Options

The appearance of the desktop, the screen area, the range of colours displayed and many other settings can be selected to suit the individual user or the requirements of particular software.

Important: Be aware that changing these display and other Control Panel settings will affect how your computer operates. Do not change any settings if you are not sure about them.

Proceed as follows.

- Select **Settings** in the **Start** menu.

- Select **Control Panel** in the sub-menu. The Control Panel window opens.

- Scroll through the Control Panel window if necessary to find the **Display** icon.

- Double click on the **Display** icon to open the **Display Properties** window.

7.2.1 Changing the Colour Settings (2.1.2.2)

To make adjustments to the desktop settings, click on the **Settings** tab in the **Display Properties** window.

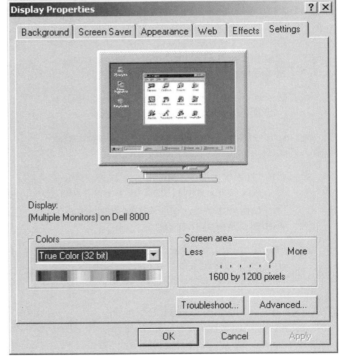

- Select the number of colours to be displayed from the menu in the **Colour** area.

- To set the screen area, drag the slider in the **Screen area** panel.

  Drag towards **Less** to show a smaller part of the desktop but at increased magnification.

  Drag towards **More** to show more of the desktop but at reduced magnification.

- Click **Apply** to make your new settings effective.

- You may be asked to **verify** that the settings are correct or to **restart** the computer.

  Follow the instructions on the screen.

The number of colours that can be displayed may vary depending on the computer and monitor. Different applications may require different settings from time to time.

- **256 colors** is still used by some multimedia programs.
- **High Color (16 bit)** can display thousands of colours for superior quality.
- **True Color (24 bit)** can display millions of colours for photographic quality.

See Module 1, Section 2.4.1 for more information on monitors.

7.2.2 Appearance

To adjust the appearance of the desktop:

- Click the **Appearance** tab in the **Display Properties** window.

- Select the scheme you want from the menu in the **Scheme** box.

- Click **Apply** to make your new settings effective.

- Click **OK**.

Examples of the scheme you select are displayed in the panel at the top of the window.

Windows Standard is shown in the illustration.

The menu in the **Item** box allows you to set the font and colour for individual items. Select the size and colour in the small boxes to the right of the Item box.

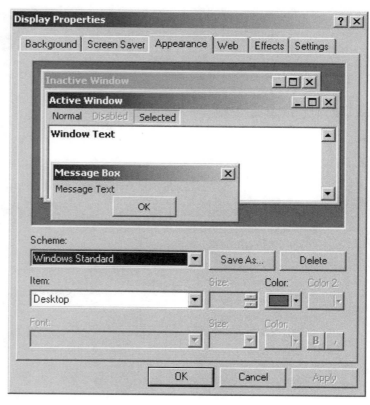

7.2.3 Background

The background – the main area of the desktop – can be adjusted as follows.

- Click the **Background** tab in the **Display Properties** window.

- To display a 'wallpaper' on the desktop, select from the list in the **Select a background picture or HTML document as Wallpaper** box.

- To display a pattern on the desktop, click on the **Pattern** button. Select an appropriate pattern and then click **OK** to return to the Display Properties window.

Click here for the Pattern window (see next page)

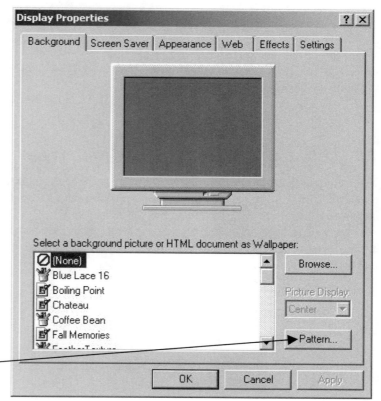

- Select **None** in either case if you do not want a pattern or wallpaper.

Your choice is displayed on the 'monitor' in the upper part of the window.

- Click **Apply** to make your new settings effective.

- Click **OK**.

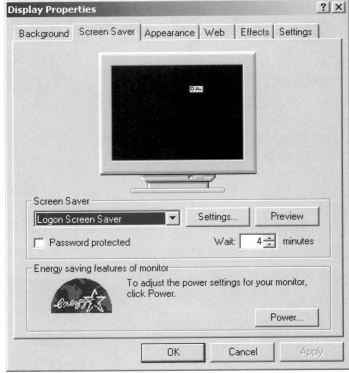

7.2.4 Screen Saver (2.1.2.2)

A **screen saver** replaces the display on the screen with an animated graphic after a set time interval when the computer is unattended.

- Click the **Screen Saver** tab in the **Display Properties** window.

- Select the screen saver you want from the menu in the **Screen Saver** box.

  If you do not want a screen saver, select **None**.

Your choice is displayed on the 'monitor' in the upper part of the window.

- Set the time before the screen saver appears in the **Wait** box.

- Click **Apply** to make your new settings effective.

- Click **OK**.

When the screen saver is in operation, touch the mouse or press any key on the keyboard to restore the original display.

7.3 Changing the Date and Time (2.1.2.2)

Your computer has an inbuilt clock and calendar that keeps track of the current date and time. The date and time is often used even without you knowing. Every time you save a file, the current date and time is recorded with the file. This can help you when you are searching for files within a particular date range. You can also insert the current date and time automatically into documents, for example using **Insert, Date** in Microsoft Word. It is important, therefore, that your computer's date and time is correctly set.

To change the date/time:

- Select **Settings** in the **Start** menu.

- Select **Control Panel** in the sub-menu.
  The Control Panel window opens.

Date/Time

- Double click on the **Date/Time** icon to open the **Date/Time Properties** window.

- Use the **Date** box to set the current month, year and day.

- Use the **Time** box to set the current time.

- Click on the **Time Zone** tab to view details of the time zone you are working in.

- From the time zone list, select an appropriate option.

- Check the **Automatically adjust clock for daylight saving changes** if you want Windows to update the times for you when the clocks go forwards or back.

- Click **OK** to accept your changes.

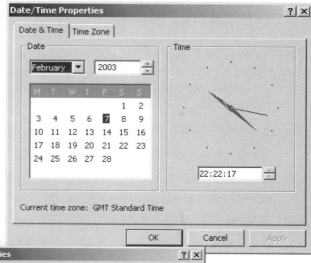

7.4   Changing the Volume Settings (2.1.2.2)

Many computers are now supplied with speakers (either internal or external units) which provide sound especially from audio files, video clips, etc. To change the volume settings for your speakers you can use the **Sounds and Multimedia** icon in the Control Panel.

- Select **Settings** in the **Start** menu.

- Select **Control Panel** in the sub-menu.
  The Control Panel window opens.

- Double click on the **Sounds and Multimedia** icon to open the **Sounds and Multimedia Properties** window.

- Use the slider in the **Sound Volume** box to control the volume.

- Check the **Show volume control on the taskbar** if you want to be able to double click the **Speaker** icon in the taskbar to increase or decrease speaker volume.

- Click **OK** to save your changes.

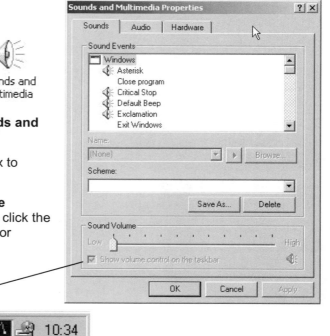

Sounds and
Multimedia

7.5   Changing the Keyboard Language (2.1.2.3)

If you work in more than one language or communicate with speakers of other languages, you may wish to change the keyboard layout to suit the language you are writing in. Each language has a default keyboard layout, but many languages have alternate layouts. Even if you work mainly with one language you may want to try other layouts. In English, for example, typing letters with accents might be simpler with the U.S.-International layout.

To change the keyboard language:

Keyboard

- Select **Settings** in the **Start** menu.

- Select **Control Panel** in the sub-menu.
  The Control Panel window opens.

- Double click on the **Keyboard** icon to open the **Keyboard Properties** window.

- Click on the **Input Locales** tab.

- The **Installed input locales** box shows the current **input languages** and **keyboard layouts** you have installed.

- To add a new **input locales** click on the **Add** button. The **Add Input Locale** box appears.

- Select a locale from the **Input locale** list.

- Select a layout from the **Keyboard layout/IME** list.

- Click **OK** to return to the **Keyboard Properties** window.

- You can use the **Hot keys for input locales** box to specify a specific key sequence you wish to use to activate an input locales. If you don't specify any hot keys, the default, **Left Alt+Shift**, can be used to switch from one input locales to another.

- Click **OK** to save your changes.

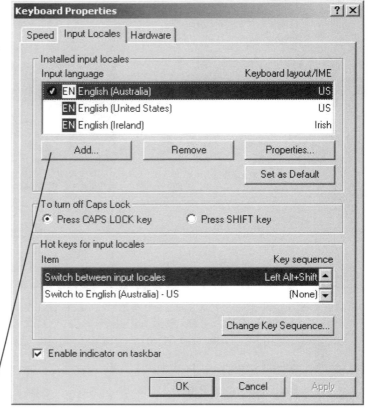

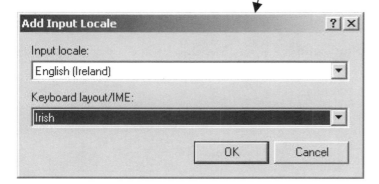

Section 8   Print Management

8.1   Set-up

Before a printer can be used for the first time it must be **set up** so that the computer knows that it is there and that it is able to use it. It is common to have one printer attached to a computer, but you may also find that you have more than one printer available to you, especially if you are working on a network. Take an example, however, of working on a machine that you may have at home. You may have two printers, a laser printer for printing large documents, such as a report or a thesis. You may also have a colour ink jet printer which you use for brochures, invitations or report covers. Before either printer can be used you need to **add the printer** into the **Printers** list so that Windows knows they are the printers you are using.

8.1.1   Viewing Available Printers

To view any printers that have been added to your **Printers** list:

- Select **Settings** in the **Start** menu.

- Select **Control Panel** in the sub-menu.
  The Control Panel window opens.

Printers

- Double click the Printers icon to open the Printers window.

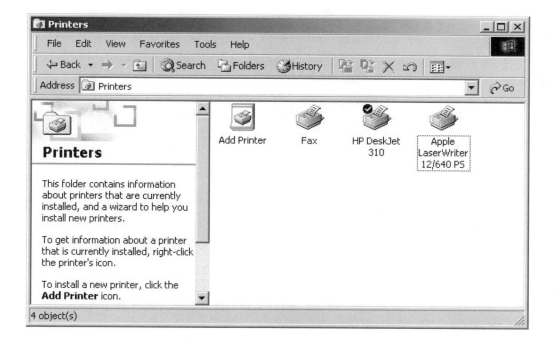

8.1.2 Changing the Default Printer (2.5.1.1)

You can have many printers added to the **Printers** list but only one printer is marked as the **default printer**. The default printer is the one automatically used for printing unless you specify that you wish to use another when working in programs such as Word, Excel and so on (see Section 8.1.3 below for more information). The default printer is identified in the **Printers** list by a **tick mark** in a dark circle beside the printer icon. In the screen shot on the previous page the **HP DeskJet 310** is marked as the default printer.

To change the default printer:

- Open the **Printers** window from the **Control Panel**.

- Click on the printer you wish to set as the new default.

- Choose **Set as Default** from the **File** menu.

- The **tick mark** will now appear next to the printer that you have specified.

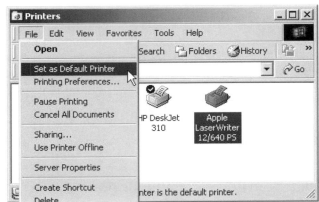

8.1.3 Changing the Printer within an Application

When you are working in an application, such as Word, Excel, PowerPoint, etc., you can temporarily change from the default printer to another printer from within the **Print** window.

- Choose **Print** from the **File** menu.

- Click on the arrow on the **Name** box.

- Select a printer from the available list.

- Change any of the remaining settings in the Print window.

- Click **OK** to commence printing.

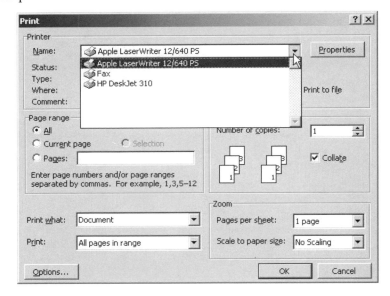

NOTE

Changing the printer in this way does not set the printer as the new default. This can only be done from the **Printers** window within the **Control Panel**.

8.1.4 Installing a New Printer (2.5.1.2)

If you purchase a new printer you must inform Windows by adding it to the **Printers** list. Windows uses a **wizard** to help you install most printers that are now on the market and even many older printers. To add a printer that is attached to your computer to your Windows environment:

Printers

- Ensure the printer you are adding is plugged into your computer.

- Double click the **Printers** icon in the Control Panel window.

- Double click the **Add Printer** icon.

Add Printer

- The **Add Printer Wizard** window will appear.

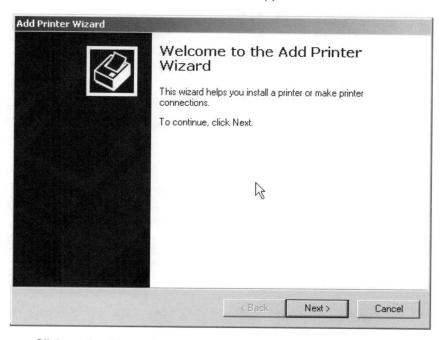

- Click on ther **Next>** button.

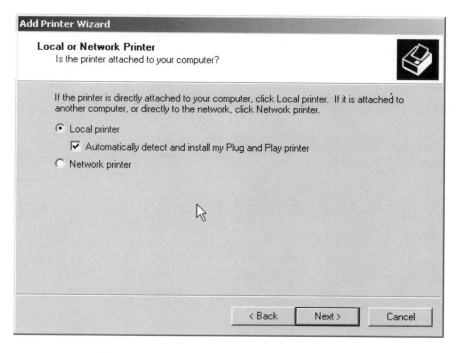

- Choose **Local Printer** and ensure the **Automatically detect and install my Plug and Play printer** is checked. This will ensure that Windows automatically detects specific settings for the type of printer you want to add.

- Click on the **Next>** button.

- Continue answering the questions proposed by the **Add Printer Wizard**. Use the **Next>** button to advance on to the next screen each time.

- When the process has been completed, click the **Finish** button to return to the **Printers** window.

- You can now make the new printer the default, if you so wish. Please see Section 8.1.2 for more information.

8.2   Printing Outputs

When a document is ready for printing it is sent from the computer to the printer. This process may vary slightly according to the software you are using. You should check that the printer is switched on before you send something to print and that it has sufficient paper.

8.2.1   Printing from a Text Editing Application (2.5.2.1)

To try out printing, type a few words in **Notepad**. Then click **Print** in the **File** menu. The page is sent directly to the printer and should print out after a short delay. Notice that Notepad is a simple, no-frills program and the user cannot set the number of copies to be printed or make any other choices in the Print window. The only preferences that can be set are those in **Page Setup**.

Now print a document in **Microsoft Word** by selecting **Print** in the **File** menu, as before. Notice that a window appears allowing the user to select page size, orientation, number of copies and so on.

The **Print** window displays numerous options.

- A different printer can be selected, if one is available.

- All or only some of the pages can be selected for printing.

- The number of copies to be printed can be set.

- The printed copies can be collated.

- Further choices can be made by clicking the **Properties** button.

- The document can be 'printed to' (saved as) a file instead of being printed. The file is a special kind of file that can be used by commercial printers.

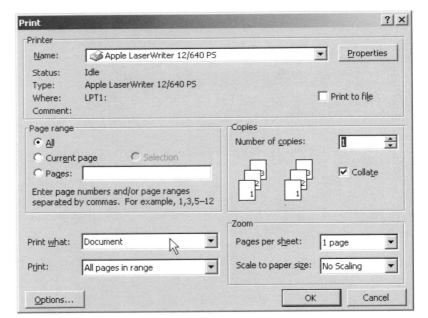

When any special options you need have been selected, click the **OK** button to start printing.

8.2.2 Print Preview

The view on the screen as you are preparing a document is not always a completely accurate representation of what will appear on paper. Using **Print Preview** presents a more accurate view of the final document.

- Click the **Print Preview** button on the toolbar or select **Print Preview** in the **File** menu.

  The document is displayed in reduced format *exactly* as it will appear when printed.

- Click the **Multiple Pages** button and drag to display several pages at once in a long document.

- Use the **Magnifier** to enlarge a page.

- Click the **Print** button to print the document or **Close** to return to the main display.

Print Preview Button

Preview
One Page   Multiple Pages

Print Magnifier

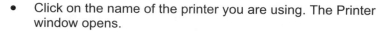

2 x 2 Pages

> **Save:** It is good practice to save your work *before* printing.

8.2.3 Monitoring Printing (2.5.2.2)

When a document is sent to a printer, a **printer icon** appears on the taskbar at the bottom right-hand corner of the screen. You can use this icon to examine print progress and to make necessary changes.

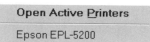

Printer Button

Open Active Printers

Epson EPL-5200

- Right click on the **Printer** icon to display a printer menu.

- Click on the name of the printer you are using. The Printer window opens.

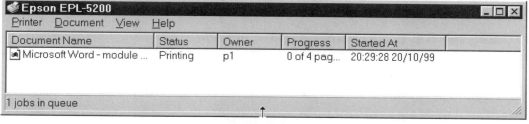

The Printer Window

Documents waiting to be printed appear in a **queue** in the window and details of progress are displayed. (You do not have to wait for one document to be printed before sending another to the printer.)

8.2.4 Managing a Print Job (2.5.2.3)

You can manage the progress of a print job from the queue in the printer's window.

- Click on the print job you wish to manage.

- Click on the **Document** menu.

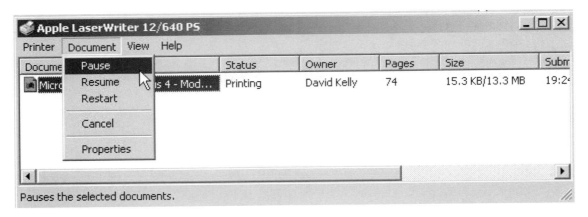

- Click **Pause** to halt the print job temporarily. Click **Resume** on the **Document** menu again to resume printing.

Or

- Click **Restart** to restart the print job from the beginning.

Or

- Click **Cancel** to end the print job all together. Again, any part of the print job that is in the printer's memory will be printed.

8.2.5 Closing a Printer Window

You can close the printer's window that you have opened to monitor the progress of a print job at any time. By closing the window you do not affect anything to do with the status of a print job. When the queue for a printer is completely empty, the **printer** icon will disappear from the taskbar until you print again.

8.2.6 Using the Keyboard Print Screen Facility (2.1.2.6)

There may be occasions when you wish to capture the contents of a particular screen or window and to then paste those contents into a file, such as a Word document. For example, you may want to send a colleague a sample of how to complete a particular screen within the Windows environment. This could be achieved using the **keyboard print screen** facility.

To capture the contents of a screen or window:

- Press **Alt+Print Screen** to capture the contents of the active window only.

Or

- Press **Print Screen** to capture the entire screen as it appears on your monitor.

To paste the contents of the captured screen or window into a document:

- Ensure you are working in the document or file where you wish to insert the captured image.

- Choose **Paste** from the **Edit** menu or click the **Paste** button on the Standard toolbar.

Module 3

Word Processing

3

MODULE 3

Module 3

Word Processing

MODULE 3

Introduction

Syllabus Goals for Module 3

Word processing requires the candidate to demonstrate the ability to use a word processing application on a personal computer. He or she shall understand and be able to accomplish basic operations associated with creating, formatting and finishing a word processing document ready for distribution. The candidate shall demonstrate competence in using some of the more advanced features associated with word processing applications, such as creating standard tables, using pictures and images within a document, importing objects and using mail merge tools.

What is Word Processing?

Word processing has replaced typing. With a typewriter you had to be a skilful typist to produce accurate, attractively laid-out work. There was only one typeface – the one used for this paragraph – and one size. If you made mistakes, it was annoying and tedious to make corrections. Even then, the amount of correction you could make was very limited. Major corrections meant typing out the whole page all over again.

The document you are reading now was prepared entirely on a word processor. The type does not always have to have the 'typewriter' appearance of the paragraph above. You will have noticed that the titles, text and paragraph headings are in different typefaces, sizes and styles. The text can be lined up neatly at both left and right margins. Illustrations can be included and lines can be drawn. This kind of presentation would have been impossible to do on a typewriter. And it is easy! Typists who change over to the computer find that their typing speed increases. The extra facilities of the computer have led to the adoption of the term **word processing**.

The computer has replaced the typewriter for all kinds of work because it is far more versatile. You still have to know how to type. The computer keyboard has replaced the typewriter keys and has given rise to a new word: keyboarding! With the computer, words and pictures can be added or deleted, paragraphs can be interchanged and the text can be arranged on the page much more attractively than when using the typewriter. In the event of changes to parts of the text, the whole document does not have to be typed out again.

A word processor application allows the computer to be used as a super-duper typewriter with many more facilities than any typewriter could ever have. The major software companies have developed word processors for both PC and Macintosh computers. Widely-used word processing applications include Microsoft Word and Word Perfect. Integrated packages such as AppleWorks and Lotus Office Suite also include word processors.

Section 1   Using the Application

1.1   First Steps in Word Processing

1.1.1   Opening and Closing a Word Processing Application (3.1.1.1)

When we want to start Microsoft Word we must click the **Start** button on the desktop and select Microsoft Word in the Programs menu or sub-menu.

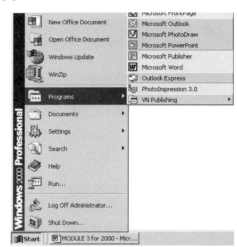

Once this has been done, the Word application window opens and presents you with a blank document. This is called the **Document window** and it is here that you can begin word processing.

There is a difference between the document window and the application window and in order to see the application window on its own you must close the document window first by clicking on its **Close** button.

Close Button

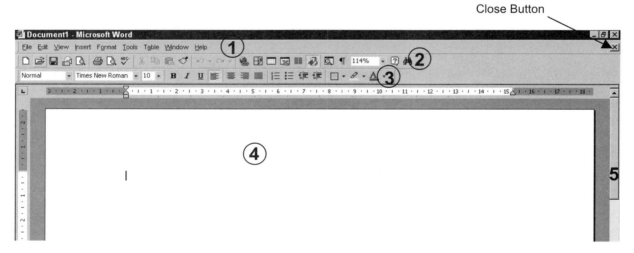

1.   Menu Bar
2.   Standard Toolbar
3.   Formatting Toolbar
4.   Document Window
5.   Scroll Bar

To close the application window use the **Exit** command in the File menu.

If you have unsaved work or if you have made changes since you last saved it, you will be reminded to save. Click **Yes** in the reminder window to save the document.

Task

Try opening Microsoft Word from the desktop and then view the different parts of each window.

1.1.2 Creating a New Document (3.1.1.3)

When you open Word it usually creates a new blank document called **Document1**. The document appears on the screen as if it were a sheet of blank white paper. If there is no document open, blank or otherwise, the main part of the screen where the document would normally appear is grey.

Click the **New** button at the left of the Standard toolbar. The button represents a blank sheet of paper.

New Button

If Word doesn't create a new blank document, you can choose the Blank Document icon from the group of templates in the **New** window which appears if you select the command. Now select the OK button and a blank document will load, ready for you to begin.

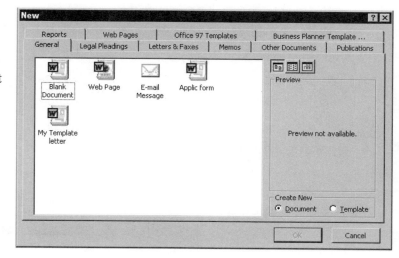

1.1.3 Saving the Document to a Location on the Drive (3.1.1.4)

When working with a document it is important to remember that in order to keep it you must save it. This procedure enables you to place your document in a location where it can be accessed if you have to amend it. By clicking on the Save in box you can choose to save to the desktop, 3½ floppy (A:), My Documents or (C:). My Documents is the default folder. (This command is fully explained in the Before You Begin section of this book.)

The first save of a document presents you with the Save As window. Once you have given the file a name you can choose the Save button on the Standard toolbar.

To save a document for the **first time**:

Save Button

- Click the Save button on the Standard toolbar or select Save in the File menu.

- The Save As window opens.

- Type a name for the document in the File Name box.

- Make sure that the **Folder**, area or floppy disk where you want to save the document appears in the Save in box.

- Click the **Save** button.

Exercise   1A

To put the document handling information you have learned into practice, do the following:

1   Create a new document.

2   Save it in your chosen location with the name **My Word 1**.

3   Close the file, but not Word itself.

4   Open the file again in Word.

5   Save the file on a floppy disk, naming it **My Disk File 1**.

6   Close both the file and Word.

1.1.4 Opening One or Several Documents (3.1.1.2)

Start Microsoft Word if it is not open. To open a document which has already been saved follow these steps:

- Click on the **File** menu and select **Open.**

- The **Look in** box should be changed to the folder where the file(s) is located.

- Select the file with the left button of mouse.

- Click on the **Open** button on the right-hand side of the window.

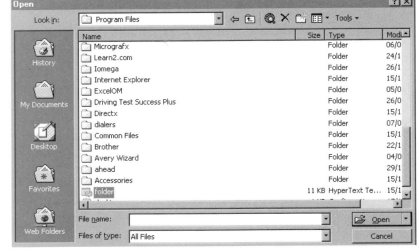

If more than one file is to be opened, hold the control key of your keyboard with your finger and select each individual file you want to open with the mouse and then click on the **Open** button in the window.

1.1.5 Saving a Document Under Another Name (3.1.1.5)

When you want to save a **copy** of a document or file under a different name, **Save As** is used. Imagine for a moment that you have typed a notice for a meeting in May called **May Meeting** that may require only minor changes for the proposed June meeting.

To save time typing out a new notice, you can edit the old one, as follows:

- Open the file for May Meeting.

- Make the changes.

- Select Save As in the File menu. The Save As window opens.

- Change the name in the File name box to June Meeting.

- Click Save.

A new copy of the document is saved with the name **June Meeting** and the new name appears on the **Title** bar. Any further work you do is now done on the new **June Meeting** file.

The original May Meeting document remains unchanged where it was originally saved.

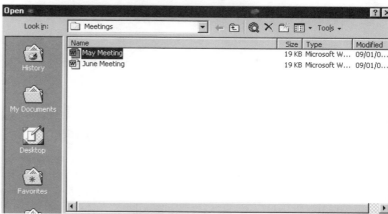

1.1.6 Saving a Document in Another File Type (3.1.1.6)

When you send a document or file to another person, they may not be able to use it if they are not using the same kind of computer and software that you used to prepare it. You should check with the recipient in advance. Then, if possible, you can save your work in a format they can use, as follows:

- Go through the **Save** process as before until the **Save As** window appears.

- Click in the **Save as type** box to display a list of available formats. Word options are shown here.

- Select the word processor version your recipient uses from the menu available in the **Save as type** options. Different version options for Word, e.g. Word 6.0, Word 97, appear as you scroll down through the options.

  - Text Only saves the file as plain text. Any formatting in the original document is discarded but the recipient will at least have access to the text that can then be inserted into other documents and reformatted if necessary. This format can be used by any word processor.

  - When you save a document as a web page you are saving it using a language known as hyper text markup language (HTML) and the document is now ready to be uploaded to the World Wide Web.

  - Rich Text Format (RTF) can be used by most word processors. It preserves common formatting options such as text size, bold, italics and so on but will not be able to reproduce some more advanced formatting.

  - Select Document Template to save a document and all the features you created, such as font size, headings, etc., for further use.

1.1.6.1 Software Specific File Extension

When you work with documents in different applications, the only way you can distinguish between the applications is by the extension which is placed automatically after you save the document. This option is used to denote the program which the file has been created and saved in.

Some examples include:

* .dwg for AutoCad

* .bmp for Bitmap files

*.wav for sound files

*.mid for MIDI files.

1.1.7 Switching between Open Documents (3.1.1.7)

It is possible to have two or more documents open on your desktop. It is also possible to see two documents displayed together. Because they then both share the desktop, a much smaller part of each document is displayed. When you switch between open documents, you normally see them displayed full size on the desktop. However, it can be useful to see and compare parts of different documents at the same time. In the following example we are going to open two documents and view the taskbar and the Window menu. These two documents are May Meeting and June Meeting.

Follow these steps:

- Open the May Meeting and June Meeting documents.

- Make sure that the two documents you want to see are open and that both of them are maximised.

- Select **Arrange All** in the **Window** menu.

- The two documents appear in the window, one above the other.

- Click on the document button for June Meeting on the taskbar. This will make the June Meeting file active.

- Click in the May Meeting document when you want to work in that one.
  To return a document to full screen size, click its **Maximise** button in the top right-hand corner of the window.
  The active document will display its **Title bar** in a darker colour.

Maximise
Button

1.1.8 Using Available Help Functions (3.1.1.8)

Help can be accessed in the Help menu, which is located above the Standard toolbar. From here you can choose to show Microsoft Word Help, Show the Office Assistant or use the What's This? features or click your mouse on the **Help button** on the Standard toolbar.

Help Button

1.1.9 Closing a Document (3.1.1.9)

When you are finished working on a document and you want to close it, follow these steps:

Program Close Button

Document Close Button

- Click the Document Close button. This is always the *lower* one. A window will appear asking you if you want to save the document.

  If you want to save the document, click **Yes** and you will then have an opportunity to give it a name if one has not already been given.

  Click **No** if you do not want to save the document before you close the document.

  Cancel can be clicked if you want to return to the document once again.

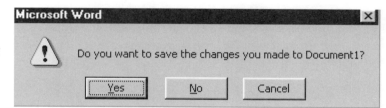

- Now click the Program Window **Close** button (the **X** button).

If you have more than one document open you can hit the Shift key of your keyboard before you open the File menu. Now select the **Close All** option. You can then make individual choices for each document in turn. Now close the program window.

Exercise 1B

1   Open document **My Word 1.**

2   Save it with the name My Word 2 as the file type **Text Only**.

3   Open My Word 1 and use Window to open My Word 2.

4   Use Help to find out information about saving a document.

5   Save and close both documents.

1.2   Adjusting Settings

1.2.1   Changing between Page View Modes (3.1.2.1)

There are several ways in which Word documents can be displayed and viewed on the screen.

Select the required format in the **View** menu. *Alternatively*, click the **View button** at the bottom left-hand corner of the screen.

The most commonly used views are **Print Layout** and **Normal**.

> **Print Layout** view displays the document as it appears on the page. It shows the actual 'page', including graphics, headers, footers and so on.
>
> **Normal** view displays only the text. Graphics do not appear. The document looks like one continuous piece of text, with dotted lines representing page breaks or divisions.

You may prefer to use **Normal** view if you have a lot of text to type. It gives you more space on the screen and it is less cluttered.

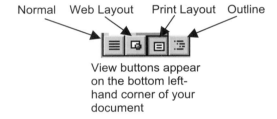

View buttons appear on the bottom left-hand corner of your document

1.2.2   Using Magnification/Zoom Tools (3.1.2.2)

Use the **zoom** control to change the magnification of the document as it is viewed on the screen. Note that changing the size of the document on the screen does not affect the size at which it will be printed. The Zoom tool can be accessed by selecting view from the menu bar and then zoom.

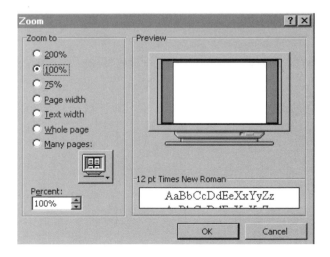

1.2.3 Displaying or Hiding Built-in Toolbars (3.1.2.3)

Word has two built-in toolbars that appear when Word is started. These are the **Standard toolbar** and the **Format toolbar.** These toolbars can be displayed either as one continuous toolbar or as two separate bars.

When a toolbar is required to complete a specific task, it can be accessed and displayed/placed for use on the application window. Activate the toolbar by using the **View** menu on the Menu bar of your program and click on the command called **Toolbars**. Glide the mouse to the right of the command and a list of different toolbars will be displayed.

In order to select a toolbar simply click on the menu to activate it.

Hiding a toolbar can be done the same way. Simply returning to the same menu and clicking the checked toolbar will remove it from the display.

Toolbars can be placed in any part of the existing window as follows:

- Clicking on the Title bar of the toolbar, hold the button of your mouse down and drag the toolbar to your preferred location.

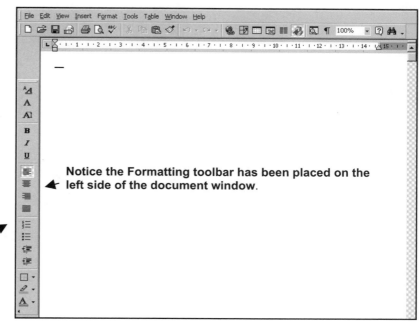

Notice the Formatting toolbar has been placed on the left side of the document window.

1.2.4 Modifying Basic Options and Preferences (3.1.2.5)

The default settings associated with any Word document, such as the user name or the location to which you want to save or from which you want to open a document, can be altered or modified. The settings can be altered through the **Tools** menu and then **Options** from the menu list.

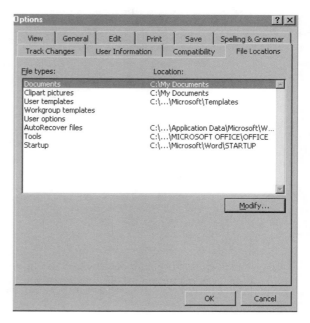

Follow these steps to modify the **Document's** file type:

- Open the **Tools** menu and select **Options.**

- Click on the **File Locations** tab.

- Click on File type – **Documents.**

- Click the **Modify** button.

- The **Modify Location** window will open. In this window you can choose to create a new folder or select a new drive to which the files can be saved.

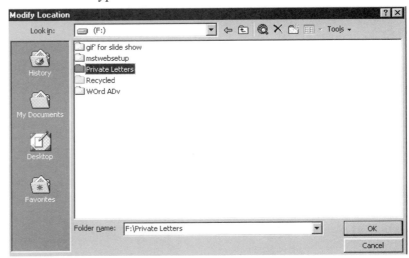

Another useful option is changing the user name should the 'default' user not be the one composing the document. To do this, simply follow these steps:

- Open the **Tools** menu and select **Options**.

- Click on the **User Information** tab.

- Replace the information appropriately.

- Click the OK button.

Exercise 1C

1   Open My Word 1.

2   Type in the text shown below (the box is not part of the exercise).

3   Save the document when you have inserted the text and close it.

Here is an example of the work of Charles Dickens

Sold for £1.99 in 1982

They turned into the wine-shop which was closed (for it was midnight) and where Madame Defarge immediately took her post at her desk, counted the small moneys that had been taken during her absence, examined the stock, went through the entries in the book, made other entries of her own, checked the serving man in every possible way, and finally dismissed him into bed.

MODULE 3

Section 2   Main Operations

2.1   Inserting Data

2.1.1 Inserting Text (3.2.1.1)

When Word opens, a screen appears with toolbars on the top and a blank area for inserting data. This area is known as a **Blank Document**. Where the cursor blinks on and off is called the **insertion point** – you can begin typing here. The default position for a new document is on the top left-hand side.

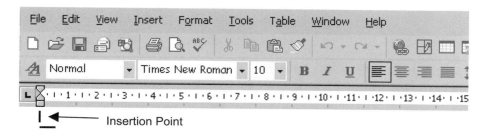

Insertion Point

If the mouse is moved about on screen it will display an **insertion bar** with an alignment icon attached to it. This insertion bar is displaying a left alignment icon.

If a specific **Alignment** button on the **Formatting** toolbar is clicked first, then when the cursor is double clicked in any area of the document it can now be moved to your chosen location with the chosen alignment. There are four different choices, Align Left, Center, Align Right and Justify. The default alignment is Align Left.

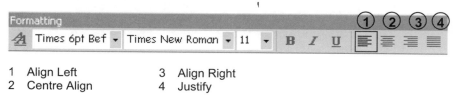

1	Align Left	3	Align Right
2	Centre Align	4	Justify

2.1.2 Inserting Special Characters and Symbols (3.2.1.2)

A word processing program is not confined to the letters or characters that appear on the keyboard keys, as in a traditional typewriter. Many special characters and symbols are also available. These include accents for different languages, special typesetting characters, copyright and registered symbols and so on.

The following are steps taken to insert the **é** in the name André:

- Place the **I-beam** cursor in the document where you want the symbol or special character to appear.

- To insert the character, select **Symbol** in the Insert menu. The Symbol window opens (see next page).

- Click the **Symbols** tab at the top of the window, if it is not already selected, to display the full set of characters available.

- Click in the Font box and select (normal text) if it is not already selected.

- Click on a character to display a magnified view, as in the illustration.

- Click the Insert button located at the bottom of the window to insert the selected character.

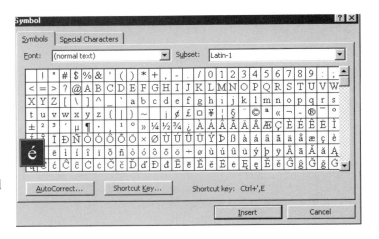

The symbol will now be inserted at the position of the typing cursor in the document.

Choosing the **Special characters** tab will give you access to trademark, copyright, registration symbols, etc.

NOTE

The **shortcut key** (*not* the Shortcut Key *button*) at the bottom of the window for inserting the character directly from the keyboard. For the selected character **é** in the illustration the shortcut keys are **Ctrl + ' + E**. It will save time if you learn the shortcut key combinations for common symbols and characters.

Control Key

The **Shortcut Key** button allows you to set your own shortcut key combinations.

Different fonts have different symbols and special characters. Click in the **Font** box to display the fonts available and look at the different characters available in each one.

2.1.3 Displaying and Hiding Non-Printing Characters (3.1.2.4)

As you type a document in Word there is a facility that flags the options you have chosen. Upon rereading or proofing your document, this can be particularly useful in checking spacing options, tabs, word spacing and so on. To display the codes click on the **Show/Hide** button.

¶

Show/Hide
Button

The following text displays some of these codes.

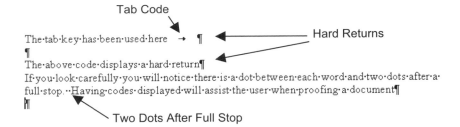

2.2   Selecting Data

2.2.1   Selecting Text (3.2.2.1)

Sometimes you'll want to manipulate the text that you have typed. You might want to move it, delete it or change its appearance in some way. To do this, you must first select the text you want to alter so that Word knows which piece of text is to be changed. The methods of selection described below use the mouse. This is usually the easiest way, although you can also use the keyboard. (When you become more familiar with the Word Help system, you can look this up yourself.)

2.2.1.1 Selecting Text with the Mouse

Place the cursor in front of the first letter of the text you want to select. Then use one of the following methods.

- Hold the left mouse button down and drag the mouse towards the end of the text you want to select.

  You will see the text being highlighted (coloured over) as you drag.

- When all the text you want is highlighted, release the mouse button.

  The text will now appear in inverse video, i.e. black is white and white is black.

  Alternatively, place the cursor in front of the first letter of the text to be selected. Hold down the Shift key while you click after the last letter of the required text. The entire text in between will be highlighted.

The Microsoft Office Suite of Applications – Word, Access, Excel, PowerPoint, Outlook and Explorer – share many common features. Opening an application, its appearance on the computer screen and the way in which you work with it are similar across the whole suite.
This chapter describes a number of the most common features which are important for the effective use of the computer. It also explains how to use them. These features and skills are important elements of the course.

Either of these two methods can also be used if you want to change your font, font size and/or orientation, insert bullets and/or change the text format to bold, italic, underline and so on. These options are to be found on the Formatting toolbar and are explained in more detail in the Before You Begin module of this book.

2.2.1.2 Shortcuts for Selecting Data

To select one word only, double click on the word.

To select one line of text on the screen:

- Move the mouse to the left margin of the text.
- The mouse pointer will change to a white arrow.
- Click once.
- The line will be highlighted.

To select an entire paragraph, move the mouse to the left margin as above and double click to select the paragraph.

2.2.1.3 Selecting All the Text in a Document

If you want to select all the text in the entire document:

- Click the **Edit** menu.
- Click on **Select All**.

When you are finished working on the selection, click anywhere outside the selected text to deselect, i.e. anywhere there is white space on the page.

2.3   Editing Data

2.3.1   Inserting and Deleting Text (3.2.3.1)

Sometimes you will want to make changes to text in a document that you have already created.

You may want to insert new text or delete some existing text.

To **insert** new text into the middle of a previously typed line, e.g. if you forgot to put in a word, do the following:

- Place the I-beam cursor where you want to insert the new text.

- Start typing. The existing text moves to the right to make room for the new text as you type.

To **replace** existing text with new text:

- Select the old text.

- Type in the new text directly.

- What you type will replace the selected text.

To **overwrite** existing text with new text:

- Place the I-beam cursor where you want to insert the new text.

- Press the **Insert** key on your keyboard. The status line located on the bottom of the document window will now display the letters **OVR** in black print. This means that Word is in **Overwrite** mode.

Insert
Key

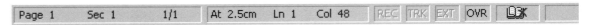

- Type the new text.
  You will see the new text *writing over* the old text.

- When you are finished, press the **Insert** key again to leave Overwrite mode.

2.3.2 Using the Undo and Redo Commands (3.2.3.2)

When a button on the Formatting toolbar appears 'greyed out' it means that option is inactive. If the Undo button looks like this it will display Can't Undo if you draw your mouse pointer beneath the button.

'Greyed Out'
Button

For example, if text is bold and you want it in plain text, first select the text. The **Bold** button will have a 'pressed in' appearance. Click it to remove the bold formatting. If you had just made the text bold a moment before, you can use the **Undo** button.

Undo
Button

2.3.2.1 Undo and Redo

If you make a mistake, e.g. delete text accidentally, you can usually undo your mistake by clicking the Undo button. Word lets you undo several previous actions by continually clicking the Undo button. Note, however, there are some actions that can't be undone, so don't rely absolutely on this button!

Redo is used to reverse Undo. For example, if you undo something then realise you should have left it the way it was, click Redo to restore the previous version.

Redo
Button

If redo is not available the button will look like this and will display Can't Redo if you draw your mouse pointer beneath the button.

Can't Redo (Alt+Shift+Backspace)

Exercise 2A

Open My Word 1.

1   Insert the following text as a final paragraph.

> Then she turned out the contents of the bowl of money for the second time, and began knotting them in her handkerchief, in a chain of separate knots, for safe keeping through the night.

2   Change the symbol for the £ sign to a € symbol.

3   Select all the text and change it to Arial font, font size 12.

4   Practise selecting different sections of text using the techniques mentioned.

5   Delete the first sentence of the text.

6   Undo your last action.

7   Overtype the words 'Charles Dickens' with the words 'C. Dickens'.

8   Redo the last action.

9   Save your work and close the document.

2.4   Duplicating, Moving and Deleting Text

2.4.1 Duplicating Text (3.2.4.1)

To duplicate text means that an electronic image is taken of the original text and placed in an area known as the **clipboard.** The process used to do this is called **copy and paste**. The buttons associated with this command are located on the Standard toolbar.

In this instance, you are copying and pasting between two separate documents instead of within the same one.

Copy   Paste
Button   Button

Open documents **My Word 1** and **My Word 2**. You can have them full size
or displayed together, as you prefer.

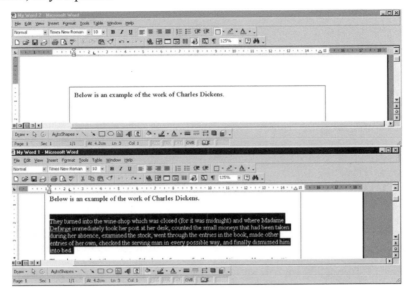

In My Word 1, select the text you want to use.

- Hold the **Ctrl** key down and drag the text into the window of My Word 2 and to the location
  you want.

- Release the **Ctrl** key.

- View the result.
  Alternatively, you can use the Copy and Paste buttons on **Standard** toolbar. This command is
  more clearly explained in the Before You Begin chapter of the book.

The Clipboard

The clipboard is an area of the computer's memory where items are stored temporarily. Text is
placed in here when using the cutting or *copying* functions. The Clipboard window can hold up
to 24 separate items at any given time. When you *paste*, you put a **copy** of what is on the
clipboard into your document. Thus, you can paste the same item many times into a document
or into many documents.

If you want to display the Clipboard Viewer, it can be found in the **Start Menu, Accessories,
System Tools menu**.

2.4.2 Moving Text (3.2.4.1)

You can move text around a document by **cutting** it from one place and **pasting** it into another. Using
this method, the user avoids having to retype the text in the new position. Follow these steps:

- Select the text you want to move with your mouse.

- **Cut** the selected text using one of the following methods.

- Click the **Cut** button on the toolbar (the scissors).

- *Alternatively*, select **Cut** in the **Edit** menu.

Cut Button

You can also use the keyboard shortcut as follows:

- Hold down the **Ctrl** key and then press the letter **X** key having selected the text.

Control Key

- The cut text is removed from its original position and stored on the **clipboard.**

- Use the mouse to place the I-beam cursor where you want the text to appear.

- Now **paste** the text, i.e. insert it into its new position. Use one of the following
  methods.

- Click the **Paste** button on the toolbar.
  Alternatively, select **Paste** in the **Edit** menu.

Paste
Button

- You can also use the keyboard shortcut, **Ctrl + V**. (Using 'V' may not seem sensible but 'P' is already used for another keyboard shortcut.)

- The text appears in its new position.

2.4.3 Deleting Text (3.2.4.3)

Deleting text can be done one of two ways. To delete one character at a time follow these steps.

- Place the cursor to the **left** of the character to be deleted and press the **Delete** key on the keyboard. Be careful when pressing the Delete key. If you hold it down too long, it will delete more characters.
  Alternatively, place the cursor to the **right** of the character to be deleted and press the **Backspace** key (above the **Enter** key).

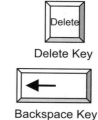

Delete Key

Backspace Key

To delete a word or a block of text:

- Select the text you want to delete and press the **Delete** key.

2.5   Search and Replace

If you have inadvertently used an incorrect word throughout a document, it is possible to search for each occurrence of the word and replace it with the correction.

2.5.1 Using the Search Command (3.2.5.1)

Use the **Find** command in the **Edit** menu to locate the word or text you are looking for. When you click on Find command the **Find and Replace** window will open.

In this example imagine you had misspelled Smith and you need to find where each instance is used within your document. Clicking on the **Find Next** button will bring you to each example of the word throughout the document.

When the last occurrence of the word is found you will be told.

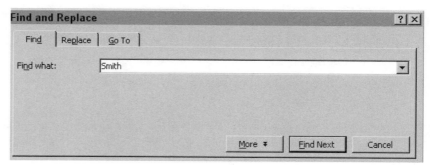

2.5.2 Using the Replace Command (3.2.5.2)

Use **Replace** when you know that you want to replace a word or phrase, not just find where it occurs in the document.

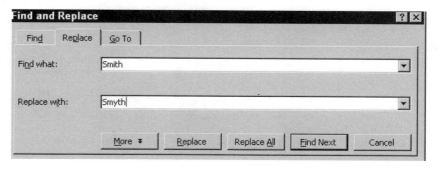

To use Find and Replace, do the following:

- Select **Find** or **Replace** in the **Edit** menu.

- In the **Find what** box, enter the text you want to search for.

- In the **Replace with** box enter the replacement text. (Click the **Replace** tab if you selected **Find** in the **Edit** menu.)

- Click **Find Next** to let Word find any occurrence of the text so you can see it before deciding whether to replace it or not.

- Click the **Replace** button to replace it.

- Click **Replace All** to replace all occurrences of the word in the document without seeing them individually.

- Once you are finished with this command this window will appear.

- Click on **OK** to finish task.

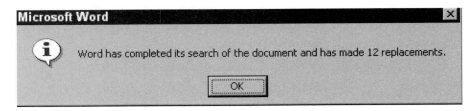

Exercise 2B

1   Open My Word 1 and My Word 2.

2   Select the first paragraph in My Word 1 and copy and paste it to My Word 2.

3   Type in your name in the My Word 2 document.

4   Cut and paste it to My Word 1.

5   Search for all instances of the word 'and' and replace it with '&' symbol.

6   Delete your name from My Word 1 using the Backspace key.

7   Undo your action and delete your name using the Delete key.

8   Save the document and close it.

Section 3   Formatting

3.1   Formatting Text

Formatting text means changing its physical appearance.

Font (or typeface) is the name given to the physical design and appearance of letters. The same letter appears differently in different fonts. There are many different fonts available in Word. Two of the most commonly used are **Times New Roman** (this typeface) and **Arial** (this typeface).

They are used throughout this manual.

The font and font size in use appear on the Formatting toolbar.

Font Size Box

Font Box ➔ Arial   10

3.1.1   Changing Text Appearance (3.3.1.1)

To use a different font from the one automatically chosen by the computer, select the text you want to change. If you want to set a font for the whole document, select the font before you begin typing. The active font can be changed at any time. You may set a font type and size before you begin typing. A new font can also be retrospectively applied to a whole document, a chunk of text, an individual word and so on. Use either of the methods below.

1 – Using the Toolbar

The quickest and easiest way to change fonts is to use the font options that are available on the Formatting Toolbar.

- Click the arrow to the right of the font name in the font box. A list of the available fonts on your computer is displayed in a drop-down menu.

- Click on the name of the font you want. Its name appears in the font box and the drop-down menu disappears.

- To change the font size, click the arrowhead in the font size box to display a list of sizes.

- Font size is measured in points, with 72 points (pt) to an inch.

- To apply a new font to a new document select the size you want.

- If your preference is not listed, select the size displayed in the Size box and type in the value you require. The size you type will replace what was in the box.

2 – Using the Format Menu

Using the Format menu gives you many more options. It also displays a preview of the font.

- Select **Font** in the **Format** menu.
  The Font window opens.
  In the top left of the window, the name of the current font appears in the **Font** box.
  Underneath is a list of available fonts.

- Use the scroll bar on the right of the box, if necessary, to see the complete list.

- Click on the font you want to use. Its name appears in the font box.

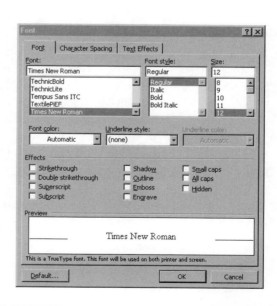

- Select the size you want in the **Size** area at the top right of the window. 10pt or 12pt are usually used for normal text.

- The **Preview** panel at the bottom of the window gives an example of the font in its selected size and style.

- Click the OK button and the options you have chosen will be applied to the selected text in your document.

3.1.2 Applying Text Formatting (3.3.1.2)

Many different aspects of the text's appearance can be changed, e.g. the size of the letters, the font, whether it's in **bold type**, *italicised* or underlined, etc.. You may want to format only some of the text or set a format for the whole document.

There are a number of options available to format text in this manner. Use the buttons on the Formatting toolbar, to do the following:

- You may choose the formatting option before you type the text. Clicking the italics key, for example, will italicise text that follows until you cancel the format by clicking the button again.

- You may return to a piece of text, select it and click the option on the Formatting toolbar. In this manner, only the selected text will be formatted. Surrounding text is unaffected. *Alternatively*, you can set the format option or return to the selected text, and using the **Fromat** menu and then **Font**, you can select these options from the **Font style** box.

If the Formatting toolbar is not visible, select **Toolbars** in the **View** menu and click **Formatting** in the sub-menu that appears. If there is a tick (✔) beside **Formatting**, it means the toolbar is already on your screen.

3.1.3 Applying Subscript or Superscript to Text (3.3.1.3)

When you wish to type in chemical symbols in your text, for example the 2 of H_2O, just follow these steps:

- Type H.
- Open the Format menu and click on Font.
- Select the Subscript box.
- Click **OK.**
- Now type 2.
- Return to the Format menu and click on Font.
- Deselect the **Subscript** box.
- Click OK.
- Now type the number 0.

Similarly, if you want to insert the symbol for a degree in a temperature, such as 21°, follow the same steps above but select the **Superscript** option.

3.1.4 Applying Case Changes to Text (3.3.1.4)

SOMETIMES WHEN YOU ENTER TEXT INTO THE MIDDLE OF A SENTENCE OF A DOCUMENT, you discover that you have turned on the **CAPS LOCK** button in error. In order to change the text to the correct case you must follow these steps:

- Highlight the text which has been typed incorrectly and then open the Format menu and select Change Case…

- When you have selected this option, a window will appear with five options.

- Choose the one you want.

- Click the OK button.

NOTE

> Word will Autocorrect your mistake if you start a sentence in the wrong case. However, it will not place capital letters for proper nouns such as a person's name within a sentence.

Exercise 3A

1   Open My Word 1.

2   Type in the following information beneath the final paragraph. (Make sure it is typed exactly as you see it typed below.

> Then she turned out the contents of the bowl of money for the second time, and began knotting them in her handkerchief, in a chain of separate knots, for safe keeping through the night. all this while defarge, with his pipe in his mouth, walked up and down, complacently admiring, but never interfering; in which condition, indeed, as to the business and his domestic affairs, he walked up and down through life.
>
> *a tale of two cities*, page 179

3   Change the text to the font Tahoma and size 12.

4   **Bold** the first word of each paragraph.

5   *Italicise* the last word of each sentence.

6   <u>Underline</u> the words 'a tale of two cities, page 179'.

7   Change the case for all the text to Title Case.

8   Type the following sentence: 'H_20 boils at at a temperature of $100^{\circ}C$.'

9   Save your work and close the file.

3.1.5   Applying Different Colours to Text (3.3.1.5)

To change the text colour do the following:

- Click the arrow on the right of the **Colour** box located on the **Formatting toolbar.**

- Select the colour you require from the palette.

- *Alternatively*, select the text first to which you wish to apply the new colour. Open the **Format** menu and select the **Font** command.

- In the window click on the Font Colour box and again select the colour you want from the palette.

- Click **OK** for the colour to be applied.

Text Colour Button

3.1.6   Copying Formatting (3.3.1.6)

When you want to apply selected formatting such as font size and style, etc., to another piece of text, it is not necessary to go through all the formatting options described above every time. You can save time by using the **Format Painter** button on the Standard toolbar.

- Select the text with the formatting you want to copy.

- Click the **Format Painter** button on the Standard toolbar. The cursor is now in the shape of the **Format Painter Tool** .

- Drag the **Format Painter tool** through the new text and release the mouse button.

Format Painter
Button

Format
Painter Tool

To apply the formatting to several pieces of text follow these steps:

- Select the text whose format you want to use.

- Double click the Format Painter button. The button will now stay selected.

- Highlight the text you wish the format to be applied to with the painter.

- When you have finished formatting, click the button again to deselect it or press the Esc key located on the top left-hand corner of your keyboard.

Escape Key

3.1.7   Applying an Existing Style (3.3.1.7)

A **style** is a selection of formatting options that determines the appearance of text in a document. When you open a new document in Word, the default style is usually Times New Roman, 10 point, left-aligned, with single-line spacing. This is known as **Normal** style.

The font name and size are given in the boxes to the right of the name.

A selection of other styles are available in a **Style menu** drop-down list. Look to the menu box. Click the arrow to view the **Style menu.** Style symbols in the list indicate the alignment and whether the style will affect the whole paragraph (¶) or selected characters only (a). You can use them to vary the appearance of your text without having to go to the trouble of setting up the formatting options yourself.

To apply a style to an existing paragraph do the following:

- Click anywhere in the text.

- Select the style from the style list on the Format toolbar. (A character style will only affect the character or text you have selected.)

- To type in a particular style, select this from the Style menu before you start to type.

To apply a style called Plain Text, for example, follow these steps:

- Open the document My Word 1.

- Select the text in the first paragraph.

- Click on the Format menu and select the command **Style…**

- Click on All Styles in the List box.

- Select Plain Text.

- Click on the **Apply** button.

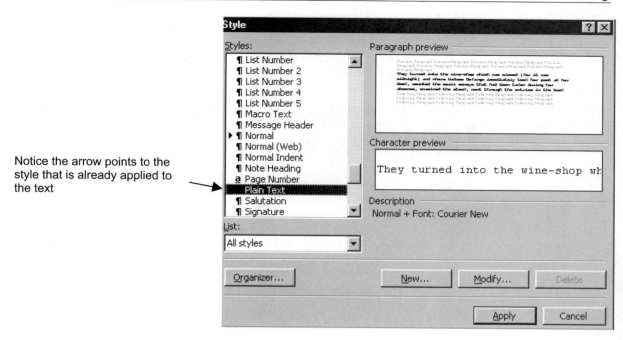

Notice the arrow points to the style that is already applied to the text

Exercise 3B

1 Open My Word 1.

2 Change the colour of the words 'A Tale of Two Cities' to blue.

3 Copy the formatting to the word Defarge in the text.

4 Apply the Style Body Text to the first paragraph of the document.

5 Use the Format Painter to apply this style to the last paragraph of the document.

6 Close the document without saving it.

3.2 Formatting Paragraphs

3.2.1 Inserting and Removing Soft Carriage Return Marks (3.3.2.2)

Say you want to type the verse of a poem into your document and because you have short lines you need to insert a **text wrapping break** at the end of each one. In Word this can be found in **Insert, Break.**

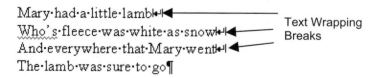

Text Wrapping Breaks

Text wrapping breaks symbols can be removed in the same way as paragraph marks, by placing your cursor to the left of the mark and pressing the Delete key. This will bring the text from the next line in line with the text where your cursor is located.

3.2.2 Aligning Text (3.3.2.3)

Alignment or Justification defines the way in which the text is lined up against the margins.

To set or change the alignment, use one of the methods below. If you are aligning text you have already typed, select the text before you can use either option.

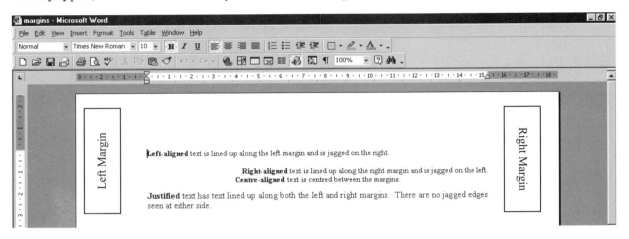

Step 1 – Using the Formatting toolbar.

Click the appropriate button on the toolbar. The 'lines of text' on the alignment buttons indicate their effect, as shown in the illustration.

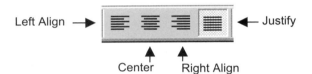

Step 2 – Using the Format menu.

Follow these steps:

- Select Paragraph in the Format menu on the Menu bar.

- The Paragraph window opens.

- In the **Alignment** box on the top left, click the arrow to select the required option.

- Look in the **Preview** box to see the effect of your selections.

- Click the **OK** button to apply your selections to the text.

- Click **Cancel** if you change your mind.

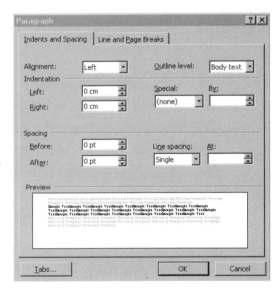

3.2.3 Indenting Paragraphs (3.3.2.4)

An indent will set the position of the text in relation to the left and right margin.

Before you go into this menu make sure that the text to which you wish to apply the formatting is selected.

- Select Paragraph in the Format menu.

- The Paragraph window appears as before.

- Make sure that the Indents and Spacing tab is clicked.

- Now choose the measurement for Left or Right indent.

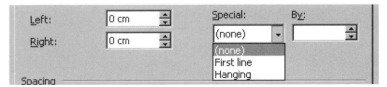

- Don't forget to look in the Preview box. If you want to choose **Special** formats such as First line or Hanging, click on the selector arrow to the right of the **By** box and choose the measurement.

- Click OK to close the window and apply the options you have chosen.

This ECDL Foundation approved courseware product incorporates learning reinforcement exercises. These exercises are included to help the candidate in their training for the ECDL. The exercises included in this courseware product are not ECDL certification tests and should not be construed in any way as ECDL certification tests. For information about authorised ECDL test centres in different national territories please refer to the ECDL Foundation website at www.ecdl.com.

Exercise 3C

1   Open My Word 1.

2   Use the Show/Hide button to reveal the formatting of the document.

3   Insert two paragraph spaces between each of the paragraphs.

4   Place four line spaces between the last paragraph and the title.

5   Remove one of the carriage returns at the end of the document.

6   Practice using the alignment buttons on the text in the document.

7   Save the document and close it.

3.2.4 Applying Line Spacing (3.3.2.5)

Line spacing refers to the amount of space between lines of text, relative to the size of the text itself. Most documents use single-line spacing. Sometimes you might want more space between lines to make the text easier to read. Double-line spacing gives the effect of an extra blank line between two lines of text. You can't change the line spacing for only a few lines in the middle of a paragraph: any change will affect the whole paragraph.

To apply double-line spacing to the second paragraph in My Word 1, follow these steps:

- Open My Word 1 and select the second paragraph.

- Click anywhere in the paragraph.

- Open **Format** on the Menu bar.

- Select **Paragraph** command.

- The Paragraph window appears. Make sure that the **Indents and Spacing** tab is clicked.

- Use the **Spacing** section to select the required spacing. (Click the arrow to display the menu.)

- Select **Double.**

- Use the **Preview** box to see the effects of the changes.

- Click **OK** to close the window.

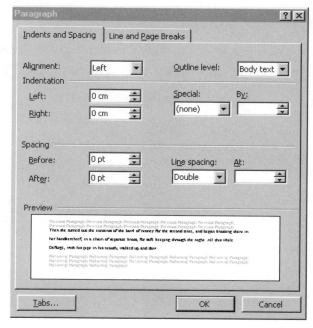

NOTE

If you select **Exactly**, the spacing is measured in **points** (as for the font size). This allows for much finer adjustment of line spacing than is possible with line-size spacing.

3.2.5 Applying Automatic Hyphenation (3.3.1.8)

If the last word on a line of text is too long to fit, Word puts it on the next line. This is known as **Wordwrap**. If the text in a document is aligned using justify this often results in a lot of white space between the words as the text is padded out with extra space to fill each line evenly.

Hyphenation is a means of improving the appearance of text in a document. It divides words to fill the lines more evenly. It reduces excess white space between words and gives a neater appearance to the text, especially when using justify alignment.

Hyphenation divides long words at the end of a line into two parts. It inserts a hyphen (-) after the first part, and places the second part on the following line. Words can only be divided in certain places. However, some words cannot be divided at all.

In the following example, notice the difference a single hyphen can make.

No Hyphenation

> You can ask Word to hyphenate your text for you or you can choose to hyphenate it yourself. You can also choose not to have any hyphenation at all. Using hyphenation reduces excessive white space between words and makes text easier to read.

Hyphenated

> You can ask Word to hyphenate your text for you or you can choose to hyphenate it yourself. You can also choose not to have any hyphenation at all. Using hyphen-ation reduces excessive white space between words and makes text easier to read.

Text can be hyphenated **automatically** or **manually**. Usually, it's better to hyphenate your document **after** you have finished writing and editing it. You can also choose to hyphenate the whole text or only certain paragraphs.

Automatic hyphenation means that Word decides where to divide the words and place the hyphens. This is quick and convenient. However, you should still check the document after automatic hyphenation to ensure that there aren't any hyphens in places where you don't want them.

If you want to hyphenate only certain paragraphs, do the following:

- Select the appropriate paragraphs.
- Select **Language** in the **Tools** menu.
- Click **Hyphenation** in the sub-menu that appears.
- The Hyphenation window opens.
- Click the **Automatically hyphenate document** box to place a tick in it.
- Click **OK**.

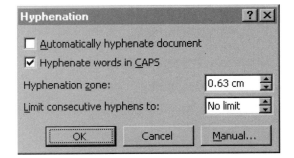

Word hyphenates the document automatically as you type.

3.2.6 Applying Spacing Above and Below Paragraphs (3.3.2.6)

Space can be added before or after a paragraph. This is useful for inserting extra space between a heading and the main text, as used throughout this manual. Paragraph spacing only affects the space

---

before the first line or after the last line of the paragraph, not the spacing between the lines in the paragraph itself.

To change the paragraph spacing, first select the paragraphs. If you only want to change the spacing for one paragraph, just click anywhere in that paragraph. Then proceed as follows.

- Select Paragraph in Format on the Menu bar.

- The Paragraph window appears as before.

- Make sure that the Indents and Spacing tab is clicked.

- In the Spacing section, select a size for the spacing in **Before** of 12pt and **After** of 6pt.

- 3pt spacing is about half the size of a normal line of text, for example.

- Use the arrows to the right to choose higher or lower values, or type in your own.

- Don't forget to look in the Preview box.

- Click OK to close the window and apply the options.

They turned into the wine-shop which was closed (for it was midnight) and where Madame Defarge immediately took her post at her desk, counted the small moneys that had been taken during her absence, examined the stock, went through the entries in the book, made other entries of her own, checked the serving man in every possible way, and finally dismissed him into bed.

This example shows line spacing of 12pt Before and 6pt After options, as chosen by the author.

3.2.7 Inserting and Removing Paragraph Marks (3.3.2.1)

Space can be added before or after a paragraph. In default mode when we press the **Enter key** on our keyboard a paragraph mark is inserted immediately after the last character typed on that line. This tells the computer to leave a line space after the last character typed in. If we select the Enter key once more a blank line space is inserted.

If·we·click·on·the·**Show/Hide**·button·on·the·**Standard· Toolbar**·paragraph·marks·will·appear·in·respect· of·any·text·written·on·screen. ··These·marks·can·be·removed·by·clicking·to·the·left·of·the·mark·and· pressing·the·**Delete·key**·on·the·keyboard.¶

¶

¶

Show/Hide
Button

3.2.8 Using Tabs (3.3.2.7)

Tabs are predefined stops set across a line in a document page. Pressing the Tab key moves the cursor along to the tabbed positions on the line. The text that you type appears at the position of the tabbed stop. Using the **Tabs** command in the Format menu is the proper way to make a list like this one shown below.

The Tab Key

Left Align	Right Align	Center Align	Decimal Align
↓	↓	↓	↓
London	March:	Monday, Wednesday	£99.00
Paris	April:	Tuesday, Thursday, Friday	£179.99

Word has default tab settings. Tabs set at ½ inch intervals (even when the ruler is set to centimetres!) from the left margin. Word default tabs are shown as small light grey dots along the bottom of the ruler. If you look carefully on the ruler you will see them.

You would normally set your own tabs, but when you are creating tabbed lists there are four different tabs available to you that align text in different ways.

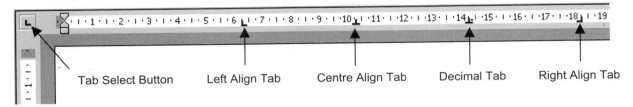

Tab Select Button   Left Align Tab   Centre Align Tab   Decimal Tab   Right Align Tab

3.2.8.1 Setting Tabs on the Ruler

You can set tabs before you begin to type, or set or change tabs in text that has already been typed. When you set a new tab, Word removes any of its own tabs to the left of the one set by you.

If you are setting tabs in existing text, select the text first.

- Click the **Tab Select** button at the left of the ruler.

- Each time you click the tab select button, a different tab appears.

- Click the tab select button until it shows the tab that you require.

- Use the **Decimal** tab for numbers with decimal points, such as prices.

- Click on the ruler at the position where you want to set the tab.

- The tab appears on the ruler at that point.

Tab	Button
Left-align	L
Centre	⊥
Right-align	⅃
Decimal	⊥

When you want to move between tabs follow these steps:

- Drag the tab along the ruler to reposition it, if necessary.

- Press the **Tab** key on the keyboard to move the cursor to the tab. Press the key again to move to the next tab, and so on.

- Press the **Backspace** key to go back.

3.2.8.2 Setting Tabs in the Tabs Window

You can set tabs at precise positions on the ruler by selecting **Tabs** in the **Format** menu, as follows:

- Select **Tabs** in the **Format** menu on the Menu bar.

- The Tabs window opens.

- Type the position of your first tab, e.g. 3cm, in the **Tab stop position** box.

- You do not have to type 'cm'. It will be added automatically later. The tab position appears in the panel underneath.

- In the **Alignment** section, click the option you want, e.g. Left.

- Click the **Set** button at the bottom of the window to place the tab on the ruler.

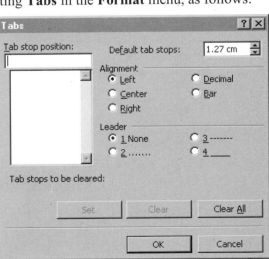

- Type the position of the next tab you want and so on until you have put in all the tab positions you require.

- Click **OK** when you are finished.

3.2.8.3 Removing Tabs

Tabs may be removed in two ways from the ruler.

Remove particular tabs, as follows:

- Click on the tab in question and drag it off the ruler.
  The tab will disappear and any text that was aligned using the tab will jump to the next right hand tabbed position.

Remove all the tabs on your ruler, as follows:

- Select **Tabs** in the **Format** menu, click the **Clear all** button and choose **OK**.

This ECDL Foundation approved courseware product incorporates learning reinforcement exercises. These exercises are included to help the candidate in their training for the ECDL. The exercises included in this courseware product are not ECDL certification tests and should not be construed in any way as ECDL certification tests. For information about authorised ECDL test centres in different national territories please refer to the ECDL Foundation website at www.ecdl.com.

Exercise 3D

1   Create a new document and save it as **Tabs 1** on your hard disk of your computer.

2   Set tabs at 5cm, 8cm and 14cm. There is no tab at the left border.

3   Type the text below using tabs on the ruler. Use Times New Roman, 10 pt.
        (The box is to frame the example only and is not part of the exercise.)
        Save your work.

Destination	Month	Days	Fare
London	March	Monday, Wednesday	€99.00
Paris	April	Tuesday, Thursday, Friday	€179.99
Amsterdam	January	Monday, Friday, Sunday	€174.50

3.2.9 Applying Bullets and Numbers (3.3.2.8 and 3.3.2.9)

Bullets are an effective means of isolating points or drawing attention to a list in a document. With Word, you can decide to type a bulleted or numbered list before you begin typing or you can add bullets or numbers to a list that you have already typed.

3.2.9.1 Typing a Bulleted or Numbered List

- Place the cursor where you want the list to begin.

- Click the **Bullet** or the **Numbering** button on the Formatting toolbar.

- The first bullet or number appears on the page.

- Complete typing the first list item and press **Enter**.

- A bullet appears on the next line.

- When the list is finished, press the **Enter** key twice.

Bullet
Button

Numbering
Button

If you have to place comments between bullets or numbers you should select the relevant button and deselect it and reselect it again if you want to continue with the style.

Should a bullet or number appear where you don't want one, click the **Bullet** or **Numbering** button again to turn off the bulleting or numbering process.

3.2.9.2 Bullet or Number an Existing List

If composing lists make sure that the Enter key has been pressed after each item in the list so that each item is recognised as a distinct new line.

To apply bullets to text, simply do as follows:

- Select the text.

- Click the **Bullet** or **Numbering** button on the Formatting toolbar.

The Bullet and Numbering buttons apply indents to achieve their effect. These indent buttons are clearly visible on the Ruler and are located to the left and right of it.

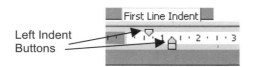

To alter the space between the bullet or number and the items in the list, select the list and move the indent buttons on the ruler.

Bulleted or numbered lists are more effective if they are indented from the left margin, as on the top of this page. To indent a list, select the list and move the **Left indent** marker on the ruler.

Word supplies a range of bullet and number formats that are suitable for most purposes but you can change them to suit your own requirements. If you don't want to have full stops after numbers or to have a bracket instead, view the following window. The **Numbered** panel has options on how the numbering appears.

You can select or change the style of bullet or numbering before you begin to type, or you can select or change the style on an existing list by selecting it first.

Proceed as follows.

- Select **Bullets and Numbering** in the Format menu.

- The Bullets and Numbering window opens.

- Click the Bulleted or Numbered tab as required.

- Click the box displaying the layout you require.

- Click OK.

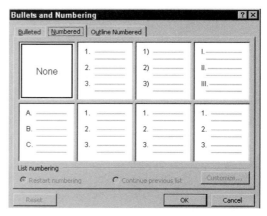

Try the following task.

1   Open a new document and call it **Bullets 1**.

2   Type the following text and make a bulleted list of the names as shown below.
        (The box is not part of the exercise.)

> The following are all writers:
>
> W. B. Yeats
>
> Charles Dickens
>
> Mark Twain
>
> Jane Austen

3   Change the bullet for a
     numbered list. Make sure that
     Restart Numbering is selected
     if you want the numbers to start
     at 1.

4   Indent the list of names by
     1.5cm (not shown above).

5   Save the document.

6   Use **Save As** to save a copy of
     Bullets 1 with the title **Bullets
     2**.

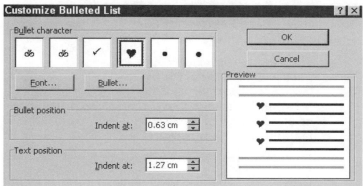

7   Practise using different styles of bullets and numbering.

8   Finish by making the list a numbered list.

9   Save your work and close the document.

To continue the numbering used in a previous list, select **Continue Previous List**. This is useful if you began a list earlier on the page and then added a few words of explanation before continuing the list again.

If none of the available options is suitable, you can set your own formats for bullets or numbering by clicking the **Customize** button and making your own choices in the window that appears.

Customising the numbered list allows you to change the number style and in the Preview window you can see the result of your choice.

Customising the bulleted list means that you can change the bullet character and, like the numbered list, you can preview your choice before applying to your text.

3.2.10 Adding Borders and Shading (3.3.2.10)

A border is a square or rectangular set of lines that surrounds an area of text or graphics. You can add a **border** to a whole page, to a selected paragraph or to a piece of text. To add a border to a paragraph or page, do the following.

- Select the paragraph or text to which you want to add the border.

- Select **Borders and Shading** in the **Format** menu on the Menu bar.

- The Borders and Shading window opens.

- Click the type of border you want in the **Setting** list on the left of the window.

- In the centre of the window, select the **Style**, **Colour** and **Width** (line thickness).

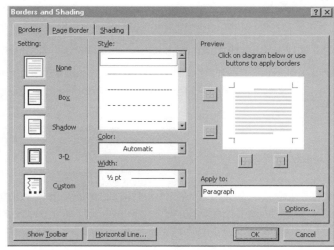

To apply shading to a paragraph, do the following:

- Select the **Shading** tab and choose from the options available.

Use the drop-down menus and scroll bars to display the various options. Use the **Preview** panel in the Borders and Shading window to draw the effect of your choices from Setting, Style Colour and Width.

The four buttons to the left of and below the **Preview** panel allow you to place or remove the border individually on the top, bottom, left or right.

- Click the **Options** button to set the distance of the text from the border. This will place a space between the border and the text.

- It is a good idea to have some space between the text and the border.

- Click **OK** in each window to return to the page.

- To apply a border to a whole page, click the **Page Border** tab at the top left.

3.3   Formatting Documents

3.3.1 Changing Document Orientation (3.3.3.1 and 3.3.3.2)

The size of the page, its text orientation, the width of the left, right, top and bottom margins and so on can all be selected according to your personal preferences and to suit the paper you use in the printer. To set your own preferences, proceed as follows:

- Select **Page Setup** in the **File** menu on the Menu bar.

- The Page Setup window appears. Tabs along the top of the window display various options. If the **Margins** tab is not already selected, click it to display the **Margins** settings window.

- Enter the margin sizes you require.

- Click in the **Top** box or use the up and down arrows to choose the distance between the top margin and the top of the first line of text.

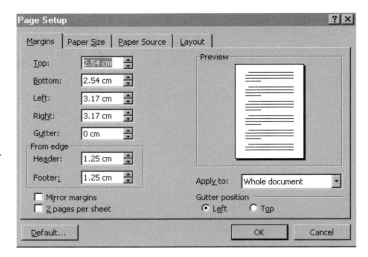

If your document is to be bound in a ring binder, increase the left margin to 3cm or more to allow for the binding area.

The **Preview** panel shows the page with the settings.

To set the **Orientation** to print down or across the page do the following:

- Click **Portrait** (vertical) or **Landscape** (horizontal).
  Portrait is used for the majority of documents.

- Click the **Paper** tab to set the paper size. The standard size in Europe is **A4**.

- Click **OK** to apply your settings to this document only.

NOTE

You may change from the default settings for individual documents, but when the next new document is created, Word will again revert to the defaults. Click the **Default** button if you want your new settings to become the default settings for all future new documents.

3.3.2 Inserting or Deleting Page Breaks (3.3.3.3)

When you have completed a paragraph, close to the end of a page you might prefer your typing to continue on a new page. To do this you can insert a **Page Break** as follows:

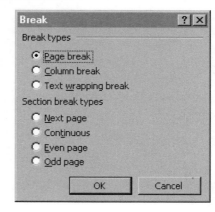

- Select **Break** in the Insert menu.

- The Break window opens. Page break is already selected by default.

- Click OK.

Word creates a new page and positions the cursor on it, ready for you to begin typing.

Using a page break means you can edit and add without affecting the layout of text and graphics on other page.

To delete the page break:

- First click on the Show/Hide button on your Format toolbar.

- Click on the choice of break, in this instance Page Break, to be deleted.

- Press the Delete key on your keyboard.

3.3.3 Headers and Footers (3.3.3.4)

Headers and **footers** are special areas on the top and bottom of a document page. Normally, any text typed or any graphic placed into these is replicated on every page in a document. They are usually used to contain a page number, a date, the document name or an author's name. Text in a **header** or **footer** can be typed, managed and formatted in much the same way as text in a normal document work area. However, the **header** and **footer** areas are outside the normal work area.

Headers and **footers** can also contain fields or autotext entries that are predefined by Word, such as the date, page number formats, author's name and so on.

To modify or add information to the header or footer follow these steps:

- Select **Header and Footer** in the **View** menu.

- The Header and Footer toolbar appears, usually in the centre of the screen.

- Select the information to be modified.

- Clicking on the **Date** or **Time** buttons inserts the current date or time.

- Press the **Delete** key on your keyboard.

- Insert the new information to replace the deleted information.

- Click on the **Close** button to the right of the Header and Footer toolbar.

Date and Time
Buttons

Note that when you return to the main page, any text in the **header** and **footer** is 'greyed out' and unavailable. To edit a header or footer, select **Header and Footer** in the **View** menu.

3.3.4 Adding Fields in Headers and Footers (3.3.3.5)

The **Insert AutoText** button is located on the left-hand side of the Header and Footer toolbar. The AutoText entries include lists of **fields** (a location in which particular data is stored) such as **Page X of Y** (page number information) and **Filename and Path** (filename and location).

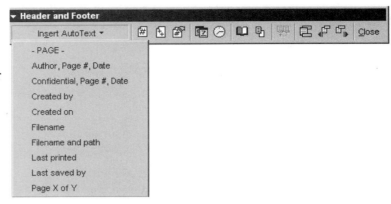

The following are screen shots of the headers and footers of a document. These include the fields date, page number format and file location.

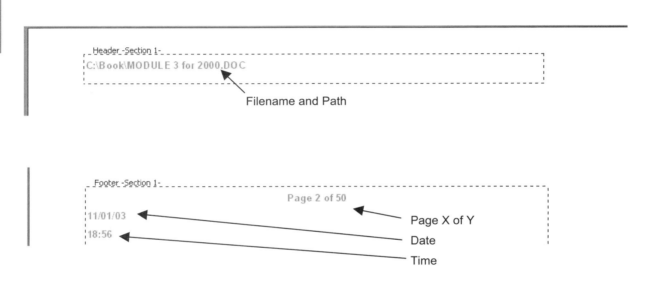

Note that headers and footers are displayed in the **Print Layout** view but not in **Normal** view. Refer to Section 1.2.1 of Module 3 dealing with different page views.

3.3.5 Applying Automatic Page Numbering (3.3.3.6)

In the Header and Footer toolbar the following buttons are very useful as they are a convenient way of inserting frequently used information.

The **Insert Page Number** button places a page number on each page. The page number is automatically increased or decreased as you add or delete pages to your document.

Insert Page
Number Button

Click to place the cursor where you want to insert the page number. Then click the **Insert Page Number** button.

The **Insert Number of Pages** button inserts the total number of pages in the document. It can be used with the Page Number button to insert text such as **Page 1 of 10**. (You must type the words 'Page' and 'of' yourself, with spaces.)

Insert Number
of Pages Button

The **Format Page Number** button allows you to choose between different numbering or indexing formats such as A, a, 1,(i) and so on.

Format
Page Number
Button

Exercise 3E

1   Open My Word 1.

2   Change the orientation of the document to Landscape.

3   Change the margins of the entire document to 3.5cm.

4   Insert a page break after the first paragraph.

5   Add a header with your own name in it.

6   Add a footer with the page number.

7   Add a time field to the footer on a new line and make it right aligned.

8   Change the contents of the header to show your initials.

9   Apply automatic page numbering to the document.

10   Save and close the document.

Section 4   Objects

4.1   Tables

4.1.1   Creating a Table Ready for Text Insertion (3.4.1.1)

A **table** is a grid of rows and columns with **cells** into which you can insert text and graphics. A table facilitates the presentation of schedules, timetables, computer lists and so on. It is also useful for many different purposes in word processing, e.g. when you want neat columns of text or numbers across the page. You can hide the grid lines of a table if your presentation appears too fussy or overcrowded. A table can be dragged anywhere on a page by using the **Table Move handle**. This is only visible when you move your mouse pointer within close proximity of the table. The handle is also useful if you want to select the full table in order to carry out some formatting within the cells.

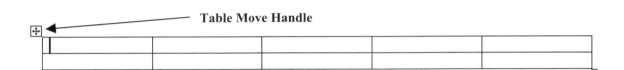

Table Move Handle

To create a table, position the insertion point on the page where you want the table to begin. Then use one of the following methods.

Step 1 – Using the Toolbar

This method is useful for creating small tables.

- Click the **Insert Table** button on the Standard toolbar.

- A grid appears below the button, as shown in the illustration.

- In one continuous movement, drag the mouse across the grid to select rows.

- The grid expands as you move the pointer around.

- In the illustration, 2 rows and 5 columns have been selected.

- Release the mouse button and the table appears in the document.

Step 2 – Using the Table Menu

This method gives more options than using the Insert Table button on the Standard toolbar. It is useful for creating larger tables.

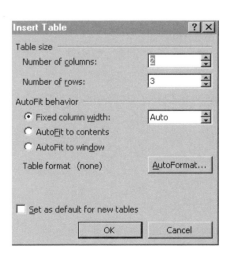

- In the **Table** menu select **Insert Table**. The **Insert Table** window appears.

- Use the arrow buttons or type in the number of columns and rows you want.

- You can specify exact measurements for the width of columns but leaving the width as **Auto** is usually sufficient.

- Click **OK**. The table appears in the document.

If a blank outline of the table does not appear when you create the table, the outline has been set to be hidden. Select **Gridlines** in the **Table** menu on the Menu bar to display it.

4.1.2 Inserting and Editing Data in a Table (3.4.1.2)

When Word inserts an empty table in a document, it positions the insertion point in the first cell. You can start typing in text right away. When you reach the end of the cell as you type, the text automatically goes on to the next line and the height of the cell changes automatically to accommodate the text. To insert text in a different cell, click with the mouse in the new cell and type the new text.

Alternatively, use one of the following.

- To move to the next cell in a row, press the **Tab** key.

- To move to the preceding cell, press **Shift + Tab**.

- To move to the next row, use the **Arrow** keys, *not* the **Enter** key.

- To go on to a new line in a cell, use the **Enter** key.

- To move to any cell, click with the mouse in that cell.

4.1.3 Selecting in a Table (3.4.1.3)

4.1.3.1 Selecting Rows

- Click once in the white area *to the left of the row* you want to select. The cursor becomes an arrow pointing towards the row. **Click** to select the row.
  Alternatively, click in any cell of the row and select **Select Row** in the **Table** menu.

4.1.3.2 Selecting Columns

- Click once in the white space *immediately above the column* you want to select. The cursor becomes a black downward-pointing arrow. **Click** to select the column.
  Alternatively, click in any cell of the column and select **Select Column** in the **Table** menu.

4.1.3.3 Selecting a Single Cell

To select an individual cell:

- Position the mouse pointer near the cell you want to select.

- When a diagonal black arrow appears click with the left button of your mouse three times.
  Alternatively, make sure the cursor is in the cell to be selected.

- Click on the Table Menu on the Menu bar Select and choose Cell option.

- To select text in a cell, click within the cell and select the text using the usual text selection method.

4.1.3.4 Selecting the Entire Table

Do not highlight all the rows and columns. You must use the following procedure.

- Click in any cell in the table.

- Select **Select Table** in the Table menu.
  Alternatively, click the Table Move handle in the left-hand corner above the table.

4.1.4 Rows and Columns (3.4.1.4)

4.1.4.1 Inserting Rows and Columns

You can insert extra rows and columns after you have created the table, if it becomes necessary.

To add an extra row:

- Select the row where you want to add a new row.

- Then select **Insert Rows Above** or **Rows Below** in the Table menu.

To add an extra column:

- Select the column where you want to add the new column.

- Then select Insert Columns to the Left or Insert Columns to the Right in the Table menu.

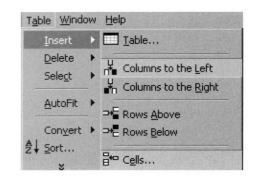

4.1.4.2 Deleting Rows and Columns

- Select the row or column as above.

- Select Table Delete Rows or Delete Columns in the Table menu.

4.1.5 Modifying Column Width and Row Height (3.4.1.5)

Should you wish to enhance the presentation of your text in a table, you might want to expand or narrow the width or height.

4.1.5.1 Changing the Width of a Column

- Move the cursor over the column border until it becomes a bar with arrows pointing right.

- Hold the left mouse button down and drag the cell border to the required width.

To set an exact width, select **Table Properties** in the **Table** menu on the Menu bar.

- Click the Column tab in the window that opens and enter the required width in the box.

- Click OK.

To make all the columns the same width:

- Select the whole Table and click on **Table Properties**, **Columns tab** in the **Table** menu,

- Now choose the preferred width of your columns.

4.1.5.2 Changing the Height of a Row

- Move the cursor over the border until it becomes a bar with arrows pointing up and down.

- Hold down the mouse button and drag to the required height.

To set an exact height, select **Table Properties** in the **Table** menu.

- Cick the **Row** tab in the window that opens and enter the required height in the box.

- Click **OK**.

To make all the rows the same height:

- Select the whole table and click on **Table Properties**, **Rows tab** in the **Table** menu.

- Now **Specify** the preferred height of your rows and click on **OK**.
  Alternatively, you could choose one of the two buttons on the Tables toolbar

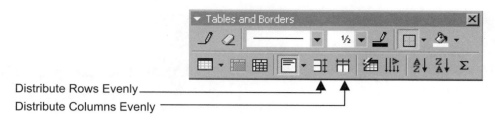

Distribute Rows Evenly
Distribute Columns Evenly

Distribute Rows Evenly – Distributes across rows to equal row height.

Distribute Columns Evenly – Distributes across columns to equal column width.

Alternatively, you could use the drag handle which appears as you place your cursor over the column border.

4.1.6 Modifying Cell Borders, Width, Style and Colour (3.4.1.6)

To change the cells' border, style or colour to a group of cells or a table, you must first select the cell(s). Now open the Format menu and select the **Borders and Shading** command.

If you click on the **Border** tab you can select the outline of the border, the line width and colour.

In the **Setting** section you choose the kind of border you require.

The **Custom** button allows you create a specific border of your own creation.

You can change the border or you can choose not to have any so that the table appears on the page with a neat, unlined appearance. To add borders proceed as follows:

- In the **Style** section select the style colour and width of the lines for the border from the drop-down menu.

- Look in the **Preview** box on the right to see the effect of the changes you've made.

- Click any or all of the option buttons at the left of and below the Preview to use partial borders, or one type of border for the top and another type for the sides and bottom, for example.

- Click a button again to remove the border.

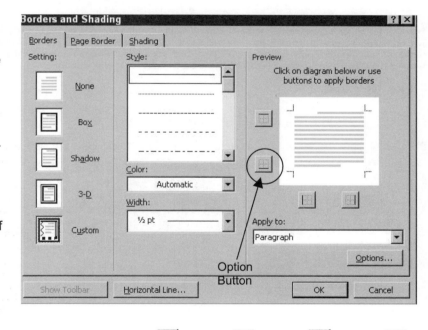

Left
Border

Top
Border

Bottom
Border

Right
Border

4.1.7 Adding Shading to Cells (3.4.1.7)

You can add shading to cells.

To add shading to cells, proceed as follows.

- Select the cell(s) that you want shaded.

- Select **Borders and Shading** in the **Format** menu on the Menu bar. The Borders and Shading window opens.

- Click the **Shading** tab to choose a colour and pattern for the cells.

- Click **OK** when you have made your choices or **Cancel** if you do not want shading.

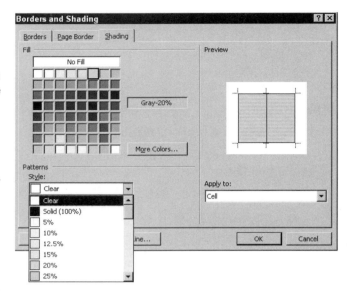

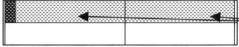 These cells are formatted with a shade style called DK Trellis.

Exercise 4A

1   Create a new document and call it **Table 1**.

2   Create the table shown below in the document. Use Times New Roman, 10 pt.
        The table on your computer may look slightly different from the illustration.

3   Don't forget to save the document.

Student Name	September Test	October Test	November Test
Jean Martin	78	56	89
John Hoyt	34	75	65
Clare Stone	69	91	47
Ted Wells	48	69	98

4.2   Pictures, Images and Charts

4.2.1   Inserting a Picture, Image or Chart into a Document (3.4.2.1)

Word comes with a selection of ready-made pictures which is referred to as **ClipArt**. These pictures may be used to enhance documents.

To insert ClipArt in Office 2000, proceed as follows.

- Select **Picture** in the **Insert** menu on the Menu bar.

- Select **ClipArt** in the sub-menu that appears.

- The Insert **ClipArt** window appears.

- Make sure the **Picture** tab is clicked.

- Icons in the main part of the window represent the different picture categories.

- Click on a category icon to display a selection of available ClipArt pictures.

- Click the picture you wish to insert.

- A vertical button menu appears with four choices.

- Click the **Insert Clips** button to place the picture in the document.

- The graphic is inserted as an inline graphic, i.e. it is treated as a piece of text on a line in a document. Close the **Insert ClipArt** window.

- The arrow buttons in the button bar allow you to move backwards and forwards through your selections.

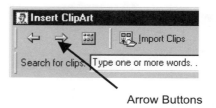

You can also search for clips by typing key words in the **Search for clips** box.

4.2.1.1 Inserting an Image

The images from a scanner or a digital camera can be placed into a Word document. The image we are going to insert is located on the desktop of the computer and you are going to follow these steps in order to insert it on a Word document.

- Click on **Insert Menu** on the Menu bar

- Click on **Picture** and **From File...** options

- The Insert Picture window opens (see next page).

- Locate the file and click on image name.

- Click on the **Insert** button.

- The image will now appear in your Word document where you cursor is located.

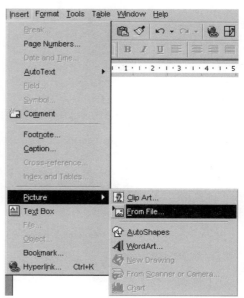

4.2.1.2 Inserting a Chart

To insert a chart into a Word document we must follow these steps:

- Click on the **Insert Menu** on the Menu bar.

- Select **Object** command.

- Click on **Microsoft Excel Chart** in the **Object** window.

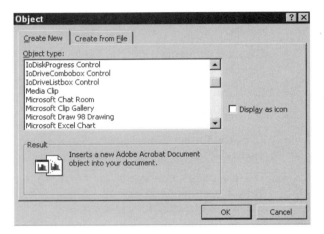

A chart is automatically placed where your cursor is located in your document. By default Microsoft provides you with a bar chart.

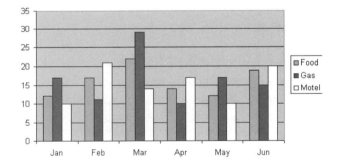

4.2.2 Selecting a Picture, Image or Chart in a Document (3.4.2.2)

If we select a picture, an image or a chart, handles will appear about the object you have selected. These handles are very useful for resizing the object. Resizing is covered in Section 4.2.5 in this module. You can also move the object with your mouse when it changes to a four-way arrow as you move it across the object. Try and click on the object and move it to a new location.

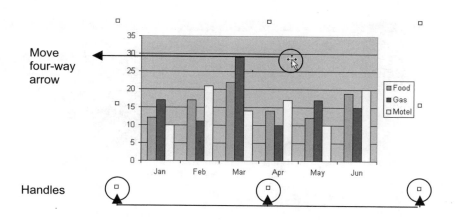

Move four-way arrow

Handles

4.2.3 Duplicating an Image, Picture or Chart (3.4.2.3)

When you want to duplicate an object it means that you want to make a copy of it. In order to do this we can use one of the following procedures.

Select the object with the left button of your mouse and use the **Copy** and **Paste** command. *Alternatively,*

- While holding the **Ctrl** key with your left hand, select the object.

- The mouse changes to a pointer with a box which displays a plus sign in it.

- Now drag your mouse to the new location and drop the object.

- Make sure you release the mouse and the **Ctrl** key.

4.2.4 Moving a Picture, Image or Chart (3.4.2.4)

When a picture, image or a chart has to be moved within a document follow these steps:

- Open the file where the picture is located.

- Select the object with the left button of the mouse.

- Use the **Cut** command.

- Place your cursor on the new location within the document.

- Click on the **Paste** command.

When you want to move the object between open documents follow these steps:

- Make sure the document which contains the object is open.

- Click the Open command in the File menu.

- Select the document to be opened.

- Go into the Window menu and select Arrange All.

- Click on the object in the source document.

- While holding the mouse button down drag the object to its new location in the destination file.

Note: The mouse changes to a pointer with a box attached to it.

4.2.5 Resizing an Image (3.4.2.5)

Should it be necessary to resize a picture, image or chart, follow these steps:

- Click anywhere on the graphic to select it.

- Small white squares, called handles, appear at intervals around the graphic.

- Drag a centre handle at the sides horizontally or at the top or bottom vertically to stretch the graphic.

Selected Graphic
Showing Handles

Stretching a graphic distorts the proportions. This is not always desirable.

- Drag a corner handle diagonally to change the size of the graphic without stretching or distorting it.

- If the graphic is distorted when you drag a corner handle, hold down the Shift key while you drag to keep the proportions correct.

- For more precise resizing, click the **Size** tab and enter the size you require.

- Click the handles at the top of the window for other options.

4.2.6 Deleting a Picture, Image or Chart (3.4.2.6)

When performing this task, select the object to be deleted by clicking on it with your mouse and press the **Delete** key on your keyboard.

Exercise 4B

1   Open My Word 1 and insert an image from ClipArt.

2   Practice resizing it and placing in different places.

3   If you have any ClipArt on a separate disk or file, insert some of it into your document.

4   Select the picture and duplicate it.

5   Open My Word 2 and copy the picture in My Word 1 to this file.

6   Delete the picture in My Word 1 and save the file.

7   Delete the picture in My Word 2 and save the file.

Section 5 · Mail Merge

5.1 Concept and Practice (3.5.1.1)

Mail Merge is used to join or **merge** two sources of information into a single document. One of the most common uses is the production of a **form letter.** A form letter is a letter with standard information that may be sent to many people but where each one contains some individual information, such as a name and address. **Mailing labels** are also produced using the Mail Merge facility.

Typically, a list of names and addresses can be used in conjunction with a form letter to prepare personalised letters for everyone on a list. The list of names and addresses can also be used to produce mailing labels for the envelopes. Form letters for different purposes and occasions can be prepared and stored on the computer and can then be merged with the name and address list as required.

Mail Merge can also be used to produce other similar label-based items, such as identity badges for conferences.

To perform a mail merge, you need two separate files – the **form letter** and a **data source**. The list of names and addresses is the data source. The data source can be created or it can be taken from an existing data source.

There are three steps involved in Mail Merge. They are as follows:

1   **Creating a form letter.**

2   **Creating a data source.**

3   **Merging the data and the letter together.**

5.1.1 Preparing a Mail Merge (3.5.1.2)

Open Word and prepare the letter as shown below. Note that **Dear** is the only word of the salutation and that there is no comma after it. Save the letter with the title **Thornton**. This is your form letter.

The James Thornton Trust School

Station Road   Abbeyvale   Beaconville

Dear

We would like to invite you to attend the next meeting of the School Management Committee which will be discussing the arrangements for…etc.

5.1.2 Preparing a Mailing List (3.5.1.3)

Make sure that the **Thornton** letter is still open on the screen before you begin.

Step 1

- Select **Mail Merge** in the **Tools** menu.

- The **Mail Merge Helper** window opens. The **Mail Merge Helper** will take you through the steps involved in performing a mail merge. They are clearly numbered 1, 2 and 3.

- Click the Create button to display a menu of options.

- Select the type of document you want to use, in this case **Form Letters**.

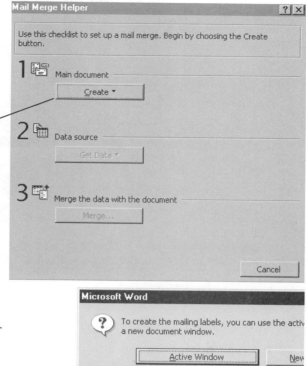

A new window asks if you want to use the **Active** window (the **Thornton** letter) or create a new document.

- Click **Active Window** to select the **Thornton** letter that is open on the desktop.

  You would click **New Main Document at this point** if you wanted to prepare a new document to use as the form letter.

- The **Mail Merge Helper** window reappears, now with an **Edit** button beside the **Create** button.

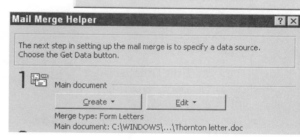

To edit a form letter and to change details since the last time you used it for a mail merge, click the Edit button before you proceed. (Do not do this now. No changes are needed.)

Select Mail Merge in the Tools menu to display the Mail Merge Helper window again. (As you did not click the Edit button, the Mail Merge Helper is still active.)

Step 2

You have no names and addresses to use with our form letter, so you shall create a new data source. Do the following:

- Click the **Get Data** button in **Step 2** of the **Mail Merge Helper** window to display a menu of options.

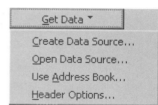

- Click **Create Data Source**.

- The Create Data Source window opens (see next page).

- The **Field Names in header row** box contains a list of prepared fields – storage areas – for Title, First Name, etc.

- To delete a field, select the field name in the Field Names in Header Row box, and then click **Remove Field Name**.

For the data source, we want the following fields: **Title, First Name, Address** and **City**. We will now add a new field to the list.

- Type E-mail in the **Field name** box.

- Click the Add Field Name button.

- The new field name will now be displayed in the **Field names in header row.**

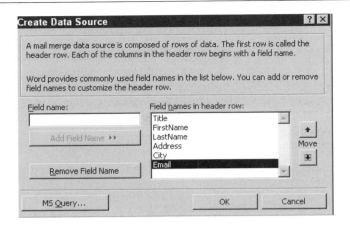

NOTE

You can change the order of the fields by using the **Move** buttons on the right as follows – click the field you want to move and then click the appropriate **Move** button.

- Click **OK** to continue.

The **Save As** window appears so that you can save the data source.

- Type **Addresses** and click **Save** to save the file.

- A message (right) appears to remind you that the data source you have just saved is empty.

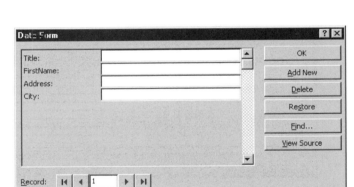

- Click the **Edit Data Source** button to begin entering information.

  The information you enter for a single person is called a **Record.**

- Click the **Add New** button to open up a new blank record each time you want to enter a new addressee.

  You will need at least two or three records to see the mail merge in operation.

- Click the arrows beside the **Record** box at the bottom of the window to move from record to record.

  This allows you to check the entries and to make any corrections that may be necessary.

- Click OK when you have finished entering all the records.

  If you made changes or corrections to the records, select **Yes** when asked if you want to save the changes.

  You are returned to the **Main Document**, in this case the Thornton letter.

You can view all the records in a table if you wish.

- Click the **View Source** button before clicking **OK** in the previous step.

You can glance through the records, scrolling if necessary.

- Click the **Close** button to return to the Main Document.

Step 3

The two items needed for the mail merge, the letter and the data, are now ready for the final step in the process, i.e. merging the data information with the form letter.

To use the data source you have just created, do the following:

- Click on the **Get Data** button – Step 2 of the Mail Merge Helper window.

- Select **Open Data Source**.

When you selected Mail Merge in the Tools menu on the Menu bar at the beginning of the process, a new toolbar, the **Mail Merge toolbar**, appeared alongside the other toolbars on the document window.

Before we complete the mail merge, we have to mark on the letter where the different items of data – the individual names and addresses – are to appear when the separate letters are printed.

First we shall insert the person's full name and address above the salutation.

Proceed as follows.

- Place the cursor where you want to start putting in the full name and address.

- In the **Thornton** letter, this is above the salutation on an empty line.

- Click **Insert Merge Field** on the Mail Merge toolbar.

- A list of the items in the data source is displayed.

- Click on the name of the item you want to insert, in this case **Title**.
  The name of the item is inserted in the document with double-pointed brackets   «Title»
  at each end:

- Press the **space bar** on the keyboard to insert a space after the title.

- Click **Insert Merge Field** again and click on **First Name** to insert it.

- Insert a space after **First Name** and then insert **Last Name**.

- Press the **Enter** key to move to the next line.

- Insert **Address 1** and press **Enter** to move to the next line.

- Insert **City**.

- Place the cursor after **Dear** and insert a space.

- Insert **Title** and **Last Name** as before, with a space between them and with a comma after **Last Name**.
  The name and address markers should now appear in the letter as shown below.

The James Thornton Trust School

Station Road   Abbeyvale   Beaconville

«Title» «First Name» «Last Name»
«Address 1»
«City»

Dear «Title» «Last Name»,

We would like to invite you to attend the next meeting of the School Management Committee which will be discussing the arrangements for…etc.

- Click the **View Merged Data** button on the Mail Merge toolbar to see the actual names and addresses appear.

View Merged Data Button

- The form letter is displayed with the markers (e.g. **«Title»**) replaced by the actual information (e.g. **Mr**).

- To view the different letters, use the arrow buttons on the Mail Merge toolbar to move back and forth through the letters.

Merge Scroll Buttons

  The names and addresses are inserted and displayed in the form letter in turn as you progress through them.

5.1.3 Merging for Printing (3.5.1.4)

The next step of mail merge is ready to be completed. Remember there are choices to be made and these are **Merge to New Document**, **Printer** and **Merge to Electronic mail.**

To merge the documents for printing, do one of the following to open the Mail Merge Helper window.

When the window appears, proceed as follows.

- Click the Merge button in Step 3 in the Mail Merge Helper window.

- The Merge window appears.

- In the Merge to box, New document is already selected.

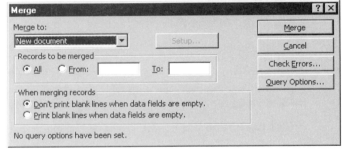

  (If you want to print the form letters immediately, click in the Merge to box and select Printer.)

  Note that **Don't print blank lines when data fields are empty** at the bottom of the window is selected. This prevents unnecessary blank lines in an address in the data source from appearing in the letter.

- Click the **Merge** button at the top right of the merge window.

A new document – the **Merge document** – with the name **Form Letters 1** is created. It consists of individual letters with the names and addresses inserted. Each letter appears on a separate page, one after the other. Use the scroll arrows or bars or the **Page Down** button on the keyboard to move from letter to letter to see the result of the merge.

Save the **Merge Document** in the usual way, giving it a name of your choice. After you have closed the document, it can be reopened later and the letters printed without having to go through the mail merge process again.

To print the letters simply click the **Print** button on the toolbar or select **Print** in the **File** menu.

The letters are printed out, one to a page, with the different personal details on each one.

5.1.4 Merging a Mailing List with a Label Document

Mailing Labels is an option which can be taken in the Mail Merge Helper window when you want to use a label document instead of a letter. **Main Document** is found in **Step 1** of **Mail Merge**. To start the mail merge with a label document follow these steps:

- Click on **Tools Menu** on the menu bar.

- Select **Mail Merge...** command.

- In the Mail Merge Helper window select **Create.**

- Choose the **Mailing Labels...** option

  The following window opens.

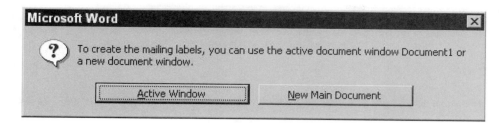

- Click on the **Active Window** button.

- The Data Source is now the next step.

- Click **Get Data** button.

- You must now select from one of two options – **Create Data Source** or **Open Data Source**.

- Click Open Data Source.

- Now the Setup button is available. This allows you to choose the type of labels for your completed task. Once you select the Setup button you can then choose from the different Label Options window.

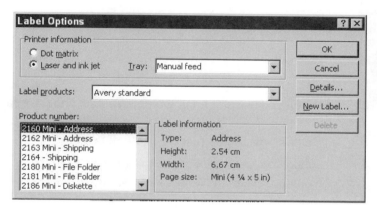

Check the box for the **Product number** so your choice of labels is correct. Having made your choices do the following:

- Click **OK**.
- The **Create Labels** window appears. **U**se the **Insert Merge Fields** button to set up the labels with the required fields.
- Now click **OK**.
- A window will appear with the fields included in it.
- Follow the final steps as for merging a form letter.

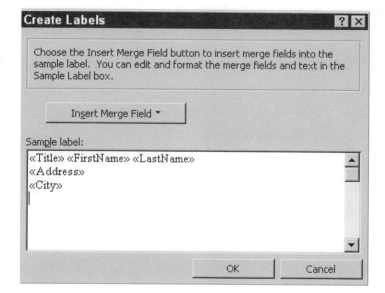

Exercise 5A

1   Open a new document and follow the instructions for the Mail Merge process to create a form letter similar to this one.

The James Thornton Trust School

Station Road   Abbeyvale   Beaconville

Dear

We would like to invite you to attend the next meeting of the School Management Committee which will be discussing the arrangements for…etc.

---

2   When you are preparing the data source, choose appropriate fields such as First Name, Surname, etc.

3   Enter at least three records in the data source.

4   When you have finished the mail merge, view the letters.
You should see the letters with the individual details inserted from the data source.

5   Preview and print the letters.

6   Close all the documents, saving any unsaved ones.

Exercise 5B

1   Use the mail merge process to make mailing labels.

2   Use the same data source as before so that you don't have to type in new details.

3   Preview and print the labels.

4   Close all the documents, saving any unsaved ones.

Section 6   Prepare Outputs

6.1   Proofreading and Preparation (3.6.1.1)

Upon completing a Word document it is important to proof it. Documents may be checked for fonts, margins, paper size, layout options, spellings and so on.

For example, formats applied to fonts will vary throughout the page if you have indented text, headings or have applied a bold, underlined or italicised format. It is possible to check through these by clicking into different text arrangements in your document and viewing the Formatting toolbar to view the active or selected options. However, using the What's This? Option in the Help menu provides access to a summary of the formatting options. Use the following procedure:

- On the **Help** menu, click **What's This?**

  The pointer becomes a question mark.

- Click into a piece of text you want to check.

  The **What's This bubble** details the formatting options.

- Click the What's This? option in the Help menu again to cancel the function.

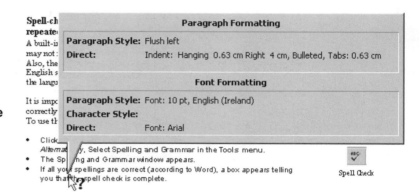

The following is a quick check list and can be accessed by selecting **Page Setup** in the **File** menu:

- **Margins** – each page has a set of non-typing areas. These can be set up by you to prevent any text being entered into them. Commonly the margins are set to 2.54 cm left and right, top and bottom. By clicking the **Margins** tab in the Page Setup window you can change the margins to suit your needs by selecting the measurement you require or by typing in the measurement. By clicking on the **OK** button, the document will reflect your chosen measurements.

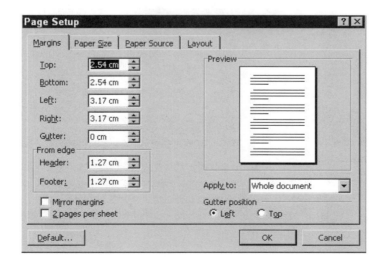

MODULE 3

- Click the **Paper Size** tab to set the paper size of your document. Select **Custom** and type in the sizes of your document's **width** and **height** if you want specific measurements. The standard size in Europe is **A4**. To set the orientation – the way the page will be viewed or printed – click **Portrait** (vertical) or **Landscape** (horizontal). Portrait is used for the majority of documents and click **OK** to apply your settings to this document only.

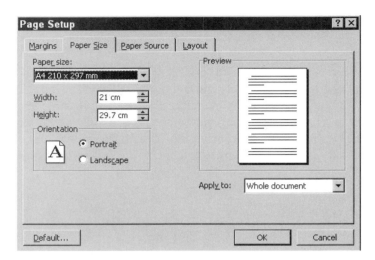

- **Layout** – in this part of **Page Setup** you can choose the **vertical alignment** of your text on a page. This means that you can have text aligned between the **top** and **bottom margins** of the document. There are four choices – **Top, Centre, Justified** and **Bottom**.

- Click **OK** to apply your settings to this document only.

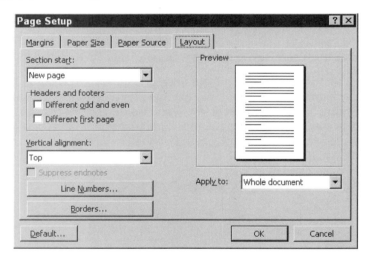

6.1.1 Spell Check (3.6.1.2)

A built-in **spell check** in Word automatically checks the spelling in your documents. However, it may not recognise some words such as local place names or words in a language other than English. Also, there are different versions of English, so if Word is set up for US English, it won't recognise English spellings such as 'colour', 'programme' and so on. See below for more details on the language used by the spell check.

To use the spell check:

Spell Check
Button

- Click the **Spell Check** button on the toolbar.
  Alternatively, Select Spelling and Grammar in the Tools menu.

- The Spelling and Grammar window appears.

- If all your spellings are correct (according to Word), a box appears telling you that the spell check is complete.

It is important to remember that the spell check does not alert you to an incorrect word that is correctly spelt – 'there' instead of 'their', for example. You still have to read through your work. A list of suggestions appears in the **Suggestions** box underneath, with the first option selected as being the most likely.

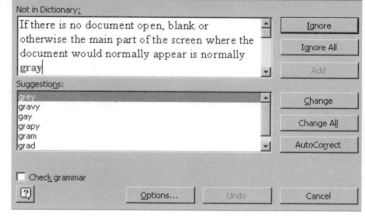

- Click on **Change** if the suggestion is appropriate and the suggested word will replace the one in your document.

- Click **Change All** to change all similarly incorrect spellings throughout the document.

- If the suggested word in **Suggestions** is not the right one, view the list and check and click on the correct word. (Scroll down if necessary.)

- Click the **Change** or **Change All** button, as appropriate.

- If no suggestions are offered, you can type in your own correction by selecting the incorrect word in the **Not in Dictionary** box and type the correction. Then, click **Change** or **Change All**.

Sometimes the word is correct but not recognised by the spell check, e.g. a place name.

- Click the **Add** button to add the word to the Spell Check dictionary and it will not be questioned again.

- Click **Ignore** or **Ignore All** if you do not want to add a word to the dictionary or you do not want it to be corrected.

- Note that clicking the **AutoCorrect** button will replace any incorrect word with what Word thinks is the correct spelling *without asking you*. This can be unpredictable so AutoCorrect should be used with care.

6.1.2 Previewing a Document (3.6.1.4)

When you've prepared your document, you will want to print it.

As the document has been prepared on the screen, not on paper, it is a good idea to make a final check before printing begins.

You can **preview** the document on screen to see what it will look like on paper when it is printed. This allows you to make any last-minute adjustments that may be necessary.

- Click the **Print Preview** button on the Standard toolbar.
  Alternatively, select **Print Preview** in the **File** menu.

Print Preview Button

- A small preview of the full page is displayed on the screen as it will appear on the paper.

- To see the next page, press the **Page Down** key on the keyboard. Press **Page Up** to see the previous page.
  Alternatively, use the **scroll bars** on the screen.

- Click the **Magnifier** button on the toolbar if the text is too small to read (see next page).

- The cursor changes to a magnifying glass with a plus (+) sign in the middle.

- Move the cursor to the part of the page you want to enlarge and click the mouse button.

- A magnified view of the text is displayed.

- The magnifying glass now has a minus sign (–) in the middle to indicate that it will reduce the size of the document if clicked.

- Click on the page with the minus (–) magnifier to return to the full-page view on the screen.

- Click the **Print** button on the toolbar to print directly from the preview screen.

- Click the **Close** button on the **Preview** toolbar when you are finished looking at the preview to return to your document window.

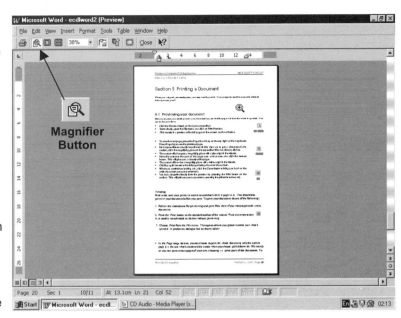

Print Button

Exercise 6A

1   Open My Word 1.

2   Check the margins and orientation of the document.

3   Do a spell check on the document.

4   Remember to ignore proper names.

5   Preview the document.

6   Save and close the document.

6.2   Printing (3.6.2.1)

In order to get a hard copy of completed work, the computer must be connected to a printer. Make sure the printer is turned on and that there is sufficient paper in the printer's paper tray.

- Click the **Print** button on the Standard toolbar of the normal Word document screen to forward the document immediately to the printer.
  Alternatively, select **Print** in the **File** menu to access the Print window with the print option.

- The **Print** window opens.

When a document consists of several pages, you may not need to print it all. To print only the pages you need, follow these steps.

- Select Print in the File menu as before.

  The **Print** window opens.

- Click **All** to print the entire document.

- Click **Current page** to print the page you are working on.

  (The current page is the one with the cursor on it when you clicked on Print.)

- Click the Pages button to print a selection of pages.

- Enter the numbers of the pages you want to print, separated by commas or hyphens.

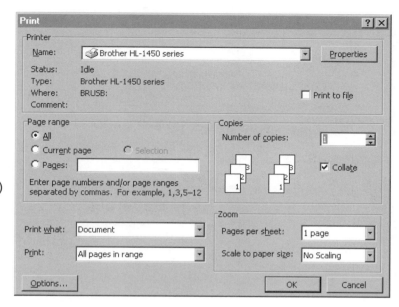

- **Use commas** to print individual pages. For example 2, 5 prints page 2 and page 5 but not pages 1, 3 and 4.

- **Use a hyphen** to print a range of pages. Typing 2-5 prints pages 2, 3, 4 and 5.

- To print more than one copy, enter the number you require in the **Number of copies** box.

- Click the **OK** button to print the pages.

6.2.1 Printing Using Defined Options or Default Settings (3.6.2.2)

The printer in use is displayed in the **Name** box at the top of the **Print** window. A single stand-alone or home computer will have a single printer connected directly to it.

In an office situation, where there are many computers connected on a network, there may also be several printers in different locations. Select the printer to use by clicking in the **Name** box to display a list of printers available and click on your choice. The selected printer's name then appears in the Name box.

If you choose the **Print to file** option, your document is stored as a file instead of a printer.

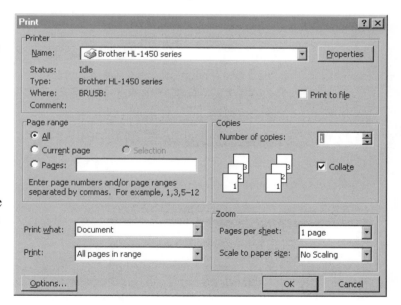

The **Copies** section of the box allow you to select the amount of copies of the document you want printed.

Exercise 6B

1   Open My Word 1.

2   Print the current page of document.

3   Check the printers attached to your computer.

4   Save your document and close it

Module 4

Spreadsheets

4

Module 4

Spreadsheets

MODULE 4

MODULE 4

Introduction

Syllabus Goals for Module 4

Spreadsheets requires the candidate to understand the basic concepts of spreadsheets and to demonstrate the ability to use a spreadsheet application on a computer. The candidate shall understand and be able to accomplish tasks associated with developing, formatting and using a spreadsheet[8] of limited scope ready for distribution. He or she shall also be able to generate and apply standard mathematical and logical formulas using standard formulas and functions. The candidate shall demonstrate competence in creating and formatting graphs/charts.

MODULE 4

What is a Spreadsheet?

A spreadsheet is composed of a large number of 'boxes' or **cells**, laid out in orderly rows and columns.

A new spreadsheet is like a large sheet of paper covered with empty cells. You can put text or numbers into the cells. A completed spreadsheet displays the information you have entered in orderly rows and columns. The cell **grid** – the lines that help you identify each cell when you enter the data – is normally omitted when you print out the spreadsheet.

The principal advantage of the spreadsheet is that it can perform actions on the data in the cells. A list of names can be easily sorted, for example. New names can be added or old ones deleted and the list is adjusted automatically.

Calculations

You can put a **formula** in a cell that will perform a calculation on information contained in other cells and display a result. You can use a formula to add up numbers, find averages and so on. It is this ability to perform calculations that makes spreadsheets so useful. Spreadsheets are widely used where lots of numbers are associated with one another, as in financial accounts.

A company budget can be prepared on a spreadsheet, with all the different items of income and expenditure laid out. A change in one item will be reflected in all the other related items, with allocations, totals, balances and so on adjusted automatically by the program.

Graphs

The data on a spreadsheet can be displayed in **graphical** form. Many different kinds of graphs and diagrams can be generated by the spreadsheet.

Spreadsheet information and graphs can be incorporated in other documents, such as Word documents or PowerPoint presentations.

---

[8] The term spreadsheet is used to denote a spreadsheet file with multiple sheet functionality. The term worksheet is used to denote a single sheet in a spreadsheet file.

Section 1   Using Excel

1.1   Introducing Excel

Excel is an electronic spreadsheet program into which you can type numbers and text and then perform a wide variety of different *calculations*. The information stored in an Excel spreadsheet can be formatted on screen with such attributes as bold, underlining, italic, borders and font styles, to name but a few.

Excel is capable of generating charts and graphics based on the spreadsheet data. There are over twenty different chart types, such as bar, line, pie, etc., available to you in the application. Charts are linked to the spreadsheet from which they were created, so any modifications to data are automatically applied to related charts.

Excel allows you to work with more than one spreadsheet at a time. This means that related sheets or charts can be compared on the one screen.

1.1.1   Opening Excel (4.1.1.1)

Open Microsoft Excel by clicking the **Excel** button on the Microsoft Office **Shortcut bar** on the desktop.

Alternatively, click the **Start** button and select **Microsoft Excel** in the **Programs** menu or sub-menu.

Excel

1.1.2   Closing Excel (4.1.1.1)

Close Excel by choosing **Exit** in the **File** menu.

Alternatively, click the **Close** icon on the Excel window.

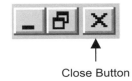

Close Button

1.1.3   A New Spreadsheet (4.1.1.3)

When you open Excel, you are usually presented with a new spreadsheet called **Book 1**. It appears on the screen as if it were a sheet of blank paper ruled with horizontal and vertical lines in the form of a grid.

If there is no spreadsheet open, blank or otherwise, the main part of the screen where the document would normally appear will be grey.

New Button

If Excel doesn't create a new spreadsheet, you can create one yourself using these steps.

- Click the **New** button at the left of the **Toolbar**.

  A new spreadsheet opens, ready for you to begin.

  Alternatively, select **New** in the **File** menu.

  The **New** window opens, as in the illustration below, with the **Workbook** icon already selected.

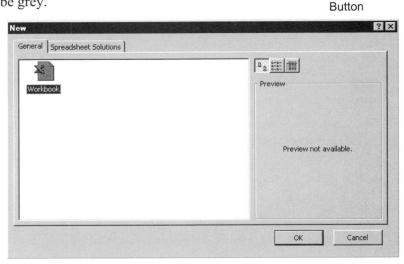

MODULE 4

- Click **OK** and a new spreadsheet appears on the screen.

1.1.4 Saving a Spreadsheet to a Location on a Drive (4.1.1.4)

The blank spreadsheet that appears is called a Workbook (see the illustration on the next page).

It is a good idea to save your new spreadsheet now, even before you begin to work on it. Then as your work proceeds, you can click the Save button from time to time and be sure that your work will not be lost in the event of a serious problem occurring.

- Click the **Save** button or select **Save** in the **File** menu.

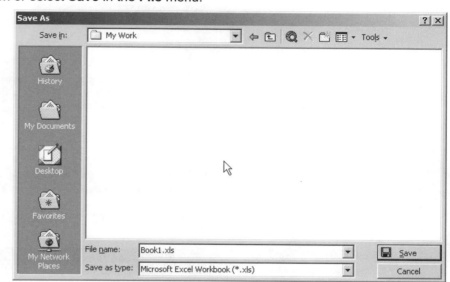

  The **Save As** window appears.

- Use to drop-down arrow in the **Save in** box to select the location in which the spreadsheet is to be saved.

- Type a name for the spreadsheet in the **File Name** box.

- Save the spreadsheet in a folder of your choice on the **hard disk**.

Exercise 1A

1   Ensure you are working in Excel.

2   Close any workbook that is currently open.

3   Create a new workbook.

4   Type your name in the cell named **A1** and press **Enter**.

5   Click the **Save** button.

6   In the **File name** box type **My First Spreadsheet**.

7   Click **Save** to save the spreadsheet.

8   Close the spreadsheet.

9   Create a new blank workbook.

1.1.5 Saving a Spreadsheet Under Another Name (4.1.1.5)

When you want to save a **copy** of a spreadsheet under a different name, **Save As** is used. To save time typing out a new spreadsheet, you can edit the old one, as follows:

- Open the file for **My First Spreadsheet**.

- Type your address in **A2**.

- Type the name of the school you attended in **A3**.

- Select **Save As** in the **File** menu. The Save As window opens.

- Change the name in the **File name** list box to **My Second Spreadsheet**.

- Click **Save**.

- Close the spreadsheet on completion.

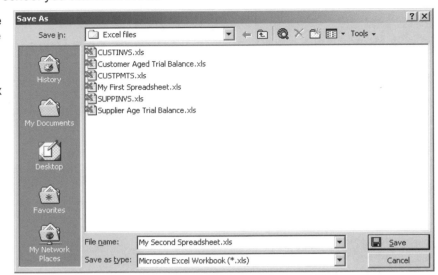

1.1.6 The Excel Window

The window that appears when an Excel document is opened is similar to the windows used in other Microsoft applications. The main features of the Excel window are shown here.

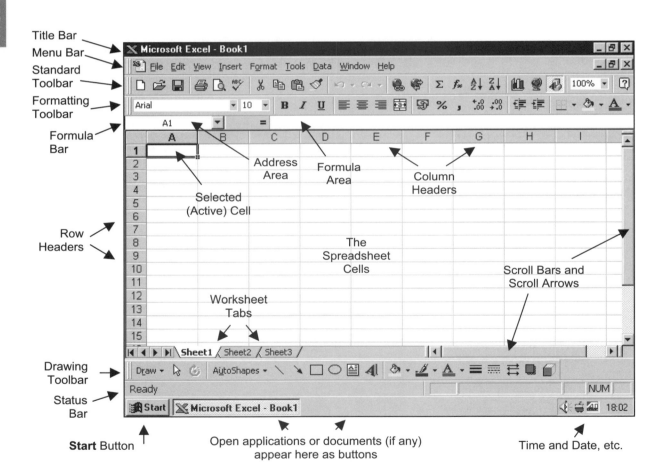

1.1.6.1 Switching Between Worksheets and Open Spreadsheets

A spreadsheet can contain multiple worksheets, up to a maximum of 256.

To switch from one worksheet to another:

- Click on the appropriate worksheet tab displayed in the lower section of the open spreadsheet window.

If you have more than one spreadsheet file open, you can switch from one file to another using the taskbar:

- Click the appropriate spreadsheet file button displayed on the taskbar.

1.1.7 Excel Window Features

The new spreadsheet that appears on the screen contains a grid of columns and rows like a ledger. The columns are labeled from left to right with letters of the alphabet, A, B, C… (called column headers) and so on. The rows are labeled from top to bottom with the numbers, 1, 2, 3… (called row headers) and so on. The lines between the cells are known as the cell **grid**.

The columns and rows divide the spreadsheet into thousands of boxes. Each box is called a **cell** and it is uniquely identified by its **address** – the letter and number of the column and row that specify its position – e.g. **A1**, the address of the cell at the top left of the spreadsheet.

- The **Title bar** displays the name of the document that you are using.

- The **Menu bar** contains menus of actions that can be performed by the computer.

- **Scroll bars and arrows** are used to move left and right or up and down over a document in the window when it is too large to see all at once.

- **The toolbars** contain buttons that you click to perform an action.

  Common actions are grouped together on separate toolbars, such as the Standard and Formatting toolbars. The **Formula bar** is unique to Excel and is briefly described below.

  – **The Formula bar** displays the address of the current cell at the left and has an area on the right where formula information is displayed.

- **The spreadsheet cells** are the actual spreadsheet or workbook area in which you will enter numbers and text for your work.

- **The Status bar** displays the page number and other information, such as the line number on which the cursor is currently placed.

- **Other items** may be displayed on occasion in separate windows.

1.1.8 Opening One or Several Spreadsheets (4.1.1.2)

To open a spreadsheet which has already been saved, follow these steps:

- Click on the **File** menu and select **Open**.

- **Look in** should be changed to the folder where the file(s) is located.

- Pick the file with the left button of mouse.

- Click the **Open** button on the right-hand side of the window.

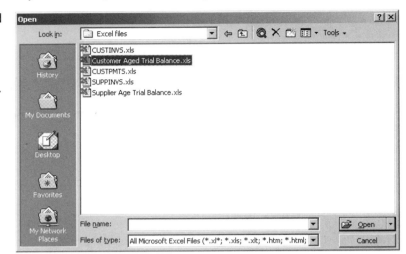

If more than one file is to be opened, hold the **CTRL** key on your keyboard with your finger and select each individual file you want to open and then click on the **Open** button in the window.

1.1.9 Saving a Spreadsheet in Another File Format (4.1.1.6)

When you send a document or file to another person, they may not be able to use it if they are not using the same kind of computer and software that you used to prepare it. You should check with the recipient in advance. Then, if possible, you can save your work in a format they can use, as follows:

- Go through the **Save** process as before until the **Save As** window appears.

- Click in the **Save as type** box to display a list of available formats.

- Excel options are shown here.

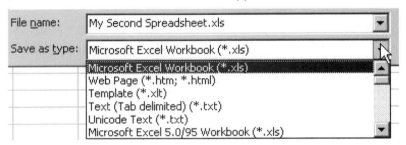

- **Web Page** – Choose this format if you want to save the spreadsheet in a web format using a language known as **hyper text markup language** (HTML). The file can then be the uploaded to the World Wide Web.

- **Template** – Use a template format if you want the layout, formatting, headings, etc. of your spreadsheet to be available as the basis of other new spreadsheets in the future. Spreadsheet templates are available when you select **New** from the **File** menu.

- **Text** – Choose this format if you want to save the spreadsheet in a text format with **tabs** separating the columns of spreadsheet data. The text can be inserted into other programs such as word processing programs or databases.

- **Unicode Text** – This is a text format which is supported by most programs that can import text.

- **Microsoft Excel 5.0/95 Workbook** – Use this format is you are sending your spreadsheet to someone who is using a release of Excel prior to Excel 2000.

1.1.9.1 Software-specific File Extensions

When you work with documents in different applications, the only way you can distinguish between applications is by the extension which is placed automatically after you save the document. This option is used to denote the program to which the file has been created and saved in.

Some examples include:

    *.dwg for AutoCad

    *.bmp for Bitmap files

    *.wav for sound files

    *.mid for MIDI files.

1.2   Adjusting Settings

Before you start working with Excel you may like to change some of the available options to suit your own requirements.

1.2.1   Changing User Options (4.1.2.4)

By choosing **Options** in the **Tools** menu you can specify various general settings on the **General** tab. For example, you may want to ensure that your name appears in the **User name** box. This information is recorded with the file when it is saved so that you can easily identify the author of the spreadsheet. You may also want to save your spreadsheets to a folder other than the one chosen by the computer. You can specify the folder of your choice in the **Default file location** box.

To specify your own options whilst working with this module, proceed as follows:

- Choose **Options** in the **Tools** menu.

- Click on the **General** tab.

- Click in the **User name** box and type your first and last names.

- Click in the **Default file location** box and enter the folder where you want to save your spreadsheets.

- Click **OK** to return to your spreadsheet.

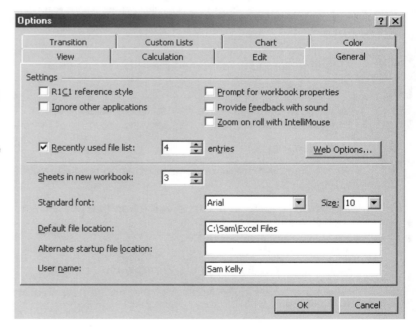

1.2.2 Freezing Row and Column Titles (4.1.2.3)

As you start to work with your Excel page or worksheet, your data can spread across many columns or down many rows. In many instances, you will find that your worksheet extends beyond the boundaries of your screen. You can *freeze*, or **reference**, specific columns or rows so that the information they contain does not disappear from the view as you move within the main body of the worksheet.

To freeze rows and columns:

- To freeze the top horizontal pane, select the row below where you want the split to appear.

  Or

- To freeze the left vertical pane, select the column to the right of where you want the split to appear.

  Or

- To freeze both the upper and left panes, click the cell below and to the right of where you want the split to appear.

- Click **Freeze Panes** on the **Window** menu.

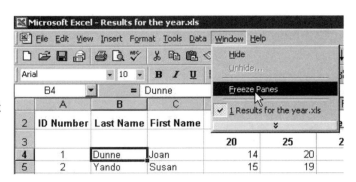

This ECDL Foundation approved courseware product incorporates learning reinforcement exercises. These exercises are included to help the candidate in their training for the ECDL. The exercises included in this courseware product are not ECDL certification tests and should not be construed in any way as ECDL certification tests. For information about authorised ECDL test centres in different national territories please refer to the ECDL Foundation website at www.ecdl.com.

Exercise 1B

1   Open the spreadsheet named **Results for the year**.

2   Click in **A4**.

3   With the arrow keys move across to the data for **Week 30**. Notice that you can no longer see the name of the student in the first few columns of the sheet.

4   Return to **A4**.

5   Using the down arrow keys move down to **row 70**. Notice that you can no longer see the week numbers.

6   Press **Ctrl+Home** to return to cell **A1** so that you are working at the top of the worksheet again.

7   Click in cell **D4**.

8   Choose **Freeze Panes** in the **Window** menu.

9   Now move around the worksheet and notice how columns **A** to **C** and rows **1** to **3** are **fixed** on the screen.

10   Choose **Unfreeze Panes** so that the rows and columns are no longer fixed.

11   Save the spreadsheet, closing it on completion.

Section 2   Working with Cells

Each cell in a worksheet has a **cell address** to identify its location within the sheet. This address is based on the intersection of a column and row. Each column has a letter identifier and each row a number. There are **256** columns in a worksheet (starting with A and ending with IV) and there are **65,536** rows – giving over **16 million** cells per worksheet – hopefully far more than you will ever need!

2.1   Inserting Data

A cell must be selected, or **active**, so information can be placed in it. To make a cell active, click inside the cell. Notice the special **cross** shape of the spreadsheet cursor. An active cell has a dark border around it and its **address** is displayed in the name box at the left of the **Formula bar**.

The Spreadsheet Cursor

What data can be input into Excel? Text, numbers, dates or a formula may be typed in a cell on the spreadsheet. By default, text aligns to the left of the cell whereas numbers, dates and formulas align to the right of the cell.

When a cell is active you can type into it, just as you would on a word processing document. As you type, the text appears in both the active cell and in the Formula bar.

A **cancel** mark (**x**) and an **enter** mark (✔) appear between the name box and the text box. Click the enter mark upon completing an entry or click the cancel mark if you change your mind about entering the data into the cell.

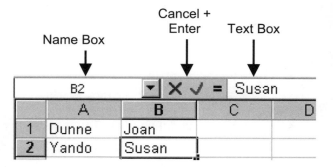

When you enter data in a cell, you must tell Excel when you have finished. Entries can be completed in a number of ways. Here are some of the ways you can do this.

- Press the **Enter** key.
- Press the **Tab** key.
- Press the **Down arrow** key to move down a cell.
- Use the **Shift** and **Enter** keys or the **Up arrow** key to move up a cell.
- Use the **Tab** key or the **Right arrow** key to move to the cell on the right.
- Use the **Shift** and **Tab** key or the **Left arrow** key to move to the cell on the left.
- Use the **Enter** mark on the **Formula bar** to enter data and stay in the same cell.
- Use the **mouse** to click in another cell.

2.1.1 Entering Numbers, Dates and Text (4.2.1.1)

Spreadsheets can be very useful for making, editing and sorting lists.

In the following set of exercises, we shall start some text, numbers and dates.

To make a list of the pupils in a class:

- Create a new, blank workbook by clicking on the **New** button on the **Standard** toolbar.

- Click in cell **A1** to make it active, if it is not already selected.

- Type the surname **Dunne** in the cell.

- Press the **Tab** key or click in cell **B1** to move to the next cell across.

	A	B	C	D
1	Dunne	Joan	10/01/1986	100
2	Yando	Susan	12/02/1986	75
3	Saxe	Carmen	16/04/1986	75
4	Zealzo	Michel	23/05/1986	50
5	Eisenberg	Wilhelm	11/01/1986	100
6	Ayers	Freda	29/05/1986	45
7	Dunne	Ciara	12/12/1985	65
8	Montuga	Charles	24/12/1985	80
9	Divorkin	Slava	09/03/1986	90
10	Brennan	Michael	04/04/1986	100
11				

- Type the first name **Joan** in the new cell.

- Press the **Tab** key or click in cell **C1** to move to the next cell across.

- Type the date **10/01/86** in the new cell.

- Press the **Tab** key or click in cell **D1** to move to the next cell across.

- Type the amount **100**.

- Press **Enter** to move to cell **A2** or click in this cell.

- Type **Yando** and then press **Tab** to move across to **B2**.

- Continue in this manner until you have completed the list of names in the illustration. **Save** the file with the title **Class List**.

2.2 Selecting Cells

Before using commands from the Excel menus, you must first select the area of the worksheet that is to be affected. A selection can be a single cell, a range of continuous cells or a range of multiple cells.

To learn how to select different areas of worksheet, perform the following.

2.2.1 Selecting Single Cells (4.2.2.1)

- Open the file named **Class List** if it is not already opened.

- Click on **D5** to select it. Now click on **A10** to select this cell.

- Move the keyboard arrow keys until you are in cell **B3**. Now move to **D1**.

- Press **Ctrl+Home** to return to **A1**.

2.2.2 Selecting the Entire Worksheet (4.2.2.1)

- Click the empty grey box that appears at the top left in the grey grid area to select the entire worksheet.

- Click on any cell to remove the selection.

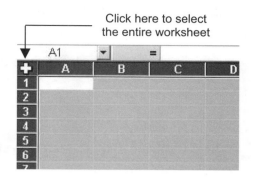

2.2.3 Selecting a Range of Adjacent Cells (4.2.2.1)

You can select a range of adjacent cells using the mouse.

- Select all of the names by first clicking in **A1** and the dragging down with the mouse to **B10**.

- Click in any single cell to clear the selection.

- Click in **A3** and then drag with the mouse to **D6** to select a range of cells.

- Click in any single cell to clear the selection.

- Highlight all of the dates by selecting **C1** to **C10**.

- Press **Home** to return to **A1**.

	A	B	C	D
1	Dunne	Joan	10/01/1986	100
2	Yando	Susan	12/02/1986	75
3	Saxe	Carmen	16/04/1986	75
4	Zealzo	Michel	23/05/1986	50
5	Eisenberg	Wilhelm	11/01/1986	100
6	Ayers	Freda	29/05/1986	45
7	Dunne	Ciara	12/12/1985	65
8	Montuga	Charles	24/12/1985	80
9	Divorkin	Slava	09/03/1986	90
10	Brennan	Michael	04/04/1986	100
11				

2.2.4 Selecting a Range of Non-Adjacent Cells (4.2.2.1)

You can select a range of non-adjacent cells using the **Ctrl** key on the keyboard.

- Click in **A1** and drag with the mouse to **A10** to select the pupils' surnames.

- Hold down the **Ctrl** key and then click and drag **C1** to **C10** to select the pupils' dates of birth.

- Click in any single cell to clear the selection.

- Select the range **B1** to **B10**.

- Holding down the **Ctrl** key, select the range **D1** to **D10**.

- Press **Ctrl+Home** to return to **A1**.

	A	B	C	D
1	Dunne	Joan	10/01/1986	100
2	Yando	Susan	12/02/1986	75
3	Saxe	Carmen	31,518.00	75.00
4	Zealzo	Michel	31,555.00	50.00
5	Eisenberg	Wilhelm	31,423.00	100.00
6	Ayers	Freda	31,561.00	45.00
7	Dunne	Ciara	31,393.00	65.00
8	Montuga	Charles	31,405.00	80.00
9	Divorkin	Slava	31,480.00	90.00
10	Brennan	Michael	31,506.00	100.00

MODULE 4

2.2.5 Selecting Rows (4.2.2.2)

You can select entire rows using the row headers in the grey grid border.

- To select row 5, click on the row header **5** in the grey grid border.

  Be sure to position the mouse cursor as centrally as possible within the row header so that the cursor is in the *selection* shape (a white cross).

- Using the grey grid area, now select row **10**.

- Click on row **3** and drag down to row **10** to select a range of rows.

- Select rows **2** to **8**.

- To select non-adjacent rows use the **Ctrl** key – click on row **2** to select it, hold down the **Ctrl** key and then click on row **6**. Hold down the **Ctrl** key again and click on row **9**.

- Click in any non-selected cell to remove the selection.

- Now select rows **3**, **5** and **10** using the **Ctrl** key.

- Press **Ctrl+Home** to return to **A1**.

2.2.6 Selecting Columns (4.2.2.3)

You can select entire columns using the column headers in the grey grid border.

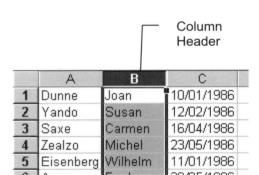

Column Header

- To select column **B**, click on the column header **B** in the grey grid border.

  Be sure to position the mouse cursor as centrally as possible within the column header so that the cursor is in the *selection* shape.

- Using the grey grid area, now select column **A**.

- Click on column **B** and drag across to column **D** to select a range of columns.

- Select columns **A** to **C**.

- To select non-adjacent columns use the **Ctrl** key – click on column **A** to select it, hold down the **Ctrl** key and then click on column **C**. Hold down the **Ctrl** key again and click on column **F**.

- Click in any non-selected cell to remove the selection.

- Now select columns **C**, **F** and **G**.

- Press **Ctrl+Home** to return to **A1**.

2.3 Rows and Columns

Rows and columns are used to divide a worksheet into **cells** where information can be entered. Each column has a letter identifier (starting at **A** and ending with **IV**). Each row has a number identifier (starting with **1** and ending with **65,536**). Sometimes it may be necessary to insert additional rows or columns *between* cells that already contain information. Other times, you may wish to delete existing columns or rows.

2.3.1 Inserting Rows and Columns (4.2.3.1)

Using the Class List file already created, you have decided to give each name on the list an identification number and to place it before the names that you have already typed in. Proceed as follows:

- Ensure the file named **Class List** is open.

- Select column **A** by clicking the column header (the letter **A** at the top of the column).

- Select **Columns** in the **Insert** menu.

  A blank column is inserted *to the left* of the selected column. You will use this column later to insert an identification number for each pupil.

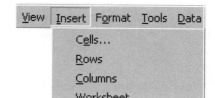

- Select column **D** by clicking the column header (the letter **D** at the top of the column).

- Select **Columns** in the **Insert** menu.

If you wish to have headings at the top of the list, it is necessary to insert a new row *above* the present first row. Proceed as follows:

- Select row column **1** by clicking the row header (the number **1** to the left of the row).

- Select **Rows** in the **Insert** menu.

A blank row is inserted *above* the selected row.

Copy the illustration to enter headings into the new row on your worksheet.

	A	B	C	D	E	F
1	ID Number	Surname	First Name		DOB	Subs
2		Dunne	Joan		10/01/1986	100
3		Yando	Susan		12/02/1986	75
4		Saxe	Carmen		16/04/1986	75

- Select row **2** by clicking the row header (the number **2** to the left of the row).

- Select **Rows** in the **Insert** menu. This will give you a blank row below the column headings.

2.3.2 Deleting Rows and Columns (4.2.3.2)

To delete an entire row or column:

- Select the row or column you wish to delete.

- Select **Delete** in the **Edit** menu.

To modify your **Class List** file, proceed as follows:

- Select row **2** by clicking the row header (the number **2** to the left of the row).

- Select **Delete** in the **Edit** menu. The blank row will be removed.

- Select column **D** by clicking the column header (the letter **D** at the top of the column).

- Select **Delete** in the **Edit** menu. The blank column will be removed.

- Click in **A1** to return to the top of the worksheet.

2.3.3 Modifying Column Widths and Row Heights (4.2.3.3)

Each time you start a new worksheet every column has a default width and every row has a default height. You can, however, change the widths and heights of columns and rows to suit the data you are entering.

There are two ways to adjust the width or height of a column/row, either by **dragging** to adjust the size on the spreadsheet itself or by using the **Format** menu.

To change the size by dragging:

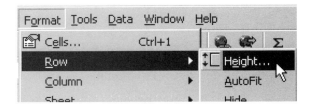

- Move the cursor slowly over the dividing line between the cells in the column or row header until it changes to a bar with an arrow at each side.

- Hold down the mouse button and drag until the cell width or height is the required size. A *tip* box appears indicating the width as you drag.

To modify a column width, proceed as follows:

- Position the mouse between the column divider of columns **A** and **B**.

- Drag across until the column width for column **A** is approximately **20 points**.

- Position the mouse between the column divider of columns **B** and **C** and change the column width to approximately **10**.

- Position the mouse between the row divider of rows **1** and **2**.

- Drag down until row **1** is approximately **25 points**.

Adjusting cells by dragging is convenient for occasional use. However, more often you will want to change the cell size of a selection of cells, or of a complete row or column. Changing them individually can be tedious as well as giving uneven results.

To change the row height using the **Format** menu, proceed as follows:

- Select row **1**.

- Select **Row** in the **Format** menu and then **Height** in the sub-menu.
  The **Row Height** window opens. The default row height, 12.75, is displayed.

- Type **20** in the **Row height** box.

- Click **OK**.

- Now select columns **A** to **E**.

- Select **Column** in the **Format** menu and then **Width** in the sub-menu.
  The **Column Width** window opens.

- Type **10** in the **Column width** box.

- Click **OK**.
  Using the **Format** menu gives precise control over cell height and width. It allows for spacing between rows and columns and can be used to give your spreadsheet a neat and ordered appearance.

- Save the current spreadsheet, closing it on completion.

2.4   Editing Data

To edit data in a cell, you can either add to the existing information or you can entirely replace the original cell contents.

2.4.1 Inserting Additional Cell Content (4.2.4.1)

To add to the cell contents, simply select the cell, type the next data and then press **Enter**. If you want to modify the contents of a cell you can double click the cell so that you can edit.

To modify an existing spreadsheet file, proceed as follows:

- Open the file named **Class List – Editing Data**.

- Double click **A1** to edit the cell. Move the cursor to the beginning of the text and type **Book** followed by a space. The title should now read: **Book Subscriptions for Class A**. Press **Enter** to complete the editing.

- Note how cell A1 is now stretched across three columns. Cells B1 and C1 still exist underneath.

- Double click the cell **B8** which contains the surname **Ayers**. Click in front of the text and type **Scott-** and then press **Enter**. The cell should now contain the surname **Scott-Ayers**.

2.4.2 Replacing Cell Content (4.2.4.1)

To replace the entire contents of a particular cell you can type over the existing cell contents.

- Click in **B2** to select the cell containing the title **Surname**. Now type **Last Name** and then press **Enter** to replace the original cell contents.

- Click in **B5** to select the cell containing the name **Saxe**. Type **Saxon** and then press **Enter** to replace the original cell contents.

- Click in **E5**, type **90** and then press **Enter** to update the subscription for **Carmen Saxon**.

- Click the **Save** button to update the spreadsheet file.

- Close the spreadsheet on completion.

	A	B	C	D	E
1	Book Subscriptions for Class A				
2	ID Number	Last Name	First Name	DOB	Subs.
3		Dunne	Joan	10/01/1986	100
4		Yando	Susan	12/02/1986	75
5		Saxon	Carmen	16/04/1986	75
6		Zealzo	Michel	23/05/1986	90
7		Eisenberg	Wilhelm	11/01/1986	100
8		Scott-Ayers	Freda	29/05/1986	45
9		Dunne	Ciara	12/12/1985	65
10		Montuga	Charles	24/12/1985	80
11		Divorkin	Slava	09/03/1986	90
12		Brennan	Michael	04/04/1986	100

MODULE 4

2.5   Sorting Data (4.2.7.1)

Lists are often more useful when they are sorted into alphabetical or numerical order. There are two **Sort** buttons on the toolbar you can use for sorting in **ascending** or **descending** order.

An **ascending** sort – the most common – sorts from **A** through to the letter **Z** or from zero to the highest number and places the contents in order, beginning at the topmost cells of the worksheet.

If you select **descending**, the cells are sorted from **Z** to **A**, or from the highest number through to the lowest. Descending sorts are useful for sorting numbers when you want the highest number to be displayed at the top of the list.

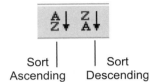

Sort Ascending   Sort Descending

To sort the data in the results table, proceed as follows:

> To begin with, you decide to sort in ascending order of the surnames in your list.

- Open the spreadsheet file named **Class List – Sorting**.

- Click on any name in the **Last Name** column.

- Click the **Sort Ascending** button.
  Now you have decided to sort the names into a descending order.

- Click the **Sort Descending** button to rearrange the last names into descending order.
  Now imagine that you want to look at who got the highest scores in the first week.

- Click anywhere in the **Week 1** column.

- Click the **Sort Descending** button.

- Now sort **Week 1** into ascending order so that you can see the lowest to highest scores.

- Save the spreadsheet, closing it on completion.

Section 3   A Spreadsheet Timetable

Spreadsheets are used mainly for their ability to analyse and calculate numbers. They can also be used to create everyday documents such as lists and school timetables. Refer to the illustration here as you follow the instructions below and on the following page.

	A	B	C	D	E	F
1						
2		Monday	Tuesday	Wednesday	Thursday	Friday
3	9	Spanish	Spanish	Spanish	Spanish	Spanish
4	9.3	Math	Drama	Math	History	Math
5	10	Math	English	English	Science	English
6	10.3	Swimming	History	Computers	Swimming	Science
7	11	Break	Break	Break	Break	Break
8	11.3	English	Geography	History	Science	Computers
9	12	English	Science	Geography	English	Art
10	12.3	Lunch	Lunch	Lunch	Lunch	Lunch
11	1	Singing	Art	Singing	Art	Geography

3.1   Duplicating, Moving and Deleting Information

You can duplicate or move information to other locations within the worksheet, using the copy, cut and paste tools.

In addition to copy/cut and paste, Excel provides an **autofill** facility using a special tool known as the **fill handle**.

3.1.1 Using Copy and Paste (4.2.5.1)

Using copy and paste in Excel is very similar to how they can be used within any other application (see Before You Begin, Section 4 for more information).

- Select the cells you wish to copy.

- Click the **Copy** button on the Standard toolbar.
  A *flashing border* appears around the outside of the selected cells.

- Click where you want a copy of the cells to appear.

- Click the **Paste** button on the Standard toolbar.
  You can continue to paste into different locations in the worksheet, if you so wish.

- When you have finished pasting, press the **Esc** key on the keyboard to end the routine.

Copy Button

| Monday | Tuesday | W |

Paste Button

NOTE

You can copy and paste in exactly the same way as shown above between different spreadsheet files, simply by switching to the appropriate spreadsheet using its button on the taskbar. Once you have pasted the copied cells, click back on the original spreadsheet button in the taskbar and press Esc to complete the copy routine.

3.1.2 Using Cut and Paste (4.2.5.3)

Using cut and paste in Excel is again very similar to how they can be used within any other application (see Before You Begin, Section 4 for more information).

- Select the cells you wish to move.

- Click the **Cut** button on the Standard toolbar.
  Cut Button
  A *flashing border* appears around the outside of the selected cells.

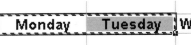

- Click where you want the moved cells to appear.

- Click the **Paste** button on the Standard toolbar.

Paste Button

NOTE

You can move cells from one open file to another in exactly the same way as shown above, simply by switching to the appropriate spreadsheet using its button on the taskbar. Once you have pasted the copied cells, click back on the original spreadsheet button in the taskbar.

To practice duplicating or moving data within a worksheet, proceed as follows:

- Open the file named **Copy and Move**.
  You would like to copy the cells containing the days of the week and duplicate the information for the remaining two terms.

- Select the cell range **B3** to **F3**.

- Click the **Copy** button.

- Click in **B16** and then click the **Paste** button.

- Click in **B30** and then click the **Paste** button.

- Press the **Esc** key to cancel the flashing border around the original cells.
  Now let's copy the times from Term 1, so that they also appear for Term 2.

- Select the range **A4** to **A11**.

- Click the **Copy** button.

- Click in **A18** and then click the **Paste** button.

- Press **Esc** to end the routine.
  Now let's move Term 2 so that it appears next to Term 1 and not below it.

- Select the cells **A15** to **F25**.

- Click the **Cut** button.

- Click in **H1** and then click the **Paste** button. Notice that you do not need to press **Esc** after moving the data, unlike when you were copying.

- Save the current worksheet and then close it.

3.1.3 Using the Fill Handle (4.2.5.2)

Using the **fill handle**, you can automatically fill in a series of dates or numbers.

The **fill handle** is a small black square at the bottom right-hand corner of the selected area or active cell.

	A	B	C	D	E
1					
2		Monday			
3		9 Spanish			

The Fill Handle

Proceed as follows to use the fill handle to complete some of the data in your timetable:

- Open the file named **Class Timetable**.

- Click in **B2** to select the cell containing the word **Monday**.

- Move the mouse pointer slowly over the **fill handle** until it turns into a cross.

- Drag the mouse over the cells to the right and you will see the names of the other days appear.

- Release the mouse button when you reach **Friday** to automatically insert the days of the week.

3.1.4 Deleting Cell Contents (4.2.5.4)

Using the **Delete** key you can remove the contents of a cell or range of cells. The data in each cell is removed but not the formatting that may have been applied to the cell. The next time you enter information into the cell all of the formatting features there will apply.

- To practice using the fill handle for inserting dates, click in **J2**, type **January** and then press **Enter**.

- Select **J2** and then, using the fill handle, drag down until you have all twelve months of the year.

- Press **Delete** to remove this data.

The fill handle can also be used to duplicate a single cell or a range to adjacent cells in the worksheet.

Proceed as follows to continue building your timetable:

- Click in **B4** to select the subject **Math**. Use the **fill handle** to drag down to **B5** so that the ten o'clock timeslot also has the subject **Math**.

- Click in **B3** to select the subject **Spanish**. Use the **fill handle** to drag across to **F3** so that **Spanish** is repeated for every day of the week.

- Click in **B7** to select the word **Break**. Use the **fill handle** to add the **Break** at this timeslot for every day of the week. Do the same for **Lunch** at 12.30.

- Select the range **B11** to **C11** which contains the subjects **Singing** and **Art**. Use the **fill handle** to drag across through cells **D11** and **E11** to repeat the entries in these cells.

    To save you from entering all of the remaining subjects, a completed timetable has been created for you.

- Save the current file, closing it on completion.

3.2   Basic Cell Formatting (4.5.1.1)

Cells can be formatted to display text and numbers in different ways. The lesson times you typed in already are not displayed as you might have expected. Excel recognises them as numbers rather than as times and it discards unwanted zeros and decimal points. To display the times correctly, we shall format the cells so that the times will always display two decimal places.

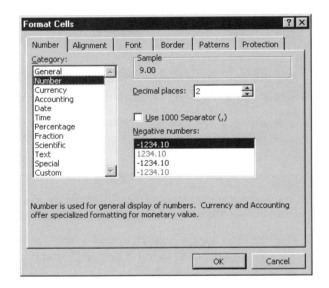

	A	B	C	D	E	F
1			Class Timetable			
2		Monday	Tuesday	Wednesday	Thursday	Friday
3	9.00	Spanish	Spanish	Spanish	Spanish	Spanish
4	9.30	Math	Drama	Math	History	Math
5	10.00	Math	English	English	Science	English
6	10.30	Swimming	History	Computers	Swimming	Science
7	11.00	Break	Break	Break	Break	Break
8	11.30	English	Geography	History	Science	Computers
9	12.00	English	Science	Geography	English	**Art**
10	12.30	Lunch	Lunch	Lunch	Lunch	Lunch
11	1.00	Singing	**Art**	Singing	**Art**	Geography

Proceed as follows:

- Open the file named **Class Timetable - Formatting**.

- Select cells **A3** to **A11**, which contain the lesson times.

- Select **Cells** in the **Format** menu. The Format Cells window opens.

- Click the **Number** tab, if it is not already clicked.

- Click **Number** in the **Category list** on the left to select it.

- Type **2** in the **Decimal places** box. Notice the sample displayed to the right.

- Click **OK**. The times should now be displayed correctly.

Using this sequence numbers can also be displayed in other formats, such as **currency**, **date** and **percentage**.

To insert commas to separate large numbers into thousands, click the **Use 1000 Separator (,)** box on the Formatting toolbar.

The number of digits after the decimal point can also be set by first selecting the appropriate cells. Then use the **Increase** or **Decrease Decimal** buttons on the toolbar.

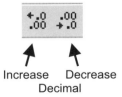

Increase Decimal   Decrease Decimal

Click the tabs at the top of the window to see further ways in which cells can be formatted to display their content.

3.3   Text Alignment and Formatting (4.5.2.1, 4.5.2.2 and 4.5.3.1)

In spreadsheets, numbers are automatically aligned to the right of a cell. Text is aligned to the left. This alignment may not always be the most suitable and it can be easily changed. To change the alignment of individual cells or ranges, proceed as follows:

- Select **B2** and then click the **Right Align** button on the toolbar.

- Select **C2** and then click the **Center Align** button on the toolbar. Now click the **Left Align** button to return it to the left of the cell.

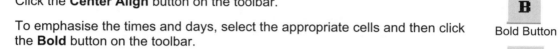

Alignment Buttons

- Select the cell range showing the days of the week.

- Click the **Center Align** button on the toolbar. The days are now aligned in the centre of the cells.

- Select the cell range showing the lesson times in **A3** to **A11**.

- Click the **Center Align** button on the toolbar.

B

Bold Button

- To emphasise the times and days, select the appropriate cells and then click the **Bold** button on the toolbar.

- To change the appearance of the times, select the cell range A3 to A11 and then click the Italics button on the Formatting toolbar.

I

Italics Button

- Select the days of the week in the cell range B2 to F2. Underline these cells by clicking the Underline button on the Formatting toolbar.

U

Underline Button

- To double underline the days of the week, again select the cell ragne B2 to F2. Choose **Cells** from the **Format** menu and click on the **Font** tab. Click the arrow for the Underline box and select **Double**. Click **OK** to continue.

- To change the font of the main part of the timetable, select the cells (**B3** to **F11**) and choose **Times New Roman** and **11pt** using the toolbar.

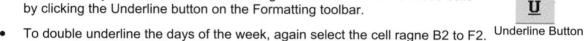

- Select the column range **B** to **F** (using the column headers) and using the **Format** menu, change the column widths to **12pt** wide.

- Select the row range **1** to **11** and using the **Format** menu, change the row heights to **20pt** high.

- Save the spreadsheet but do not close it.

3.3.1   Text Alignment and Orientation (4.5.3.1 and 4.5.3.3)

In addition to changing the horizontal alignment of data within a cell or range of cells, you can also manipulate the vertical alignment of data and/or its orientation. Use this sequence to apply formatting options to cell contents:

- Select the five days of the week (**B2** to **F2**). Select **Cells** in the **Format** menu. The Format Cells window opens (see next page).

- Click on the **Alignment** tab to display the alignment options.

- Click on the arrow on the **Vertical** box and select **Centre**. Click **OK**.

  Perhaps now you would also like to *angle* the orientation of the headings down by 45 degrees.

- Select the five days of the week (**B2** to **F2**). Select **Cells** in the **Format** menu.

- Click on the **Alignment** tab if it is not currently selected.

- **To angle the text**, drag the 'hand' around the 'clock face' in the **Orientation** panel until it reaches **-45 degrees**. Click **OK**. The height of the row needs to be adjusted to fit the angled text.

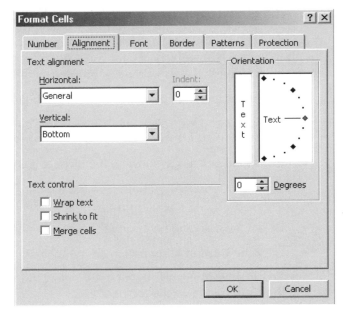

- Ensure the days of the week are still selected.

- Choose **Row** in the **Format** menu and click the **AutoFit** option in the sub-menu to adjust the row height. The row should now accommodate the information it contains.

	A	B	C	D	E	F
1						
2		*Monday*	*Tuesday*	*Wednesday*	*Thursday*	*Friday*
3	9.00	Spanish	Spanish	Spanish	Spanish	Spanish

3.3.2 Adding a Border (4.5.3.4)

A border can be added to the entire spreadsheet or around selected cells as follows:

- Select the cells containing the days of the week (**B2** to **F2**).

- Click on the arrow beside the **Borders** button on the toolbar to display a menu of different border styles.

- Click on the **All Borders** style.

- Select the timeslots in the cells **A3** to **A11**.

- Click the **Borders** button to apply the **All Borders** style.

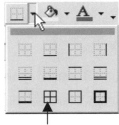

All Borders Button

3.3.3 Adding a Heading (4.5.2.1 and 4.5.3.2)

We shall enter a heading in cell **A1** at the top of the sheet.

- Select **A1** and type the heading **Class Timetable** and then press **Enter**.

- Select the new heading in **A1**.

- Select **Times New Roman, 18pt** on the toolbar to emphasise the heading. Make the heading **bold**.

- To centre the heading evenly across our timetable columns, you can use the **Merge and Center** option. Select **A1** to **F1** and then click the **Merge and Center** button on the toolbar.

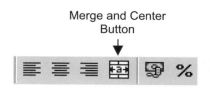

Merge and Center
Button

- Adjust the row height if necessary.

3.3.4 Multiple Lines of Text within a Cell (4.5.2.5)

Using the wrap text feature, you can display multiple lines of text within a cell rather than having to use additional cells to display the text.

- Click in **A14**, type **Additional Activities** and then press **Enter**.

- Select **A14** and then select **Cells** in the **Format** menu.

- Click the **Alignment** tab if it is not currently selected.

9	12.00	English	Science	Geography	English
10	12.30	Lunch	Lunch	Lunch	Lunch
11	1.00	Singing	Art	Singing	Art
12					
13					
14	Additional Activities	Drama, Tennis and Hockey		Speech and Cookery	
15					

- Check the **Wrap text** option in the **Text control** panel.

- Click **OK** to continue.

  The text has now spread across multiple lines within cell A14.

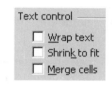

Text control

☐ Wrap text
☐ Shrink to fit
☐ Merge cells

- Click in **B14**, type **Drama, Tennis and Hockey** and then press **Enter**.

- Using the **Format Cells** window, select the **Wrap text** option to display the text across multiple lines in the cell.

- Click in **D14**, type **Speech and Cookery** and then press **Enter**.

- Using the **Format Cells** window, select the **Wrap text** option to display the text across multiple lines in the cell.

3.3.5 Applying Different Colours and Backgrounds (4.5.2.3)

To further enhance your work, selected areas of a worksheet can have different font colours and cell backgrounds.

- Select the days of the week in **A2** to **F2**.

- Click on the arrow on the **Fill Colour** button on the toolbar and select **tan**.

- Select the timeslots range **A3** to **A11** and then click on the **Fill Colour** button again to select **tan** (the **Fill Colour** button remembers the last colour you used so that it can be quickly applied without having to select it from the extended menu).

- Select the main area of the timetable (**B3** to **F11**) and change the **Fill Colour** to **light green**.

- Select the days of the week in **A2** to **F2**.

- Click on the arrow on the **Font Colour** button on the toolbar and select **red**.

- Select the timeslots in **A3** to **A11** and then click on the **Font Colour** button again to select **red** (the **Font Colour** button also remembers the last colour you used so that it can be quickly applied again if necessary).

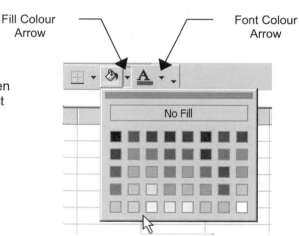

Fill Colour
Arrow

Font Colour
Arrow

No Fill

MODULE 4

- Click on the heading **Class Timetable** and set the **Fill Colour** to **light green** and the **Font Colour** to **red**.

- Save the spreadsheet but do not close it.

3.3.6 Copying Formatting to Other Cells (4.5.2.4)

Data can easily be copied within a worksheet using copy and paste or using the fill handle method. You can also copy the formatting of a cell or group of cells to other cells within the worksheet.

- Select **B7** which contains the word **Break**.

- Using the **Font Colour** button, change the colour of the text to **red**. Now make the text **bold** and **italised**.

- Ensure **B7** is selected and then click on the **Format Painter** button on the toolbar.

Format Painter

- Drag the mouse across the range **C7** to **F7** to format the remaining text at this timeslot.

- Use the **Format Painter** to format the **Lunch** breaks with the same formatting as the breaks at **11.00**.

- Imagine that you teach **Art** as one of your subjects and you want to make this subject stand out on the timetable. Select the word **Art** in **F9**. Change the **Fill Colour** to **light yellow**. Change the **font size** to **12pt** and make the text **bold**.

- Select **F9** and then double click the **Format Painter** button. By double clicking on the Format Painter you can then click or drag on more than one cell or range to apply formatting to multiple cells or cell ranges.

- Click on any other occurrence of the subject **Art** until all have been formatted.

- Press the **Esc** key to turn the Format Painter off.

- Save the spreadsheet and close it.

	A	B	C	D	E	F
1			Class Timetable			
2		Monday	Tuesday	Wednesday	Thursday	Friday
3	9.00	Spanish	Spanish	Spanish	Spanish	Spanish
4	9.30	Math	Drama	Math	History	Math
5	10.00	Math	English	English	Science	English
6	10.30	Swimming	History	Computers	Swimming	Science
7	11.00	*Break*	*Break*	*Break*	*Break*	*Break*
8	11.30	English	Geography	History	Science	Computers
9	12.00	English	Science	Geography	English	**Art**
10	12.30	*Lunch*	*Lunch*	*Lunch*	*Lunch*	*Lunch*
11	1.00	Singing	**Art**	Singing	**Art**	Geography
12						
13						
14	Additional Activities	Drama, Tennis and Hockey		Speech and Cookery		
15						

3.4   Using Find and Replace (4.2.6.1 and 4.2.6.2)

There may be times when you need to search through a spreadsheet for a particular piece of data, such as a word, phrase or number. Rather than scanning through yourself, you can use the **Find** option to help you look. In addition, there may be occasions when you also wish to look for a particular item and replace it throughout the entire spreadsheet. For example, in your timetable you may wish to change the subject **Singing** and replace it with **Music**.

We will start by looking for a single word:

- Open the file named **Class Timetable - Find and Replace**.

- Click in **A1**.

- Select **Find** in the **Edit** menu.

- Type **Hockey** in the **Find what** box.

- Click **Find Next** to locate the first occurrence of the word **Hockey**. Once a match has been found, click **Find Next** again to see if there is another match (there should only be one).

- Click the **Close** button to close the **Find** window.

Now let's look for the word **Singing** and replace it with **Music**. Proceed as follows:

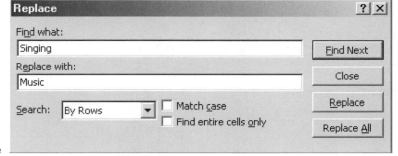

- Select **Find** in the **Edit** menu.

- Type **Singing** in the **Find what** box.

- Click the **Replace** button and the Find window is changed to the **Replace** window.

- Enter **Music** in the **Replace with** box.

- Click **Find Next** to locate the first occurrence of the word **Singing**. Click the **Replace** button to replace it with **Music**.

- To replace all remaining occurrences of the word **Singing**, click the **Replace All** button.

- Check the contents of your timetable.

3.4.1 Other Options

To search rows or columns, select **By Rows** or **By Columns** from the menu in the **Search** box.

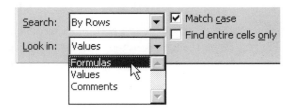

The menu in the **Look in** box allows you to search in **Formulas** as well as in **Values** and **Text**. This option only appears in the **Find** box and not in the **Replace** window.

Uncheck **Match case** so that both uppercase and lowercase occurrences of the word are found.

Click **Find entire cells only** to find an exact match. Leaving it unchecked will find, for example, the number **8** in cells that contain **8**, **182**, **2845** and so on.

Save your spreadsheet and close it.

Section 4   Working with Formulas and Functions

One of the most powerful features of a spreadsheet application such as Excel is the ability to create *formulas* based on data in a worksheet. Simple formulas can be used to perform calculations such as adding, subtracting, multiplying and dividing. A formula is entered into a cell and the result is then displayed in the cell, not the actual formula that produced it.

This is the formula used to display the answer in **B5** on the Formula bar

4.1   Creating a Basic Formula

All formulas should begin with an equals sign (=). Thereafter, formulas are usually based on cell references (such as A1, A2, A3, etc.). An example of a simple formula would be:

=A3+A4
or
=A10*350

The basic mathematical operators that you can use with formulas are:-

Description	Operator
Addition	+
Subtraction	-
Multiplication	*
Division	/

There are two main methods used for **building** a formula – you can either **type** the cell references you wish to include in the formula or you can **point** to the references, i.e. **A1**, **B1**, etc.

4.1.1 Typing Cell References in Formulas (4.4.1.1)

As you already know, each cell in a spreadsheet has its own unique address – such as **A1**, **B1**, **C1**, etc. These cell references can be typed into a formula to perform a calculation on existing spreadsheet data.

Proceed as follows:

- Open the file named **Working with Formulas**.

  Take a few moments to familiarise yourself with the **Book Subscriptions** worksheet.

  Your students have purchased various textbooks and they have been paying off different amounts over a four-week period. You need to find out how much they have paid and the balance that is remaining.

	A	B	C	D	E	F	G	H
1	**Book Subscriptions**							
2								
3	Student	Total Due	Week 1	Week 2	Week 3	Week 4	Total	Balance
4	Brennan M	125	25	32	15	10		
5	Dunne C	95	40	20	10	5		
6	Ayers F	82	10	20	35	15		
7	Saxon C	111	20	50	20	20		
8	Yando S	65	20	20	20	20		
9	Zealzo M	78	10	15	10	15		
10	Divorkin S	130	20	15	35	40		
11	Eisenberg W	76	20	10	10	25		
12	Montuga C	32	5	5	5	17		

- To calculate the total for **M. Brennan**, click in **G4** and type the following formula: **=C4+D4+E4+F4** and then press **Enter**. The answer should be **82**. If not, delete the formula and try it again.

  Notice that the formula appears in the **Formula bar** while the *result* of the formula appears in the cell **G4**.

- To calculate the total for **C. Dunne**, click in **G5** and type the following formula: **=C5+D5+E5+F5** and then press **Enter**. The answer should be **75**. If not, delete the formula and try it again.

- Delete the answer in **G5**.

  Rather than typing the same type of formula for each student, you can use the **fill handle** to copy the first formula.

- Click on **G4** and use the **fill handle** to drag down to **G12**. Click on each of the answers and note how the formula is displayed in the **Formula bar**.

	A	B	C	D	E	F	G	H
1	**Book Subscriptions**							
2								
3	Student	Total Due	Week 1	Week 2	Week 3	Week 4	Total	Balance
4	Brennan M	125	25	32	15	10	82	
5	Dunne C	95	40	20	10	5	75	
6	Ayers F	82	10	20	35	15	80	
7	Saxon C	111	20	50	20	20	110	
8	Yando S	65	20	20	20	20	80	
9	Zealzo M	78	10	15	10	15	50	
10	Divorkin S	130	20	15	35	40	110	
11	Eisenberg W	76	20	10	10	25	65	
12	Montuga C	32	5	5	5	17	32	

- Click in **C4** and change the first week's amount paid by **M. Brennan** to **55**. Notice that the answer in **G4** has automatically updated to **112**.

- Click in **D5** and change the second week's amount paid by **C. Dunne** to **10**. Notice that the answer in **G5** has automatically updated to **65**.

  Now it's time to work out the balance that each student has to pay.

- Click in **H4** and type the following formula: **=B4-G4** and then press **Enter**. The answer should be **13**.

- Use the **fill handle** to copy the formula down to **H12** so that the balance for the other students is calculated.

  Has anyone paid their amount in full? Has anyone overpaid?

- Save the spreadsheet but do not close it.

4.1.2 Selecting Cell References in Formulas (4.4.1.1)

As you have already learned, you can type cell references directly into a formula. However, this can sometimes lead to errors, especially when you are working with large worksheets as you may misread the cell reference you wish to use. By **pointing** to the cell references you wish to use, you can ensure the accuracy of your formulas.

Proceed as follows:

- Click on **Sheet 2** in the **Working with Formulas** spreadsheet.
  This takes you to the **Book Orders** worksheet.

- Take a few moments to familiarise yourself with the worksheet.

You need to order some reference books and you need to calculate the total value for each title based on the price multiplied by the number of books required.

	A	B	C	D
1	**Book Orders**			
2				
3	Title	Price	No Required	Total
4	Cottage Crafts	15.6	10	
5	The Industrial Revolution Ed.7	14.2	12	
6	Wilsons Anatomy and Physiology	30	10	
7	Potions and Lotions	27.99	5	
8	Ready, Steady, Draw	24.3	7	
9	Introduction to Computers	12.25	15	
10	Learning the Guitar - Marksons	14.65	6	
11	Science Made Easy	26.4	2	
12	Design and Drawings	21.25	14	

- To calculate the total for the **Cottage Crafts** book, click in **D4** and type an equals sign (=) to start the formula.

- Now, using the mouse, click on **B4** which contains the price for the **Cottage Crafts** book.

- Type a multiplication symbol (*) into the formula and then click on **C4** which contains the number of books required. Press **Enter** to complete the formula. The answer should be **156**.
  Notice that the formula appears in the **Formula bar** while the *result* of the formula appears in the cell **D4**.

In addition to using the mouse to **build** a formula, you can also use the cursor arrow keys on the keyboard.

Proceed as follows:

- Delete the answer in **D4** and type an equals sign (=) to start the formula again.

- Now, move the cursor arrow left until you are in **B4** which contains the price for the **Cottage Crafts** book.

- Type a multiplication symbol (*) into the formula and then move the cursor arrow left until you are in **C4,** which contains the number of books required. Press **Enter** to complete the formula. The answer should again be **156**.
  Rather than typing the same type of formula for each student, you can use the **fill handle** to copy the first formula.

- Click on **D4** and use the **fill handle** to drag down to **D12**. Click on each of the answers and view the formula it is based on in the **Formula bar**.

Exercise 4A

1   Click on **Sheet 3** to access the **General Class Supplies** worksheet.

In this example you have a number of class supplies with the total value for each item. You want to work out how many items you have in stock based on their total value and the unit price for each.

2   Click in **D4** where the first **Amount of Stock** calculation should appear.

3   Create the following formula either by pointing at the cell references or typing them in. Remember to start with an equals sign first (**=**): **=B4/C4** and press **Enter**. The **/** sign is used for **division** within Excel.

The answer should be **101.82** – don't worry about the decimal places as these will be fixed later.

4   Use the **fill handle** to calculate the remaining stock amounts.

5   Click back on **Sheet 1** and then save the spreadsheet file, closing it on completion.

	A	B	C	D
1	**General Class Supplies**			
2				
3	**Item**	**Total Stock**	**Price Per Item**	**Amt of Stock**
4	Pens	56	0.55	101.82
5	Pencils	111	0.23	482.61
6	Erasers	36	1.22	29.508
7	Disks	50	5.5	9.0909
8	Exercise Books	110	6.3	17.46
9	Highlighters	23	2.5	9.2
10	Stapler Packs	35	4.8	7.2917
11	Folders	46	4.9	9.3878
12	Rulers	29	0.75	38.667

4.2   Working with Functions

Functions are used to create special type of formulas within a spreadsheet program such as Excel. Each function performs a specific task, such as adding a range of numbers (the **SUM** function) or finding the highest number in a range (the **MAX**) function and so on.

Functions can be accessed through the **Paste Function** button on the Standard toolbar or by using **Function** in the **Insert** menu on the Menu bar.

f_x

Paste Function Button

4.2.1   Using the SUM Function (4.4.3.1)

The **SUM** function is used to add a range of numbers and provide a total.

To work with the **SUM** function proceed as follows:

- Open the spreadsheet named **Working with Functions**.

  Take a few moments to familiarise yourself with the **Book Subscriptions** worksheet – it is similar to the worksheet you used for creating basic functions.

- Click in **G4** where the total for **M. Brennan** should appear.

- Click the **Paste Function** button on the toolbar.

  The **Paste Function** window appears.

- Select **Most Recently Used** in the **Function category** box as this will display the **SUM** function.

- Select **SUM** in the **Function name** box.

- Click **OK**.

  The **SUM** window appears.

An explanation of the **SUM** function appears in the bottom of the window. It is in mathematical terms, however, and may not be very useful.

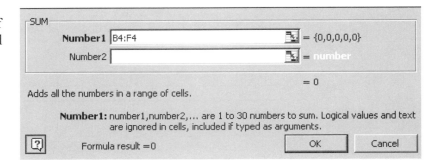

Excel assumes that you want to find the **total** for the range **B4** to **F4** and has entered that cell range into the **Number 1** box. In this instance the cell range is incorrect as you only want to add the individual payments for the four weeks and not the initial amount due (which is in **B4**).

- To select a different range, click on the **selector button** at the right-hand end of the **Number 1** box to reduce the **SUM** box to the **Number 1** box.

- Using the mouse, select the range **C4** to **F4** and then press the **Enter** key to return to the **SUM** box.

  The cell range you selected appears in the **Number 1** box.

  Selector Button

- Click **OK** to complete the formula.

  The answer should be **112**. Notice the formula in the **Formula bar** – it should read **=SUM(C4:F4)**.

- Use the **fill handle** to copy the formula in **G4** down to **G12**.

	A	B	C	D	E	F	G	H
1	**Book Subscriptions**							
2								
3	Student	Total Due	Week 1	Week 2	Week 3	Week 4	Total	Balance
4	Brennan M	125	55	32	15	10	112	13
5	Dunne C	95	40	10	10	5	65	30
6	Ayers F	82		20		15	35	47
7	Saxon C	111	20	50	20	20	110	1
8	Yando S	65	20	20	20	20	80	-15
9	Zealzo M	78	10	15		15	40	38
10	Divorkin S	130		15	35	40	90	40
11	Eisenberg W	76	20	10	10	25	65	11
12	Montuga C	32	5	2	4	17	28	4
13								
14	Totals							

Now let's use the **SUM** function again to calculate the total amount **due** for all of the students.

- Click in **B14** where the total should appear.

- Click the **Paste Function** button on the toolbar.

- Ensure **SUM** is selected in the **Function name** box and then click **OK**.
  This time, Excel has selected the range **B4** to **B13** as the cells where the numbers are to be added. This is correct for the formula you are creating.

- Click **OK** to complete the formula.
  The answer should be **794**.

For practice, let's see again what happens when Excel does not suggest the correct cell range when using a function such as **SUM**.

- Click in **C14** where the total for **Week 1** should appear.

- Click the **Paste Function** button on the toolbar.

- Ensure **SUM** is selected in the **Function name** box and then click **OK**.
  Excel has selected the range **C11** to **C13** as the cells where the numbers are to be added. This is not correct as you want to include all of the numbers for Week 1.

- To select a different range, click on the **Selector button** at the right-hand end of the **Number 1** box.

- Using the mouse, select the range **C4** to **C13** and then click **Enter** to return to the **SUM** box.

- Click **OK** to complete the formula.
  The answer should be **170**.

Whilst you could use the **fill handle** to copy the total in C14 across to the other weeks, we will look at two other ways of performing the **SUM** function.

4.2.1.1 Typing in the SUM Function

You can type a **SUM** function directly into a cell in much the same way as you did when creating basic formulas.

- Click in **C14** where the total for **Week 1** should appear and press **Delete** to remove the total.

- Ensure you have **C14** selected and then type the following formula into the cell:
  =sum(c4:c13).

- Press **Enter** to complete the formula – the answer should again be **170**.

4.2.1.2 Using AutoSum

Because the **Sum** function is one of the most regularly used of all the available functions, Excel has included an **AutoSum** button on the Standard toolbar.

AutoSum
Button

To use **AutoSum** proceed as follows:

- Click in **C14** where the total for **Week 1** should appear and press **Delete** to remove the total.

- Ensure you have **C14** selected.

- Click on the **AutoSum** button on the toolbar.

- Select the range **C4** to **C12**.

- Press **Enter** to complete the formula – the answer should again be **170**.

- Use the **fill handle** to copy the formula across to **H14** to calculate the remaining totals.

- Save the spreadsheet but do not close it.

	A	B	C	D	E	F	G	H
1	**Book Subscriptions**							
2								
3	Student	Total Due	Week 1	Week 2	Week 3	Week 4	Total	Balance
4	Brennan M	125	55	32	15	10	112	13
5	Dunne C	95	40	10	10	5	65	30
6	Ayers F	82		20		15	35	47
7	Saxon C	111	20	50	20	20	110	1
8	Yando S	65	20	20	20	20	80	-15
9	Zealzo M	78	10	15		15	40	38
10	Divorkin S	130		15	35	40	90	40
11	Eisenberg W	76	20	10	10	25	65	11
12	Montuga C	32	5	2	4	17	28	4
13								
14	Totals	794	170	174	114	167	625	169

4.2.2 Using the AVERAGE Function (4.4.3.1)

The **AVERAGE** function is used to calculate the *average* for a list of numbers.

To work with the AVERAGE function proceed as follows:

- Ensure the spreadsheet named **Working with Functions** is open.

- Click in **C16** where the average payment for **Week 1** should appear.

- Click the **Paste Function** button on the toolbar.
  The **Paste Function** window appears.

- Select **Most Recently Used** in the **Function category** box.

- Select **AVERAGE** in the **Function name** box.

- Click **OK**.
  The **AVERAGE** window appears.

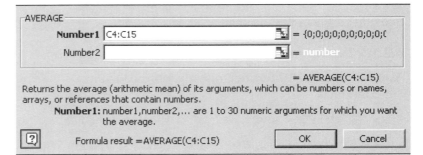

Excel assumes that you want to find the **average** for the range **C4** to **C15** and has entered that cell range into the **Number 1** box. This would not be correct as it would include the cell containing the weekly total (in C14) as well as the individual payments.

- To select a different range, click on the **Selector button** at the right-hand side of the **Number 1** box.

- Using the mouse, select the range **C4** to **C12** and then click **Enter** to return to the **AVERAGE** box.

- Click **OK** to complete the formula. The answer in **C16** should be **24.286**.

- Use the **fill handle** to copy the formula across to **F16** to calculate the remaining averages for each week.

- Select the averages in the range **C16** to **F16** and then use the **Decrease Decimal** button on the Formatting toolbar to remove all decimal places for each average, leaving just whole numbers.

Decrease Decimal Button

4.2.3 Using the MAX Function (4.4.3.1)

The **MAX** function is used to find the highest number in a list of numbers.

To work with the **MAX** function proceed as follows:

- Ensure the spreadsheet named **Working with Functions** is open.

- Click in **C17** where the maximum payment for **Week 1** should appear.

- Click the **Paste Function** button on the toolbar.
  The **Paste Function** window appears.

- Select **Most Recently Used** in the **Function category** box.

- Select **MAX** in the **Function name** box.

- Click **OK**.
  The **MAX** window appears.

- To select a different range, click on the **Selector button** at the right-hand side of the **Number 1** box.

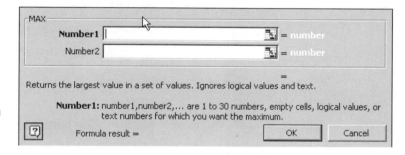

- Using the mouse, select the range **C4** to **C12** and then click **Enter** to return to the **MAX** box.

- Click **OK** to complete the formula.
  The answer in **C17** should be **55**.

- Use the **fill handle** to copy the formula across to **F17** to identify the remaining maximum values.

4.2.4 Using the MIN Function (4.4.3.1)

The **MIN** function is used to calculate the lowest number from a list of numbers.

To work with the **MIN** function proceed as follows:

- Ensure the spreadsheet named **Working with Functions** is open.

- Click in **C18** where the minimum payment for **Week 1** should appear.

- Click the **Paste Function** button on the toolbar.
  The **Paste Function** window appears.

- Select **Most Recently Used** in the **Function category** box.

  Notice the **MIN** function is not currently listed in the **Most Recently Used** box.

- Click on **Statistical** in the **Function category** box.

- Scroll down through the **Function name** list until you can see the **MIN** function. Click on this function and then click **OK**.

  The **MIN** window appears.

- To select a different range, click on the **Selector button** at the right-hand side of the **Number 1** box.

- Using the mouse, select the range **C4** to **C12** and then click **Enter** to return to the **MIN** box.

- Click **OK** to complete the formula.
  The answer in **C18** should be **5**.

- Use the **fill handle** to copy the formula across to **F18** to calculate the remaining minimum values.

- Save the spreadsheet but do not close it.

4.2.5 Using the COUNT Function (4.4.3.1)

The **COUNT** function is used to calculate how many entries are within a list of numbers.

To work with the **COUNT** function proceed as follows:

- Ensure the spreadsheet named **Working with Functions** is open.

- Click in **C19** where the number of payments for **Week 1** should appear.

- Click the **Paste Function** button on the toolbar.
  The **Paste Function** window appears.

- Select **Most Recently Used** in the **Function category** box.

- Click on the **COUNT** function in the **Function name** box.

- Click **OK**.
  The **COUNT** window appears.

- To select a different range, click on the **Selector button** at the right-hand side of the **Number 1** box.

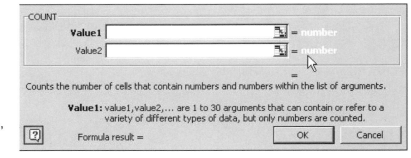

- Using the mouse, select the range **C4** to **C12** and then click **Enter** to return to the **COUNT** box.

- Click **OK** to complete the formula.
  The answer in **C19** should be **7**.

- Use the **fill handle** to copy the formula across to **F19** to calculate the remaining number of payments per week.

- Save the spreadsheet, closing it on completion.

4.3   Cell Referencing

When you create a formula, cell references **direct** Excel where to look for data or values. There are two ways in which data and values in cells are accessed or referred to, i.e. using **relative references** or **absolute references** in a formula.

4.3.1   Relative References (4.4.2.1)

Relative cell references are used when the cells containing data or values you want to use are positioned 'relative' to the cell containing the formula.

In the diagram over, for example, **B4** and **C4** are positioned relative to **D4** containing the formula =**B4+C4**. The next row down shows how **B5** and **C5** are positioned relative to **D5** containing the formula =**B5+C5**. Both cell references are **relative references**. When you copy the formula, Excel automatically adjusts the references in the copied formula to refer to different cells relative to the position of the formula. In the example, when the formula in **D4** is copied down to **D5**, the formula in **D5** performs the same calculation relative to where its answer is to go – that is two to the left plus one to the left.

	A	B	C	D
1				
2				
3		Jan-Jun	Jul-Dec	Total
4	Class A	100	50	=B4+C4
5	Class B	75	93	=B5+C5

When you copy a relative reference, it automatically adjusts the cell references.

4.3.2   Absolute References (4.4.2.1)

Absolute references are less frequently used in simple spreadsheets than relative references but you need to understand how they work as there may be occasions when a formula requires an absolute reference as well.

An absolute reference does not adjust in any way when you copy the formula. For example, using the diagram, if you want to find the total cost for each book title for all 27 students, you would need to use the absolute reference **B4** so that when you copy the first formula (in B8), the reference **B4** appears in all calculations.

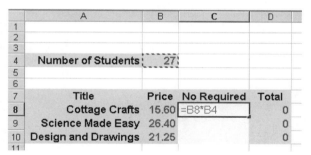

	A	B	C	D
1				
2				
3				
4	Number of Students	27		
5				
6				
7	Title	Price	No Required	Total
8	Cottage Crafts	15.60	=B8*B4	0
9	Science Made Easy	26.40		0
10	Design and Drawings	21.25		0
11				

4.3.3   Switching Between Relative And Absolute References (4.4.2.1)

You can switch between relative and absolute references as you are creating a formula. In the **Formula bar**, highlight, or click in, the reference you want to change and then press the **F4** function key. Each time you press **F4**, Excel *toggles* through the combinations: absolute column and absolute row (for example, **B4**); relative column and absolute row (**B$4**); absolute column and relative row (**$B4**); and relative column and relative row (**B4**). For example, if you select the address **A1** in a formula and press **F4**, the reference becomes **A$1**. Press **F4** again and the reference becomes **$A1**, and so on.

Exercise 4B

To work with relative and absolute references, proceed as follows:

1   Open the spreadsheet named **Working with Relative and Absolute References**.

2   Click in **C6** where the first total should appear.

3   Create the following formula: **=B6*B3** and then press **Enter**.

        The answer should be **421.20**.

4   Use the **fill handle** to copy the formula down to **C14**.

        Click down each total and view the formula in the **Formula bar**. The answers are incorrect. This is because **B3** should be an absolute reference in the original formula and not a relative reference.

5   Select **C6** to **C14** and press Delete to remove the formulas.

6   Click in **C6** and create the following formula: **=B6*B3** and then press **Enter**. Remember that you can use the **F4** function key to make the B3 reference absolute.

7   Use the **fill handle** to copy the formula down to **C14**.

        Click down each total and view the formula in the **Formula bar**. The answers are now correct as each total is multiplied by the number of students in **B3**.

8   Save the spreadsheet but do not close it.

Exercise 4C

To work with a formula where only the row reference or column reference is absolute, proceed as follows:

1   Ensure the spreadsheet named **Working with Relative and Absolute References** is open and click on **Sheet 2**.

        In this example you want to calculate **how much of a discount** you will receive off each book dependent on the number of copies you order.

2   Click in **C7** where the first total should appear.

3   Create the following formula: **=$B7*C$5** and then press **Enter**. Remember that you can use the **F4** function key to make the reference absolute – each press alters the type of reference you are creating.

        The answer in **C7** should be **0.31** discount.

4   Use the fill handle to copy the formula across to E7.

5   With the range **C7 to E7** still selected, use the **fill handle** to copy the formulas down to **E15**.

        Click on each total and view the formulas in the **Formula bar**. Notice the use of mixed references.

6   Save the spreadsheet, closing it on completion.

4.4   Working with the Logical IF Function (4.4.3.2)

Excel provides a range of **logical functions** to enable you to specify *conditions* within a formula. One of the most frequently used logical functions is the **IF** function.

The **IF** function allows you to *test* for a **condition** and then carry out an action depending on whether the condition is found to be true or false. There are three *arguments* in an **IF** function:

=IF(logical_test,value_if_true,value_if_false)

For example:

Students must pay a €100 subscription fee. We want to create an IF function that *tests* to see if they have paid that amount. If they have, we want the **value_if_true** argument to display the words "paid in full". If they have not paid the full amount, we want the **value_if_false** argument to calculate how much they owe.

In this example, imagine that the amount paid by the first student is in the cell **B2**:

=IF(B2=100, "paid in full",100>B2)

When creating a **logical test condition**, the following operators can be used:

Operator	Explanation
=	Equal to
>	Greater than
>=	Greater than or equal to
<	Less than
<=	Less than or equal to
<>	Not equal to

NOTE

When referring to text entries within an **IF** function, the text must be enclosed in quotation marks.

To work with the **IF** function, proceed as follows:

Step 1 – In this step you will select the IF function from the Paste Function window.

- Open the spreadsheet named **Working with Logical Functions**.
  In this example you want to find out if any students have overpaid and by how much.

- Click in **H4** where the first logical function should be created.

- Click the **Paste Function** button on the toolbar.
  The **Paste Function** window appears.

- Select **Logical** in the **Function category** box.

- Select **IF** in the **Function name** box.
  (Note that the **IF** function may also have been listed under the **Most Recently Used Functions** category.)

- Click **OK**.
  The **IF** window appears.

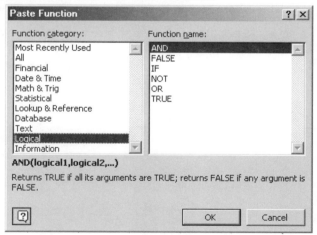

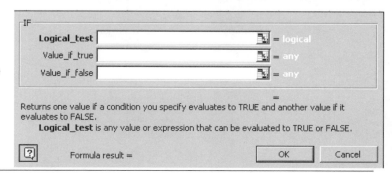

Step 2 – In this step you will specify the logical test condition. You want to find out whether the total paid by M. Brennan (in cell G4) is more than the amount that is due (in cell B4).

- To create the **logical_test** condition, click on the **Selector button** at the right-hand end of the **Logical_test** box.

- Click on **G4** which contains the **Total Paid** by **M. Brennan**.

- Now type the greater than symbol **>** and then click on **B4** which contains the **Total Due** for **M. Brennan**. The logical_test should now read **=IF(G4>B4)**.

- Now press **Enter** to return to the **IF** window.

Step 3 – In this step you want to specify what to do if M. Brennan has overpaid. If so, you want to find out how much M. Brennan has overpaid. You will achieve this by typing the argument G4-B4 (the total paid minus the total due) as the value_if_true.

- Click in the **Value_if_true** box.

- Click on the **Selector button** to the right-hand end of the **Value_if_true** box to access the worksheet.

- Click on **G4**, type a minus sign (**-**) and then click on **B4**. The formula should now read **=IF(G4>B4,G4-B4)**.

- Press **Enter** to return to the **IF** window.

Step 4 – In this step you want to specify what to do if M. Brennan has not overpaid. In this case you want to display a zero (0) for the value_if_false argument.

- Click in the **Value_if_false** box.

- Type a **zero** (**0**) meaning that if the student hasn't overpaid the **Amount Overpaid** cell will show **0** for them.

- Click **OK** to complete the formula.
  The answer for **M. Brennan** (in **H4**) should be **0** as he/she has not overpaid.

Step 5 – In this step you want to apply the formula to the other cells in column H.

- Use the **fill handle** to copy the formula in **H4** down to **H12**.
  There should be four students who have overpaid.

- Save the spreadsheet, closing it on completion.

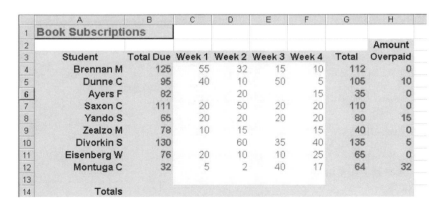

	A	B	C	D	E	F	G	H
1	**Book Subscriptions**							
2								Amount
3	Student	Total Due	Week 1	Week 2	Week 3	Week 4	Total	Overpaid
4	Brennan M	125	55	32	15	10	112	0
5	Dunne C	95	40	10	50	5	105	10
6	Ayers F	82		20		15	35	0
7	Saxon C	111	20	50	20	20	110	0
8	Yando S	65	20	20	20	20	80	15
9	Zealzo M	78	10	15		15	40	0
10	Divorkin S	130		60	35	40	135	5
11	Eisenberg W	76	20	10	10	25	65	0
12	Montuga C	32	5	2	40	17	64	32
13								
14	Totals							

4.5   Special Symbols and Characters

The majority of special characters you may require for formulae are available on the keyboard. Some keys have two characters, upper and lower. For the upper character, hold down the **Shift** key while pressing the character key (just as you would to obtain a capital letter).

Remember, if you are creating a formula yourself (that is, you are not using the Paste Function button or AutoSum button), always type an equals sign (=) before you enter the **formula** or **function** in the cell.

4.5.1 Mathematical Symbols

*   The asterisk is used for multiplication. Use it to multiply two numbers, such as in **100*17**. You can also use it to multiply the contents of two cells by typing the cell addresses, such as in A3*B1.

/   The forward slash is used for division. For example, **C6/8** divides the value of cell C6 by 8.

-        The minus sign, or hyphen, is used to subtract one value from another, as in **8-4**.

+   The plus sign is used for addition of two or more values, as in **8+4**.

^   The caret is used to raise the power of one number to another. For example, **3^2** (3 to the power of 2) gives a value of 9.

You can combine mathematical operations in Excel as you would in any normal mathematical exercise. The rules regarding multiplication, division, addition and subtraction and the use of parentheses are the same, as in an expression such as **=(A5+(B6-F3)/D7**.

4.5.2 Other Symbols

:   The colon is used to designate a range of cells, as in **A5:A12**. It can also designate a range of cells over more than one row or column, as in **A5:C7**.

,   The comma may be used as a thousands separator in large numbers, as in **1,000,000**.

.   The full stop is used to denote decimal values, as in **24.68**.

\#   The hash character is used in two ways.

        In the first, a number of hash characters appear in a cell to indicate that the cell is not wide enough to display all the characters required.

        In the second, it indicates that an error has occurred (see Section 4.6 below).

5E+08   This is scientific notation, a way of writing large numbers. It is used by Excel when a cell is not wide enough to display a number in the usual way. If you increase the width of the cell sufficiently, the number will be displayed normally. **(5E+08 is five hundred million)**.

~   The tilde character may be used when searching for an asterisk in a worksheet. In the **Find what** box, the asterisk would be preceded by the tilde as follows. **~*34**. It behaves like a wildcard.

4.6   Error Messages (4.4.1.2)

From time to time an **error message** may appear. Some common ones are described here. Use Excel **Help** to find more information on error messages.

- **####**   The column is not wide enough to display the number.

- **#DIV/0!**   The formula is trying to divide by zero, which is not possible.

- **#Value!**   Text has been entered when the formula expects a number.

- **#Name!**   Text has been entered in a formula, which is not allowed.

- **#N/A**   The value is not available.

Section 5   Formatting Numbers

In Excel, you can use **number formats** to change the appearance of numbers, including dates and times. The number format you apply does not affect the actual cell value that Excel uses to perform calculations, it simply changes the appearance of values in the worksheet.

Excel uses a **General** format for numbers entered into a spreadsheet. The General format is the default number format and can be found in the Format Cells window on the **Number** tab. When the General format is used, the number you enter in a cell is formatted as per the example below:

You enter:	The General format displays:
12	12
12.10	12.1
12.12	12.12
12.120	12.12
12.1201	12.1201

5.1   Using the Format Menu or the Formatting Toolbar

Using the **Numbers** tab in the Format Cells window, you can apply any of the available number formats.

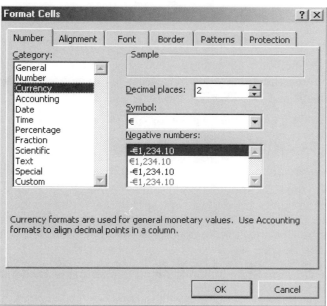

You can also use the available number formats on the Formatting toolbar.

Number Formatting
Buttons

5.1.1   Using Commas to Indicate Thousands (4.5.1.1)

You can nominate whether or not to include a comma for values above a thousand.

- Select the cells to be formatted.

- Choose **Cells** in the **Format** menu.

- Ensure the **Number** tab is selected.

- Click on the **Number** option in the **Category** list.

- Check or uncheck the **Use 1000 Separator (,)**.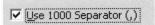

- Click **OK** to format the cells.

You can also use the **Comma Style** button on the Formatting toolbar. However, this button only turns the comma style on, not off. You would need to turn the commas off using the Format Cells window.

Comma Style Button

To include commas in your number formatting, proceed as follows:

- Open the spreadsheet named **Working with Number Formats**.

- Select the range **B4** to **H14**.

- Click on the **Comma Style** button on the Formatting toolbar.
  Notice that Excel inserts the comma symbol but also adds two decimal places to each number.

- Use the **Decrease Decimal** button on the Formatting toolbar to remove the decimal places.

5.1.2   Using the Currency Symbol (4.5.1.3)

You can format numbers to include your country's currency symbol. If you use the **Format Cells** window, you can also nominate how many decimal places are to be used and how you would like negative numbers to be displayed.

To include the currency symbol in your worksheet, proceed as follows:

- Select the range **B4** to **H19**.

- Click on the **Currency** button on the Formatting toolbar.
  Note: When using the **Currency** button to format numbers, Excel actually uses the *Accounting* number format which aligns the currency symbols to the left of the column. If you prefer the currency symbols to be directly in front of the number, use the *Currency* format option instead in the Format Cells window (please see below).

Currency Button

- Click back on the **Comma Style** button to return to a format without the currency symbol.

- Choose **Cells** in the **Format** menu. Ensure the **Number** tab is selected.

- Click on **Currency** in the **Category** box.

- Set the **Decimal places** to **0**.

- If necessary, change the setting in the **Symbol** box if it does not currently display your country's appropriate currency symbol.

- Select a setting from the **Negative numbers** box for how you would like negative numbers displayed.

- Click **OK** to format your worksheet.

5.1.3 Formatting Numbers as Percentages (4.5.1.4)

You can format numbers as a percentage using the Formatting toolbar or the Format Cells window.

To format numbers as percentages, proceed as follows:

- Click on **Sheet 2**.

- Select the range **C5** to **E5**.

- Click on the **Percent Style** button on the Formatting toolbar.

- Click the **Undo** button to reverse the formatting you have just applied.

- Ensure the range **C5** to **E5** is still selected.

- Choose **Cells** in the **Format** menu.

- Ensure the **Number** tab is selected.

- Click on **Percentage** in the **Category** box.

- Set the **Decimal places** to **0**.

- Click **OK** to format your worksheet.

- Save the spreadsheet file but do not close it.

Percent Style
Button

5.1.4 Formatting Cells to Display a Date Style (4.5.1.2)

Excel treats dates and times as numbers. The way that a time or date is displayed on a worksheet depends on the number format applied to the cell. When you type a date or time that Excel recognises, the cell's formatting changes from the *General* number format to a *built-in date or time format*. By default, dates and times are right aligned in a cell. If Excel does not recognise the date or time format, the date or time is entered as text and it is left aligned in the cell.

To format dates, proceed as follows:

- Click on **Sheet 1**.

- Click in **D1**.

- Type **01/01/03** and then press **Enter**.
  Excel will recognise the entry as a date and formats it accordingly. If you don't like the date format that Excel has used, proceed as follows to change the format of the date:

- Select **D1**.

- Choose **Cells** in the **Format** menu.

- Ensure the **Number** tab is selected.

- Click on **Date** in the **Category** box.

- Select an appropriate date format in the **Type** box.

- Click **OK** to format your worksheet.

- Save the spreadsheet file, closing it on completion.

Section 6   Multiple Spreadsheets and Worksheets

6.1   Handling Worksheets

When a **workbook** (a *spreadsheet*) is opened in Excel, it automatically contains *three* **worksheets**, although often only one of them is used.

A **tab** for each **sheet** is displayed at the bottom of the screen. The tabs can be used to move from one sheet to another. You can create extra worksheets, name them and even delete unwanted sheets.

Worksheet Tabs

To work with a spreadsheet file containing multiple worksheets proceed as follows:

- Open the file named **Working with Multiple Worksheets**.

- Click between the *two* available worksheets.

  Notice that this file has only two sheets – **Sheet1** and **Sheet2**. The first sheet contains **Book Orders** for **Class A**. The second sheet is currently empty.

Using multiple sheets within a workbook is a useful way of organising data relating to specific subjects, such as a school, student, etc. For example, imagine that you are looking after the book orders for three classes. You want to record the orders for each class and keep that information all in one spreadsheet file for ease of access. Each class will have its own worksheet within the file.

6.1.1   Inserting New Worksheets (4.3.1.1)

You can insert additional worksheets until you have a maximum of **256** (if you would ever need that many!).

In your sample spreadsheet, you need a total of four worksheets (one each for **Class A**, **B**, **C** and **D**). To insert two new worksheets, proceed as follows:

- Ensure **Sheet1** is active.

- Select **Worksheet** in the **Insert** menu.
  A new worksheet is added and the **Sheet3** tab appears at the bottom of the screen.
  Note that the new worksheet is added before the currently selected sheet, which in this case is **Sheet1**.

- Add one extra worksheet so that you have four in total.

6.1.2   Moving Worksheets within a Workbook (4.3.1.5)

Once you start to work with multiple worksheets you may wish to reorganise the order in which they appear at the bottom of the screen.

To move a worksheet within a workbook, proceed as follows:

- Click on the **tab** for **Sheet3** and then drag the mouse across the sheet names until the **black move triangle** symbol appears *after* **Sheet2**.

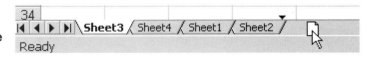

- Release the mouse to complete the move.

- Now move **Sheet4** so that it appears after **Sheet3**. The order of the sheets should now be **Sheet1**, **Sheet2**, **Sheet3** and then **Sheet4**, working from left to right.

6.1.3 Copying or Moving Data between Worksheets (4.2.5.1 and 4.2.5.3)

Using copy, cut and paste, you can copy or move information from one worksheet to another within the same workbook. This avoids having to recreate information all over again.

To create a similar worksheet for **Class B**, you have decided to use a copy of the information in **Class A's** worksheet and then modify it.

- Ensure you are working on **Sheet1**.

- Select the range **A1** to **D12**.

- Click on the **Copy** button on the Standard toolbar.

- Click on the **tab** for **Sheet2**.

- Click in **A1** on **Sheet2** and then click the **Paste** button.

- Press the **Esc** key to end the copy function.
  Notice how the original data from **Class A's** worksheet has been copied, along with the cell formatting but NOT the column widths or row heights. As you want **Class B's** worksheet to look exactly the same as **Class A's** (with the exception of the number of books required), you may wish to use a different method of duplicating the original data.

- Select all the data on **Sheet2** and delete it by pressing the **Delete** key.

- Save now.

- Click on the **tab** for **Sheet1**.

6.1.4 Duplicating Worksheets within a Spreadsheet (4.3.1.4)

In a similar way to that used for *moving* a worksheet within a workbook, you can also *duplicate* a worksheet.

To duplicate **Sheet1** which contains the **Class A** data, proceed as follows:

- Click on the **tab** for **Sheet1**, hold down the **Ctrl** key on the keyboard and then drag the mouse across the sheet names until the **black copy triangle** symbol appears *after* **Sheet1**. A **plus sign (+)** will appear in the worksheet icon at the bottom of the screen as you are copying.

- Release the mouse to complete the duplication.

  The duplicate sheet has the same tab name as the original sheet with a number **2** in brackets, e.g.: **Sheet1 (2)**. You can rename tabs to something more meaningful. See below for more information.

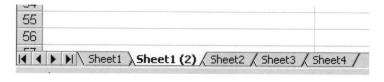

- Click on the **tab** for **Sheet1**, hold down the **Ctrl** key on the keyboard and then drag the mouse across the sheet names until the **black copy triangle** symbol appears *after* **Sheet1 (2)**. Release the mouse – you should now have another worksheet called **Sheet1 (3)**.

6.1.5 Renaming Worksheets (4.3.1.2)

Worksheet tabs can be renamed so that they more clearly identify the information they contain.

- Double click the tab for the sheet you wish to rename.
  The selected tab's name will be highlighted.

- Type the new name and then press **Enter**.

To rename the sheets within your workbook, proceed as follows:

- Double click the **tab** for **Sheet1** and type **Class A**.

- Press **Enter**.

- Rename **Sheet1 (2)** so that it is named **Class B**.

- Rename **Sheet1 (3)** so that it is named **Class C**.

- Save the spreadsheet but do not close it.

- Click on the tab for **Class B**. Select **C1** and change the cell contents so that they read **Class B**. Using the illustration, enter the data in the **No Required** column for **Class B**.

- Click on the tab for **Class C**. Select **C1** and change the cell contents so that they read **Class C**. Using the illustration, enter the data in the **No Required** column for **Class C**.

- Save the spreadsheet but do not close it.

C Class B	C Class C
No Required	No Required
2	6
7	5
4	6
6	3
11	4
2	2
11	1
3	3
14	10

6.1.6 Deleting Worksheets (4.3.1.3)

You can remove worksheets that are not required from a workbook at any time.

- Click on the **tab** for the sheet you wish to delete.

- Choose **Delete Sheet** in the **Edit** menu.
  A warning box will appear.

- Click **OK** to proceed with the deletion.

> ⚠ Microsoft Excel
>
> The selected sheet(s) will be permanently deleted.
>
> • To delete the selected sheets, click OK.
> • To cancel the deletion, click Cancel.
>
> [OK] [Cancel]

To delete the unused worksheets in your workbook, proceed as follows:

- Click on the tab for **Sheet2**.

- Choose **Delete Sheet** in the **Edit** menu.

- Click **OK** to proceed with the deletion.

- Now delete the two remaining empty sheets – **Sheet 3** and **Sheet 4**.
  You should now have three sheets – **Class A**, **Class B** and **Class C**.

- Save the spreadsheet under the new name of **Book Orders** but do not close it.

6.1.7 Duplicating a Worksheet between Open Spreadsheets (4.3.1.4)

In addition to duplicating a worksheet within the **same** workbook (spreadsheet), you can also duplicate a worksheet into another spreadsheet file.

Imagine that you have also been asked to look after the book orders for **Class D**. Their information has already been entered into a worksheet in a different spreadsheet file. To insert **Class D's** worksheet into your existing spreadsheet, proceed as follows:

- Ensure the **Book Orders** spreadsheet is still open.

- Now open the spreadsheet named **Class D – Book Orders**. This spreadsheet has only one sheet in it – **Sheet 1**. Ensure that this is now the **active** spreadsheet (that is the one that you are working in).

- Choose **Move or Copy Sheet** in the **Edit** menu.
  The Move or Copy window appears.

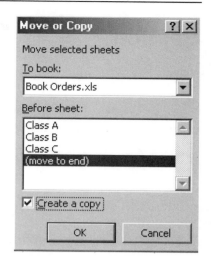

- Click on the arrow for the **To book** box and select **Book Orders.xls** (note that the spreadsheet file must be open for this procedure to work).

- In the **Before sheet** box select **(move to end)** to indicate where the sheet is to be placed.

- Click the **Create a copy** box so that Excel knows to **copy** the sheet and not to move it.

- Click **OK** to complete the procedure.

  You will now be working in the **Book Orders** spreadsheet. **Sheet1** containing **Class D's** data will appear as the last sheet in the workbook.

- Click on the icon in the taskbar for the **Class D – Book Orders** spreadsheet to make it active. Close the spreadsheet as it is of no further use. Save any changes, if you are prompted.

- Double click the tab name **Sheet1** in the **Book Orders** spreadsheet and type **Class D**. Press **Enter** to update the sheet name.

- Click back on the **Class A** tab.

- Save the spreadsheet file but do not close it.

6.1.8 Moving a Worksheet between Open Spreadsheets (4.3.1.5)

In addition to duplicating a worksheet between open spreadsheets, you can also **move** a worksheet from one open spreadsheet to another open one.

Imagine that you are no longer looking after book orders for **Class C**. You would like to move their information into another spreadsheet looked after by **Tutor 1**.

- Ensure you have the **Book Orders** spreadsheet still open.

- Now open the spreadsheet named **Tutor 1 - Book Orders**.
  Notice that **Tutor 1** looks after **Class E**, **Class F** and **Class H**.

- Click back into the original **Book Orders** spreadsheet to make it active.

- Click on the tab for **Class C**.

- Choose **Move or Copy Sheet** in the **Edit** menu.

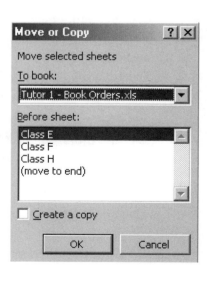

- Click on the arrow for the **To book** box and select **Tutor 1 - Book Orders.xls** (note that the spreadsheet file must be open for this procedure to work).

- In the **Before sheet** box select **Class E** to indicate that the sheet is to be placed at the beginning of the existing sheets.

- **DO NOT** click the **Create a copy** box as this will tell Excel to **copy** the sheet and not to move it.

- Click **OK** to complete the procedure.

  You will now be working in the **Tutor 1 - Book Orders** spreadsheet. The **Class C** sheet will appear as the first sheet in the workbook.

- Save this spreadsheet, closing it on completion.

- Ensure you are working in the **Book Orders** spreadsheet.
  Notice that **Class C** has been removed as it was *moved* and not *copied*.

- Save the spreadsheet file, closing it on completion.

Section 7   Preparing Output

7.1   Worksheet Set-up

If you want to print a copy of a worksheet you may wish to control how it appears on paper. For example, you may want to use certain margins, include page numbering or change the orientation of the paper.

7.1.1 Previewing a Worksheet (4.7.2.2)

It is recommended that you use the **Print Preview** option before printing a worksheet. This way you can see how it will print with the current page settings and know whether or not there are things you need to change.

To preview a worksheet you can:

Print Preview
Button

- Choose **Print Preview** in the **File** menu

Or

- Click the **Print Preview** button on the toolbar.

Exercise 7A

1   Open the spreadsheet named **Printing Worksheets**.

2   Click the **Print Preview** button.
     The **Print Preview** window opens. Notice how the worksheet is separated onto two pages.

3   Click **Next** to view page 2 and then **Previous** to return to page 1.

4   Click the **Zoom** button to *zoom in*. Click **Zoom** again to *zoom out*.

5   Click on the previewed page with the mouse (the mouse pointer will be in the shape of a **magnifying glass**).
     The page will zoom in.

6   Click on the page again (the mouse pointer will be in the usual mouse arrow shape).
     The page will zoom out.

7   Click the **Close** button to return to the worksheet.

7.1.2 Changing Worksheet Margins (4.7.1.1)

You can change the top, bottom, left and right margins of the page to suit the type of worksheet you wish to print.

To alter margin settings, you must access the **Page Setup** window using one of the two available methods:

- Click on the **Print Preview** button on the Standard toolbar and select **Setup**.

Or

- Choose **Page Setup** in the **File** Menu on the Menu bar.

To change the margin settings for the current worksheet, proceed as follows:

- Click on the **Setup** button on the **Preview** toolbar.

- Click on the **Margins** tab.

- Change the **top** margin to **3.5** (cms) using the direction buttons.

- Change the **left** and **right** margins to **0.9** (cms).

- Click **OK** to return to the **Preview** window.

    Notice how the margins have changed in size. Altering the left and right margins, however, has not been enough to enable the entire worksheet to fit onto one page. You may want to fit a worksheet onto one page rather than across a number of pages.

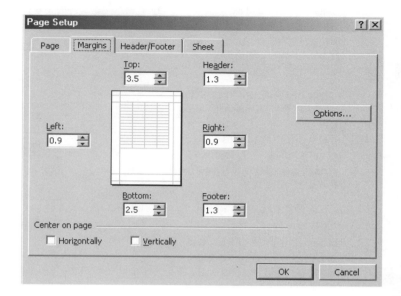

- Click the **Margins** button on the **Preview** toolbar.

    Notice how a *marker* for each margin appears and also for each column. You can use these markers to increase or decrease margins or columns by hand. The size you are setting is displayed in the bottom left of the screen.

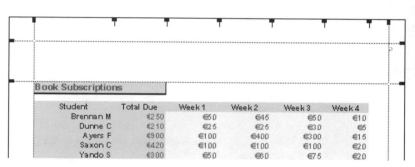

- Place the mouse pointer over the left margin until the **crosshair** pointer appears. Drag the crosshair with the mouse until the width of the left margin is a suitable size.

- Click the **Margins** button again to turn the margin markers off.

- Click the **Close** button to return to your worksheet.

7.1.3 Changing the Page Settings (4.7.1.2 and 4.7.1.3)

Changing the margins may not enable you to fit the current worksheet on one page. There are a few other options available that can help you. *Scaling* or *fitting* the worksheet to one page, specifying a number of pages (in the case of a much larger worksheet), or altering the page *orientation* are the main options.

To fit the current worksheet to one page:

- Click on the **Print Preview** button to access the **Preview** window.

- Click on the **Setup** button on the **Preview** toolbar.

- Click on the **Page** tab in the **Page Setup** window (see next page).

- Click the **Fit to** button in the **Scaling** section.

- Ensure the **Fit to** settings are **1** page(s) wide by **1** tall.

- Click **OK** to return to the **Preview** window to view the changes.

Notice that Excel has *condensed* the worksheet to fit it onto one page. Excel does this by scaling down all the dimensions of the worksheet. You can change this percentage scaling manually, if you wish, to condense the worksheet further or to *expand it*.

- Click on the **Setup** button again and ensure the **Page** tab is selected so that we can continue adjusting the scaling.

- Click the **Adjust to** button and set the **% normal size** back to **100** – this returns the worksheet to its original size. Any number ABOVE 100 would enlarge the worksheet.

- Click **OK** to return to the **Preview** window.

  Notice that the worksheet is back to its original size and still split across two pages. Perhaps now you should try altering the page orientation for your printed worksheet.

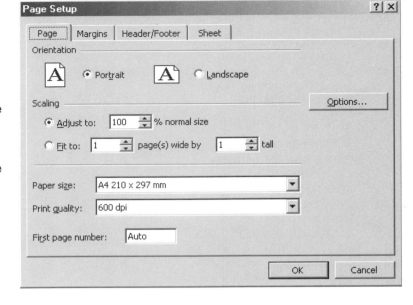

- Click on the **Setup** button and ensure the **Page** tab is selected.

- Click on the **Landscape** option in the **Orientation** section. Landscape is used when you want to print width-wise across the page.

- Click **OK** to preview the changes.

  Notice that the worksheet now fits onto one page but there is a little bit more blank space on the right than perhaps you want. You could solve this by:

  – centring the worksheet horizontally on the page,

  – by changing the left and right margins,

  – or by *expanding* the scaling of the worksheet.

- Click the **Setup** button and then click on the **Margins** tab.

- Tick **Centre horizontally** in the **Centre on page** section.

- Click **OK** to view the changes in the **Preview** window.

- Click the **Setup** button again and click on the **Page** tab.

- Set the **Adjust to** box to **115 % normal size**.

- Click **OK** to preview the changes.

NOTE

In addition to the suggestions above, you can also change the paper size although **A4** paper is often the standard used by most printers. You can change the **Paper size** on the **Page** tab of the **Page Setup** window.

7.1.4 Using Headers and Footers (4.7.1.4 and 4.7.1.5)

To help the reader identify with the contents of a printed worksheet, you can include extra information in the **header** and **footer** areas of the page. You can, for example, include a detailed heading, page numbering, a date and/or time, the file name or worksheet name and other relevant details.

The **Page Setup** window contains a **Header/Footer** tab where you can specify the settings you wish to use for your headers and footers. Excel provides some *predefined* headers and footers for you to use or you can design your own **custom** headers and footers.

To add a *predefined* header and footer to your printed worksheet, proceed as follows:

- Click on the **Setup** button in the **Preview** window.

- Click on the **Header/Footer** tab in the **Page Setup** window.

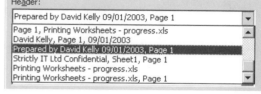

- Under the **Header** section, click on the arrow to display the available list of predefined headers.

- Select the predefined header that starts with **"Prepared by"**. In the header box above, a sample of the predefined header text will be displayed.

- Under the **Footer** section, click on the arrow to display the available list of predefined footers.

- Select the **predefined footer** that will display the file name **ONLY** (the file name should be **Printing Worksheets.xls**).

- Click **OK** to view the header and footer information in the **Preview** window.

7.1.5 Creating Custom Headers and Footers (4.7.1.5)

In addition to the predefined headers and footers provided by Excel, you can also create your own *custom* headers or footers. By clicking the **Custom Header** or **Custom Footer** buttons on the **Header/Footer** tab, you can access a window where you can customise your header or footer to include special **codes** or any of your own text that you wish to enter. The custom header or footer area is separated into three sections. Information in the **Left section** appears on the left margin, in the centre of the page for the **Centre section** and on the right margin for the **Right section**.

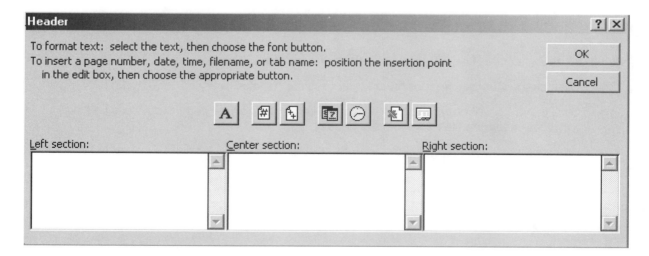

The buttons in the Header or Footer window can be used to insert field codes or to format text or field codes within each of the sections.

Button	Description
A	The **Font** button. Use this button to format selected text or field codes with different font attributes.
🔲	The **Page Number** button. Inserts the field code **&[Page]** and inserts the current page number when printing.
🔲	The **Total Pages** button. Inserts the field code **&[Pages]** and inserts the total number of pages in the printout.
🔲	The **Date** button. Inserts the field code **&[Date]** and inserts the current date into the printout.
🔲	The **Time** button. Inserts the field code **&[Time]** and inserts the current time into the printout.
🔲	The **File name** button. Inserts the field code **&[File]** and inserts the spreadsheet file name.
🔲	The **Tab name** button. Inserts the field code **&[Tab]** and inserts the sheet name for the worksheet you are printing. If you have not renamed the tab, this field will display **Sheet1**, **Sheet2**, etc.

Rather than using the predefined headers, to create your own proceed as follows:

Step 1 – Turning off the predefined header.

- Click on the **Setup** button in the **Preview** window.

- Click on the **Header/Footer** tab in the **Page Setup** window.

- Under the **Header** section, click on the arrow to display the available list of predefined headers.

- Select **(none)** to turn off the predefined header.

Step 2 – Adding a code that will insert the file name on the left margin of the header.

- Click on the **Custom Header** button to access the **Header** window.

- Click in the **Left section** and then click the **Filename** button to add the field code **&[File]**, which will insert the file name into the header.

- Highlight the field code and click the **Font** button. Select **Bold** from the **Font style** list and then click **OK**.

Step 3 – Adding a code that will insert the page number in the centre of the header and the current date on the right margin of the header.

- Click in the **Centre section** and type the word **Page** followed by a space. Click the **Page Number** button to insert the code **&[Page]**.

- Click in the **Right section** and click the **Date** button to insert the field **&[Date]**.

- Highlight the field code and click the **Font** button. Select **Bold** from the **Font style** list and then click **OK**.

Your custom header should look like the example below:

- Click **OK** to return to the **Header/Footer** tab.
  Now you can create a custom footer.

Step 4 – Turning off the predefined footer.

- Under the **Footer** section, click on the arrow to display the available list of predefined footers.

- Select **(none)** to turn off the predefined footer.

- Click on the **Custom Footer** button to access the **Footer** window.

Step 5 – Adding text on the left margin of the footer.

- Click in the **Left section** and then type **ECDL Training**.

- Highlight the text and click the **Font** button. Select **Bold** from the **Font style** list and then click **OK**.

Step 6 – Adding text on the right margin of the footer.

- Click in the **Right section** and type **Syllabus 4**.

- Highlight the text code and click the **Font** button. Select **Bold** from the **Font style** list and then click **OK**.

- Your custom footer should look like the example below:

- Click **OK** to return to the **Header/Footer** tab.

- Click **OK** again to accept the changes in the **Page Setup** window and to preview your worksheet.

- Close the Preview window and return to your spreadsheet.

- Save and close the spreadsheet.

7.2 Preparation

Before you send a worksheet to print there are a few additional settings you may wish to make.

- To practise these topics, open the spreadsheet named **Printing Wide Report**.

- Click the **Print Preview** button.

- Use the **Next** and **Previous** buttons on the Preview toolbar to view the different pages of the report.

7.2.1 Gridlines and Row/Columns Headings (4.7.2.3)

Using the **Sheet** tab in the **Page Setup** window, you can control whether or not you want to print **gridlines** on the printed page or whether you wish to include the row and column headings as well.

To add gridlines and row/column headings to your printed worksheet, proceed as follows:

- Click on the **Setup** button to return to the **Page Setup** window.

- Click on the **Sheet** tab.

- Tick the **Gridlines** box in the **Print** section to select it.

- Tick the **Row and column headings** box to select it. This option will print the column letters and row numbers against the columns and rows in your printout.

- Click **OK** to preview your worksheet.

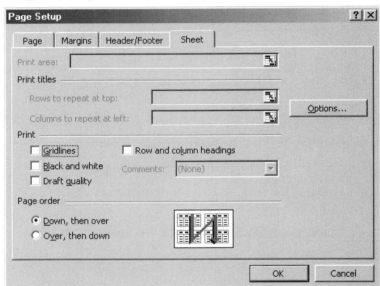

7.2.2 Repeating Title Rows/Columns on Every Page (4.7.2.4)

If you are working with information that spreads across more than one page, you may find that it is useful for certain columns or rows from the first page to be repeated on all of the subsequent pages.

For example, in the current worksheet when you print or preview the information, the student names appear on page 1 but not on subsequent pages. The same is true of the column headings, **Week1**, **Week2**, etc. They are not repeated on every page. This can make the information difficult to read when printed onto paper.

To solve this problem, you can repeat information in specific columns and rows so that it appears on **all** pages of the printout and not just the first. This is known as *repeating title rows and columns*. You can repeat rows and columns in the **Print titles** section of the **Sheet** tab in the **Page Setup** window.

NOTE

> You can ONLY use the **Print titles** section if you access the **Page Setup** window by choosing **Page Setup** from the **File** menu. You cannot use **Print titles** from the **Setup** button on the **Preview** window.

To repeat students' names on each page of a printout, proceed as follows:

- Click the **Close** button to leave the Print Preview window.

- Choose **Page Setup** in the **File** menu.

- Click on the **Sheet** tab.

- Click on the **Selector box** to the right of the **Columns to repeat at left** box so that you can access the worksheet.

- Click and drag anywhere from **Column A to C** to select the **ID Number** column and the **Last Name** and **First Name** columns.

- Press **Enter** to return to the Sheet tab.
  Now let's select the rows containing the week numbers so that they will be repeated at the top of every page.

- Click on the **Selector box** to the right of the **Rows to repeat at top** box so that you can access the worksheet.

- Click and drag anywhere from **Row 1 to 3** to select the headings.

- Press **Enter** to return to the Sheet tab.

- Click **Print Preview** to access the **Preview** window.

- Use the **Next** and **Previous** buttons on the toolbar to view each page. Notice that the rows and columns we specified are repeated on every page.

- Click on the **Setup** button in the **Preview** window.
  Notice that the **Print titles** boxes are greyed out and cannot be used.
  Remember, they can only be accessed through the **Page Setup** option in the **File** menu.

- Click **OK** to exit the **Page Setup** window and then click **Close** to return to the worksheet.

7.2.3 Preparing to Print (4.7.2.1)

Before you finally send a worksheet to print, it is highly recommended that you check the spreadsheet calculations and the surrounding text.

Once you are happy that you have checked the validity of the worksheet data and you have defined the way in which the worksheet will print (using the Page Setup options previously discussed), the information is finally ready to be sent to the printer.

To print your worksheet, proceed as follows:

- Click **Save** to save the current spreadsheet.
  It is always a good idea to save your spreadsheet just before you print it just in case you have any problems with the printing process.

- Choose **Print** from the **File** menu.

- To print the current worksheet, ensure **Active sheet(s)** is clicked in the **Print what** section.
  If you want to print more than one copy of the current

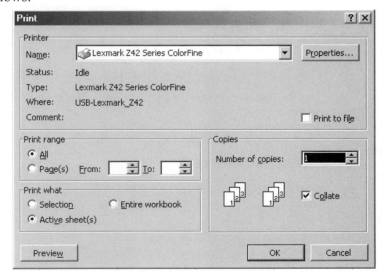

worksheet, you can increase the **Number of copies** in the **Copies** box.

To print every page of a worksheet if it spans across more than one page, click **All**. Alternatively, you can specify a **From** and **To** page number in the **Page(s)** box.

- If you are attached to a printer, click **OK** to start printing. If, however, you are not attached to a printer, click **Print to file** first and then click **OK**. You will be asked to name the file to which you are printing. Type **Printing Wide Reports** and then click **OK**. This method does not physically print the file, it actually creates a special output file that could be printed at a later stage. These files have the file extension **.PRN**.

NOTE

> If you print a worksheet or range within a worksheet once, thereafter the **Print** button on the toolbar will automatically repeat the last printout without taking you into the **Print** window. If you wish to redefine any of the settings in the **Print** window you **MUST** choose **Print** in the **File** menu before printing, rather than using the **Print** button.

7.2.4 Printing a Cell Range (4.7.3.1)

There may be times when you want to print only a selected area of the worksheet and not the entire sheet.

To print a range within your worksheet:

- Select **A1** to **G23** so that only a portion of the worksheet is selected.
- Choose **Print** in the **File** menu on the Menu bar to access the **Print** window.
- Choose **Selection** in the **Print what** box.
- Click **OK** to start printing.
- Click back on **A1** to unselect the range.
- Save the spreadsheet and then close it.

7.2.5 Printing an Entire Workbook (4.7.3.1)

If a workbook contains more than one worksheet, you can print all of the worksheets within the workbook in one easy step.

To print the contents of three worksheets in one spreadsheet file:

- Open the spreadsheet named **Printing Multiple Sheets**.
- Choose **Print** in the **File** menu to access the **Print** window.
- Select **Entire workbook** in the **Print what** box.
- Click **Preview** to view the results rather than printing onto paper.
- Click the **Next** and **Previous** buttons on the toolbar in the **Preview** window to move between pages.
- Click **Close** to return to the worksheet.
- Click back on **Sheet1**.
- Save the spreadsheet and then close it.

Section 8   Charts and Graphs

8.1   Using Charts and Graphs

A **chart** (also known as a **graph**) can be used to provide a *graphical* representation of the data in a worksheet. Excel offers an extensive range of different chart types to choose from so that you can quickly and easily create charts for any of your worksheet data.

8.1.1 Creating Charts (4.6.1.1)

Excel can create charts and graphs in three different ways:

- On the **worksheet** currently being used.

- In a **separate sheet** in the workbook being used.

- In a **separate workbook**.

Chart Wizard
Button

We shall use our **book subscription** data again to create a simple graph.

Step 1 – Selecting the data to use for the chart.

- Open the **Working with Charts** file.

- Ensure you are on the **Book Subscriptions** worksheet.

    You have decided to create the chart so that it shows the amounts paid by each student for the four weeks. You do NOT want to include the total amount that each of them owes in the finished chart.

- Select the cells **A3** to **A7** – the cells containing the student names.

- Hold down the **Ctrl** key while selecting cells **C3** to **F7** (Week1 to Week4).

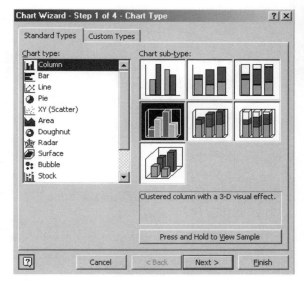

Step 2 – Using the Chart Wizard to create a chart.

- With the two sets of cells selected, click the **Chart Wizard** button on the toolbar.

- The Chart Wizard displays the first of four windows that will lead you through the process of creating the graph.

- Select **Column** as the **Chart type** if it is not already selected.

- Select the **fourth** box in the **Chart sub-type** (this chart sub-type is known as *Clustered column with a 3-D visual effect*).

- Click **Next** to go on to the next step.

Chart Types

In the **Step 1** window above, **Column** is selected in the **Chart type** panel on the left. Different kinds of column charts are displayed in the panel on the right. Click on a column type to see a description underneath.

Click on other chart types in the **Chart type** panel to see them illustrated. Popular chart types are **bar** charts, **pie** charts and **line** charts. These are illustrated in the exercises that follow.

MODULE 4

The **Step 2** window shows how the final graph would be displayed at this stage. Notice that the **category axis** at the bottom of the chart sample shows the week numbers and the **legend**, on the right, shows the student names.

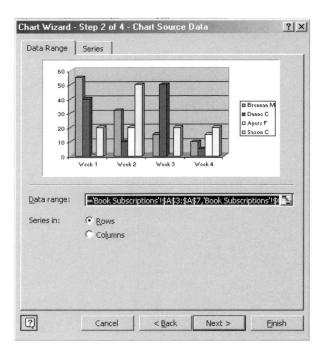

Step 3 – Customising the chart.

- Choose **Columns** in the **Series in** box so that the student names appear on the **category axis**.

- Click **Next** to go on to **Step 3**.

- In the **Step 3** window, we will add a **Chart title** and **labels** for the **axes**.

- Click in the **Chart title** box. Type **Subscription Payments**.

- Type **Class A** in the **Category (X) axis** box.

- Type **Euro** in the **Value (Z) axis** box. Note: the **Z axis** is used to label values in a **3-D** chart and the **Y axis** is used in a **2-D** chart.

- Click on the **Legend** tab and change the **Placement** of the box to **Bottom**.

- Click **Next** to go to the final step, **Chart Location**.

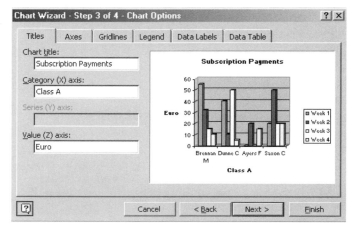

Step 4 – Placing the chart on a Chart sheet within the workbook.

- Click **As new sheet** so that your chart appears on a separate sheet, known as **Chart1**.

- Click **Finish**.

  The chart appears on its own sheet in your workbook.

- Double click the sheet name **Chart1** and rename the sheet **Book Payments Chart**. Remember to press **Enter** after you have typed the name.

8.1.2 Modifying Charts

When you are working with a chart, for example when working in a chart sheet, Excel slightly changes the Menu bar and some of the toolbar buttons. The Menu bar includes a **Chart** option and most of the other menu options are related to working with the chart rather than the worksheet data.

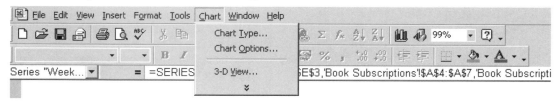

You can use the Menu bar and toolbar buttons to modify your chart, however, there is a very easy way to make modifications to any part of a chart. Simply by double clicking the element of the chart you want to change, you will open a window providing all of the options that can be applied to that element.

8.1.3 Changing the Background Colour in a Chart (4.6.1.3)

By default, the standard background colour for a chart is grey. To change the background colour for your chart, proceed as follows:

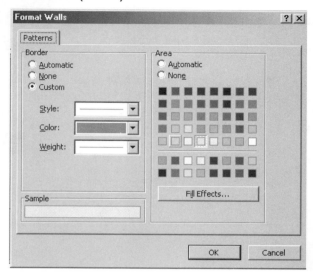

- Hover your mouse over the *grey* background on your chart.

  You will see a small yellow box appear containing the word **Walls**. This is identifying the chart element you will modify if you are to double click.

- Double click on the **Walls** area and the **Format Walls** window appears.

- In the **Area** section, select a **pale green** shade.

- Click **OK** to return to your chart.

8.1.4 Changing the Colour of Chart Series (4.6.1.4)

You can format the **series** in a chart such as the columns, bars, lines, pie slices and so on. If you have created a different type of chart, such as a bar, line or pie chart, you can format the lines, bars or pie slices in the same way you format a column.

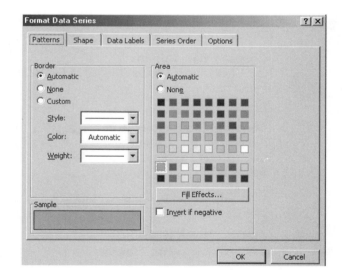

- Hover your mouse over the first column in your chart.

  You will see a small yellow box appear showing that the column refers to the **Series** Week 1. This is identifying the chart element you will modify if you are to double click.

- Double click on the first column and the **Format Data Series** window appears.

- In the **Area** section, select a **dark green** shade.

- Click **OK** to return to your chart.

  Now, double click on the next column and format the **Series** for Week 2 with another shade of green. Continue with the remaining two columns so that you have recoloured all of the columns in your chart.

8.1.5 Changing the Chart Type (4.6.1.5)

When you create a chart the first step in the Chart Wizard asks you to choose the **type** of chart you wish to display. You can choose from a variety of different chart types, such as **column**, **bar**, **line**, **pie**, etc. Once you have created your chosen chart, you can, if you so wish, change the format to a different type of chart again.

To change your column chart to a line chart, proceed as follows:

- Select the chart you want to edit by clicking on the chart sheet.

- Choose **Chart Type** in the **Chart** menu.

- Select **Line** for the **Chart type** and then select the **first** box in the **Chart sub-type** section.

  Now let's change the chart to a bar chart.

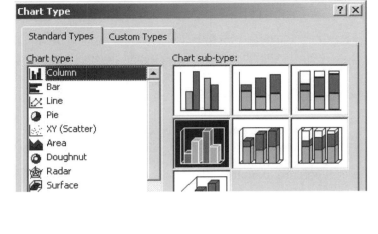

- Click **Cancel**.

- Choose **Chart Type** in the **Chart** menu.

- Select **Bar** for the **Chart type** and then select the **first** box in the **Chart sub-type** section.

  Now let's change the chart back to a 3D column chart.

- Choose **Chart Type** in the **Chart** menu.

- Select **Column** for the **Chart type** and then select the **fourth** box in the **Chart sub-type** section.

- Click **OK**.

8.1.6 Deleting Titles and Labels from a Chart (4.6.1.2)

When you create a chart using the **Chart Wizard**, step 3 of the process is where you can assign titles and labels to your chart. Once the chart has been finished, you can also add or remove titles and labels for the existing chart.

- Select the chart you want to edit by clicking on the chart sheet.

- Choose **Chart Options** in the **Chart** menu on the menu bar.

- Highlight the title **Subscription Payments** in the **Chart title** box and press **Delete** to remove the contents.

- Click **OK** to return to the chart.

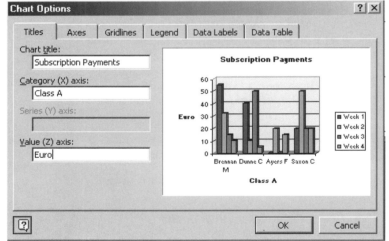

- Click the **Undo** button on the toolbar to reinsert the title.

  In addition to using the **Chart Options** window for inserting or deleting titles/labels, you can also delete directly within the chart.

- Click on the label **Euro** on the **Z axis**. A selection box will appear around it.

- Press **Delete** to remove the label.

- Click **Undo** to reinsert the label.

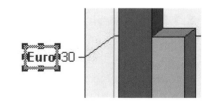

8.1.7   Creating a Pie Chart (4.6.1.1)

Pie charts can be created in just the same way as any of the other chart types available within Excel.

To create a pie chart that shows the total amount due for each student, proceed as follows:

Step 1 – Selecting the data for the pie chart.

- Click on the **Book Subscriptions** sheet.

- Select the cells **A3** to **B7** – this range includes the student names' and their corresponding total amounts.

- Click on the **Chart Wizard** button.

- Select **Pie** in the **Chart type** box and then select the second box in the **Chart sub-type** to create a **3-D** pie.

- Click **Next** to proceed to step 2.

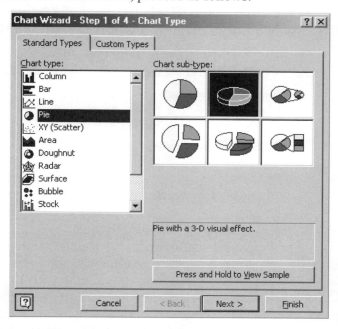

Step 2 – Customising the pie chart.

- As there is nothing to change in step 2, click **Next** again to proceed to step 3.

  The **Chart title** has already been inserted for you as you included the heading in the cell selection at the start.

- Edit the title so that it reads **Total Payments Due**.

- Click on the **Data Labels** tab. Click the **Show percent** option in the **Data labels** section.

- Now click **Show label and percent**.

- Click on the **Legend** tab.

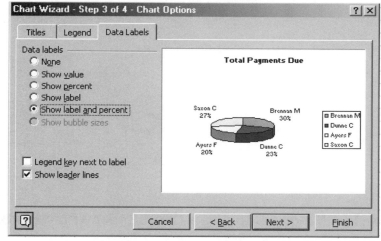

- Click in the **Show legend** box to uncheck it. The legend is not needed as the labels are shown around the outside of the pie slices.

- Click **Next** to proceed to step 4.

Step 3 – Adding the chart to a worksheet.

This time, instead of creating the chart in a separate sheet, we will place it on the original worksheet.

- Ensure **As object in** is selected in the **Chart Wizard** box. Ensure the **Book Subscriptions** sheet appears in the box to the right of the option.

- Click **Finish** to create the chart.

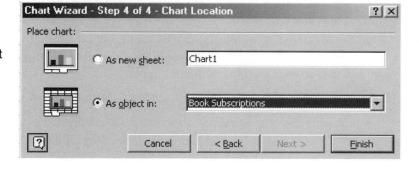

A chart **object** will appear on the worksheet.

- To move the chart, simply select it and drag it so it appears **below** the main data in the **Book Subscriptions** sheet.

8.1.8   Moving/Copying a Chart Object within the Same Workbook (4.6.1.6)

If you have created a chart object that appears on a worksheet, you can move it or copy it to other locations on the same sheet using the following sequences.

- Click on the chart object to select it.

- Move the chart so that it appears below the worksheet data.

- Hold down the **Ctrl** key and drag the chart object across to the right and then release the mouse button. A duplicate of the original chart will appear.

  If you so wished, you could change the chart type for either of the two pie charts but for now we will leave them both the same.

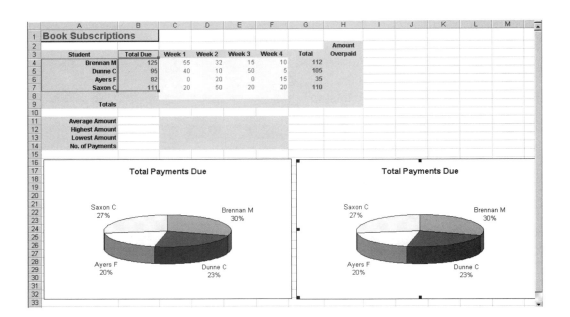

8.1.9   Moving/Copying a Chart Sheet within the Same Workbook (4.6.1.6)

If you have created a chart that is displayed in a separate **sheet**, you can move the chart sheet tab to another location in the workbook. For example, your chart sheet may be displayed on the third tab in a workbook and you would prefer that it appeared in the first tab position instead.

To move the **Book Payments Chart** sheet so that it appears **after** the **Book Subscriptions** worksheet tab:

- Click on the **Book Payments Chart** tab and drag across so that the **Move triangle** appears after the **Book Subscriptions** sheet. Release the mouse button to complete the move.

  Now let's copy the chart to another separate sheet and change the duplicate chart to a bar chart.

- Click on the **Book Payments Chart** tab and hold down the **Ctrl** button. Drag across with the mouse so that the **Copy triangle** appears after the **Book Payments Chart** sheet. Release the mouse button to complete the copy.

Here we will change the chart type for the new chart sheet.

- Double click the tab **Book Payments Chart (2)** and type **Book Payments Bar Chart**. Remember to press **Enter** to finish the renaming process.

- Ensure you are working on the **Book Payments Bar Chart** sheet.

- Choose **Chart type** in the **Chart** menu.

- Select **Bar** for the **Chart type** and then select the **first** box in the **Chart sub-type** section.

- Click **OK** to change the chart.

- Save the current workbook but do not close it.

8.1.10 Moving/Copying a Chart Sheet to a Different Workbook (4.6.1.6)

In addition to moving or copying a chart sheet within the same workbook, you can also move/copy the sheet to another workbook. The chart is still **linked** to the original workbook so that if the data in the sheet is changed, the chart will also update the next time it is accessed.

To copy the **Book Payments Chart** sheet to another workbook:

- Ensure you are working with the workbook named **Working with Charts**.

- Open the workbook named **Class A Book Subscription Charts**.

- Switch back to the **Working with Charts** spreadsheet.

- Click on the **Book Payments Chart** tab to display the **column chart**.

- Choose **Move or Copy Sheet** in the **Edit** menu.

- In the **To book** box select the **Class A Book Subscription Charts.xls** file.

- In the **Book sheet** box select **(move to end)**.

- Check the **Create a copy** box so that you copy the sheet rather than move it.

- Click **OK** to complete the copy.

  The **Book Payments Chart** tab should now appear in the **Class A** spreadsheet.

- Double click the tab **Book Payments** and type **Class A - Column Chart**. Remember to press **Enter** to finish the renaming process.

- Save the spreadsheet and return to the **Working with Charts** spreadsheet.

8.1.11 Resizing and Deleting Chart Objects (4.6.1.7)

To resize a chart, do the following:

- Click on the chart to select it. **Handles** appear around it.

- Hold down the **Shift** key and drag one of the corner handles to change the size.

  (Holding down the Shift key keeps the proportions correct).

To delete a chart:

- Click on the chart object to select it.

- Press the **Delete** key.

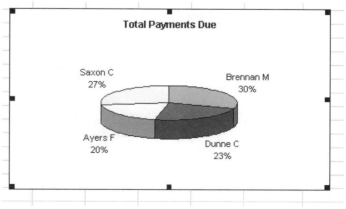

To delete the duplicate chart object on the **Book Subscriptions** sheet, proceed as follows:

- Click on the **Book Subscriptions** tab.

- Click on duplicate copy of the pie chart (that is the one on the right-hand side) and then press the **Delete** key.

To resize the pie chart object, proceed as follows:

- Hold down the **Shift** key and drag one of the corner handles to change the size.

8.1.12 Deleting a Chart Sheet (4.6.1.7)

You can delete a chart sheet in the same way that you can delete a worksheet within a workbook.

To delete the **Book Payments Bar Chart** sheet, proceed as follows:

- Click on the **Book Payments Bar Chart** tab.

- Choose **Delete Sheet** in the **Edit** menu.

- Click **OK** to confirm the deletion.

- Save the spreadsheet but do not close it.

8.1.13 Printing Charts (4.7.3.1)

Printing charts is much like printing worksheets. The worksheet data and chart may be printed together. The chart may also be printed on its own.

To preview and print the worksheet and chart data together, proceed as follows:

- Click on the **Book Subscriptions** tab.

- Click outside the chart to deselect it if you want to print both spreadsheet and chart.

- Click the **Print Preview** button on the toolbar.

- You could change the **setup** for the page, if you so wish, using the **Setup** button on the toolbar.

- Click the **Print** button to print the spreadsheet.

To print the chart sheet, proceed as follows:

- Click on the **Book Payments Chart** tab.

- Click the **Print Preview** button on the toolbar.

- Click **Print** to print the chart.
  You could change the **setup** for the page, if you so wish, using the **Setup** button on the toolbar.

- Save the workbook, closing it on completion.

Module 5

Database

5

Module 5

Database

MODULE 5

MODULE 5

Introduction

Syllabus Goals for Module 5

Database requires the candidate to understand the basic concepts of databases and demonstrate the ability to use a database on a personal computer. The module is divided in two sections: the first section tests the candidate's ability to design and plan a simple database using a standard database package, while the second section requires the candidate to demonstrate that he or she can retrieve information from an existing database by using the query, select and sort tools available in the database. The candidate shall also be able to create and modify reports.

This module begins with an explanation of a number of important concepts associated with Access. Use this section to support your understanding as you work through the various tasks.

A Computer Database

Data is **information**. A database is an information store. A computer database is an electronic store of information. A computerised database application such as **Access** is essentially the same as a filing cabinet or card index but the data is stored electronically rather than on pieces of paper.

This a blank database called Golf Club

Card Index for Golf Club

There are major advantages in a computerised filing system over a manual system. The information still has to be gathered and entered into the computer but the entry of some items can be automated. In addition, the computer has the ability to search for and present the information with great speed.

For example, a user can use the computer to sort all the orders sent in May or June, or both, at the touch of a button. The information is listed instantly and can then be printed out, if necessary. The librarian can find all the members whose name begin with 'McN' and print out a full list, if required.

Compared to a paper-based system, an electronic database takes up no physical space. Large numbers of records that would require hundreds of thousands of catalogue cards will fit easily on a computer's hard disk.

The computer may even be used to display the information in the database in other documents such as letters, lists and reports. There is enormous flexibility with the management and presentation of information in a database that is quite simply beyond traditional filing systems.

It will help to be familiar with some commonly used terms.

Database   This is a storage area for tables, forms, queries and reports that contain data that is organised in various ways.

Field   In a computer database, a field is an area where a single item of information, such as a membership number, a last name and so on may be stored.

Membership Number	Last Name	First Name
1	Janis	Steve
2	Relman	Cathy
3	Nelson	Michael
4	Gonzales	Fred

This is a Field called Membership Number

Record   One or more fields (e.g. membership number, last name, first name, street address and town) are stored in a record, corresponding to one card in a card index. All the information pertaining to a single member of a club would comprise a record.

A Single Record →

Membership Number	Last Name	First Name	Street Address	Town
1	Janis	Steve	9 Bachelors Walk	Dundalk
2	Relman	Cathy	92 Arlen Road	Dundalk
3	Nelson	Michael	229 Drogheda Rise	Dundalk

File   All the records for a particular table are stored in a database file.

Folder   On a computer, different files are stored in separate folders, corresponding to individual suspension folders in the drawers of a filing cabinet.

Table   A database table holds the database records. Once the table structure has been completed, its contents can be used fully or partially to construct the other objects in the database such as forms, queries, reports and so on. A single database may contain one or several related tables.

Form   This database object can be based on a table you created or on a query that has been created. Essentially, it presents the information you require in a more readable form than a table.

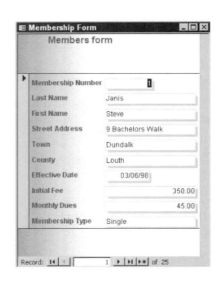

Query   A query is an object that can be based on data in the table or on the data in another query. Typically, a query selects out information and presents a modified table containing only the information you require for a particular purpose.

MODULE 5

Report   A report is a database object that can be based on data in either a table or data in a created query. It is a summary of information that can be stored or printed in a particular manner.

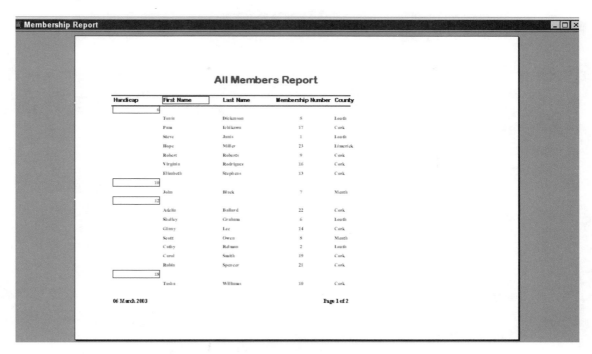

This is a Preview of a Completed Report.

Setting up a Database

The database program you will use on this course is **Microsoft Access**. You will start with an empty database, give it a name and save it in a folder on the hard disk.

Before you can start entering information, you will need to set up a table with fields for each category of information.

Access can sort the information in the database in many different ways. To help it do this, it must know what kind of information is stored in each field, i.e. whether it is text, numbers, dates and so on. This is done with the click of a button when you are setting up the table.

Names and Addresses

To store people's names in the database, you may need up to three fields, typically one each for the title, the first name and the last name.

With different fields, the database can separate the names by title, such as Mr, Mrs, Ms, Dr and so on. Lists of people with similar names can be made. You may even use this data to prepare address labels for envelopes.

It is also a good idea to divide addresses into different fields, such as street address, town, county and perhaps country. In this way, you will then be able to search for information by town, county or street address. You can also use the town name in the body of a letter or document prepared for multiple recipients.

Using the Database

Once the database has been set up and information entered, it can then be put to work. The data can be sorted in a variety of ways to interpret the information. Access can use the information in the database documents for numerous purposes, many of which you will discover as you progress through this course. Access can also perform calculations such as adding numbers, calculating averages and much more.

Section 1   Using the Application

1.1   Database Concepts (5.1.1.1)

A database is a file that stores objects such as tables, forms, queries and reports. The tables are the 'primary structure' from which the fields can be used to create tables, forms and reports. They can also be interrogated using queries.

Examples of a database are:

- the telephone directory;
- a membership list of a golf club;
- a list of cars for sale in a garage;
- a list of an electorate; or
- a list of suppliers in a supermarket stock list.

1.1.1 How a Database is Organised (5.1.1.2)

A database is a file like any other document file. This file is made up of a group of **tables**. These tables contain a number of **records,** which are in turn made up of **fields**.

In a typical database of people who are members of a golf club, a person's first name would be a single field and their surname would be another. The other related information such as their address, telephone number and so on in other fields altogether make up a single person's record.

Many different types of data can be stored in a database. **Access** allows you to specify the type of data stored in a table field. Only a single data type, such as numeric, date, time and so on, can be selected for each field created. You must specify the correct data type when creating the field.

1.1.2 Understanding the Primary Key (5.1.1.3)

A primary key is a special function that Access has to assign a unique identification to each record in a database. Primary keys can be assigned to a particular field, such as a membership number. Alternatively, Access can generate a special field and automatically assign unique identification numbers to each record.

Primary Key Button

1.1.3 Relating Tables in a Database (5.1.1.5)

Access is a very powerful application that allows you to create multiple tables within a single database.

This multiple tables facility is very useful as you don't need separate database files for different departments with different requirements. Sales, accounts or personnel may access the same database but have related tables that contain only the information they are interested in. Separate tables within a database can be linked together – or *related* – to create a **relational database**. This insures that changes at any level in the database are updated in the other related tables.

1.1.4 Setting Rules to Ensure Relationships between Tables are Valid (5.1.1.6)

When working with tables that are related, Access uses a set of rules to ensure that the relationships between records in different tables of a database are maintained and that you don't accidentally alter or remove data inappropriately. This is referred to as **referential integrity** for a relationship. You ensure the relationships between fields and data across different tables in a database are maintained.

1.2 First Steps with Databases

1.2.1 Opening and Closing a Database (5.1.2.1 and 5.1.2.2)

Access can be opened from the **Start menu** on your desktop by selecting **Programs Microsoft Access** or by double clicking the program shortcut icon if it appears on the desktop of your computer.

Shortcut to Access

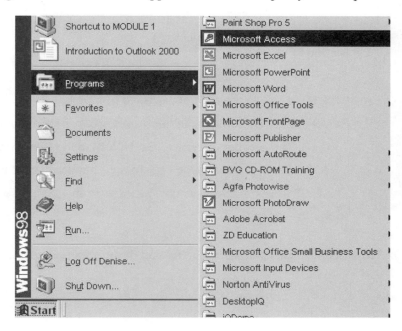

When the application program window opens, you will be presented with a window that will allow you various choices, as follows.

1.2.1.1 Blank Access Database

This function allows you create a new database from scratch.

1.2.1.2 Access Database Wizards, Pages and Projects

With this choice, you generate the required tables, forms and reports for the Microsoft Access database you choose.

1.2.1.3 Open an Existing File

Sometimes you may need to open a database that has already been created in order to access, add or delete information.

When the Access window appears follow these steps:

- Click the **Open an existing file** option in the window.
  If the file is not listed in the window beneath this area, then double click the **More Files...** option.
  An Open window will appear. Here you can locate the file you want to open.

- Select the file you want.

- Click the **Open** button.
  The file now opens up on your screen.

1.2.2 Creating and Saving a Database (5.1.2.3 and 5.1.2.4)

In this section you are going to create a new database called 'Golf Club' and save it using the following steps:

- Open the Access application.

- When the program starts, the Microsoft Access window opens to create a new blank Access database.

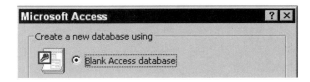

- Select Blank Access database.

- Click the OK button at the bottom of the window.

- The File New Database window opens.

- Click the arrow to the right of the **Save in** box.

- Select the **My Documents** folder on your **(C:)** drive in the extended **Save in** box.

- Type the name of the database (**Golf Club**) in the **File name** box.

- Click the **Create** button in the bottom right-hand corner of the window.

- The **Golf Club** database window will now open.

- **Close** the database.

In Office 2000, buttons in a panel at the left of the window replace the buttons on top of the window in earlier versions of Access.

Section 2   Tables

2.1   Main Operations

2.1.1   Creating, Saving and Closing a Table (5.2.1.1 and 5.2.1.9)

For the purposes of this exercise you will open the **Golf Club** database. The table you will create will be called **Membership List**. The database will be saved in the **My Documents** folder. In order to open the database follow these steps:

- Start Access by using Start button and selecting Microsoft Access from the Programs menu. The Access window appears.

- Select **Open** an existing file. The **Open** window opens.

- Locate the file **Golf Club** in the My Documents folder.

- Click the database file called **Golf Club**.

- Click the **Open** button. The Golf club database window appears.

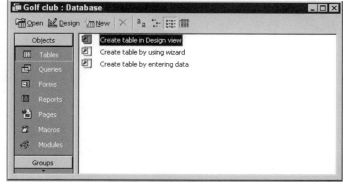

Golf club database window

This Golf Club database window shows the name of the new database which you have just opened and also the different objects associated with databases are displayed on the left hand side of the window. The next step in creating the database is to compose a table.

2.1.1.1 Creating a Table

To create the database table, use the following steps:

- Click the **Tables** button in **Objects.**

- Click the **New** button in this window.

  The **New Table** window opens. You are presented with the choice of creating a new table in **Datasheet View**, **Design View** or by using **Table Wizard**.

- Select Design View.

- Click **OK.**

MODULE 5

The table **Design** window opens. Now take a few moments to examine the window. This window has a few features that are important to note.

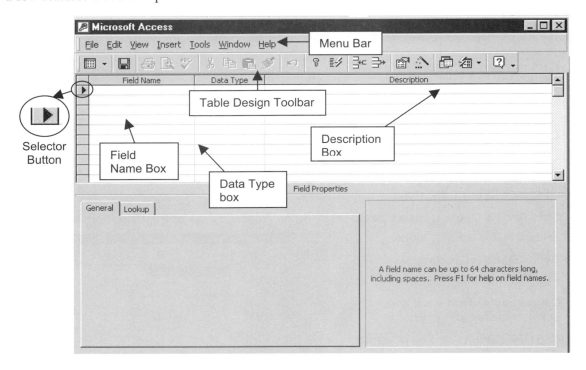

Scenario: You have been asked by your golf club captain to create a database. In this database you must include the full name, street address, town, county, effective date of membership and initial fee paid for membership of the golf club.

To begin with, you will now insert the field names and include their correct data type. It is important to remember that field names can be typed in uppercase or lowercase. Make sure to keep it uniform.

To insert the field names and data types follow these steps:

- Click the first row of the Table Design window beside the **Row Selector.**

- Type in the words 'Membership Number'.

- Press the **Tab** key on your keyboard.

- Click the Selector button which appears to the right of the **Data Type** box and choose **AutoNumber** as your **Data Type.**

- Press the Tab key once again and then press the Tab key once more to place the cursor immediately below the field you have just inserted.

The cursor should now appear below the first field name on a new row. Now you will type in the remainder of the fields and choose their data types.

Membership Number	AutoNumber
Last Name	Text
First Name	Text
Street Address	Text
Town	Text
County	Text
Effective Date	Date/Time
Initial Fee	Currency

When you have inserted all the field names and chosen their data types you will have to save the table.

To save the table follow these steps:

- Click the File menu on the Menu bar.

- Select the **Save** command.

- In the **Save As** box type in the words **Membership List.**

- Click **OK.**

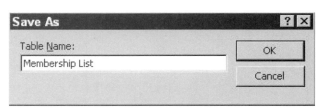

You will now be prompted to add a **primary key**. We will ignore this option for the moment, so select **No**.

The name of the table will now appear in the Table window and also the golf club Database window.

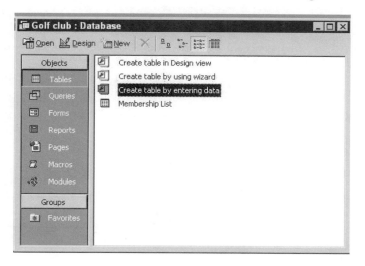

2.1.2 Displaying and Hiding Built-in Toolbars (5.1.3.2)

The toolbars are similar in appearance to the toolbars in other Office applications but contain buttons specific to Access and to the Access object in use at a particular time. You will learn to recognise and use them as you proceed through the module.

To display the appropriate toolbar, you can open the **View** menu on the Menu bar and then select the **Toolbars** command. *Alternatively*, you can select to the right of the Menu bar with the right button of your mouse and then choose the toolbar to insert.

Remember that each section (form, queries or report) in the database will have its own specific toolbars associated with it.

If you want to hide a toolbar you can click on the **Close** button on the right-hand corner of the toolbar, or alternatively, open the **View** menu and select **Toolbars**. Now click the name of the toolbar to be deselected.

Close Button

2.1.3 Adding and Deleting Records in a Table (5.2.1.2)

When you have created and saved your table you can then start to add records. However, you cannot add records while in **Table view**. You must change from the Table View to a new one called **Datasheet view**. This view option is available if you click on the **View** button, located to the left of your Standard toolbar.

Alternatively, you can select the table and click on the **Open** button in the database window to go directly to the table in Datasheet view.

When you are in Datasheet view you will notice that the window displays two toolbars, i.e. **Table Datasheet** and **Formatting (Datasheet).** The field names you created in your table are also visible in the datasheet area.

Table/Datasheet Toolbar →

Formatting (Datasheet) Toolbar

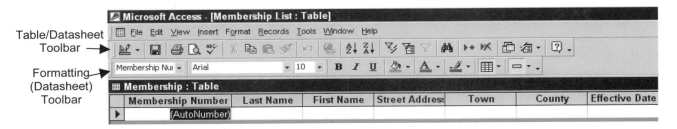

Notice that the Membership Number field has AutoNumber written in it. This field can be ignored because Access will automatically insert a number each time you include a new record. However, by pressing the Tab key on your keyboard you will now find that your cursor will appear in the **Last Name** field.

Navigation of the datasheet is by means of your Tab key. When you press the Tab key your cursor will go from one field to the next.

Insert the following information into each of the relevant fields, then save and close the table.

Membership Number	Last Name	First Name	Street Address	Town	County	Effective Date	Initial Fee
1	Janis	Steve	9 Bachelors Walk	Dundalk	Louth	03/06/1998	€350.00
2	Relman	Cathy	92 Arlen Road	Cork	Cork	13/06/1997	€350.00
3	Nelson	Michael	229 Route 55	Dundalk	Louth	04/04/1998	€350.00
4	Gonzales	Fred	Parkgate Street	Drogheda	Louth	16/04/1996	€350.00
5	Dickenson	Tonia	92 Main Avenue	Ennis	Clare	25/05/1995	€350.00
6	Graham	Shelley	1 Henry Street	Dundalk	Louth	01/06/1996	€350.00
7	Black	John	11 River Rd.	Adare	Limerick	27/04/1997	€350.00
8	Owen	Scott	72 Yale Way	Slane	Meath	10/05/1999	€350.00
9	Roberts	Robert	56 Water St.	Borris	Tipperary	21/05/2001	€350.00
10	Williams	Tasha	1 Spring St	Mallow	Cork	28/06/1998	€350.00

2.1.4 Adding a Field to an Existing Table (5.2.1.3)

When you want to add a field to an existing table you must first open the table in Design view. To open the table in Design view follow these steps:

- Click the table to be opened, i.e. Membership List.

- Click the **Design** button on the **Table Datasheet** toolbar.

Follow these steps to add three new fields to your Membership List table:

- Type in the field names below and set the data types as listed.

Field Name	Data Type
Monthly Dues	Currency
Membership Type	Text
Handicap	Number

Monthly Dues	Membership Type	Handicap
€45.00	Single	6
€55.00	Couple	12
€55.00	Couple	20
€55.00	Couple	20
€65.00	Family	6
€45.00	Single	12
€45.00	Single	10
€45.00	Single	12
€45.00	Single	6
€65.00	Family	18

- Type the information into each of the new fields in the table using **Datasheet view.**

- Save the table and close it.

2.1.5 Modifying Data in a Record (5.2.1.4)

From time to time it may be necessary to update information, such as change of address, telephone number and so on. Open the Membership List table by clicking on the Open button in the database window.

If you want to alter the information in a record, select the appropriate field and type in the new information. Save your work when you have completed this task. The information in record 1 for Steve Janis is shown incorrectly. The address should read 9 Bachelors Walk and not Batchelors Walk, as displayed. Amend the information and save your datasheet.

2.1.6 Deleting Data in a Record (5.2.1.5)

In order to delete data in a record you must first select the information and then use the **Delete** command in the Edit menu on your menu bar. Delete the word Yankee in the record for Scott Owen and now type in Yale.

2.1.7 Using the Undo Command (5.2.1.6)

You discover that the word Yale was not correct and you want to revise the information. Instead of retyping the word you can use the **Undo** command, which is displayed as a button on the toolbar or as a command in the **Edit** menu on the Menu bar. Try both these options to undo your last command now. Save your datasheet and close it.

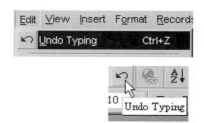

2.1.8 Navigating a Table (5.2.1.7)

Viewing the information on an individual club member in table layout means that you have to scroll over and back across the table to see all the available field columns.

In order to do navigate the table you must follow these steps:

- Display the Membership List table in **Datasheet** view.
- View the bottom of the datasheet window and you will see a set of navigational buttons.
- Use your mouse to click on any of the buttons to move in the direction you require.

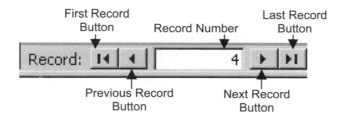

If you want to go to a specific record, click where the record number is displayed in the navigational box and type in the number to which you want to go to.

You can also use the **Go To** command in the **Edit** menu on the Menu bar to navigate your contents in the table datasheet.

2.1.9   Deleting a Table (5.2.1.8)

If you delete a table, the contents of table design, the design elements and all the records will be lost. If you want to do so, follow these steps:

- In the database window click on the object, i.e. table, you want to delete.

- Open the Edit menu on the Menu bar.

- Select the **Delete** command
  An alert box will open.
  If you click on **OK,** Access will proceed with the deletion.

- Click on **No** to cancel the operation.

2.2   Define Keys

2.2.1   Primary Key (5.2.2.1)

A primary key field is one that uniquely identifies each record in a table. Access does not allow duplicate primary key fields, so each one is unique. They are particularly important with related tables (explained later on in the module).

Primary Key
Button

Most tables have a single primary key field. In a golf club, each person could have a unique membership number and this would be a good choice for the primary key field.

Access allows you to select a primary key or it will choose one for you. This option is presented to you when you create the fields in the Design view of your table. In order to insert the primary key after you have created the table, follow these steps:

- Open the Table Membership List in Design view by clicking on the Design button in the Database window after selecting the table.

- Select the Membership Number field.

- Click the **primary key** in the **Table Design** toolbar.
  A key will now appear beside the field name in the Design window.

- Click the Save button on the Table Design toolbar.

- Close the window.

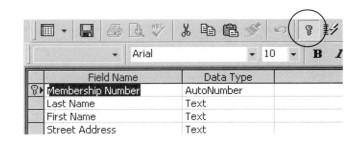

2.2.2 Indexing (5.2.2.2 and 5.1.1.4)

An **index** helps to quickly find and sort records in large databases. Like the index in a book that directs you to particular pages, indexed fields make it easier for the database to find the information.

An index can be set up on fields that you search or sort frequently. To set up an index, you mark a field (or fields) as indexed. Indexes operate in the background when you use sorts, queries or grouping, as described in this section.

To create an index, do the following:

- Open the **Membership** table in Design view if it is not already open.

- Click the field you want to index, such as **Last Name**.

- In the lower part of the window, click in the **Indexed** box.

- A button appears at the right of the box.

- Click the button to display a menu.

- Click **Yes (Duplicates OK)** if you are happy that more than one record can have the same data in this field. There may be several employees with the same last name.

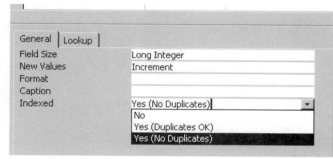

    Otherwise, Click **No (No Duplicates)** if you want to ensure that no two records are the same. You may want every stock item to have a unique name.

- Close the table.

- Click **Yes** when asked if you want to save the changes.

- The index is saved with the table.

If you frequently search or sort using more than one field at a time, such as **Last Name** and **First Name**, you can create a multiple index for those fields. This is done in the **Indexes** window.

Proceed as follows:

- Open the **Membership List** table in Design view if it is not already open.

- Select **Indexes** in the **View** menu.

    The Indexes window opens. Notice that the primary key field is automatically indexed.

- Type Full Name in the Index Name box.

- Click in the **Field Name** box to display a button at the right.

- Click the button to display a list of fields.

- Enter **Last Name** in the **Field Name** box.

- Enter **First Name** in the **Field Name** box *on the next line*, as in the illustration.

- Close the Indexes window.

- When you close the table, click **Yes** when asked if you want to save the changes.

2.3   Table Design and Layout

2.3.1   Changing Field Format Attributes (5.2.3.1)

When you work in Table Design view, you will notice that there is a section on the bottom of the window that is called **Field Properties**. This section is very useful when you are creating fields, because it is here you can define formatting features for your fields such as field size, number format and date format. These formats do not alter the size of the text.

2.3.1.1 Changing the Attributes of a Text Field

In our table we created a field called **Last Name.** If you look in the Field Properties section of the design window you will notice that it has been allowed a **Field Size** of 50. This means that when you are inputting data into this field, you can insert a name with up to 50 characters only. Text field size in Access can have up to 64 characters, which includes spaces.

In order to compact the size of the file we should alter this size to 30, as this allows for very large last names to be inserted.

Follow these steps to reduce the field size:

- Click on Last Name field.

- Click on Field Properties Field Size option.

- Alter 50 to read 30.

- Click the Save button.

    An alert window will now be visible.

    As the properties for Last Name are to be changed and you know that the longest Last Name is less than 30 characters, click **OK**.

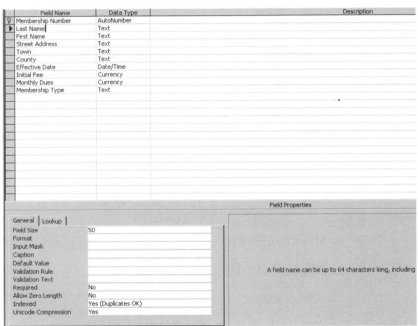

In normal circumstances ensure that the field is wide enough to accept the new size. Access will delete the additional characters from data if the field size is not wide enough.

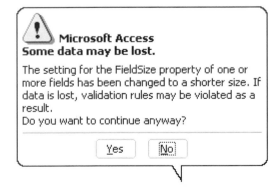

2.3.1.2 Changing the Attributes of a Number Field

If you are going to change a field which
has number as its data type, **Field
Properties** offers you a choice of
different number attributes.

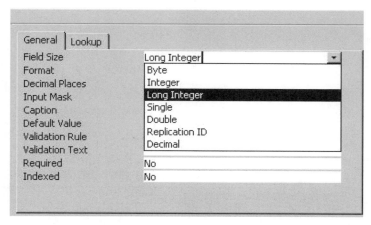

The most common settings for a number
field are **Long Integer** and **Double**. If you
select Long Integer, no decimal places
will be shown and the number will be
rounded to the nearest decimal place, i.e.
6.7 becomes 7.

However, selecting Double Integer means
you can show up to 15 decimal places
after the decimal point.

If you alter the attribute and the data information will be changed, the Alert window will appear
prompting you to reconsider before applying.

2.3.1.3 Changing the Attributes of a Date Field

To change the format of a date field follow these steps:

- You must first select the field to be altered,
  in this instance the **Effective Date** field.

- In the Field Properties window select
  Format.

- Now you can choose **Short Date** from the
  list of options for this field.

  An Alert window will not appear here when
  altering this option because the dates have
  already been typed into the records.

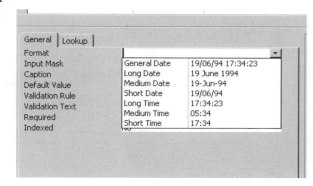

NOTE

Remember to always choose a date format for a field that has to show a date.

2.3.2 Validation Rules (5.2.3.3)

Microsoft Access does not support text in a field whose data type has been specified as number, for
examle. In order to avoid incorrect data being typed into a field, you can apply a **validation rule**.
When you apply a rule to a field, you can additionally use **validation text** to specify the message to be
displayed should a violation of the rule occur (located in the **Field Properties** pane of the table Design
view). The following are examples of validation rules applied to number, text, date/time and currency
fields.

2.3.2.1 Before You Begin

Before you start working with the validation rule tasks, you must make a copy of the Membership List
table. Follow these steps:

- Click the Membership List table in the Database
  window.

- Click on **Edit menu** on the Menu bar.

- Select the **Copy** command.

- Select the **Paste** command.

- In the **Paste Table As** window type in the name
  Membership in the **Table name** box.

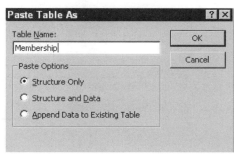

- Select the option **Structure Only.**

  This means that the different field names of the Membership List table will be copied and the data will not.

- Click **OK.**

2.3.2.2 Validation Rule for a Number

In the Membership table change the data type for the Membership Number field to number and remove the primary key. Save your table.

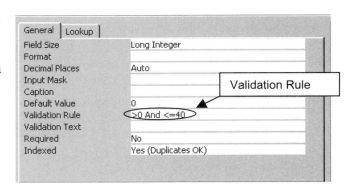

If you want to limit the amount of members in the club to 40 only, you can type in **>0 And <=40** in the **Validation Rule** box in **Field Properties**. Make sure you enter the field data type as **Number**. Try the following task:

- In the Datasheet view of the table, type in the number 41 in the Membership Number field and then observe the error reading.

- Press **Esc** key on your keyboard.

  This should stop the error reading.

- Delete the rule.

2.3.2.3 Validation Rule for Text

If you want to use a validation rule for text, you must first decide what you want to limit the insertion information to. In the following example you have decided you do not want people with last names beginning with the letter L and any characters after this letter. Follow these steps:

- Open the **Membership** table in Design view.

- Select the **Last Name** field.

- In the Field Properties section of the table select the **Validation Rule** box.

- Type in L?????????? in the box.

  This means that you want to restrict any last name beginning with L and any other text up to 11 characters after that.

- Save the table.

- Change the view to **Datasheet view.**

- Click **Yes** when Access reports there may be problems.

- Open the **Insert** menu on the Menu bar.

- Insert New Record.

- Type information into the fields and attempt to insert a last name of Leahy.

- Observe the error reading (see next page).

- Press the **Esc** key on your keyboard.

- This should stop the error reading.

- Delete the new rule.

2.3.2.4 Validation Rule for Date/Time

If you entered a rule in the Effective Date field that confined the date range to 1998, you would receive an error message since the table contains dates outside this year.

Follow these steps:

- Open the **Membership** table if it is not already open.

- Change the view to **Datasheet.**

- Delete any records that have an Effective Date other than 1998.

- Return to the **Design view** of your table.

- Select the **Effective Date** field.

- Click in the Validation Rule box in Field Properties.

- Now enter >=01/01/98 And <=31/12/98

- Save the table.

- Change the view to **Datasheet view.**

- Click **Yes** when Access reports there may be problems.

- Type information into the various cells and attempt to insert an **Effective Date** of 10/06/03.

- Observe the error reading.

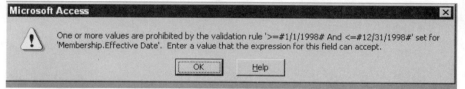

- Press the **Esc** key on your keyboard.

  This should stop the error reading.

- Delete the rule.

2.3.2.5 Validation Rule for Currency

If you wanted to accept only **initial fees** of between €300 and €500 you would need to place the validation rule **>300 And <500** in the box in **Field Properties,** otherwise attempting to enter a fee outside this range of numbers would get an error reading when the information was placed in the field cell in the **Table Datasheet.**

Finally, when you have tried the above tasks, close the **Membership** table.

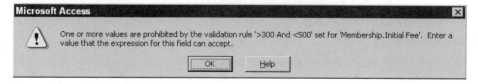

2.3.3 Change Column Width (5.2.3.5)

The basic structure of datasheet is columns and rows. When you put information into them, you will find that the data can be obscured because the column is not wide enough. In order to widen the columns you must follow these steps:

- Select the Membership List table in the Database window.

- Click the **Open** button.

  You will see that the fields **Membership Number** and **Street Address** need to have their columns widened.

- Bring the pointer of your mouse to the column border between the **Membership Number** and **Last Name** fields. The mouse will change to a two-way arrow.

- Click on your mouse and drag the border to the right until you reveal all the data.

- Release your mouse button.

  Alternatively, you can follow these steps to change the width of the **Street Address** column in the Datasheet view of the Membership List table as follows:

- Click the Field Selector button for the Street Address field. This is located to the left of the field name.

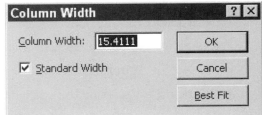

- Open the **Format menu** on the Menu bar.

- Select the **Column Width...** command.

- Click on **Best Fit** option.

- Click **OK.**

2.3.4 Moving a Column within a Table (5.2.3.5)

From time to time you may want to reorganise your table. Moving a column in a table can be tricky. Make sure that you know where you are going to place the column. In this instance you are going to move the column called **Last Name** and place it after the column **First Name**. To do this task, follow these steps:

- Open the **Membership List** table in Datasheet view.

- Select the Field Selector button for Last Name.

- Keep your finger down on the mouse button.

- Drag the column to just beyond the First Name column.

- Release the button of your mouse to drop the column in place.

  Notice how the pointer of the mouse has a different look. Also when you move the column an enhanced black line appears as you move your mouse.

2.3.5 Closing a Database (5.1.2.6)

When you have saved your database, follow these steps to close it:

- Open the **File** menu on the Menu bar.

- Click the **Close** command.

The database will close and you will be left with the Access application window still open. Close this in turn if you are finished with Access.

2.4   Table Relationships

2.4.1   Relationships between Tables (5.2.4.1)

When you create a relationship between tables within a database, a link is established between fields across the tables. This link is called a **relationship.** A relational database is a set of linked tables that share information. For your example, you have a table that includes all the information for the members of a golf club. It is a fairly big table with lots of information. Should you wish to handle handicaps within the database, it would be appropriate to generate a modified version of the main table extracting only the information you need for your purpose. The second table might contain the fields from the first table, which could include only members' names, their membership number and their handicap. The two most common relationships are the **one-to-one** and the **one-to-many**.

When one record in a table is linked to the same record in other tables, it is referred to as a one-to-one relationship. One-to-many relationships occur when one record in a table is linked to several records in other table. Relationships are created when links are established between matching fields in different tables.

In the following exercise you are now going to create a **one-to-one** relationship, but before you begin you must create a new table. To create the new table follow these steps:

- Click the **Tables** button in the Database window.

- Click the **New** button.
  The **New Table** window will open.

- Select the Datasheet view.

- Click on OK.

- Minimise the Datasheet window by selecting the Minimise button on the Title bar.

Here, you will copy across a selection of information to the new table as follows:

- Double click the **Membership List** table to open it.

- Change the view to **Design view.**

- Drag the **Handicap** field to appear below the First Name field.

- Save the table.

- Change the view of the table to **Datasheet view.**

- Highlight the Membership Number, Last Name, First Name and Handicap fields.

- Click on the highlighted area with the right button of your mouse.

- Select **Copy** from the Shortcut menu of your mouse.

- Double click on the minimised icon of Table1 (remember this is in Datasheet view).
  The table should open.

- In this sequence, you will paste the information across to the second table.

Field Name	Data Type
Membership Number	Number
Last Name	Text
First Name	Text
Handicap	Number
Street Address	Text
Town	Text

Membership List : Table

Fields Highlighted

This is the Table1 minimised **icon**

- Highlight the first four columns.

- Click the highlighted area with the right button of your mouse.

- Click on **Paste** from the Shortcut menu of your mouse.
  A Warning window will now open and alert you to the fact that you are about to paste 10 record(s).

- Click the **Yes** button.

You will now close the Membership List table and adjust and save the new table.

- Click the **Close** button on the Title bar for the Membership List table.

- Click on the **Design view** button for Table1.
  You are prompted to save the table.

- In the **Save As** window type in **Membership**.

- Click **OK.**
  You will now be prompted that there is no primary key.

- Select **No**,as you will add a primary key yourself.
  The table Design window will now open.

- Replace Field1, Field2, Field3 and Field4 with the following: Membership ID, Last Name, First Name and Handicap.

- Click on the Field Selector button for Membership ID.

- Click the **Primary Key** button on the toolbar to assign it to this field.

- Click on Field Properties and ensure that **no duplicates** are accepted for this field.

- Save the table.

- Close the table.

2.4.1.1 One-to-One Relationships

In the database window you should now have two tables, i.e. Membership and Membership List. You will now create a **one-to-one relationship** following these steps:

- Select the **Relationships...** command from the **Tools** menu on the toolbar.
  The Relationships window should now open.

- Open the **View** menu and select the **Show Table...** command.

- Select both tables by selecting one and then holding the Shift key on the keyboard down and selecting the other table.

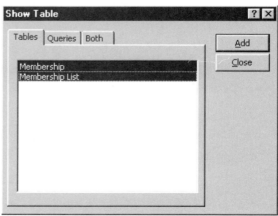

- Click the **Add** button.

The two tables will now appear in the Relationships window.

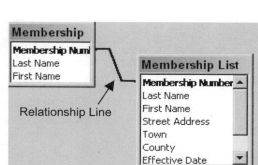

- Drag and drop the Membership Number field in the Membership box to the Membership Number field in the Membership List box.

  The Edit Relationship window will open.

- Click the **Create** button.

  You will now see a **relationship line** linking both fields together in the Relationship window.

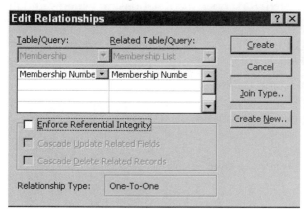

Now that you have completed these tasks you need to save the relationship as follows:

- Open the **File** menu on the Menu bar.
- Click the Save command.

2.4.1.2 One-to-Many Relationships

- Open the Membership List table in **Design view.**
- Deselect the **Primary Key** button on the toolbar.
- Save the table.
- Close the table.

To create the relationship follow these steps:

- Click the **Relationships** button on the **Database** toolbar in the Database window.

- Add the Membership and Membership List tables by clicking the **Add Table** button on the **Relationship** toolbar.

Add Table Button

- Click and drag the Membership Number field in the Membership box to the Membership Number field in the Membership List box

  The **Edit Relationships** window will open. Notice on the bottom of the window that the **Relationship Type** is displaying **One-To-Many**.

- Click the **Create** button.

  You can now see that One-To-Many will appear at the bottom of the window and a relationship line will appear between the two tables.

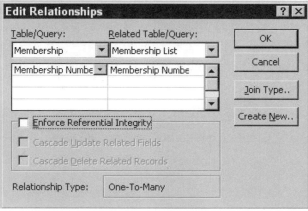

MODULE 5

- Save your work and close the Relationship window.

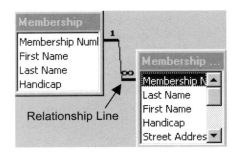

Relationship Line

2.4.2 Deleting Relationships between Tables (5.2.4.2)

Relationships that have been created can be deleted. First open the Relationship window and then follow these steps:

- Click the **Add Table** button and add both the Membership and Membership List tables.

- Click on the **relationship line** and select the **Delete** command from the **Edit** menu on the Menu bar.
  Access will now display an alert window with a warning.

- Click **Yes** to continue.

The relationship line has been deleted. Now you need to save the change as follows:

- Select **Hide** from the **Relationships menu** on the Menu bar and hide both tables.

- Now select the **Close** command in the **File** menu on the Menu bar.
  The alert window will appear and click **Yes**.

2.4.3 Applying Rule(s) to Relationships (5.2.4.3)

When you work with relationships you can include rules. For example, you can make sure that fields in joining tables are not deleted as long as links to another table exist. **Referential integrity** is the rule structure to ensure that relationships between records in related tables are maintained. When referential integrity is enforced, you must observe the following rules:

- You cannot enter a value in the second-level field of the related table that doesn't exist in the primary key of the primary table.

- You cannot delete a record from a primary table if matching records exist in a related table. (Any table containing a unique field is a primary table.)

- You cannot change a primary key value in the primary table if that record has related records.

Should you want Microsoft Access to enforce these rules for a relationship, select the **Enforce Referential Integrity** check box in the **Edit Relationship** window when you create the relationship.

If referential integrity is enforced and you try to break one of the rules with related tables, Microsoft Access displays a message and doesn't allow the change.

To work with referential integrity, follow these steps:

- Open the Relationships window.

- Add the Membership and Membership List tables to the window.

- Create a one-to-one relationship between the two tables.

- Click the Enforce Referential Integrity box.

You will see that a relationship line also displays the type of relationship that has been applied. If it is a one-to-one relationship the line appears like this one.

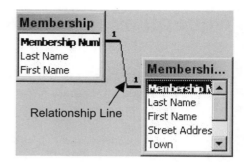

Relationship Line

Section 3   Forms

In this section you are going to create a form. Forms have been explained in some detail in the introduction to this module.

3.1   Working with Forms

3.1.1   Opening a Form (5.3.1.1)

The database table contains **all** the information about members of the golf club. In many cases, however, you do not need to see all the data in a record at the same time.

For example, you may only need a list of names and addresses, or you may only need a list of club members in a particular town. A **form** uses some or all of the data contained in an existing table and presents it in a user-friendly layout.

NOTE:

While you are working with a form, any changes made to the data in the form will also be updated in the table.

To open a form that is already created, make sure that you click **Forms** in the Objects menu section of the Database window. You can then select the form you require from the list of forms presented and click Open on the Menu bar.

3.1.2   Creating and Saving a Form (5.3.1.2)

A **wizard** is available to help you create a new form using fields and data from an existing table.

To create a new **form** in Office 2000:

- Click the **Forms** button in the panel at the left of the window.

- Double click **Create form by using wizard** in the main part of the window.
  The Form Wizard window opens.

The **Form Wizard** lets you select those fields you want to display in the form.

- In the **Table/Queries** box make sure that it shows the **Membership List** table.

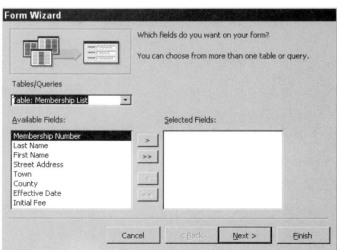

The **Available Fields** panel lists all the fields available in the table.

The **Selected Fields** panel on the right will list the fields you select for inclusion on the form.

To include a field:

- Click the field in the **Available Fields** box list to select it.

- Click the single arrow button at the top between the two panels.
  The field is moved across to the Selected Fields panel.

- Click the double arrow button to move all the fields across.
  The two lower buttons enable you to remove one or all of the fields back should you change your mind.

> | > | Move One |
> | >> | Move All |
> | < | Remove One |
> | << | Remove All |

For the purpose of this exercise, move **all the fields** across to the Selected Fields panel.

- Click **Next** when you have moved all the fields.
  A new window gives you a choice of layout. Click the different options to see examples.

- Select **Columnar** and click **Next**.

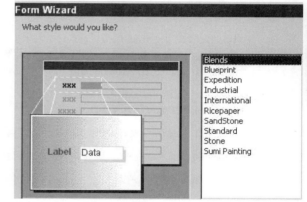

The next window gives a choice of form style.

- Click the different options to see examples.

- Select **Blends** and click **Next**.

- The last window asks for a **Title** for the form.

- Type the name Membership Form.

In the last window you are presented with two options, as follows:

- Open the form to view or enter information.

- Modify the form's design.
  By default option 1 is checked. You will keep this option to view the form as soon as you have finished.

- Click **Finish**.
  The completed form is displayed.

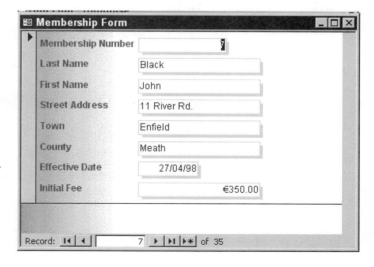

To save the form, follow these steps:

- Open the **File** menu on the Menu bar.

- Select the **Save** command.
  The form is now saved within the database for the golf club.

MODULE 5

3.1.3 Entering, Modifying and Deleting Records (5.3.1.3)

When you work with **Form view** you can enter, modify and delete records on the database. Information changed here will be saved to the table. For practice, you are going to enter an additional record.

A new member has joined the golf club – Patricia O'Connor, 1 Clonskeagh Avenue, Goatstown, Dublin on 21/01/03 and she has paid an initial fee of €200. As secretary of the golf club it is up to you to add her name to the form.

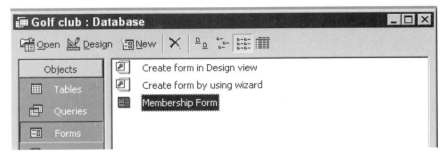

Follow these steps :

- Click on the Forms button in the Database window.
  Now the **Membership Form** is visible in the Database window.

- Double click on the form name.
  The form window opens.

- Click on **Insert** menu and select the **New Record** command.

- Type in P. O'Connor's details.

- **Save** the form by clicking on the **Save** button on the **Form View** toolbar.

Upon viewing the records in the form you noticed record 3 for Michael Nelson was showing the incorrect information for his street address. This should read 229 Ravensdale Court and not 229 Route 55 as shown. In order to modify this record, you must follow these steps:

- Change the view to **Datasheet view** by clicking on the **View** button on the **Form View** toolbar.

- Select the incorrect address for Michael Nelson.

- Type in the correct address as 229 Ravensdale Court.

- Click the **Save** button.

- Change the view back to **Form View** again by using the **View** button.

Steve Janis has emigrated so his name has to be removed from the list of members. To delete his record follow these steps:

- Open the form in **Datasheet** view.

- Select the full contents of Steve Janis' record by clicking the **Selector button** to the left of the contents of record 1. A black arrow appears.

- Open the **Edit** menu on the Menu bar.

- Click the **Delete Record** option.
  A warning window will appear and inform you that if you delete a record then it will be permanent.

- Select **Yes.**

- **Save** your records and return to **Form** view.

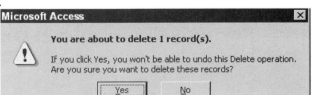

3.1.4 Navigating Forms Using Form Display (5.3.1.4)

Navigating forms can be very awkward if there are a lot of records to go through. To work efficiently and with some ease through records, you can use the navigational buttons. These are located on the bottom of the form. Open the Membership Form if it is not open already. When you scroll down to the bottom of the form the **Navigational buttons** will be visible. Click on each to move to another record. If you want to go to a specific record number, click the record number box, overtype the record number you want to go to and press the **Enter** key on your keyboard.

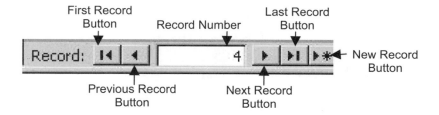

3.1.5 Headers and Footers in a Form (5.3.1.5)

Forms can be enhanced by using headers or footers. Headers and footers in forms can contain titles, dates, pictures and so on. The form header already exists at the top of the form and the form footer is located at the bottom. To work with these areas you must first of all change the view to **Form Design** using these steps:

- Click the **Forms** button in the database window.

- Select the form called Membership Form.

- Click the **Design** button.
  The form will now open in Design view.

To add text in the header of your form, do the following:

- Widen the **form header** first by dragging the **Detail bar** downwards when the double arrow appears.

- Make the **Toolbox** active by selecting it from the toolbar.

Toolbox Button

- Select the **Label** button from the toolbox and draw a rectangle shape in the **Form Header** area.

Label Button

- Type the words **Members Form**.

- View the result in the **Form Design view.**

- Change the view to **Form View** by clicking the **View** button on the toolbar.

- View the form.

To place text in the **form footer,** repeat the process you used for the form header except choose the form footer option.

You are now going to change the text in the label to bold 12pt Arial and centre align the text. You will also place the label into the form footer.

Change the view to **Form Design** view and then follow these steps:

- Click on the border of the label located in the form header to make it active (see next page).

- Click on the **Formatting (Form/Report) toolbar** beneath the Menu bar and select the Arial font and font size as 12pt.

- Click the **Center align** button on the toolbar.

- Click the border of the label and a black hand will appear.

- Drag and drop the label into the **form footer.**

- Save your work.

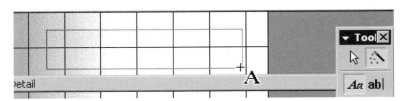

The Label in the Form Header is Active

Return to **Form view** by selecting the view button and choosing **Form view** and you will see that the label is now at the foot of the form.

3.1.6 Deleting a Form (5.3.1.6)

You can delete a form when you are working in Access. Simply open the database window, choose Forms in the object list and select the form you wish to delete. Click the Delete button on the window toolbar. Choose the Yes button in the Alert window. This will not delete the information that you used from the table – the records' information will remain intact – but if you choose **Yes** the form will be deleted permanently.

Do not choose **Yes** in the alert window because you will not be able to use the undo function following the deletion. Click the **No** button.

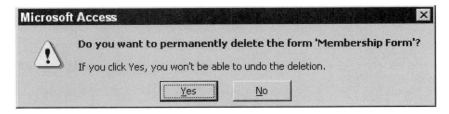

3.1.7 Saving and Closing a Form (5.3.1.7)

When you are finished working on the form you must save to preserve any additional formatting you have done. Make sure you are in **Form** view and follow these steps:

- Open the File menu and choose the **Save** command.

- Open the File menu once more and choose the **Close** command.

You will now be back in the Golf Club Database window.

Section 4   Retrieving Information

4.1   Main Operations

4.1.1   Using the Search Command (5.4.1.1)

Details of each record can sometimes be difficult to view or find, but there is a find function within Access. To locate information regarding a member called Spencer follow these steps:

- Click on **Tables** in the Database window.

- Click the **Open** button in the Database window.
  You should now see your information in **Datasheet view**.

To find information in respect of Robin Spencer, choose the **Find** command in the **Edit** menu on the Menu bar. The **Find and Replace** window will open.

- Type the word Spencer into the **Find What** box.

- Change the **Look In** box to show Membership List : Table by clicking the Selector button.

- Now click the **Find Next** button.

Once Access locates the record, click the **Cancel** button in the Find and Replace window. Do not close the table.

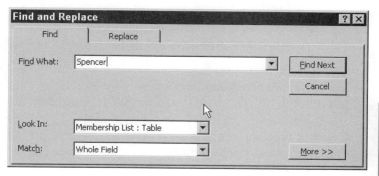

4.1.1.1 Searching for a Date (5.4.1.1)

When searching for a date there are a limited number of date format options that Access can interpret. Valid date formats are 5-April-98; 5/4/98; April 5, 1998; 05/04/1998. Entering any of these formats in the **Find what** box will successfully match the date in any of the other formats providing the Whole Field option is selected in the Match box and the appropriate column label is selected in the Look in box.

It is important to note that the **Search Fields As Formatted** box, accessed using the **More>>** button, must be deselected.

Otherwise, you will need to match the format of the date you enter in the Find What box with the format of the date you are searching for.

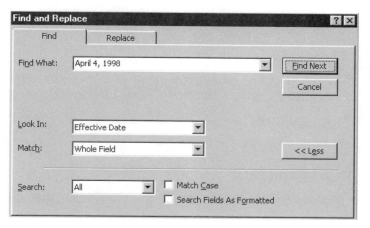

4.1.1.2 Searching for a Number (5.4.1.1)

In searching for a number, the Find Replace option may be used to narrow down or widen out the search. For example, to search for the number 11 in the address 11 River Road there are two options to locate the number.

First you may select **Any Part of Field** in the Match box. Should the number 11 appear anywhere in a field, it will be located no matter what other text is there.

Alternatively, selecting **Start of Field** will locate the number 11 only where it occurs at the very beginning of a field. Should the number be preceded by a currency label, it won't be recognized.

Choosing **Whole Field**, will locate the number 11 only where the number itself is the entire field entry. Numbers with currency symbols will not be recognized with this option.

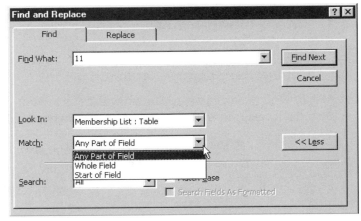

4.1.2 Applying Filters to a Table and Form (5.4.1.2 and 5.4.1.3)

If your database is very large, you will use a command known as **Filter** instead of **Find** because this can be more focused and you can be more specific as to the information you want to recall. The filter function can be performed if you are in the Datasheet view of a table or in Form view of a form. For our examples we are going to use the table called Membership List. If the table is not open in datasheet view, open it now.

4.1.2.1 Table Filter

You are now going to use a filter to find out how many of golf club members live in the county of Cork. Follow these steps:

- Highlight the word Cork in a **County** field.
- Click on the **Records** menu on the Menu bar.
- Click on the **Filter** command and move your mouse to the Selector button to the right.
- From the list of commands choose the **Filter By Selection** command.

The datasheet will now display the answer by showing the corresponding data for your filter.

If you look to the bottom of the Datasheet window in the table, you will notice that Access has also told you that 14 records were filtered.

Now that you have your information filtered you can remove the filter by clicking the **Remove Filter** button on the **Form View** toolbar.

- Click the Remove Filter button now.
- Save and close your table.

4.1.2.2 Form Filter

A filter can also be done within forms. To perform the same filter, follow these steps:

- Click the **Forms** button in the Database window.
- Open the Membership form in **Form** view.
- Click the **Filter by Form** button on the **Form View** toolbar.
  A blank form will appear.

- Type the word 'Cork' in the County field.

- Click on the **Apply filter** button on the **Form View** toolbar. (This button is called the **Remove Filter** button when the filter is completed.)

  The result will be displayed and you can check the results by means of the Navigational toolbar.

- Click the **Remove Filter** button.

- Save the filter result.

- Close your form.

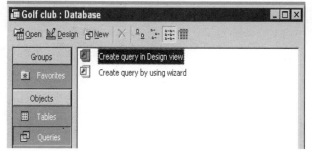

4.2   Queries

4.2.1   Creating a Single Table and Two-Table Query (5.4.2.1 and 5.4.2.5)

Using the query function allows more flexibility than using filters or sorting when working with forms. It allows you to choose which fields to display and search only for particular information. You can also save the query and when more people are added to the membership list you can run the query again to update it. If the new records have information that matches the query, the answer will reflect it when the query is run.

4.2.1.1 Single Table Query

Step 1 – Creating the query.

To create a query to isolate the names and addresses of all the members in the golf club who live in County Meath, follow these steps:

- Click the **Queries** button in the Database window.

- Double click on **Create query in Design view.**

  The Query Design window will open.

- Click the **Membership List** table in the **Show Table** window.

- Click the **Add** button.

- Click the **Close** button.

  The Membership List table will be displayed in the Query window.

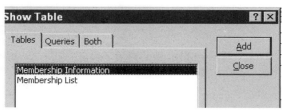

Step 2 – Setting up the query.

You now have to select the First Name, Last Name, Street Address, Town and County fields.

- Double click the **First Name** field with the left button of your mouse.
  The field will now appear in the grid.

- Double click each of the other fields until each field appears once in the grid.
  Make sure that you do not duplicate any field name.

- Type the word 'Meath' into the **Criteria** beneath the County field (see next page).

- Press the **Enter** key on your keyboard.
  The word Meath will now appear with inverted commas before and after it.

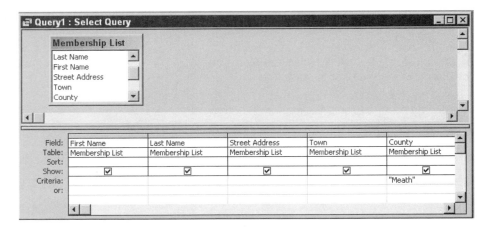

Step 3 – Running the query.

The next step in the process is to apply the criteria and run the query.

Run
Button

- Click the **Run** button in the **Query Design** toolbar.

The result will be displayed in **Query Datasheet** view shown here.

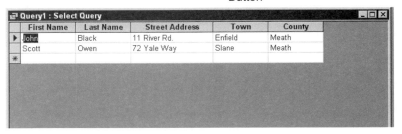

Step 4 – Saving the query.

- Type the words 'Members living in Meath' in the **Save As** window.

- Close the Query window.

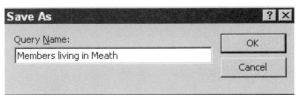

4.2.1.2 Two-Table Query

Queries can be created using more than one table in a database. Even if you haven't created relationships, Microsoft Access will automatically create a link if you add two tables to a query.

- Click the **Create a query in Design View** option in the database window.
  The **Query** window opens.

- Click the **Add Table** button from the **Query Design** toolbar.

- Select both the Membership List and Membership Information tables from the **Show Table** window.

Add Table
Button

- Click the **Add** button.

- Click the **Close** button.

The two tables will now appear in the **Query** window.

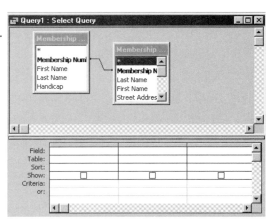

- Include the First Name and Last Name fields from the Membership List table. Include the Membership Number field from the Membership Information table.

- In the **Sort** for the Last Name field select Ascending from the Selector button and then click the **Run** button.

  The result will be displayed in the **Datasheet view** for the query. **Save** the query as Members Last Names in ascending order.

- Close the Golf Club Database.

The two queries will now appear in the Queries window of the Golf Club database.

4.2.2 Adding Criteria to a Query (5.4.2.2)

In adding criteria to queries, you can more precisely specify the information you require. Operators such as less than, greater than, or a combination of greater than and/or equal to or less than and/or equal to are commonly used to define criteria. Specific mathematical symbols are used to express these criteria.

Greater than	>	Less than	<
Greater than and equals	>=	Less than and equals	<=
Equals	=	Not equal to	<>
And, or			

You are going to interrogate the Membership List table using some of these operators. Together we will work on the first of them. Follow these steps:

- Open the Golf Club database.

- In the Database window click the **Queries** tab.

- Double click Create query in Design view.

- Add the **Membership List** table to the Query window.

- Close the **Add** window.

- Double click the First Name, Last Name and Handicap fields.

- Click with your mouse on the Criteria for Handicap.

- Type >12

- Press the **Enter** key on your keyboard to log the query.

- **Run** the query by using the Run button on the Query toolbar.

- Save the query as '**Over 12 handicap**'.

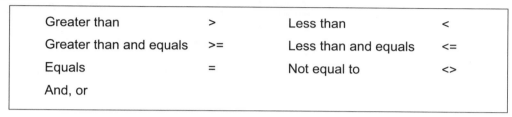

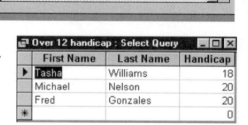

The following are a few exercises that you might try:

1. List all members whose handicap is greater than 12.

2. List all members whose handicap is less than 20.

3. List all members whose monthly dues are greater than or equal to €45. (Remember that because you have already told Access the field is a currency one, you do not have to include the currency symbol in the criteria section.)

4. What are the details of members whose monthly dues was not equal to €55?

5. List all members who live in Cork **or** Galway.

6. What members joined the club in the month of May?

7. Name all the members who live in Louth and Limerick.

4.2.3 Editing a Query by Criteria (5.4.2.3)

You can further refine the information you require by changing, adding to or removing existing criteria. To edit the criteria in the Over 12 Handicap query so as to display the new criteria greater than or equals to 12, follow these steps:

- Double click on the query in the Database window.

- Change the view to **Design view**.

- Select the >12 information in the criteria for handicap.

- Type in >=12.

- Open the **File** menu on the Menu bar.

- Select the **Save** command.

- Select **Yes** from the window.

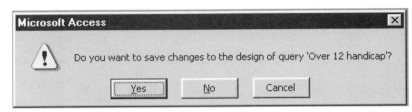

You will now be returned to the Database window. Run the query and note that the handicap rating of 12 is included in the result.

To remove criteria, simply return to Design View, click anywhere in the **Criteria row** and then select **Delete Rows** in the **Edit** menu. Your table returns to the original state before you ran the criteria.

4.2.4 Editing a Query by Fields (5.4.2.4)

If you want to edit a query so that fields inappropriately positioned are moved, removed, hidden or unhidden, you must work in the query **Design view**.

Open the query created for exercise 5 above and carry out the following tasks.

Step 1 – Place the Members Number field at end of the fields displayed.

- Highlight the column associated with the field by clicking once when the black arrow appears above the column header.

- While holding down the left button of the mouse, a box will appear attached to the cursor. Drag the Membership Number column to the end beyond the last field – Membership Type is displayed on the grid.

- Release the mouse button.

Column Header

Field:	Last Name	First Name	Town	County	Membership Type	Membership Number
Table:	Membership List	Membership List	Membership List	Membership List	Membership List	Membership List
Sort:						
Show:	☑	☑	☑	☑	☑	☑
Criteria:				"Cork" Or "Galway"		
or:						

Step 2 – Remove the Handicap field.

- Select the Handicap field.

- Open the **Edit** menu on the Menu bar.

- Select the **Delete** command.

Step 3 – Hide the Town field.

If you remove the check from the check box beneath the Town field when in Query view, the information associated with that field is hidden from view when you run a query.

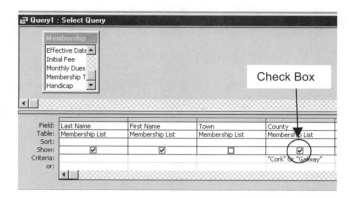

- Open the exercise 5 query in Design view.

- Remove the tick from the check box with the left button of your mouse.

- Run the query.

The result of the query is shown over. Note how the field name and its contents are not displayed in the Datasheet window.

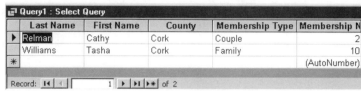

4.2.5 Deleting a Query (5.4.2.6)

From time to time as you manage your database, you may want to discard old and unused queries. In order to delete a query, follow these steps:

- Open **Queries** in the Database window.

- Select the query to be deleted.

- Click the **Delete** button or **Delete** command in the **Edit menu** on the Menu bar.

Delete Button

- Click **Yes** in the **Delete Alert** box to proceed, click **No** to cancel.

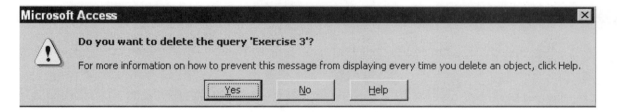

4.2.6 Saving and Closing a Query (5.4.2.7)

Having run a query, you can close it by using the **File** menu and selecting the **Close** command. However, if the query has not been saved you will be prompted with the message below.

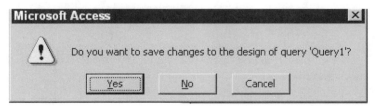

4.3   Sorting Records

4.3.1   Sorting Data (5.4.3.1)

Data in a table, a form or a query can be sorted into numeric or alphabetical order. If the field has the data type *text*, it can be sorted alphabetically from A to Z (ascending) or Z to A (descending). Numeric data can also be sorted in ascending (1 to 10) or descending (10 to 1) sequence using the same buttons.

4.3.1.1 Sorting Text Data in a Table

To sort data in a table in alphabetical order from A to Z follow these steps:

- Open the Golf Club database.

- Open the Membership List table in Datasheet view.

- Select all the contents of the Last Name field.

- Click the **Sort Ascending** button on the **Table Datasheet** toolbar.

- Deselect the column.

- Save and close the table.

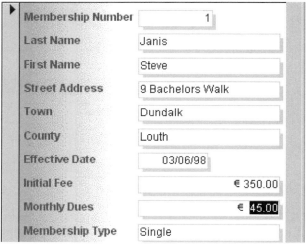

Sort Ascending and Descending Buttons

If you want to sort numeric data in a table, you could follow these steps selecting a field with numbers in it. Date and time fields could also be sorted providing they have the field property of **Short Date** or **Short Time**.

It is important to remember that all related data is sorted along with the fields in the related column when you use the Sort command.

4.3.1.2 Sorting Numeric Data

To sort data in a form in numeric order from 1 to 10 (A to Z), follow these steps:

- Open the Membership Form in **Form view**.

- Highlight the contents of the **Monthly Dues** field.

- Click the **Sort Ascending** button on the **Form View** toolbar.

- Change the view to **Datasheet view**.

- Save and close your form.

If you want to sort text data in a form, you could follow these steps in the text field containing the data you need to sort.

Membership Number	1
Last Name	Janis
First Name	Steve
Street Address	9 Bachelors Walk
Town	Dundalk
County	Louth
Effective Date	03/06/98
Initial Fee	€ 350.00
Monthly Dues	€ 45.00
Membership Type	Single

4.3.1.3 Sorting Data Using a Query Output

If you are sorting data using a query output, you will have to change to **Queries** in the Database window as follows:

- Double click the Create Query in Design view option.

- **Add** the Membership List table to the Query window.

- Click the **Close** button.

- Select the Membership Number, First Name, Last Name and Effective Date fields and insert them on the grid.

- Click on the Sort row beneath the **Effective Date** field.

- Click the Selector button to the right of the box.

- Select the **Ascending** option.

- Click the **Run** button.

- Save and close your query.

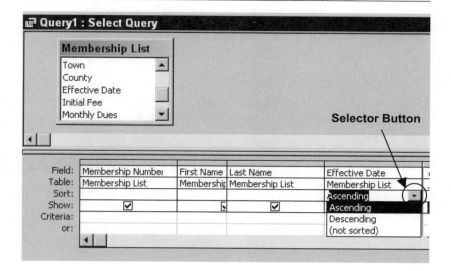

MODULE 5

Section 5   Reports

In this section you are going to learn about reports and their manipulation. If you are unsure as to what a report is, refer to the introduction section of this module. When you create a report you will follow these steps:

- Choose the Report Wizard from the New Report window.

- Choose the fields to be included in the report.

- Select one or more fields if you want to group information on the report.

- You can sort the information in one or more fields in the report in alphabetical or numerical order.

- You can choose the layout of the report.

- You can choose the style of the report.

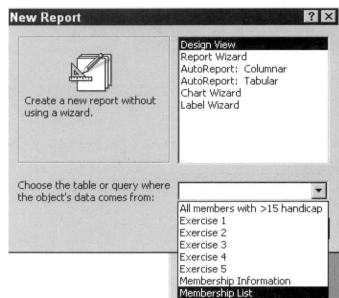

- You will view your work in the **Report Preview** window if you choose the former option and you will view the report in **Report Design** view if you choose the latter option.

- You must give the report a name. You will be prompted with a name the program suggests.

- At this stage you can also choose to preview or modify the report's fields by using the radio buttons – you must select one or the other.

- Click the **Finish** button to complete the report.

5.1   Working with Reports

5.1.1   Creating a Report (5.5.1.1 and 5.5.1.3)

Reports are used to present information from a table or query in a format suitable for printing. You can, of course, print directly from a table or query but the data is printed as it appears in the table. The report assists you in managing and arranging the output from the table.

- Click the **Reports** tab in the **Database window** and then click the **New** button. The **New Report** window opens.

- Select **Report Wizard** in the panel on the right.

- Click the **Choose the table or query...** box in the lower part of the window. Select the table or query in the menu that contains the data you want to use. In this case, select the **Membership List** table.

- Click **OK.**

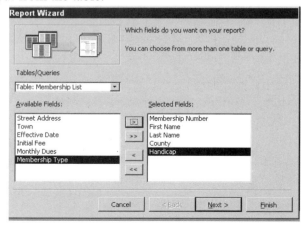

In the Report Wizard that appears, select the fields you want to display in the report.

- Click the **single arrow** button to add the selected fields to the right-hand box. *Alternatively*, double click a field to move it across to the **Selected Fields panel.**

- Add the Membership Number, First Name, Last Name, County and Handicap fields.

- Click the **Next** button to continue.

The next window in the wizard lets you group the data.

For example, members with the same handicap can be linked together in the report layout using this sequence:

- Click **Handicap** in the grouping panel.

- Click the arrow button to move it across to the preview window.

- Click the **Next** button to continue.

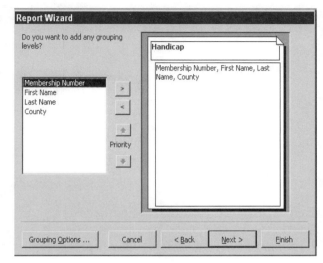

In the new window you can sort the records using one of the chosen fields. The last name of the members of each group can then be arranged in alphabetical order.

- Select **Last Name** from the menu in the first **Sort Field Order box**.

- Click **Next** to continue.

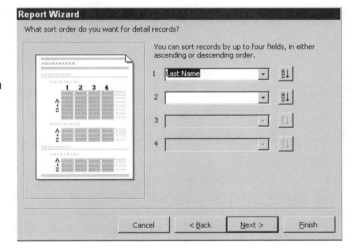

In the next window you will choose a layout option for your report.

- Select Stepped.

- Click Next.
  You may view the effects and choose **<Back** if you want to choose another layout.

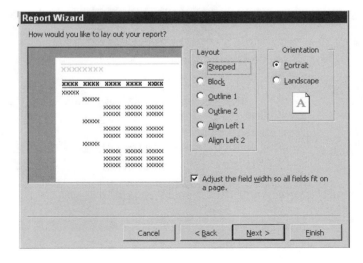

MODULE 5

The next window wants you to choose a **style** for the report.

- Select **Bold.**
- Click **Next.**

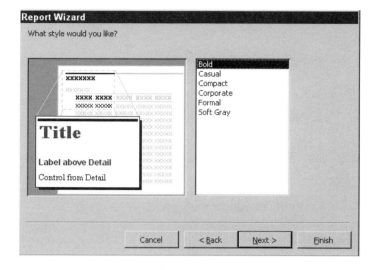

The final window allows you to give the report a name.

- Type in Membership Report.
- Click Finish.

There is no particular difference between choosing to create a report based on a table and a report based on a query, other than the amount of available fields you have to choose from.

5.1.2 Changing Report Layout (5.5.1.2)

If you are unhappy with the final layout having completed the wizard, it is possible to view the report using three views. These are **Print Preview, Layout Preview** and **Design View.** The **Print Preview** window allows you view the report as it will appear when you go to print. The **Layout Preview** window gives you a quick view of the simplified layout of a report. The **Design View** window allows you to change the arrangement of data fields and headings within a report layout.

In the Print Preview of the report you can also see that the members' first name and last name have been separated. The heading would look better if it was placed in the centre of the page, so before you print the report you will adjust these using the following steps:

- Click the **View** button on the **Print Preview** toolbar.

- Click the **Design View** option.

- Click on the label for the heading.
  You can see that **handles** appear about the label.

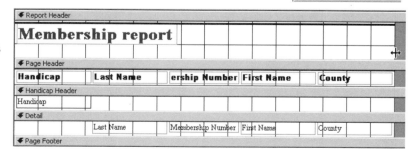

When you move your
mouse toward the label the
cursor changes into a **hand**.

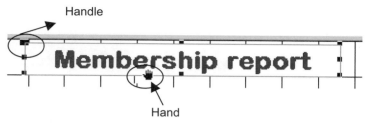

Handle

Hand

- Click and hold the mouse
  and drag the label to the
  centre of the **Report
  Header** grid.

- Drop the label by letting go of the mouse button.

Now you must make room for the First Name field so that it appears before the Last Name field.
Follow these steps:

- Widen the grid for the **Page Header** by dragging the grid border on the right-hand side of the
  window further to the right.

- Hold down the **Shift** key on
  your keyboard and select the
  Label Toolbox and **Text Box**
  for the Last Name, Membership
  Number, First Name and
  County fields.

  Handles will appear around all
  of the fields you have selected.
  As they are all active, they will
  move together.

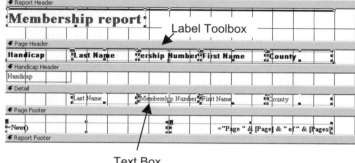

Label Toolbox

Text Box

- Drag the fields to the right,
  leaving space for the **First Name** field.

- Click away from the fields to deselect them.

- Select the **First Name** field Label Toolbox and Text Toolbox.

- Drag them into the space left beside the **Last Name** field.

- Adjust the fields so that the Label and Text boxes are fully visible.

- Click the **View** button and select Print Preview.

- Save your report by using the **Save** command in the **File** menu on the Menu bar.
  You will now see the Database window.

5.1.3 Presenting Specific Fields in a Grouped Report (5.5.1.4)

When you present specific fields in a
grouped report, you may avail of a
number of options that summarise
numeric information. For example, you
can display the information in the fields
as sum, minimum, maximum, average or
count at appropriate break points.

Follow these steps:

- Double click **Create report by
  using wizard** in the Report
  Wizard window.

- Select the Membership List
  table.

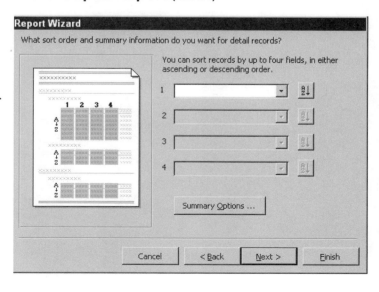

MODULE 5

- Select the First Name, Last Name, County, Initial Fee, Monthly Dues and Handicap fields.

- Click **Next**.

- Select the County field for the report to be grouped by.

- Click **Next**.
  Because you have chosen to group your information by county, the next window will allow you summarise some of your fields. However, if you do not group a specific field, this option will not be available here.

- Click the **Summary Options...** button.
  The **Summary Options** window opens.

In this window we are going to select the different types of summary we want for the balance of the fields which were not grouped, i.e. Initial Fee, Monthly Dues and Handicap.

- Select the **Sum** option for Initial Fee, the **Min** option for Monthly Dues and **Avg** option for Handicap.

- Click the **Detail and Summary** radio button.

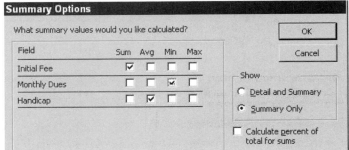

- Click **OK**.
  You will now return to the Report Wizard.

- In the window that asks How would you like to lay out your report?, select Landscape.

- Follow the usual steps for completing the wizard and when you are on the final window of the wizard, type in the name Summary Report for Members.

  The report will now display in **Print Preview**. When you look at the report you will notice that the different summary options are displayed below each county, as the county field was chosen by you in the **Group By** option in the wizard (see next page).

- **Save** and close the report.

Summary Report for Members

County	First Name	Last Name	Initial Fee	Monthly Dues	Handicap
Cork					
	Robert	Roberts	IR£350.00	IR£45.00	6
	Tasha	Williams	IR£350.00	IR£65.00	18
	Kendra	Majors	IR£350.00	IR£65.00	21
	Shawn	Kelly	IR£350.00	IR£55.00	33
	Elizabeth	Stephens	IR£350.00	IR£45.00	6
	Ginny	Lee	IR£350.00	IR£45.00	12
	Crystal	Stevens	IR£350.00	IR£65.00	20
	Virginia	Rodriguez	IR£350.00	IR£45.00	6
	Pam	Idukawa	IR£350.00	IR£55.00	6
	Gail	Paxton	IR£350.00	IR£45.00	20
	Carol	Smith	IR£350.00	IR£45.00	12
	Peter	Kane	IR£350.00	IR£45.00	20
	Robin	Spencer	IR£350.00	IR£45.00	12
	Adelia	Ballard	IR£350.00	IR£55.00	12

Summary for 'County' = Cork (14 detail records)
Sum   IR£4,900.00
Avg   14.571 43
Min   IR£45.00

Galway					
	Jeffrey	Chavez	IR£200.00	IR£55.00	33

12 February 2003   **Page 1 of 3**

Print Preview of Report

5.1.4 Headers and Footers in a Report (5.5.1.5)

It is appropriate to add text to the header or footer of a report to clearly label it. Use the following steps:

- Select the Membership Report.

- Click the Preview button in the Database window.
  The report will now open in **Design view**. Note the different elements of the report presented in this view.

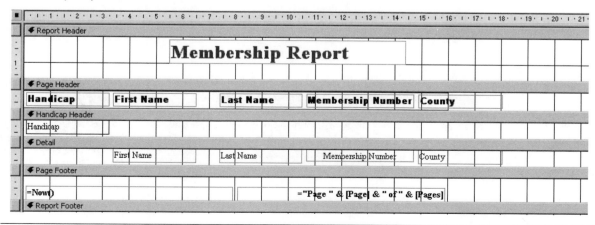

- The **Report Header** displays the title of the report as it will appear.

- The **Page Header** shows the page headers.

- The **Handicap Header** displays the handicap label. When you view the report in Preview you will see that it contains the contents of the handicap field. *Remember this field was used when you chose to group the information by this field.*

- The **Detail** section displays the data for each record that will be listed.

- The **Page Footer** displays the footer information, such as the data and page numbers.

- The **Report Footer** would show an additional level of footer information should you require it.

You are now going to add new text to the label in the header and change the font to Arial Rounded MT Bold. You will also change the alignment of the text to Center. Follow these steps:

- Click the label and select text with the I-beam of your mouse.

- Click on Font in the Formatting toolbar and select Arial Rounded MT Bold.

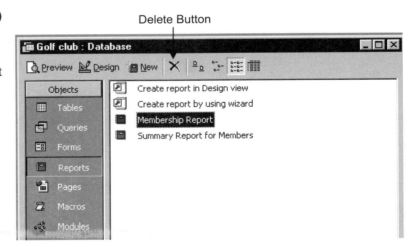

- Delete the text and type in the words All Members Report.

- Deselect the label.

- Click on the label border.

- Select the Center Align button on the formatting toolbar.

- Deselect the label.

- Save and close the report.

These steps can be applied to any text labels in your report whether they are in the header or footer areas.

5.1.5 Deleting a Report (5.5.1.6)

You can delete a report by selecting it in the Database window and using the **Delete** button. Just remember that you cannot use **undo** to retrieve it.

Delete Button

5.1.6 Saving and Closing (5.5.1.7)

Saving a report is done in the same manner as with other Access objects. Remember that if you make alterations to a report, it is important to save your changes if you want to keep them. Closing a report does not keep the changes unless you save them first. Always use the **Close** command in the File menu if you are unsure which button to use in the application windows.

Close Program Window

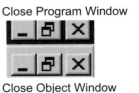

Close Object Window

Section 6   Printing

Before you start this section of the module ensure that you have paper in your printer and also that it is ready to receive information.

6.1   Preparing to Print

6.1.1   Previewing a Table, Form or Report (5.6.1.1)

It is important to always to view your table, form or report before you print. This option is known as **preview**. To use the preview option you can either access it through the **File** menu on the Menu bar, or you could use the **Print Preview** button on the toolbar.

Generally, when you choose to preview an object you will first open the object and then click on the **Preview button**. The Preview window will open and you can view the document as it will appear in print. You can also use the Navigation buttons to move through the object's pages. A **View** button is available on each toolbar for you to look at the document in an alternative view. If you are looking at the table, form or report in their respective Preview windows, you will notice that the toolbars options are similar (with the exception of the View button).

Print Preview
Button

Table Print Preview Toolbar

Form Print Preview Toolbar

Report Print Preview Toolbar

MODULE 5

6.1.2 Changing Orientation (5.6.1.2)

Sometimes you may find that the information as displayed could be improved by changing the document's orientation and adjusting margin settings. You can either display the information in **portrait** or **landscape** format. You can choose a paper size. If you choose an inappropriate size for the margins, Access will prompt you accordingly. For example, the summary report for the members

would be displayed far better if you changed the orientation of the report to landscape and changed the margins so that the information displayed evenly on a page.

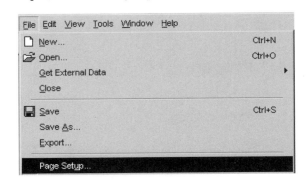

To do this, follow these steps:

- Click on **Reports** in the objects on the Database window.

- Double click on the **Summary Report for Members** report.

- Open the **File** menu on the Menu bar.

- Select **Page Setup**.
  The Page Setup window opens.

- Select the **Margins** tab.
  The margins for the sheet are displayed. These show the left, right, top and bottom margins as 24.99 mm by default.

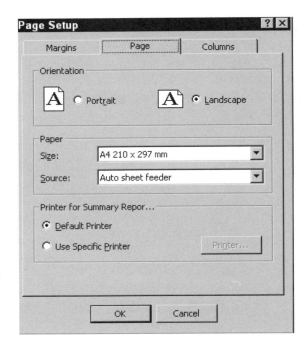

- Change the margins to 12.5 mm left and 12.5 mm right by clicking on the measurements box.

- Click the **Page** tab.

- Click the **Landscape** button.

- Click the drop down arrow in the Size box.

- Select A4 210 X 297 mm – if this is the paper size you are using. Otherwise select from the other size options.

- Click **OK**.
  The report will now be displayed with the new margins and in landscape orientation.

- Save your report.

6.2   Print Options

6.2.1 Printing (5.6.2.1)

The **Print** button on the toolbar will print what Access assumes you require, i.e. the selected table, form, report or datasheet *without* showing the **Print** window. If you want to be more specific in your choices, then you use the Print command in the File menu to access the print options.

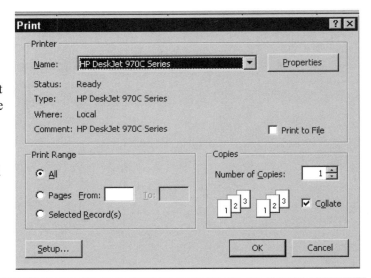

- Choosing the **All** option in the **Print Range** box means that all the contents of the table would be printed.

- Choosing the **Pages From** option means that you can choose which pages you want to print, i.e. if you type in 1 in the **From** box and type in 5 in the **To** box, pages 1,2,3,4, and 5 would print.

- By clicking the **Selector** button when you are in the Datasheet view of the table, you can select more than one record to be printed by highlighting them first and then using the **Selected Record(s)** option in the Print window.

6.2.2 Printing Using Form Layout (5.6.2.2)

As in the previous section, when printing forms you have three options available to you. If you need to print using the form layout, make sure that you are in **Form view** for a form per page. If you want to print using the form layout, you must insert a **Page Break** beneath the last field in the form.

Follow these steps:

- Open the Members form in **Design view.**

- Click the **Toolbox** button on the **Form Design** toolbar.

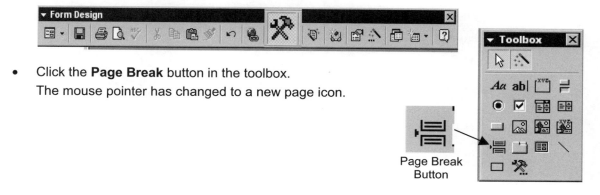

- Click the **Page Break** button in the toolbox.
  The mouse pointer has changed to a new page icon.

Page Break Button

- Click beneath the last field in the form design, i.e. Membership Type.
  A page break has been inserted.

- Now choose between the **All, Pages From** and **Selected Record** options as appropriate.

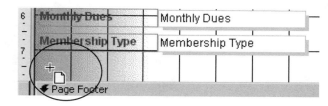

6.2.3 Printing the Result of a Query (5.6.2.3)

If you want to print the result of a query, simply print using the first and third options explained above.

6.2.4 Printing Specific Pages (5.6.2.4)

When you want to print specific pages in a report you can use the option of typing in the page number from which you want to begin in the **From** box and the last page in the **To** box. *Alternatively*, if you choose the **All** options, all of the pages of the report will be printed.

6.2.5 Using Help Functions (5.1.2.5)

When you work with Access, assistance and explanations are available by either using the **Help menu** on the Menu bar or by using the **F1** key at the location of your problem. For example, should you select the Blank Database option in the opening stages of Access and then press **F1**, Help will give you some information on the blank database choice you made.

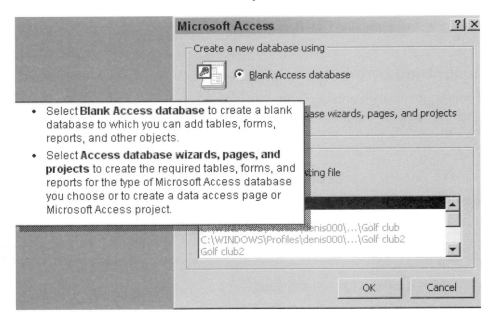

NOTE:

Help is covered in more detail in Before You Begin, Section 7.

6.2.6 Changing between View Modes (5.1.3.1)

Database objects such as Tables, forms and reports all have different view options. To change to other views, select the **View menu** on the Menu bar and select **Database Objects.** Now slide your mouse over to the right of the command and you can choose from the list of objects which window you wish to open.

Alternatively, use the shortcut button of the object in the database window.

Module 6

Presentation

Module 6

Presentation

MODULE 6

MODULE 6

Introduction

> ## Syllabus Goals for Module 6
>
> **Presentation** requires the candidate to demonstrate competence in using presentation tools on a computer. The candidate shall be able to accomplish tasks such as creating, formatting, modifying and preparing presentations using different slide layouts for display and printed distribution. He or she shall also be able to duplicate and move text, pictures, images and charts within the presentation and between presentations. The candidate shall demonstrate the ability to accomplish common operations with images, charts and drawn objects and to use various slide show effects.

Presentations

The professional presentation of information is an integral part of modern communication. A clear and effective presentation of important points facilitates the understanding of new projects and ideas. Information presented in a lively and colourful manner stimulates an audience. People's attention is caught and retained more easily. In the past, the range of techniques available to do this was limited.

Traditional blackboard and chalk gave way to the flipchart, which made it possible to prepare material in advance. The overhead projector extended the possibilities of the flipchart. Now it is the computer's turn.

Computers

A computer presentation offers several advantages over traditional methods. Presentations can be prepared on-screen, edited, sorted and transported with ease on a floppy disk, for example. Instead of the old static displays, animation can be added. Sound and video clips can be used. Audience reaction can be anticipated and suitable material can be displayed in response to it, or kept hidden if not needed.

Displays

Computer presentations are intended to be displayed on a big screen. While it is possible to use an ordinary computer monitor, this is only suitable for a very small group. Large monitors are very expensive and even the largest monitors are not big enough for a very large audience.

Making a presentation to a large audience requires the use of a screen and a special projector that can be plugged into the computer. The operator can then view the presentation on the computer monitor while behind him or her, as it is projected onto a large screen for the audience.

Projection

Two means of projection are commonly used for computer presentations. The first uses a projection panel in conjunction with an overhead projector (OHP). This is a very inefficient method, however. The area of the panel is far smaller than the area of the light tray on the overhead projector, so a lot of light is wasted. In addition, a standard overhead projector is not bright enough and a special OHP with high-power light output has to be purchased in addition to the projector.

The best solution is a data projector. This is a special projector with its own light source, designed so that no light is wasted. Modern projectors are compact and can be easily transported and set up.

MODULE 6

Section 1   Getting Started

What is PowerPoint?

PowerPoint is a presentation tool increasingly used by lecturers, teachers, conference speakers and businesspeople. It improves the quality of their presentations by using high-quality text, graphics and pictures. Presentations are usually structured by displaying the most important, relevant points during the talk, with the speaker themselves outlining these points in greater detail.

The completed presentation can be shown in many ways. It can be presented on a computer screen, or projected on a large conference screen using a computer data projector. It can also be printed out on paper for distribution as handouts or on transparent acetate sheets for use on conventional overhead projectors. 35mm slides of the presentation can be prepared for use with a standard 35mm photographic slide projector.

There are also many educational applications for PowerPoint apart from its use as a presentation tool. Many teachers have used the simple multimedia elements of the package to create short projects with their students. These and other applications of the package will become apparent as you become more familiar with the program.

Slides

A PowerPoint presentation is made up of a number of **slides**. Each slide typically has a title with supporting text in bulleted list format and/or graphics. The drawings can be created with PowerPoint or imported as standard ClipArt from the supplied library or from other sources.

Presentations can be made more attractive with the use of **transitions** – special effects to switch from one slide to another – and **builds** which use animation effects to reveal bullet points one at a time rather than displaying them all at the beginning.

1.1   First Steps with Presentations

1.1.1   Opening PowerPoint (6.1.1.1)

Open Microsoft PowerPoint by clicking the **PowerPoint** button on the Microsoft Office **Shortcut** Bar on the desktop.

Alternatively, click the **Start** button and select **Microsoft PowerPoint** in the **Programs** menu or sub-menu.

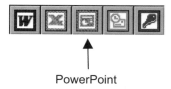

PowerPoint

A window will appear. This will offer several options:

- To open an existing presentation, choose **Open an existing presentation**. This will make the files area active.

- Select a file to open it.

- Click **OK** to open the file.

To close the presentation application:

- Click **Exit** on the **File** menu.

- If you have made any changes to the presentation you will be asked if you want to save them.

1.1.2 Opening One or Several Presentations (6.1.1.2)

If you have started PowerPoint and the window shown above does not appear, the **Don't show this window again** option has previously been selected as the default option. This forces PowerPoint to go straight into the blank presentation. In this case you will have to use the **Open** option on the **File** menu to access the PowerPoint window.

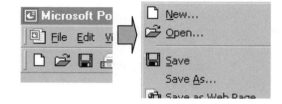

If you want to open several presentations at one time, hold down the **Ctrl** key while you pick the required files in the **Open an existing presentation** section of the window.

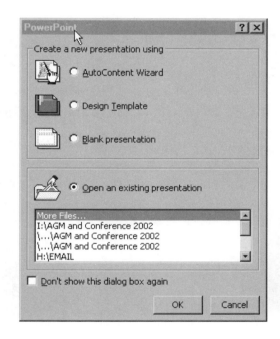

1.1.3 Creating a New Presentation (6.1.1.3)

You can create a new, blank presentation either when you first start PowerPoint or from within the open PowerPoint window.

- If you have just started PowerPoint, select **Blank Presentation** to begin a brand new presentation and click **OK**.

Or

- If PowerPoint is already open, click the **New** button on the Standard toolbar.

  In each instance, the **New Slide** window appears (see next page).

New Button

A number of different types of slides are presented for you to chose from. Click the samples in turn to see a description in the panel at the bottom right of the window of each type of slide.

The first slide on the top row – a **Title slide** – is already selected.

- Click **OK**.

The first slide appears on the screen.

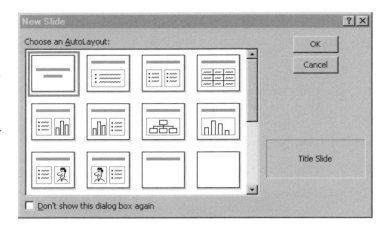

1.1.4 Save a Presentation to a Location on a Drive (6.1.1.4)

When you start to create a presentation, it is good practice to **save** it from the beginning and at regular intervals as you proceed. If you don't and a problem occurs, any unsaved work may be lost and you will have to start all over again. If you save after preparing each slide, you will only lose one slide in the event of a major problem occurring.

To save a presentation for the first time, do one of the following.

- Select **Save** from the **File** menu on the menu bar.

- Click the **Save** button on the toolbar.
  Alternatively, press **Ctrl + S** on the keyboard.

Whichever option you choose, the **Save** window appears. PowerPoint allocates a suggested file name, such as Presentation 1, 2, 3, etc. You may use this or replace it by typing a name in the **File name** box.

PowerPoint automatically assigns the extension **.ppt** to the file name.

- Click the **Save in** box to select a suitable location for the presentation.

- If necessary, click the **New Folder** button to save the presentation in a new folder.

- Click the **OK** button.

- In this situation the file will now be saved to the default drive into the **My Documents** folder.

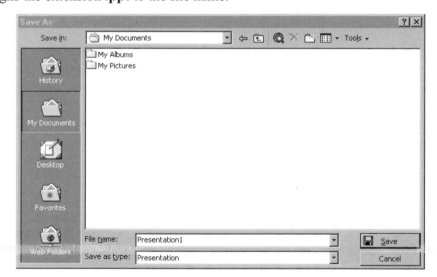

When you have named the file and saved it on disk, you can save any further additions or changes without having to go through the whole Save procedure again. Use one of the following methods.

- Click the **Save** button on the toolbar.

- Select **Save** in the **File** menu.
  Alternatively, press **Ctrl + S** on the keyboard.

Save
Button

1.1.5 Save a Presentation under Another Name (6.1.1.5)

Sometimes you may need to save your PowerPoint presentation under another name.

- Choose **Save As** in the **File** menu.

- Select an appropriate folder where you wish to save the file.

- Give a name to the presentation in the **File name** box.

- Click **Save**.

1.1.6 Save a Presentation in Another File Type (6.1.1.6)

A PowerPoint presentation is normally saved as a presentation but it can be saved in several other different formats, if required. You can, for example, save the presentation as a **template** that you can use later to prepare similar presentations without having to set up everything from the beginning.

Current versions of PowerPoint allow presentations to be saved in **HTML**, a format for use on the World Wide Web.

- Click in the **Save as type** box in the **Save** window.

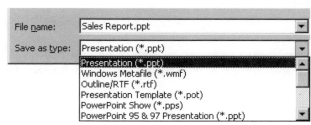

- Select the format you require from the menu.

The file will now be saved in the format you have specified.

Some of the PowerPoint file options are as follows:

- **Web Page** – Choose this format if you want to save the presentation in a web format using a language known as **hyper text markup language** (HTML). The file can then be the uploaded to the World Wide Web.

- **PowerPoint Version Number** – If you are sending your presentation to someone who is using a release of PowerPoint prior to PowerPoint 2000, you can choose a different version number, such as **PowerPoint 95**, **PowerPoint 97-2000 & 95** or **PowerPoint 4.0**.

- **Design Template** – Use a template format if you want the layout, formatting, headings, etc. of your presentation to be available as the basis of new presentations in the future. Your file will be added to the other design templates available within PowerPoint 2000.

- **Image File Formats** – You can save your presentation in a number of different image file formats which are supported by other graphics programs. Some of the available image formats are: **GIF** (graphics interchange format), **JPEG** (file interchange format), and **Windows Metafile** (a metafile image format).

- **Outline/RTF (Rich Text Format)** – Use this format if you want to save only the text contained on your slides so that it can be imported into a text editing program such as a word processing program, Notepad, etc.

1.1.6.1 Software-specific File Extensions

When you work with documents in different applications, the only way you can distinguish between applications is by the extension which is placed automatically after you save the document. This option is used to denote the program to which the file has been created and saved in.

Some examples include:
   *.dwg for AutoCad
   *.bmp for Bitmap files
   *.wav for sound files
   *.mid for MIDI files.

1.1.7 Switching between Open Presentations (6.1.1.7)

As outlined above, it is possible to open several presentations and have them running at the same time. In order to switch between several open presentations, select **Window** from the menu bar. This will show a list of the presentations that are currently open. The one with the tick beside it is the one that is active. Clicking on any of the presentations on the list will make it active, bringing the window containing the selected presentation to the forefront.

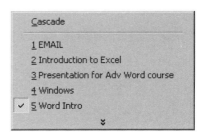

1.2 Adjusting Settings

1.2.1 Using Magnification/Zoom Tools (6.1.2.1)

Sometimes it may be necessary to take a closer look at your work. PowerPoint is equipped with a zoom option that allows you to magnify the work on screen.

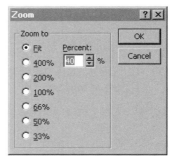

To magnify the screen click **View** and **Zoom.** There are two options to pick a zoom value a predefined percentage may be picked or a percentage value may be entered into the box provided. Picking the **Fit** option will resize the screen to fit into the original window. No matter which option is chosen, the **OK** button must be clicked for the zoom to take effect.

1.2.2 Displaying and Hiding Built-in Toolbars (6.1.2.2)

As with all the programs in the Office suite, PowerPoint has many tools that have been designed to make this powerful application easy to use. These tools are kept on toolbars. Because of the screen size, PowerPoint and the other applications in the Office suite cannot display all the toolbars at once. If all the toolbars were switched on at the same time, they would take up too much screen space and make using the program very difficult. As the manipulation of toolbars is common to all programs in the Office suite, Before You Begin, Section 5 covers this area in detail.

1.2.3 Modifying Basic Options (6.1.2.3)

When PowerPoint is first started it loads with a set of default options, for example the location where files will be stored, spelling and style, user information and a range of settings, which can be changed to suit your own needs.

To make these changes:

- Select **Options** in the **Tools** menu.

- Click any of the tabs to access the item to change.

- Here the user name is **Blackrock Training**, with the initials **BT**. These details can be changed by typing the new information in the **Name** and **Initials** boxes.

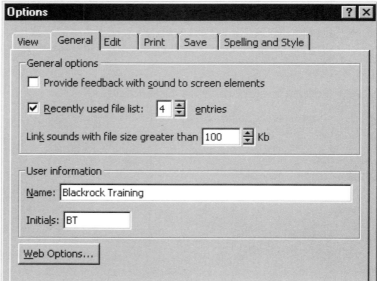

PowerPoint presentations can be saved in many formats. The default format option is a PowerPoint Presentation. This setting can be changed by clicking on the **Save** tab and choosing from the range of options displayed in the **Save PowerPoint files as** box.

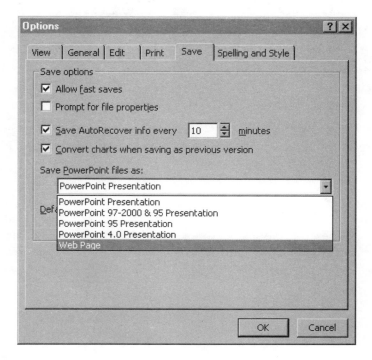

Another feature of this Save window is an area where the default folder is shown, i.e. the place where files are saved by default. Typing in a new path can change this default. Typing **C:\work** will change the default folder to work on the C: drive.

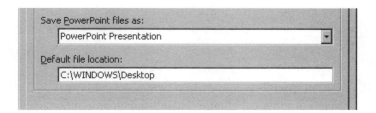

Section 2   Developing a Presentation

2.1   Presentation Views

PowerPoint comes with different views to help you while you are creating a presentation. The two main views you use in PowerPoint are **Normal** view and **Slide Sorter** view.

2.1.1 Normal View (6.2.1.1)

The **Normal** view is usually the most frequently used view, especially when you are designing your slides. The Normal view contains three panes: the **Outline** pane, the **Slide** pane and the **Notes** pane. These panes let you work on different aspects of your presentation in one screen. You can adjust the size of the different panes by dragging the pane borders.

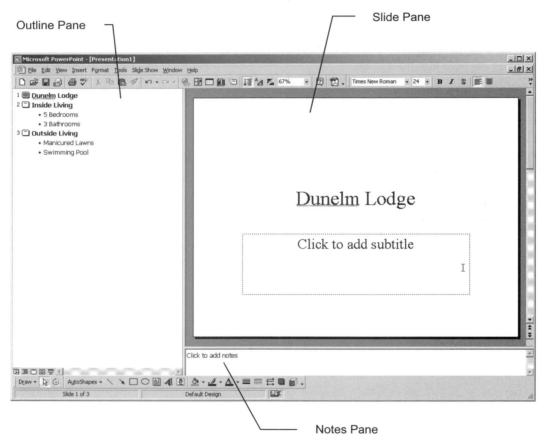

2.1.1.1 Outline Pane

The Outline pane can be used to organise and develop the content of your presentation. You can type all of the text of your presentation and rearrange bullet points, paragraphs and slides.

2.1.1.2 Slide Pane

In the Slide pane, you can see how your text looks on each slide. You can add graphics, movies and sounds, create hyperlinks and add animations to individual slides.

2.1.1.3 Notes Pane

The Notes pane allows you to type your own speaker notes relating to each slide. This information can then be printed before giving a presentation.

2.1.2 Outline View (6.2.1.1)

The Outline view can be used to quickly plan the main content of your presentation. As the Outline view only displays text, you can easily add slides and type in the main titles, coming back later in another view to fill in the detailed content.

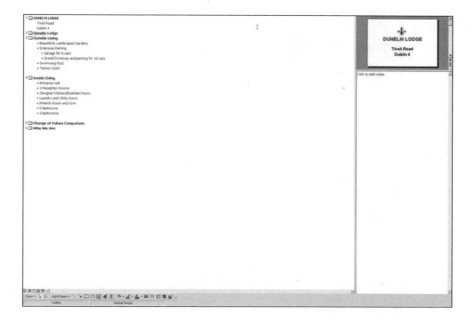

2.1.3 Slide View (6.2.1.1)

Slide view can be used to work with the overall look and content of a slide. You can concentrate on how and where graphics/text is placed without seeing any of the other elements otherwise displayed in the Normal view.

MODULE 6

2.1.4 Slide Sorter View (6.2.1.1)

Using the Slide Sorter view, you can see all the slides in your presentation on screen at the same time, displayed as *miniatures*. This makes it easy to add, delete and move slides, add timings and select animated transitions for moving from slide to slide.

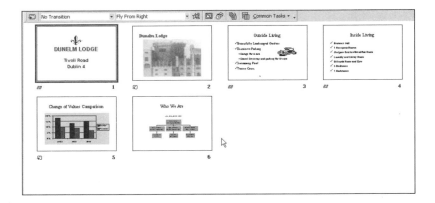

2.1.5 Slide Show (6.2.1.1)

The Slide Show view can be used at any time to start your onscreen presentation. Here you can preview how your presentation will appear to the audience.

2.1.6 Switching Between Views (6.2.1.2)

To easily switch between views, click the buttons at the lower left of the PowerPoint window. *Alternatively*, you can access all of the views, except the **Outline** view, from the **View** menu.

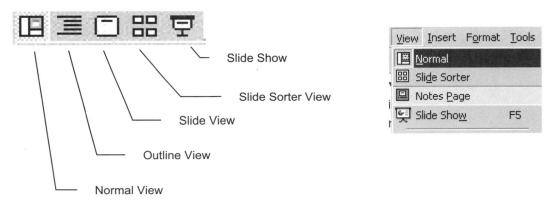

There is also a **Slide Show** menu option that can be used to switch to the Slide Show view. Slide Shows will be covered in more detail in Section 5 of this module.

Exercise 2A

In this exercise we will work with one of the built-in presentations so that we can use the views available in PowerPoint.

1   Choose **New** in the **File** menu.

2   Click on the **Presentations** tab.

3   Select the presentation named **Marketing Plan** and then click **OK**.

4   Switch to the **Slide Sorter** view.

5   Using the **Zoom** button on the toolbar, change the zoom to **75%**.

6   Take a few moments to briefly look at the content of a few slides.

7   Click on **slide 2** and then switch to the **Slide view**.

8   Using the pane on the left of the Slide view, look at the content of **slide 10** by clicking on the miniature for this slide.

9   Click onto **slide 1**.

10   Click on the **Slide Show** button to run the presentation. Click the left mouse button to advance to the next slide. When you have finished looking at the content of some of the slides in the show, press the **Esc** key to return to the **Slide view**.

11   Close the presentation without saving any changes.

2.2   Working with Slides

2.2.1   Adding a New Slide (6.2.2.1)

You can add a new slide into a presentation in a number of ways. The new slide will be added *after* the current slide on the screen.

- Click the **New Slide** icon on the Standard toolbar.

  Or

- Select **New Slide** in the **Insert** menu.

  Or

- Select **New Slide** on the **Common Tasks** toolbar, if it is displayed.

  Or

- *Alternatively*, use the keyboard shortcut, **Ctrl+M.**

  The New Slide window opens.

  Here you can use the **AutoLayout** feature to choose the slide type you want to use. There are 24 options to choose from.

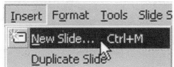

New Slide
Button

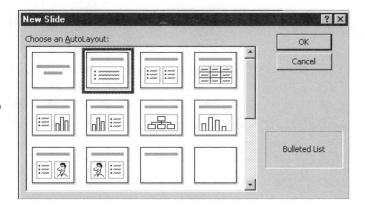

MODULE 6

2.2.2 Using AutoLayouts (6.2.2.2)

The AutoLayouts within the New Slide window provide different default layouts for the various types of slide you may wish to create. Each layout has one or more default **placeholders**. Placeholders are special boxes, often preformatted, guiding you as to where text, bullets, charts and so on are to be added.

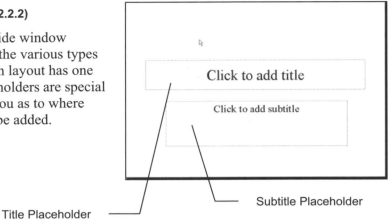

Title Placeholder

Subtitle Placeholder

When you click on one of the **AutoLayout** boxes, a description of that box appears in the lower right corner of the New Slide window. To create a slide based on that layout, click **OK** to continue.

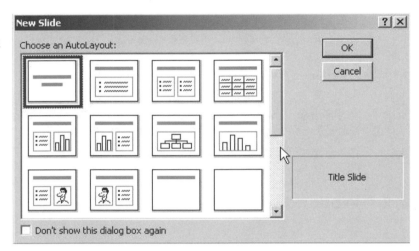

2.2.3 Changing the Slide Layout

Once you have inserted a slide based on a particular layout, you can easily change the layout to a different one of your choice. This is particularly useful if you have already added text to your slide as the text will remain but it will be adjusted to suit the new slide layout.

- Choose **Slide Layout** in the **Format** menu.

- Choose a new layout using the available samples.

- Click **Apply** to update the current slide layout with your new selection.

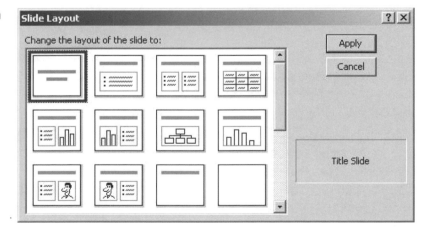

MODULE 6

2.2.4 Changing Background Colour (6.2.2.3)

The slide background colour can be changed for either an individual slide or for all slides. To change a slide background colour:

- Choose **Background** in the **Format** menu. The Background window appears. This box allows you to choose from a range of colours and fill effects.

- Click on the arrow to display colours in the current *colour* scheme.

- Select a colour from the available colour scheme options or choose a colour/effect using **More Colors** and **Fill Effects**.

- Choose **Apply** to change the current slide or **Apply to All** to change all the slides in the presentation.

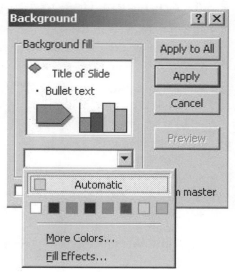

Exercise 2B

1   Create a new blank presentation.

2   Select the **Title Slide** layout for the first slide and click **OK**.

3   Use the **Click to add title** placeholder and type the following heading: **My Presentation**.

4   Choose **Slide Layout** from the **Format** menu.

5   Select the **Title Only** layout and then click **Apply**. Notice that your original title has now been moved into the title placeholder for the new slide layout.

6   Insert a new slide based on the **Organisation Chart** layout.

7   In the title placeholder type **Statistics for 2002**.

8   Choose **Slide Layout** from the **Format** menu.

9   Select the **Chart** layout and then click **Apply**.

10   In this part of the exercise, we will change the background colour for all slides in the presentation.

11   Choose **Background** in the **Format** menu.

12   Click on the arrow and select a colour from the available colour scheme colours.

13   Click Apply to All.

14   Switch between slide 1 and slide 2 to check that both slides have been updated.

MODULE 6

2.3   Using Design Templates

2.3.1   Applying a Design Template (6.2.3.1)

An effective background design can add a professional look to your presentation. PowerPoint is supplied with an extensive range of pre-prepared templates. A template can be selected when starting a presentation.

- Choose **New** from the **File** menu.

- Select **New Presentation** when the window appears.

- Select the **Design Templates** tab.

- Click on the available templates to display an example of its design attributes in the Preview box.

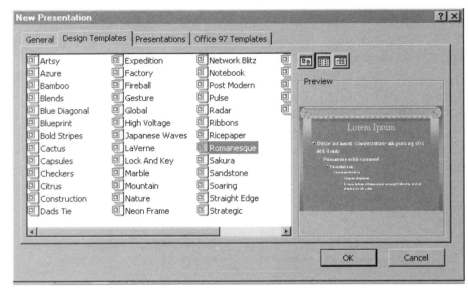

- Click **OK** when you have selected the template for your new presentation.

2.3.2   Changing the Design Template (6.2.3.2)

Once you have started to develop your presentation, you may decide that the design template should be different from your initial choice. To change the design template for an existing presentation:

- Select **Apply Design Template** in the **Format** menu. The **Apply Design** window appears.

- Choose the required template and click on **Apply** to change the current template.

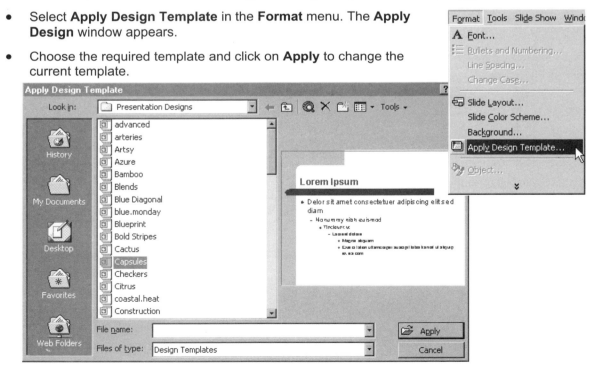

Exercise 2C

1   Close the current presentation without saving.

2   Choose **New** in the **File** menu.

3   Click on Design Templates.

4   Select **Artsy** from the available template list and click **OK**.

5   Choose the **Title Slide** layout and click **OK**.

6   Add the following title to the first slide: **ECDL Training**.

7   Insert a new slide using the **Title Only** layout.

8   Add the following title to the new slide: **Module 1**.

9   Choose Apply Design Template in the Format menu.

10   Select **Blends** from the available template list and click **Apply**.

11   View the changes for slides 1 and 2.

12   Change the design template to **Cactus** and view the changes in your presentation.

13   Select the **Title Slide** layout for the first slide and click **OK**.

2.3.3 Adding Notes to a Slide (6.3.1.2 and 6.6.1.3)

Each slide has a notes page available. You can use the notes page to add any relevant details relating to each slide, such as "speaker notes", reminders, and so on. The information on the notes pages can be printed for your own reference but will not be displayed during the presentation.

The best view for entering speaker notes is the **Normal view**. Use the **Notes pane** to enter your notes.

MODULE 6

Exercise 2D

1   Select **slide 1** in your presentation.

2   Ensure you are working in the Normal view.

3   Click in the **Notes pane**.

4   Make up a sentence relating to the first slide.

5   Select slide 2.

6   Make up another sentence for this slide.

7   Close the presentation without saving the changes.

2.4   Manipulating Tools

As with the other programs in Microsoft Office, you can copy, move, resize and delete objects within any slide. Objects are anything that can be inserted into a slide, such as text, a picture, an image, a chart, a drawn object and so on.

Before an object can be copied, moved, etc., it must be selected. You can select an object simply by clicking on it. However, if the object is contained within a *text placeholder*, you may need to click on the border of the placeholder a second time to ensure that it is correctly selected. On the second click, the border around the placeholder will change from this style ///// to this style :::::: as is more clearly seen in the example below.

Style of border around text placeholder after it has been clicked once.

Style of border around text placeholder after it has been clicked twice. The placeholder is now completely selected.

2.4.1   Duplicating Objects (6.3.3.1 and 6.4.4.1)

To duplicate an object within a presentation:

- Click on the object and then click the **Copy** button on the toolbar. If the object you are copying is in a *placeholder*, click on the border of the placeholder to select its entire contents.

Copy Button

- Select the slide into which you want to place the copied object.

- Click the **Paste** button on the Standard toolbar.

Paste Button

If you want to copy an object to another presentation, open the presentation and select the appropriate destination slide before clicking the **Paste** button.

NOTE

You can also copy objects using the mouse. Click on the object to select it. Hold down the Ctrl key and drag with the mouse to the new location. Release the mouse on completion.

2.4.2   Moving Objects (6.3.3.2 and 6.4.4.2)

To move an object within a presentation:

- Click on the object and then click the **Cut** button on the toolbar. If the object you are moving is in a *placeholder*, click on the border of the placeholder to select its entire contents.

Cut Button

- Select the slide into which you want to place the moved object.

- Click the **Paste** button on the toolbar.

Paste Button

If you want to move an object to another presentation, open the presentation and select the appropriate destination slide before clicking the **Paste** button.

NOTE

You can also move objects using the mouse. Click on the object to select it. Drag with the mouse to the new location. Release the mouse on completion.

2.4.3 Deleting (6.3.3.4 and 6.4.4.3)

To delete an object within a presentation:

- Click on the object and then press **Delete**.

  If the object you are deleting is in a *placeholder*, click on the border of the placeholder to select its entire contents.

Exercise 2E

1   Create a new presentation based on the **Presentation** design called **Selling a Product or Service**.

2   Select **slide 6** which has the title **Our Strengths**.

3   Using the mouse drag the three images to move them closer to the title on the slide.

4   Using **Ctrl** and the mouse, create a fourth image that appears below the other three.

5   Select the fourth image and now press **Delete** to remove it.

2.4.4 Resizing Objects (6.3.3.3 and 6.4.3.7)

You can resize any object within a slide using the mouse.

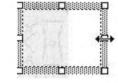

- Click on the object to select it.

- Hover the mouse over one of the selection boxes that appear around the object.

- Click on the box and drag with the mouse to resize the object.

You can also resize proportionally using the following keys in conjunction with the mouse.

Proportionally from a corner	**Shift** and drag a corner sizing handle
Vertically, horizontally or diagonally from the centre outward	**Ctrl** and drag a sizing handle
Proportionally from the centre outward	**Ctrl+Shift** and drag a corner sizing handle

Exercise 2F

1   Practise resizing any of the objects (including the placeholders) in the current presentation.

2   Close the presentation without saving it.

MODULE 6

Section 3   Text and Images

Presentations are usually based on a combination of text, images, pictures, charts and drawings. Text communicates the main points of your presentation to the target audience. Images are a useful way of visually enhancing your presentations and a combination of both images and text can help you to develop professional-looking and attractive presentations.

Scenario

For the remainder of this module, we will create a presentation using the following example:

We are working for an estate agent and have a prestigious period property we wish to sell. We are going to advertise the usual way but we also want to show prospective buyers a presentation for the property which they can take away with them if they have a computer.

3.1   Inputting and Formatting Text

To work with this section you will need to create a new presentation. Proceed as follows:

- Close any presentation that is currently open in PowerPoint.

- Choose **New** on the **File** menu.

- Select **Blank Presentation** in the **New Presentation** window.

- When the **New Slide** window appears, select **Title Slide** for the first slide layout in your presentation.

- Click **OK** to continue.

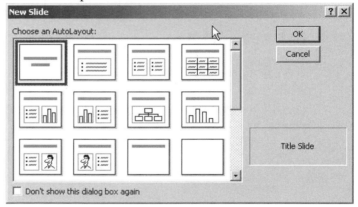

3.1.1 Adding Text to Placeholders (6.3.1.1)

Text can be added to a slide using the sample placeholders available on each slide's layout. Text is usually added when you are working in the **Normal view**, **Slide view** or **Outline view**.

- Click on the **Slide View** button to view the current slide on the entire screen.

- Click in the **Click to add title** box.

- Type the name of the property we are selling – **DUNELM LODGE**.

- Click in the **Click to add sub-title** box.

  Type the address of the property – **Tivoli Road
  Dublin 4**

  The first slide has been created. It should appear as in the

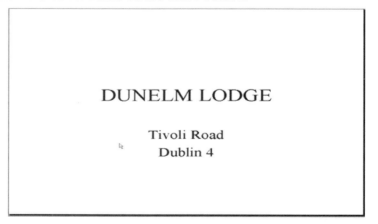

illustration. At the moment it only contains a title and sub-title on a blank background.

The next step would be to add a new slide. For the next slide we will use a different view.

- Click on the **Normal View** button to switch to an alternate view in PowerPoint.

New Slide Button

- Choose **New Slide** from the **Insert** menu or click the **New Slide** button on the Standard toolbar to insert a new slide into your presentation.

- Select **Title Only** for the second slide. This slide will contain the name of the property again, but later on you will add an *image* of the property to the slide.

- Click in the text placeholder and type **Dunelm Lodge**. Do not use all uppercase for this heading as we will change the *case* later on.

- Click on **slide 1** in the **Outline Pane** to view its content.

- Click back on **slide 2** in the **Outline Pane**.

3.1.2 Adding a Bulleted List Slide

A **bullet point** is a short piece of text with a black dot (•) in front of it to catch the eye, as demonstrated in numerous places in this manual. PowerPoint adds the bullets automatically when you are using a **Bulleted List** slide layout.

When you click in the **Click to add text** box on a Bulleted List slide, the first bullet is already in place. Type the first line of text and then press **Enter** to start the next bulleted line.

> • Click to add text

If you want to create a sub-point, use the **Tab** key to indent to the next bullet level or **Shift+Tab** to demote to the previous tab level.

> • **This is a main point**
>   – This is a sub-point

Use the **ENTER** key at the end of each line except the last.

To update your presentation, proceed as follows:

- Add a new slide which uses the **Bulleted List** layout.

- Enter the following text onto the new slide.

Inside Living

- Entrance Hall
- 3 Reception Rooms
- Kitchen/Breakfast Room
- Utility
- Billiards Room and Gym
- 5 Bedrooms
- 3 Bathrooms

- Add another **Bulleted List** slide to your presentation. The new slide should be slide number **4**.

MODULE 6

- Enter the text shown in the following illustration to your new slide.

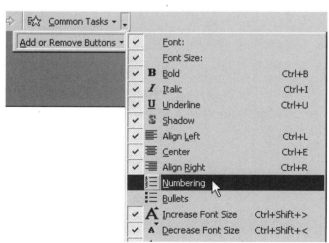

3.1.3 Using Numbers instead of Bullets

You can select numbering instead of bullets for your slides. There are two ways to select numbering.
Start with a bulleted list:

- When the first bullet appears on the slide, press the **Backspace** key to delete it.

- Type the number one (1) followed by a full stop or a bracket.

- Type the text you want and press **Enter**.
  The numbering continues automatically.

Alternatively, you can use the buttons on the toolbar:

- Click the **Numbering** button on the toolbar.
  To change back to bullets from Numbering, click the **Bullets** button.

Bullets and
Numbering Buttons

If the **Bullets** and **Numbering** buttons do not appear on the toolbar, display them as follows.

- Click the arrow beside the **Common Tasks** button at the right of the toolbar (arrowed in the illustration).

- Click on the **Add or Remove Buttons** option.
  A selection of extra buttons is displayed.

- Click on the **Numbering** or **Bullets** button as required.
  The buttons will then appear on the Formatting toolbar.

Bullets can be of different shapes, sizes and styles for different effects. To format the bullets, do the following:

- Select **Bullet** (or **Bullets and Numbering**) in the **Format** menu to make your own choices.

For more information, see Section 3.1.9 in this module.

3.1.4 Editing the Text Content of a Slide (6.3.1.2)

You can easily modify the content of a slide by adding to the text or deleting existing text. To update your sample presentation, proceed as follows:

- Save the presentation, naming it **Dunelm Lodge**.
- Select **slide 1**, which is the main title slide.
- Change the address from **Tivoli Road** to **Tivoli Avenue**.
- Select **slide 3**.
- Change the line **Kitchen/Breakfast Room** so that it reads **Designer Kitchen/Breakfast Room**.
- Change the line **Utility** so that it reads **Laundry and Utility Room**.
- Change the content of **slide 4** so that it reads **Garage for 6 Cars**.
- Save the presentation but do not close it.

3.1.5 Text Formatting (6.3.1.3, 6.3.1.4 and 6.3.1.7)

Text can be formatted in the same ways that it can in other programs, such as Word and Excel.

- To format portions of text, highlight the text using the mouse.
  Alternatively, to format the entire contents of a text placeholder, click on the placeholder border that surrounds the text.
- Use the **Font** option on the **Format** menu to change the appearance and formatting of text.

Or

- Use the available buttons on the **Formatting toolbar**, as shown below.

Exercise 3A

1   Select **slide 1**.

2   Select the text placeholder that surrounds the main title (**Dunelm Lodge**).

3   Choose **Font** from the **Format** menu.

4   Change the font to **Arial**, the font style to **bold**, the size to **54pt** and also select **Shadow**.

5   Click **OK** to return to your slide.

6   Select the text placeholder that surrounds the sub-title (**Tivoli Avenue**).

7   Using the Formatting toolbar change the font to **Arial**, the font style to **bold**, the size to **44pt** and also select **Shadow**. Click the **Underline** button to underline the text.

8   Select slide 3, Inside Living.

9   Click in the word **Designer** and then click the **Italics** button on the Formatting toolbar.

10   Save the presentation but do not close it.

3.1.6 Text Alignment and Case (6.3.1.5 and 6.3.1.8)

Depending on the text placeholder that you are using, text will automatically align, usually either to the left or to the centre of the placeholder. To change the paragraph alignment, do the following:

- Select the paragraph you want to align by clicking anywhere in it.

Alignment Buttons

- Click the appropriate **Alignment** button on the toolbar.

  Alternatively, select **Alignment** in the **Format** menu. The Alignment sub-menu appears.

  Click **Left, Center, Right** or **Justify** to align the paragraph as desired.

  Note the keyboard shortcuts in the Alignment sub-menu:

  - **Ctrl + L** for left alignment

  - **Ctrl + R** for right alignment

  - **Ctrl + E** for centred text

To change the case of text without having to type it all out again, do the following.

- Select the text you want to change.

- Select **Change Case** in the **Format** menu.

- Click to select the format you require.

- Click **OK**.

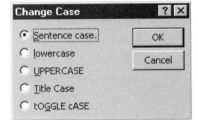

Exercise 3B

1   Select **slide 2**.

2   Select the text placeholder that surrounds the title (**Dunelm Lodge**).

3   Choose **Change Case** in the **Format** menu.

4   Select **UPPERCASE** and then click **OK** to return to the slide.

5   Now change the case for this text placeholder back to **Title Case**.

6   With the text placeholder still selected, left align the text using the appropriate button on the **Formatting toolbar**.

7   Save the presentation but do not close it.

3.1.7 Applying Different Colours to Text (6.3.1.6)

Depending on the template that your presentation is based on, PowerPoint provides a set of predefined colours in a **colour scheme** to simplify the choice of colours for your presentation. When changing the colour of text, you should try to select from the colours provided in the colour scheme. However, you can choose from the **More Colours** option on the Colour menu but these may not all be complementary to the existing colours in your colour scheme.

To change the colour of text within your slide:

- Select the text or click on the text placeholder you wish to apply a new colour to.

- Choose **Font** in the **Format** menu.

- Click on the arrow for the **Colour** box.

- Select a colour from the row of colours in the current **colour scheme** or click on **More Colors** to select any colour of your choice.

- Click **OK** to return to your slide.

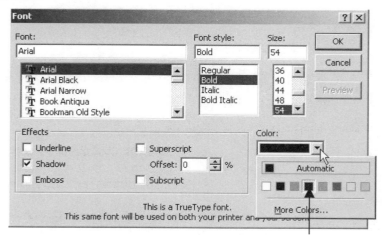

Colour Scheme Colours

3.1.8 Adjusting Line Spacing (6.3.1.9)

To change the line spacing in a paragraph, first click in the paragraph in question. *Alternatively*, select all the paragraphs if there is more than one.

- Select **Line Spacing** in the **Format** menu.
  The Line Spacing window appears.
  Line spacing controls the space between the lines in a paragraph.

- Click in the right-hand box to select either **Lines** or **Points** as the unit of measurement. Points allow finer control over the spacing.

- Set the number of lines or points in the left-hand box.
  Before paragraph controls the space *between* a paragraph and the paragraph that comes *before* it.
  Set your preferences as for line spacing.
  After paragraph controls the space *between* a paragraph and the paragraph that *follows* it. Set your preferences as for line spacing.

- Click **OK**. Your line and paragraph spacing choices are applied.

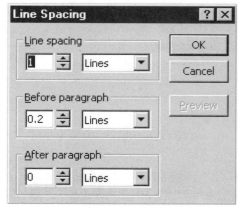

The menus that appear let you set the line spacing in either lines or points. A line is the current line height, based on the text size in use. Spacing can be set in full lines or half lines. Points are the preferred unit used by designers and printers to measure text. There are 72 points to an inch so much finer spacing is possible.

MODULE 6

Exercise 3C

1   Select **slide 1**. Select the text placeholder that surrounds the title (**Dunelm Lodge**).

2   Choose **Font** in the **Format** menu.

3   Click on the **Colour** arrow.

4   Select the blue shade that displays the label **Follow Accent Scheme Colour**. Click **OK** to return to your slide.

5   Select **slide 2**.

6   Select the text placeholder. Change the colour of the heading to the same as the one used on **slide 1**.

7   Select **slide 4** (**Outside Living**). Select the text placeholder for the bulleted information.

8   Choose **Line Spacing** in the **Format** menu. Change the **Before paragraph** to **0** lines and the **After paragraph** to **.5** lines.

9   Click **OK** to return to the slide.

10   Select **slide 3**. Change the line spacing for the bulleted information in the same way as for slide 4. Remember to select the text placeholder first.

3.1.9 Changing the Style of Bullets and Numbers (6.3.1.10)

You can easily change the style of the bullets or numbers that you are using in a bulleted or numbered list using the following sequence:

- Select the placeholder for the bulleted or numbered list if you wish to change the bullet/number style for the entire placeholder.

  Alternatively, you can select just the line or lines you want to modify.

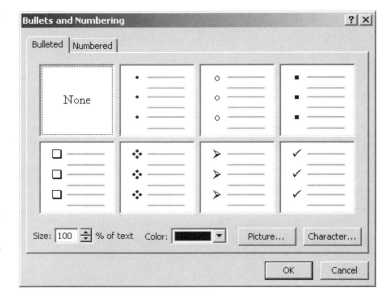

- Choose **Bullets and Numbering** in the **Format** menu.

- Select the appropriate tab, either **Bulleted** or **Numbered** depending on the current information you are changing.

- Choose a style from one of the predefined samples.

- Use the **Size** box to increase the bullets or numbers in ratio to the text. For example, setting the size to 110% of text means that the bullets/numbers would be **10% greater** than the text size. Setting the size to **90%** would mean that the bullets/number would be **10% smaller** than the text size.

- Use the **Color** button to select a colour for the bullets or numbers.

- If you are working on the **Bulleted** tab, you can use the **Picture** button to select a bullet style from a gallery of picture bullets.

  Alternatively, you can use the **Character** button to select a bullet based on the characters in the fonts that are currently available.

- If you are working on the **Numbered** tab, you can use the **Start at** box to control the first number for the current list. All subsequent numbers in the list are also updated in sequence, based on the starting number.

- Click **OK** to update your bulleted/numbered list.

Exercise 3D

1   Select **slide 3** (**Inside Living**). Click on the text placeholder to select the entire bulleted list. If you do not select the entire placeholder, only one line of the bulleted list will be updated as you continue with the next few steps.

2   Choose Bullets and Numbering in the Format menu.

3   Click on the **Numbered** tab. Select the **A. B. C.** style and then click **OK** to return to the slide.

4   Ensure the text placeholder is still selected and access the Bullets and Numbering window.

5   Click on the **Bulleted** tab. Select the tick mark style (✓). Set the **Size** to **100% of text**.

6   Click **OK** to return to the slide.

7   Select **slide 4** (**Outside Living**). Format the text placeholder so that the bullets are the same as for slide 3.

     Once you have formatted the entire placeholder, notice that even the indented bullets have used the same tick mark as the first level bullets. Let's change them to something different.

8   Select only the two sub-level bullet lines.

9   Choose **Bullets and Numbering** from the **Format** menu. Select the square bullet style from the available samples. Change the **Size** to **90% of text**.

10   Click **OK** to return to the slide.

3.2   Working with Pictures and Images

Pictures and images can help to place emphasis within your presentations or simply enhance the overall visual effect.

Some of the slide layouts you can choose from have placeholders that can be used to assist you when you wish to insert such items as **ClipArt**, **media clips** or **objects** (an **object** can be any saved file, such as a photo, drawing, chart, spreadsheet and so on).

Text & ClipArt Placeholders

Text & Media Clip Placeholders

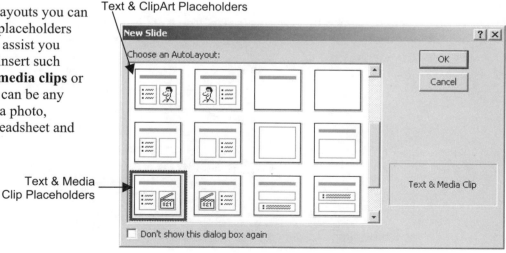

NOTE

For the purposes of this syllabus, the term *picture* refers to a visual representation available from an inbuilt gallery, such as pictures in the **ClipArt Gallery**. The term *image* refers to a visual representation that is inserted from a file, such as a scanned photograph or drawing.

MODULE 6

3.2.1 Inserting a Picture Using the Slide Layout (6.3.2.1)

To insert a picture using the Slide layout, follow this sequence:

- Click the **New Slide** button on the Standard toolbar.

- Select an AutoLayout from the **New Slide** window that contains a placeholder for **ClipArt**.

- Click **OK** to add the new slide.

- **Double click to add ClipArt** in the placeholder that is displayed.

- **The Microsoft ClipArt Gallery** will appear.

- Using the **Pictures** tab, click on a **Category** to open a set of ClipArt pictures.

- Click on the picture you wish to use and choose **Insert clip**.

NOTE

Once you have inserted a picture in this way, you can replace the picture simply by deleting it and then double clicking again to access the ClipArt Gallery.

3.2.2 Inserting a Picture onto Any Slide (6.3.2.1)

In addition to using the picture placeholders to insert a ClipArt picture, you can also add a picture to any slide within your presentation using these steps:

- Select the slide where the picture is to be added.

- Choose **Picture** from the **Insert** menu.

- Choose **Clip Art** from the sub-menu that appears.

- Click on the **Pictures** tab.

- Click on a **Category** you wish to use.

- Click on the picture you wish to insert.

- Choose **Insert clip**.

- Close the **Insert ClipArt** window or minimise it for later use.

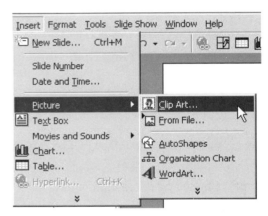

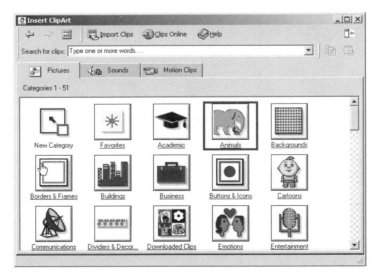

Exercise 3E

In this exercise we are going to insert a picture on the title slide that represents a decorative symbol associated with the property.

1   Select **slide 1**.

2   Choose **Picture** from the **Insert** menu. Select **Clip Art** from the sub-menu.

3   Click on the Category known as Dividers & Decorations.

4   Click on the **ornaments** picture and choose **Insert clip**.

       If you don't have this picture, find one that you would like to use instead.

5   Close the **Insert ClipArt** window if necessary.

6   Move the picture so that it appears above the title and resize it slightly.

7   Save the presentation but do not close it.

DUNELM LODGE

Tivoli Road
Dublin 4

Exercise 3F

In this exercise we are going to insert another picture onto the **Outside Living** slide. If you don't have exactly the same picture as used in the example, find one that you would like to use instead.

1   Select **slide 4 (Outside Living)**.

2   Choose **Picture** from the **Insert** menu. Select **Clip Art** from the sub-menu.

3   Click on the **Category** named **Transportation**.

4   Click on the cars picture and choose **Insert clip**.

       Close the **Insert ClipArt** window if necessary.

5   Move the picture so that it appears in a similar location to the illustration.

       Resize the picture if you so wish. If you have used a different picture than the one in this exercise, the size of the picture you have chosen may already be suitable for the slide.

6   Save the presentation but do not close it.

Outside Living

✓Beautifully Landscaped Gardens

✓Extensive Parking

   ▪ Garage for 6 cars

   ▪ Gravel Driveway and parking for 10 cars

✓Swimming Pool

✓Tennis Court

MODULE 6

3.2.3 Inserting an Image into a Slide (6.3.2.2)

As we have already discussed, for the purposes of this Syllabus an image is a visual representation that is brought into PowerPoint as a file.

To insert an image into a slide:

- Select the slide where the image is to be added.

- Choose **Picture** from the **Insert** menu.

- Choose **From File** from the sub-menu that appears.

- Use the **Look in** box to select the folder where the image is located.

- Select the appropriate image.

- Click **Insert**.

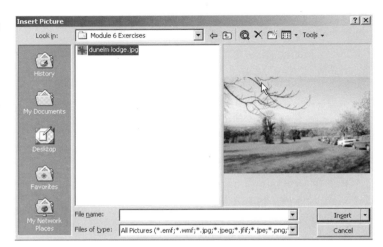

Exercise 3G

In this exercise we are going to insert a photograph of the view from Dunelm Lodge onto the second slide.

1   Select **slide 2**.

2   Choose **Picture** from the **Insert** menu. Select **From File** from the sub-menu.

3   Using the **Look in** box, select the folder where the photograph is stored. Your instructor will advise you of this location.

4   Choose **Dunelm Lodge** and then click **Insert**.

5   Resize the picture and move it if necessary.

6   Save the presentation but do not close it.

MODULE 6

Section 4   Charts, Graphs and Drawn Objects

4.1   Using Charts and Graphs

PowerPoint includes a program called Microsoft Graph that can help you prepare effective charts, also known as graphs, for use in a presentation.

This module of the Syllabus covers the basics for creating a chart in PowerPoint. For more information on charts, see Module 4.

4.1.1 Inserting a Chart (6.4.1.1)

- Add a new slide that includes a chart placeholder. Use the **Double click to add chart** placeholder to add the new chart to the slide.

Or

Select the slide where the new chart is to be inserted. Click the **Insert Chart** button on the toolbar.

Insert Chart
Button

A sample graph appears on the slide with a **Datasheet** window in front.

The datasheet is like a small spreadsheet with rows, columns and cells. It contains sample information.

You can move the datasheet to any part of the screen to give a clear view of the chart by dragging its Title bar.

Datasheet Window

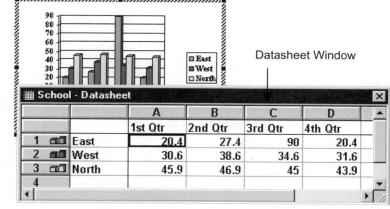

- Click on the cells in turn and enter your own information to replace what is there.

The graph in the background adjusts automatically as you enter the information.

- When you have entered all the information, close the Datasheet window.

- The graph remains on the slide.

- **Position** and **resize** the graph on the slide, as required.

- To return to the slide, click anywhere outside the graph.

4.1.2 Editing a Chart

When you have finished working on a chart you can return to your normal slide functions by clicking outside of the chart, i.e. on any area of the slide. If you want to make additions or changes to an existing chart, simply double click on the chart object to return to chart mode.

MODULE 6

4.1.3 Working with Datasheets

To amend data on a chart, you first have to display the datasheet.

- Ensure you are working in chart mode.
- Click the **View Datasheet** button on the Chart toolbar.

View Datasheet
Button

The first row and the first column of the datasheet are reserved for titles by default. In our example the first row contains **1st Qtr**, **2nd Qtr** and so on. The first column contains **East**, **West** and **North**. Numbers can be entered in all the other cells on the datasheet.

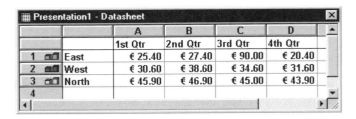

While the datasheet behaves like a spreadsheet, its functions are limited. It is not possible to use formulas in the cells, for example. You can, however, reformat the data if necessary.

- Select the cells that you want to reformat.
- Select **Number** in the **Format** menu.
- The **Format number** window appears.

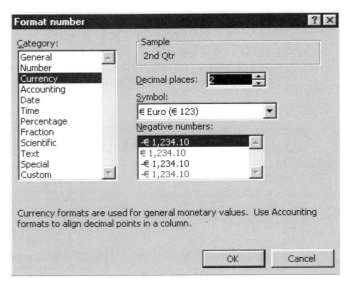

In the illustration, the Euro currency format has been selected. The font in selected cells can be formatted in a similar manner.

Exercise 4A

In this exercise we are going to create a chart which shows a comparison in the increase percentage values of property in Dublin versus the national statistics.

| 1 | Select **slide 4**. |

New Slide
Button

2	Click the **New Slide** button to insert a new slide.
3	In the New Slide window select the **Chart** AutoLayout and then click **OK**.
4	In the Click to add title, type the heading Change of Values Comparison.
5	Use the **Double click to add chart** placeholder to create your new chart.
6	Enter the data shown in the illustration into the datasheet for your new chart (see next page).

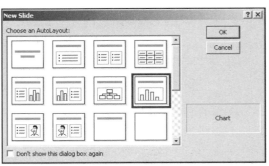

7   To delete the contents of **Column D**, click on the letter **D** and then press **Delete**.

8   To delete the contents of **Row 3**, click on the number **3** and then press **Delete**.

Look at how your chart has been designed. Microsoft Graph has automatically formatted the chart using a number of default values.

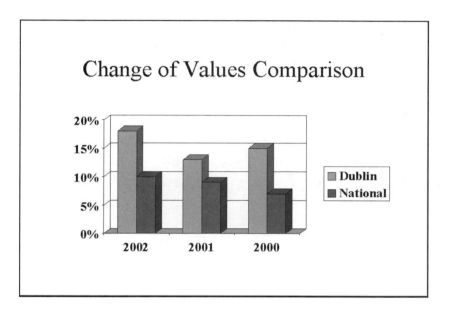

9   Click outside of the chart to return to your slide.

4.1.4 Changing Chart Types (6.4.1.4)

When you enter data into the datasheet for a new slide, PowerPoint automatically bases the chart on a default chart type, which is usually a three-dimensional column chart. You can, however, change the type of chart to a different style of your choice.

- Choose **Chart Type** from the **Chart** menu.

- Click on the **Standard Types** tab.

- Make a selection from the **Chart type** panel.

- Make a sub-selection using the **Chart sub-type** panel.

    If you only want the settings to affect a selection you have previously made in the chart (such as by clicking on a particular column, line, pie slice, etc.), click the **Apply to selection** box.

    If you have applied any of your own formatting to the current chart but decide that you want only the default settings for the chart type you have selected, click the **Default formatting** box.

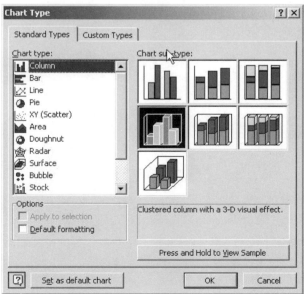

To view how your chart will appear with the selections you have made in the **Chart Type** window, click and hold on the **Press and Hold to View Sample** button.

- If you want the chart type and sub-type to become the new default, click the **Set as default chart** button.

- Click **OK** to change your chart to the new chart type settings.

- Click outside of the chart to return to chart mode if you have finished making changes to the chart.

This ECDL Foundation approved courseware product incorporates learning reinforcement exercises. These exercises are included to help the candidate in their training for the ECDL. The exercises included in this courseware product are not ECDL certification tests and should not be construed in any way as ECDL certification tests. For information about authorised ECDL test centres in different national territories please refer to the ECDL Foundation website at www.ecdl.com.

Exercise 4B

In this exercise we are going to change the chart type and sub-type.

1   Double click in the existing chart so that you are working back in chart mode.

2   Choose **Chart Type** in the **Chart** menu.

3   Select **Bar** in the **Chart type** panel.

4   In the **Chart sub-type** panel select the sub-type with the description **Clustered bar with 3-D visual effect**.

5   Click **OK** to create the chart.

6   Now change the **Chart Type** to a line chart. Select a sub-type of your choice. View the resulting chart on completion.

4.1.4 About Chart Types

As you already know, the chart type that appears by default when a chart is inserted on a slide is a columnar chart. It can display all the information in all the cells in the datasheet at the same time.

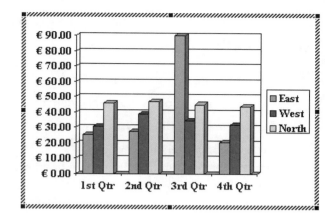

Not all charts are able to display all such information. If you want to use a different kind of chart, be sure that the chart type you select is able to display information in the datasheet that you want it to show.

A pie chart, for example, would be unable to show all the information in the datasheet together. It would only be able to display the information in the cells of one row only.

To make a graph using one column or one row in the datasheet, the other columns or rows can be deselected, leaving the rest of the data *live*. To deselect a column or row, double click the appropriate column or row header. The chart is adjusted automatically to reflect the changes.

The following examples demonstrate how different graphs may be produced from selected data by modifying the datasheet.

The datasheet shows the data in column **B** as live, the other data having been deselected **by double clicking the column headers**.

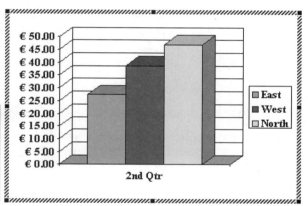

The chart displays the **2nd Qtr** data in column B

Presentation1 - Datasheet		A	B	C	D
		1st Qtr	2nd Qtr	3rd Qtr	4th Qtr
1	East	€ 25.40	€ 27.40	€ 90.00	€ 20.40
2	West	€ 30.60	€ 38.60	€ 34.60	€ 31.60
3	North	€ 45.90	€ 46.90	€ 45.00	€ 43.90
4					

This datasheet shows the data in row **3** as live. The other data has been deselected **by double clicking the row headers**.

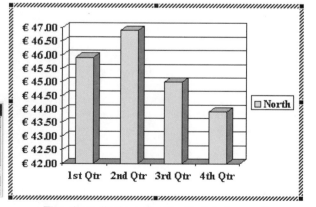

The chart displays the **North** data in row 3

Presentation1 - Datasheet		A	B	C	D
		1st Qtr	2nd Qtr	3rd Qtr	4th Qtr
1	East	€ 25.40	€ 27.40	€ 90.00	€ 20.40
2	West	€ 30.60	€ 38.60	€ 34.60	€ 31.60
3	North	€ 45.90	€ 46.90	€ 45.00	€ 43.90
4					

MODULE 6

Exercise 4C

In this exercise we are going to create a pie chart based on only the national statistics for 2000 to 2002.

1   Choose **Chart Type** in the **Chart** menu.

2   Select **Pie** in the **Chart type** box and select the first pie sample in the **Chart sub-type** box.

3   Click **OK** to create the chart.

             Notice that the **Dublin** figures have been selected in the datasheet (**Dublin**
             should have a small pie sample next to it in the datasheet).

4   Double click **row 1** to turn off the **Dublin** figures. The **National** figures will now be activated.

5   Now change the chart type to a **Column** chart using the first **chart sub-type** and clicking **OK**
             to draw the chart. Notice that only the **National** figures are displayed.

6   Double click **row 1** to turn the **Dublin** figures back on.

7   Click outside of the chart to return to the slide.

4.1.5 Changing the Background Colour in the Chart (6.4.1.2)

You can change the background colour in the chart to a colour of your choice. The default for a chart is for it to have no background fill colour so that it takes on the appearance of the background of the slide. You may, however, have occasions when you wish to change the background colour to emphasise the details of the chart. To do so, follow this sequence:

- Ensure that you are working within the chart. Double click on the chart to select it.

- Close the datasheet so that the chart itself is active.

- A border surrounds the outside of the chart. Hover your mouse
  near this border and a **tip box** will appear on the mouse labeled
  Chart Area. Click to select the **Chart Area**.

- Click on the arrow for the **Fill Colour** button on the toolbar.

- Select a colour from the available list.

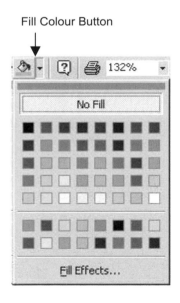

Fill Colour Button

4.1.6 Changing the Colour of a Chart Series (6.4.1.3)

The elements in a chart (such as the lines, bars, columns, pie slices, etc.) are known as the data **series**. Each series represents a different category of data for your chart. For example, in your chart you have a series for **Dublin** and another series for **National** figures. To change the colour of a series, simply click once on the series element (the line, bar, column, etc. that represents that series). You can then use the **Fill Colour** button to select a new colour for the series.

This ECDL Foundation approved courseware product incorporates learning reinforcement exercises. These exercises are included to help the candidate in their training for the ECDL. The exercises included in this courseware product are not ECDL certification tests and should not be construed in any way as ECDL certification tests. For information about authorised ECDL test centres in different national territories please refer to the ECDL Foundation website at www.ecdl.com.

Exercise 4D

1   Double click the chart to return to chart mode.

2   Close the datasheet if it is still displayed.

3   Click on the **Chart Area** for your current chart.

4   Using the **Fill Colour** button, change the colour of the background to **ice blue**.

5   Click on the first column for the **Dublin** series.

6   Using the **Fill Colour** button, change the colour of the series to **dark blue**.

7   Click on any of the columns for the **National** series.

8   Using the **Fill Colour** button, change the colour of the background to **violet**.

9   Click outside of the chart to return to the slide.

10   Save the presentation but do not close it.

4.2   Working with Organisation Charts

An **organisation chart** can be used to show, for example, the management structure of an organisation. Within PowerPoint, you can use an inbuilt **Organisation Chart** program provided by Microsoft.

4.2.1 Creating an Organisation Chart (6.4.2.1)

To add a new slide with an organisation chart on it, do the following:

- Click the **New Slide** button on the toolbar.
  The New Slide window opens.

- Select the **Organisation Chart** slide (see illustration) and click **OK**.
  The new slide appears.

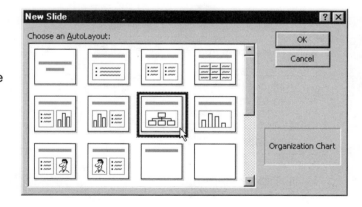

- Add a title to the slide, if required.

- Double click in the lower box on the slide to add the chart.

  The Organisation Chart window opens (see below).

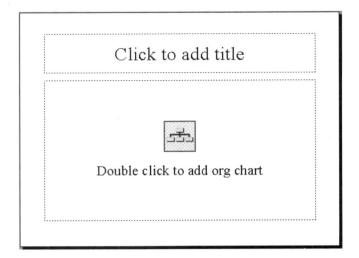

To add an organisation chart to an existing slide, do the following:

- Display the slide on which you want to place the chart.

- Select **Object** in the **Insert** menu.

- The **Insert Object** window opens.

- Scroll through the **Object type** list and click **MS Organization Chart 2.0**.

- Click **OK**.

- The Organisation Chart window opens.

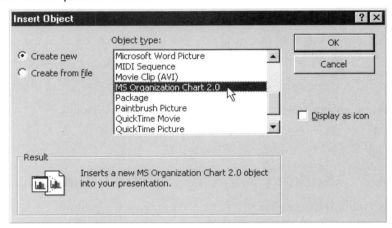

4.2.2 The Organisation Chart Window (6.4.2.1)

Some boxes are displayed in the chart window containing sample text. **Type name here** is already selected in the box at the top (which overlaps the box underneath temporarily). We shall replace the sample text to illustrate the administrative structure of Broadstar Technologies.

- Click the top box to select it.

- Type **Sam Kelly**.
  It replaces **Type name here** in the central box.

- Press **Enter** and type **Managing Director**.

- Click in the box on the left.

  The three subordinate boxes now appear under the Managing Director's box.

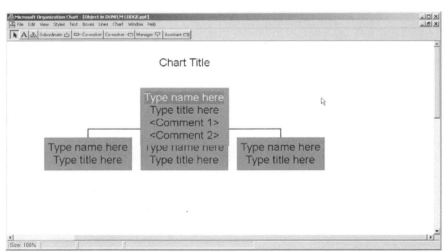

- Type **Drew Wilson** to replace **Type name here** in the left-hand box.

- Press **Enter** and type **Residential Sales**.

- Repeat the previous two steps to enter **Cody Cooper**, **Residential Rentals** and **Brooke Peters**, **Commercial** in the other two boxes.

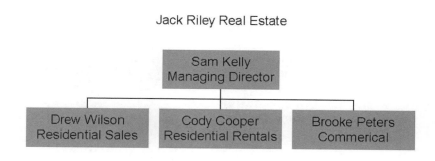

- Select **Chart Title** and replace it with **Jack Riley Real Estate**.

- Click outside the boxes to see the completed chart.

- Select **Exit and Return to** in the chart window **File** menu (*not* the PowerPoint **File** menu) to return to the slide and insert the chart.

- Click **Yes** to the **This Object has been changed** message.

4.2.3 Editing an Organisation Chart

An organisation chart on a slide can be edited or changed at any time as follows:

- Display the slide that contains the chart you want to change.

- Double click the organisation chart.
  The chart window opens

- Make the changes that you require by clicking on each in turn and entering new text.

- Select **Exit and Return to** in the chart window **File** menu to return to the slide and insert the chart.

- Click **Yes** to the **This Object has been changed** message.

4.2.4 Adding Managers, Co-Workers and Subordinates (6.4.2.3)

Buttons at the top of the Chart window make it easy to add extra boxes to the chart. The icons and text on the buttons indicate the positions in which they can be added to an existing box.

The chart can be expanded before or after it is placed on the slide. To update our organisation chart, proceed as follows:

- Double click the chart to reopen the Organisation Chart window.

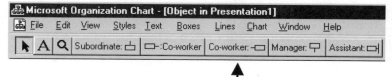

- Click the right **Co-worker** button (arrowed) to select it.
  The cursor assumes the shape of the icon on the button.
  Note the small connecting line on the icon that indicates that this box can be added to an existing box on the left.

- Click in the **Brooke Peters** box.
  A new box is added.

- Click in the new box and enter **Kim Slade**, **Finance**.

Now let's add two subordinates to Drew Wilson.

- Click the **Subordinate** button on the toolbar. Click on **Drew Wilson** to add the new box.

- Click in the new box and enter **Jay Clarke**, **Valuer**.

- Add another new subordinate for Drew Wilson. The details for the new box are **Jo Green**, **Consultant**.

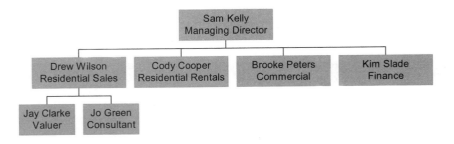

Now let's add a new manager above Jay Clarke.

- Click the **Manager** button on the toolbar. Click anywhere on the **Jay Clarke** box to add a new manager above him.

- Click in the new box and enter **Mel Smith**, **Valuation Manager**.

- To remove a manager, co-worker or sub ordinate, you must first select the box you wish to remove. Let's remove the new manager named **Mel Smith**.

- Click on the **Mel Smith** box and press **Delete**.

Now let's remove the sub-ordinate named **Kim Slade**.

- Click on the **Kim Slade** box and press **Delete**.

- Choose **Undo Delete** from the **Edit** menu to reverse the deletion.

- Select **Exit and Return to** in the chart window **File** menu to return to the slide and insert the revised chart.

- Click **Yes** to the **This Object has been changed** message.

4.2.5 Changing the Hierarchical Structure of the Chart (6.4.2.2)

You can change the hierarchical structure of an organisation chart simply by moving the boxes around and attaching them to other managers, co-workers and so on in the chart.

- If the chart is on a slide, double click the chart to reopen the Organisation Chart window.

- In our chart, **Jo Green** should work with **Cody Cooper** and not **Drew Wilson**. Click and **hold** with the mouse anywhere in the **Jo Green** box. It is important that you keep holding the mouse button down, otherwise you will not be able to move the selected box.

- With the mouse button still held down, drag the box into the lower part of **Cody's** box to make **Jo** a *subordinate* attachment (if you move further up into the box and move left or right, **Jo** would become a **co-worker**). Release the mouse to make the move.

- Now move **Kim Slade** so that this person is now a *subordinate* of **Brooke Peters**.

- Select **Exit and Return to** in the chart window **File** menu to return to the slide and insert the revised chart.

- Click **Yes** to the **This Object has been changed** message.

- Resize/move the organisation chart until it fills more of the available slide.

- Add a title to the slide – **Who We Are**.

- Save the presentation but do not close it.

See next page for finished chart.

Who We Are

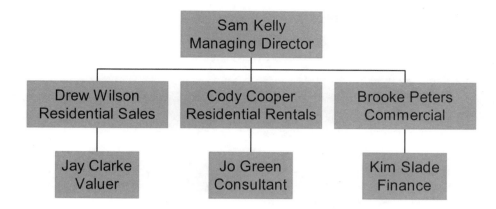

4.3   Drawn Objects

The **Drawing toolbar**, displayed along the bottom of the screen in **Slide view**, has a range of drawing tools which will help you to enhance your presentation graphically. Different kinds of lines, including freehand lines and basic shapes such as boxes, circles and so on, can be draw on slides.

The Drawing toolbar is the same one that is available in other Office applications. The Drawing toolbar and its functions are described in detail in Module 3.

If the Drawing toolbar is not visible, select **Toolbars** in the **View** menu bar and then click **Drawing** in the list of toolbars.

4.3.1   Drawing Objects (6.4.3.1)

The general procedure for drawing an object is the same, no matter which object you draw.

- Click the button on the **Drawing** toolbar for the line or shape you want to draw.

- Move the mouse pointer to where you want the line or one corner of the shape to begin.

- Hold down the mouse button and drag to draw the line or shape.

  To draw a square, use the **Rectangle** tool on the Drawing toolbar but hold down the **Shift** key as you drag with the mouse. To draw a circle, use the **Oval** tool and also use the **Shift** key as you drag with the mouse.

- Release the mouse button. The object appears on the page.

- To modify the line or shape, select the object first and then click one of the **Line buttons** on the toolbar and choose from the menu that appears.

Line Buttons

MODULE 6

Exercise 4E

In this exercise we will practise using some of the basic drawing tools.

1   Ensure you are working on **slide 6** in your presentation.

2   Insert a new slide based on the **Blank** AutoLayout.

3   Using the drawing tools on the Drawing toolbar, create the following objects. If you aren't happy with an object you have drawn, simply click on it and press **Delete** to remove it from the slide. You can then try again.

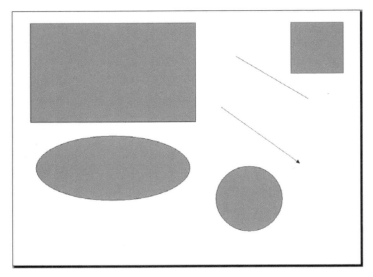

4.3.2 Formatting a Drawn Object (6.4.3.2, 6.4.3.3 and 6.4.3.4)

Using some of the buttons on the Drawing toolbar, you can format a drawn object. Simply select the object and then select the button with the option you require.

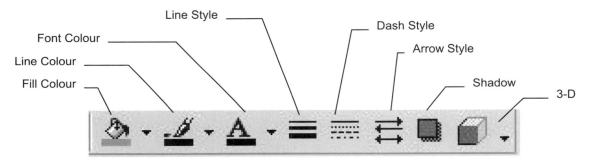

4.3.3 Working with Objects

Working with objects in PowerPoint is the same as working with objects in other applications.

Here are some reminders.

- To **select** an object, click on it.

- To **delete** an object, select it and press the **Delete** key.

- To **move** an object, select it and drag it to its new position.

- To **resize** an object, select it and drag one of its handles.

- To **copy** an object, hold down the **Ctrl** key and drag to where you want the copy to appear.

- To **draw a uniform object** (a circle or square), hold down the **Shift** key while drawing.

- To draw an object starting from the centre rather than from a corner, hold down the **Ctrl** key while drawing.

Exercise 4F

In this exercise we will practise formatting some of the drawn objects.

1   Ensure you are working on **slide 7** in your presentation where the drawn objects are displayed.

2   Change the **Fill Colour** for the rectangle and oval. Use any colour from the colour scheme choices or **More Colours**.

3   Select the drawn line and change its **Line Style** to **6pt**. Change the **Line Colour** to another colour of your choice. Change the **Dash Style** to **Square Dots**.

4   Select the arrow line and change its **Line Style** to **4 ½ pt**. Change the **Arrow Style** to **Arrow Style 9**.

5   Select the square and change its **Shadow** to **Shadow Style 5**. Change it then to **Shadow Style 6**.

6   Select the rectangle and change its **3-D** effect to **3-D Style 10**. Now change it to **3-D Style 2**.

4.3.4   Text Boxes and WordArt (6.4.3.1)

The Drawing toolbar contains buttons for inserting **Text Boxes** and **WordArt**. WordArt is described in Module 3.

Text and WordArt Buttons

Text that is not typed directly into a text placeholder can be added to a slide using a **text box**. A text box is like a graphic in that it can be moved and positioned anywhere on the slide.

Inserting Text

When you click on the border of a text box or on one of the handles, the border becomes a 'dotted' border, indicating that it can now be moved or resized.

Drag the border of the text box (between the handles) to move the box. Drag a handle to resize it. When a text box is resized, the size of the text in the box does not change. PowerPoint wraps text automatically as needed to fit in the text box, but the text box may have to be resized to display it all.

To delete a text box, select it and when the handles appear around it, press the **Delete** key.

Drag to resize

Drag to move box

4.3.5 Formatting Text Boxes

The text boxes that appear on slides usually have no border or shading. This means that the text appears to have been typed directly on the slide with nothing to indicate that it is actually in a box.

If you wish, you can add borders and shading to text boxes.

- Select the text box to which you want to add a border or shading by clicking on its border. (Click on the text first to display the border and then click on the border so that the entire placeholder is selected.)

- Select **Text Box** at the bottom of the **Format** menu option on the Menu bar.

    The **Format Text Box** window appears.

    Notice that **No Fill** and **No Line** are specified.

- To fill the text box with colour, click in the **Colour** box and select a colour from the palette that appears.

- To add a line border to the text box, first select a colour for the line and then select from the other options in the **Line** panel.

- Click **OK** when you have finished formatting the text box.

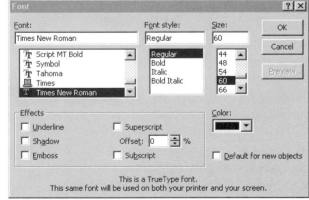

4.3.6 Formatting Text in a Text Box

Text in a text box can be edited or changed in the same way as you would edit or change it in a word processing application. You can change the font, size, style and so on by using the menus and buttons on the toolbars.

Further font options are available in the **Format** menu. First click anywhere in the text to select the text box.

- Select **Font** in the **Format** menu.

- The Font window opens.

    Here you can set the font, size and style effects such as **shadow** and **emboss**, as well as **superscript** and **subscript**.

    The text **colour** can also be set.

- When you drag over text to select it, PowerPoint selects whole words.

    To select individual characters, select **Options** in the **Tools** menu. Then select **Automatic Word Selection** to turn it off.

    Then click **OK**.

Insert, **delete**, **cut**, **copy** and **paste** text as you would in a word processing application.

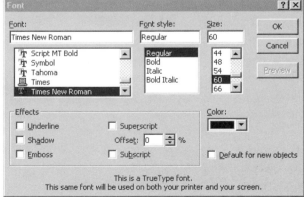

MODULE 6

Exercise 4G

1   Ensure you are working on **slide 7** in your presentation where the drawn objects are displayed.

2   Click on the **Text Box** tool and create a text box on an empty area of the slide. Type the following text into the text box: **Jack Riley Real Estate**.

3   Select the text box.

4   Choose **Text Box** in the **Format** menu option on the menu bar.

5   Set the **Fill Colour** to a light colour of your choice.

6   Set the **Line Colour** to red.

7   Click **OK** to return to the slide.

4.3.7   Adding Text to a Drawn Object

Text can be added to any drawn object on a slide, not just a text box.

- Select the object in which you want the text to appear.

- Type the text. As you type, the text appears in a single line across the object.

- Click outside of the object when you have finished adding text.

- You can format either the text or the entire object in the usual ways.

4.3.8   Rotating an Object (6.4.3.5)

Objects added to slides can be rotated for extra effect as follows:

- Select the object you want to rotate.

- Click the **Rotate** button on the **Drawing** toolbar. **Circular handles** appear at the corners of the object.

- Click and drag one of the circular handles until the object is in the desired position.

- Release the mouse button.

- Click away from the object to complete the rotation.

If you rotate an AutoShape that has attached text, the text rotates with the shape.

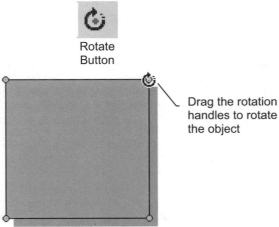

Rotate Button

Drag the rotation handles to rotate the object

4.3.9 Flipping an Object (6.4.3.5)

You can flip an object horizontally or vertically, or you can flip the object to the right or left. If you flip an AutoShape that has attached text, the text flips with the shape.

- Select the object you want to flip.

- Click the **Rotate** button on the **Drawing** toolbar.

- Select **Rotate or Flip** from the available menu.

- Select one of the flip options from the sub-menu that appears.

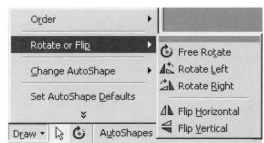

Exercise 4H

1   Click on the oval shape on **slide 7**.

2   Click the **Rotate** button on the Drawing toolbar.

3   Drag one of the circular rotation handles to rotate the object upwards on the slide.

4   Click away from the oval to end the rotation.

5   Click on the text box containing **Jack Riley Real Estate**.

6   Click on the **Draw** button and choose **Rotate or Flip**.

7   Choose Rotate Left.

8   Now rotate the text box back to the right.

4.3.10 Aligning an Object on the Slide (6.4.3.6)

You can *align* an object or group of objects on a slide, such as to the left, centre, bottom or top in the following way:

- Select the object or objects you wish to align on the slide.

- Click on the **Draw** button on the **Drawing** toolbar.

- Choose **Align or Distribute**.

- Ensure **Relative to Slide** is checked at the bottom of the sub-menu if you want to adjust the objects relative to the slide rather than relative to each other. If you do not

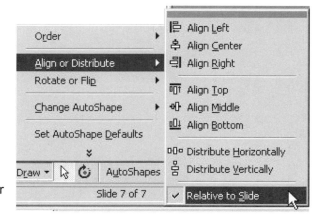

check this option, all the other options on the **Align or Distribute** pop-up menu are greyed out.

- Choose an alignment option from the available list.

4.3.11 Controlling the Order of an Object (6.4.3.8)

Objects automatically stack in individual layers as you add them to a slide. You see the stacking order when objects overlap – the top object covers a portion of objects beneath it. If you "lose" an object in a stack, you can press **Tab** to cycle forward (or **Shift+Tab** to cycle back) through the objects until it is selected.

You can move individual objects or groups of objects in a stack. For example, you can move objects up or down within a stack one layer at a time, or you can move them to the top or bottom of a stack in one move. You can overlap objects when you draw to create different effects. You don't have to draw the bottom object first – you can always move it later.

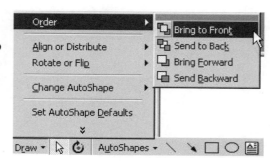

To change the order for an object:

- Select the object you want to reposition in the stack.

- Click the **Draw** button on the **Drawing** toolbar.

- Choose **Order**.

- Select an appropriate option from the sub-menu.

Exercise 4I

1   Ensure you are working on **slide 7**.

2   Select the circle and the square objects.

3   Click the **Draw** button and choose **Align or Distribute**.

4   If Relative to Slide is checked, choose Align Top.

5   If **Relative to Slide** is not checked, check it now. Then click the **Draw** button again. Choose **Align or Distribute** and then select **Align Top**.

6   Practise moving several of the objects one on top of each other.

7   Use the **Order** option using the **Draw** button to bring an object to the front and then to the back.

8   Delete the current slide by choosing **Delete Slide** in the **Edit** menu. You should now only have six slides remaining.

Section 5   Slide Shows

You can use all of the PowerPoint special effects and features to make an automated presentation known as a **slide show**. You can use such things as slide transitions, timings, movies, sounds, animation and hyperlinks to enhance your presentation.

This ECDL Foundation approved courseware product incorporates learning reinforcement exercises. These exercises are included to help the candidate in their training for the ECDL. The exercises included in this courseware product are not ECDL certification tests and should not be construed in any way as ECDL certification tests. For information about authorised ECDL test centres in different national territories please refer to the ECDL Foundation website at www.ecdl.com.

Exercise 5A

1   Before we start to work with some of the special slide show effects, let's have a look at how our current presentation appears on-screen in a slide show.

2   Go to **slide 1** in your current presentation.

3   Save the presentation before you begin the slide show.

4   Click the **Slide Show** view to start the on-screen presentation.

5   Click the mouse to advance from one slide to the next until the presentation has been completed. *Alternatively,* move from slide to slide using the **PageUp** and **PageDown** buttons.

        While the presentation would be fine to deliver as it is, we can enhance it further using some preset animation and transition effects.

5.1   Preset Animation (6.5.1.1)

PowerPoint has many features that can add simple animation to the text and graphics of your slides. It is best to add preset animation using the **Normal view**, **Slide view** or **Slide Sorter view**. If you use the **Normal view** or **Slide view**, you can apply preset animation effects to **any** placeholder or object on the slide simply by selecting it first. If you use the **Slide Sorter view** to apply animation effects, the effect you select applies to the **entire** slide.

Once an animation effect has been added to a slide or object on a slide, you can easily change it using the same steps as you did to apply the animation initially.

Be aware however, that overuse of transitions and animations has an irritating effect on the viewer. An effective presentation uses the many facilities that are available sparingly.

5.1.1 Applying Preset Animation in the Normal View or Slide View

To add a preset animation effect, such as the Camera effect which flashes the slide onto the slide show, proceed as follows:

- Select the placeholder or object you wish to apply the animation to.

- Choose **Preset Animation** in the **Slide Show** menu.

- Select an effect from the available sub-menu. If you have previously set an animation effect and wish to turn it off, click the **Off** option.

- Select the next placeholder, if appropriate, and apply another animation effect.

- Repeat for each slide where necessary.

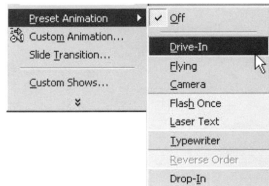

5.1.2 Applying Preset Animation in the Slide Sorter View

- Click on the **Slide Sorter** view button to access this view.

- Click on the slide you wish to apply animation to.

- Click on the **Preset Animation** button on the **Slide Sorter** toolbar.

- Select an animation from the available options.

- Repeat for each slide where necessary.

In the Slide Sorter view, slides with animations have an animation icon underneath. You can click this icon to view the animation effect on the slide in the Slide Sorter view.

This ECDL Foundation approved courseware product incorporates learning reinforcement exercises. These exercises are included to help the candidate in their training for the ECDL. The exercises included in this courseware product are not ECDL certification tests and should not be construed in any way as ECDL certification tests. For information about authorised ECDL test centres in different national territories please refer to the ECDL Foundation website at www.ecdl.com.

Exercise 5B

1   Ensure you are working in the **Normal view** and that you are currently viewing **slide 1**.

2   Click on the main title placeholder containing the text **Dunelm Lodge**.

3   Choose **Preset Animation** in the **Slide Show** menu. Choose the **Flying** animation effect.

4   Select the placeholder that contains the property's address.

5   Choose **Preset Animation** in the **Slide Show** menu. Choose the **Drop-in** animation effect.

6   Switch to the Slide Sorter view.

7   Click on the **Animation icon** below slide 1. Watch the animation effects you have selected.

8   Switch back to **Normal view**.

9   Click on the placeholder containing the property's address.

10   Change the animation for this slide to **Drive-in**.

11   Switch to the **Slide Sorter view**. Click on the **Animation icon** below slide 1. Watch the animation effects you have selected.

     Now let's try adding an animation effect for an entire slide.

12   Ensure you are still working in the **Slide Sorter view**.

13   Click on **slide 3** containing the **Inside Living** bullets.

14   Using the **Preset Animation** button on the **Slide Sorter** toolbar, set the animation for this slide to **Fly From Left**.

15   Apply this animation effect to **slide 4** as well.

5.2   Transitions (6.5.2.1)

PowerPoint can add **slide transitions** to vary the way in which one slide follows another. Transition effects differ from animation effects in so much as transitions affect what happens **between** slides, rather than within the slide itself.

You can specify two settings for a transition, the **effect** and the **timing.**

The **effect** will apply when changing from the previous slide to the current slide.

The **timing** will apply from the current slide to the next slide.

To apply a slide transition, follow these steps.

- Display the slide to which you want to add a transition.

- Select **Slide Transition** in the **Slide Show** menu.
  The Slide Transition window appears.

- Click in the box in the **Effect** panel – showing **No Transition** in the illustration – to display a list of effects.

- Click on an effect in the list to see it demonstrated in the panel above.

- Click the **Slow**, **Medium** or **Fast** button underneath to set the desired speed for the transition.

- **On mouse click** is already selected in the **Advance** panel. This means that the transition will not take place until you click the mouse button.

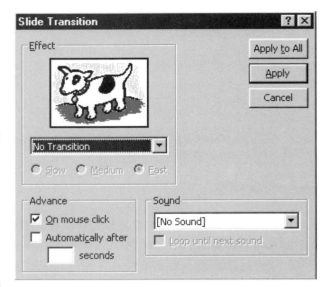

- Click **Automatically after** to cause the transition to occur after a certain time. Type the required number of seconds in the **seconds** box.

- To select a sound to accompany the transition, select a sound from the **Sound** list.

- Click the **Apply** button for this slide only or **Apply to All** for all the slides.

- Click the **Transition icon** that appears below a slide in the **Slide Sorter view** to see the transition in practice.

NOTE

In addition to using the **Slide Transition** option in the **Slide Show** menu, you can also use the **Slide Transition Effects** button when you are working in the **Slide Sorter view**. Select the slide for which you want to set a transition and then use the button.

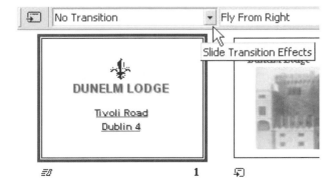

Exercise 5C

1   Ensure you are working in the **Slide Sorter view**.

2   Select **slide 2,** which contains the photograph.

3   Using the **Slide Transition Effects** button, set the transition to **Cover Down**.

4   Use the **Transition icon** below the slide to try the transition out.

5   Now change the transition for this slide to **Box in**.

6   Select **slide 5,** which contains the chart.

7   Set the transition for this slide to **Dissolve**.

8   Save the presentation but do not close it.

5.3   Delivering a Presentation

5.3.1   Starting a Slide Show (6.6.3.2)

As we have already seen, you can run a slide show using the **Slide Show** view button or by choosing **View Show** in the **Slide Show** menu. If you want to see the entire slide show, make sure you select slide 1 beforehand. If you want to run the show starting from another slide, display that slide in **Normal view** or click on it in the **Slide Sorter view**. You can then click the **Slide Show** view button or **View Show** in the **Slide Show** menu.

When running your slide show, there are some useful ways of moving around within the presentation:

- To display the next slide, click the left mouse button.

- *Alternatively*, press the right **arrow** key or the **Page Down** key on the keyboard.

- Use the left **arrow** key or the **Page Up** key to display the previous slide.

- To quit the slide show, press the **Esc** key.

5.3.2   On-Screen Assistance

An **on-screen menu** is available to assist the presenter during a slide presentation. Click the **semi-transparent button** at the bottom left-hand corner of the screen to reveal the menu.

The Semi-Transparent Button

If the button is not visible, move the cursor down to the corner first. Alternatively, right click anywhere on the slide.

The menu items are generally self-explanatory but note the following.

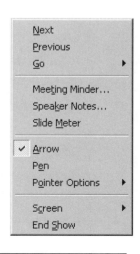

- **Meeting Minder** allows the presenter to insert notes that are saved with the slide. (Click Meeting Minder again to display them.)

- **Speaker Notes** allows similar notes to be inserted that then appear on the **Notes** pages.

  The speaker's notes can be displayed and/or amended at any time during the presentation.

- The **Pen** allows you to draw on the slides.

- The **Slide Meter** displays information on the timing of the presentation.

5.3.3 Hiding and Showing Slides (6.6.3.1)

Before you give a presentation, you should try to anticipate questions from your audience and be prepared to answer them. It is possible to create slides to support your answers and then keep them hidden until you need them. You can hide slides in **Slide**, **Outline** or **Slide Sorter** view.

To hide one or more slides, do the following.

- Display or select the slide you want to hide.

- Select **Hide Slide** in the **Slide Show** menu.

Hidden Slide Number

- In **Slide sorter** view, the number of the hidden slide appears with a line through it in a box beneath the slide.

To display a hidden slide during a presentation, do the following.

The Semi-Transparent Button

- Click the **semi-transparent** button at the bottom left on the slide *before* the hidden slide.

  Alternatively, right click the slide *before* the hidden slide.

- Select **Go** in the menu that appears and then **Hidden Slide** in the sub-menu.

  The hidden slide is displayed.

Slide Navigator allows you to display any hidden slide at any point during a presentation. You can also use it if **Hidden Slide** is not available in your version of Office. Proceed as follows.

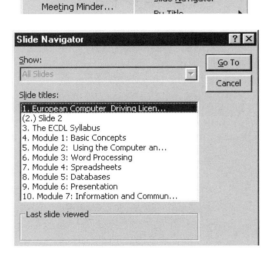

- Right click any slide in the presentation, or click the semi-transparent button at the bottom left of the current slide.

- Select **Slide Navigator** in the menu that appears.

  A list of slide numbers is displayed, with the numbers of hidden slides in brackets.

- Double click the number of the hidden slide you want to display.

Exercise 5C

1   Select **slide 1** in the **Slide Sorter view**.

2   Click the **Slide Show** button to run the presentation.

3   Advance from one slide to the next until the end.

4   On completion, click on **slide 3**.

5   Run the slide show starting from this slide.

6   When the slide show has been completed, click on **slide 5**, which contains the chart.

7   Select **Hide Slide** in the **Slide Show** menu.

8   Run the presentation until the end, checking that slide 5 has been omitted.

9   Select slide 5 again and use **Hide Slide** in the **Slide Show** menu to unhide the slide.

10   If time permits, practise making some additional transition and animation effects to your slides.

MODULE 6

Section 6   Preparing Outputs

6.1   Preparation

Before you print a presentation, there are a number of preparation options you should undertake to ensure that the finished results are correct and presented in the right way.

6.1.1 Duplicating and Moving Slides within a Presentation (6.6.1.5)

You may wish to move slides around in your presentation before printing it. You can also easily duplicate slides in the presentation, making changes to the copy of the slide.

To move or duplicate slides in a presentation:

- Ensure you are working in the **Slide Sorter view**.

- To move a slide within the presentation, click and drag the slide to its new location.

- As you move with the mouse, a vertical line appears indicating where the slide will be positioned when you release the mouse.

- To copy a slide, hold down the **Ctrl** key and drag the slide to its new location. As you move with the mouse, a vertical line appears indicating where the slide will be positioned when you release the mouse. A **plus sign (+)** also appears on the mouse, indicating that you are copying the slide and not moving it.

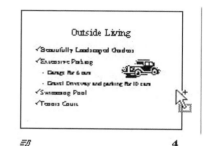

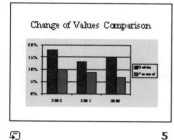

6.1.1.1 Duplicating and Moving Slides between Open Presentations (6.6.1.5)

Slides can be copied or moved between different presentation files. Again, it is best to use the Slide Sorter view so that you can easily see the overall structure of your presentation, especially when you are pasting in a copied/moved slide.

To copy or move a slide between open presentations:

- Start by working in the presentation file containing the slide you wish to copy or move.

- Ensure you are working in the **Slide Sorter view**.

- Click on the slide you wish to copy or move.

- Click the **Copy** button on the Standard toolbar or the **Cut** button if you want to move the slide.

- Using the taskbar at the bottom of the screen, click on the presentation button where the slide is to be inserted.

- Ensure you are working in **Slide Sorter view** in the destination file.

- Click on the slide after which the inserted slide is to be placed.

- Click the **Paste** button on the Standard toolbar.

- To return to the original presentation file, click on its button in the taskbar.

6.1.2 Deleting Slides (6.6.1.6)

You can delete one or more slides from a presentation.

- If you are working in the **Slide Sorter view**, click on the slide to be deleted or use **Ctrl** and click to select multiple slides. Press the **Delete** key to remove the slides.

- If you are working in the **Normal view** or **Slide view**, display the slide you wish to delete and choose **Delete Slide** in the **Edit** menu.

Exercise 6A

1   Ensure you are working in the **Slide Sorter view**.

2   Move the **Outside Living** slide so that it appears before the **Inside Living** slide.

3   Move **slide 2** so that it appears after the **Inside Living** slide.

4   Using the **Ctrl** key, move the fourth slide (the slide that you have just moved) so that a copy of the slide appears after the first slide.

5   Select **slide 5** (the slide that you have just taken a copy of) and press **Delete** to remove it from the presentation.

6   Save the presentation but do not close it.

6.1.3 Spell Checking a Presentation (6.6.1.2)

Before you print a presentation or run a slide show, you should spell check the content for any spelling errors or repeated words.

To check your presentation:

- Select the first slide in your presentation so that you spell check from the start.

- Choose **Spelling** in the **Tools** menu or click the **Spelling** button on the toolbar.

- Use the options in the **Spelling** window to correct your presentation.

- For more information on spell checking, please see Module 3, Section 6.1.

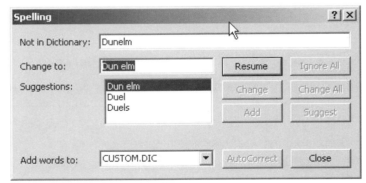

Exercise 6B

1   Spell check your presentation and make any necessary corrections.

2   Save your presentation on completion.

6.1.4 Changing the Slide Setup (6.6.1.1 and 6.6.1.4)

If you intend printing your presentation, it is important to check the format and the orientation of the slides and the paper you will be using beforehand so that the printed slides are correctly placed on the paper.

To change the slide setup:

- Choose **Page Setup** in the **File** menu. The Page Setup window will appear.

- Use the arrow on the **Slides sized for** box to indicate what the slides will be used for. The options are outlined below. The **Width** and **Height** settings will automatically update depending on the choice you make for the **Slides sized for** box.

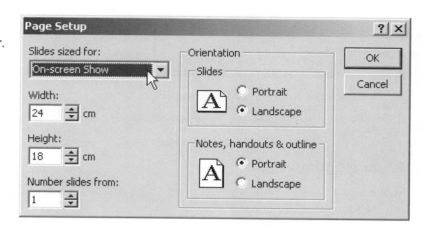

- If you have included automatic slide numbering on the slide master upon which your slides are based, you can set the first number to be printed in the **Number slides from** box. The default setting is **1**.

- Change the orientation for the **Slides** or the **Notes, Handouts & Outline**. You can select **Portrait** or **Landscape**.

- Click **OK** to complete the settings.

Slides Sized For Options

On-screen Show	This is the default option. Slides are set for an on-screen presentation/slide show.
Letter Paper (8.5 x 11 in)	The slides are formatted for letter size paper – 8.5" by 11".
A4 Paper (210 x 297 mm)	The slides are formatted for A4 paper – 210mm by 297 mm.
35mm Slides	The slides are formatted for the dimensions necessary to create 35mm slides. A service bureau can transform your electronic slides into 35mm slides. Contact your local service bureau for instructions.
Overhead	You can create a presentation that uses overhead transparencies by printing your slides as black-and-white or colour transparencies. You can design these slides in either landscape or portrait orientation.
Banner	As with 35mm slides, a service bureau can transform your electronic slides into a banner or large poster. Contact your local service bureau for instructions.
Custom	Use the **Custom** option if you want to set the width and height measurements to dimensions of your choice.

Exercise 6C

In this exercise we will format our slide setup for output onto A4 paper.

1   Choose **Page Setup** in the **File** menu.

2   Set the Slides sized for box to A4 Paper (210 x 297 mm).

3   Set the orientation for the slides and the notes, handouts and outlines to **Landscape**.

4   Click **OK** to update your slide setup.

5   View the slides to see the effect that the changes have made.

6.1.5   Printing (6.6.2.1)

When you are ready, you can print your slides, handouts for your audience, your speaker notes or an outline view of presentation.

To print:

- Choose **Print** in the **File** menu.

- To control what type of printout you produce, use the **Print what** box. Depending on your selection, other settings within the Print window will become available.

- Use the **Print range** settings to control whether you want to print the entire presentation, the current slide, a selection of slides (slides should be selected in the Slide Sorter view), or a number of slides.

- Use the **Copies** box to control how many copies of the printout are produced.

- Click **OK** to start printing.

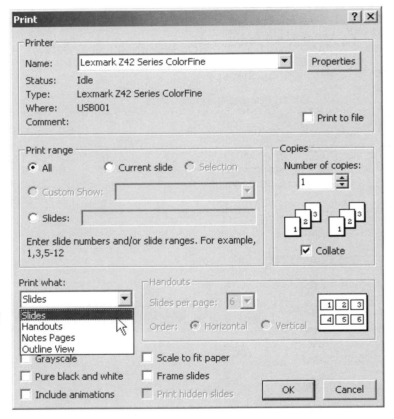

Exercise 6D

1   Print a hard copy of your slides.

2   Save the presentation and then close it.

Section 7   Master Slides

7.1   Master Slides

As you have seen, basing a presentation on an existing design template gives your presentation a consistent look and feel, which is important for your audience.

However, whether you are using a design template for your presentation or starting a blank presentation, all of your slides are based on a **master** format which includes such elements as the slide background, slide numbering, standard graphics, the format of text and so on. Master slides may also hold items such as graphics that you want to appear on every slide. Any change you make to a slide master is reflected on every other slide in the presentation file. If you want an individual slide to look different from the master, you can make changes to that slide without changing the master.

There are four predefined **master formats** for any presentation you are creating. These masters are:

- Slide Master
- Title Master
- Handout Master
- Notes Master

The **Slide Master** controls the format and placement of the titles and text you type on all slides in the same presentation file, while the **Title Master** controls the format of any slide based on the **title** slide layout. Changes you make to the **Handout Master** only affects handouts that you print for your audience. Changes you make to the **Notes Master** only affects notes pages you create and print.

Exercise 7A

1   Choose **New** in the **File** menu. Click on **Design Templates**.

2   Select **Cactus** from the available template list and click **OK**.

3   Select the **Title Slide** layout for the first slide and click **OK**.

4   Add the following title to the placeholder: **Presentations**.

5   Add the following sub-title: **Working with PowerPoint**.
        Look at the elements of the title slide. This slide is using the formatting of the **Title Master**.

6   Now insert a new slide based on the **Bulleted List** layout.

7   Add the following title to this slide: **Presentation Techniques**. This slide is using the formatting of the **Slide Master**.

8   Add another new slide based on the **Table** layout and add the following title to this slide: **Types of Slides**. This slide is also using the formatting of the **Slide Master**.

9   Insert one final new slide based on the **Title Slide** layout. Add the following title: **Section One** and the following sub-title: **Getting Started**. This slide is using the formatting of the **Title Master**.

MODULE 6

7.1.1 Working with Objects on the Slide Master (6.2.4.1)

The slide master controls certain text characteristics – such as font type, size and colour – called master text, as well as background colour and certain special effects, such as shadowing and bullet style.

The slide master contains text placeholders and placeholders for footers, such as the date, time and slide number. When you want to make a global change to the look of your slides, you don't have to change each slide individually. Just make the change once on the slide master, and PowerPoint automatically updates the existing slides and applies the changes to any new slides you add. To change the formatting of the text, select the text in the placeholders and make the changes you want.

To have art or text – for example, a company name or logo – appear on every slide, put it on the slide master. Objects appear on slides in the same location as they do on the slide master. To add the same text to every slide, add the text to the slide master by clicking the **Text Box** button on the **Drawing** toolbar – do not type in the text placeholders. The look of text you've added with the **Text Box** button is not governed by the master.

To access the slide master:

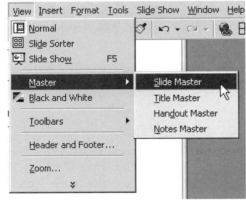

- Choose **Master** in the **View** menu.

- Select **Slide Master** from the sub-menu. The slide master will be displayed, including all its placeholders, etc.

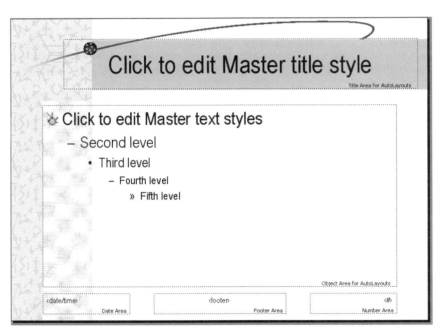

- Make any necessary changes to the slide master. In addition to adding standard text or formatting the existing placeholders, you can insert or remove images and pictures. For more information, please see Section 3.2 in this module.

- Click the **Close** button to exit the slide master and return to your normal view.

Close Button

MODULE 6

Exercise 7B

In this exercise we will add some objects and formatting to the slide master for our presentation.

1   Choose **Master** in the **View** menu.

2   Select **Slide Master** from the sub-menu.

3   Click in the **Click to edit Master title** style.

4   Set the font size to **48** and click the **bold** button.
      In this part of the exercise we will insert a ClipArt picture into the slide master.

5   Choose **Picture** from the **Insert** menu.

6   Select **Clip Art**.

7   Click on the **Shapes** category and then click on the picture called **compasses**.

8   Choose Insert clip.

9   Close the **Insert Clip Art** window on completion.

10   Drag the inserted shape into the top right of the slide master.

11   Click the **Close** button on the **Master Slide** toolbar to return to our presentation.

12   Move from one slide to another. Notice that all slides except the title slides have been updated with our formatting and the insertion of the shape picture.

7.2   Adding Text and Numbering to the Footer (6.2.4.2 and 6.2.4.3)

In PowerPoint the **footer** is an area at the bottom of the slide that may contain information that can appear on all slides or on specific slides.

Typically, the footer may contain date information, slide numbering and/or other text of your choice.

- Choose **Header/Footer** in the **View** menu.

- Check the **Date and time** box if you want to insert a date and/or time into the footer. If you select **Update automatically**, you can choose the format for the date/time you wish to use. PowerPoint will ensure the date/time is automatically updated every time the presentation is opened or printed. If you choose **Fixed**, you can enter a date/time of your choice but it will remain fixed whenever the presentation is viewed or printed.

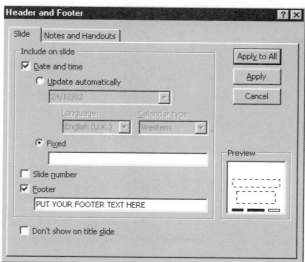

- If you wish to number your slides, check the **Slide number** box.

- To add freeform text into the footer area, check the **Footer** box and then type your text in the box provided below it.

- To add your changes to every slide in the presentation, click **Apply to All**. To update only the current slide, click **Apply**.

MODULE 6

Exercise 7C

1   Choose **Header/Footer** from the **View** menu.

2   Ensure the **Date and time** option is checked and then choose **Update automatically**.

3   Select a date format of your choice using the list box available.

4   Check the **Slide number** box so that your slides are automatically numbered in the footer area.

5   Ensure the **Footer** box is checked and type the following text in the box provided: **ECDL Training**.

6   Click **Apply to All** to add the changes to every slide in our presentation.

7   View each of the slides in our presentation to see that the footer has updated on each one.

8   Save the current presentation, naming it **Using Masters**.

9   Close the presentation on completion.

Module 7

Information
and
Communication

7

MODULE 7

Module 7

Information and Communication

MODULE 7

MODULE 7

Introduction

Syllabus Goals for Module 7

Information and Communication is divided into two sections. The first section, Information, requires the candidate to accomplish basic web search tasks using a web browser application and available search engine tools, to bookmark search results and to print web pages and search reports. The second section, Communication, requires the candidate to demonstrate their ability to use electronic mail software to send and receive messages, to attach documents or files to a message and to organise and manage message folders or directories within electronic mail software.

E-mail

One of the most widely used features of networks is the ability to send and receive electronic mail, or **e-mail**. Messages can be sent worldwide in a matter of seconds and at minimal cost. Other documents and files can be attached to e-mail messages and sent to addresses in virtually any part of the world. Long-distance, cheap, instant communication makes it possible to exchange messages as never before, whether between friends and family or in the world of big business.

The Internet

The successful use of networks by universities and corporations for the exchange of information led to the network idea spreading to the private sector, giving birth to the Internet. The Internet is a worldwide network of separate computers and computer networks connected together so that information can be exchanged between them.

The Internet was completely text-based until the late 1980s. Then a group of scientists, looking for a more convenient way to share documents, conceived the idea of an easy-to-use World Wide Web of information. Clicking on a word in a document on the screen would automatically connect to related documents on other computers, a technique known as hypertext. This development greatly increased the opportunities for accessing information and led to the expanded use of the Internet as we know it today.

The World Wide Web

The expansion of the simple text systems to include the use of hypertext and the ability to incorporate sounds, images and video led to the rapid development of a new branch of the Internet known today as the World Wide Web (WWW).

The World Wide Web is now an enormous library of information. The ease with which it can be used has led to the term the Information Superhighway. It provides opportunities for global communication between individuals and groups. The WWW is used by universities, government agencies, libraries, commercial companies and individuals.

MODULE 7

Section 1   Information

1.1   Internet Concepts and Terms (7.1.1.1, 7.1.1.2 and 7.1.1.3)

1.1.1 The Internet

The first and most widely believed story is that the Internet is primarily a product of the Cold War between America and Russia. In order that information the Americans held would not be destroyed in the event of war, the Americans decided to decentralise it. In the early 1960s **J.C.R. Licklider** of Massachusetts Institute of Technology (MIT) wrote papers on a concept he termed **Galactic Networks**. He envisaged this network as interrelated computers on a worldwide scale across which information could be transferred. Around the same time important research was being done in computer networking that could accelerate the development of this 'global network'.

The successful use of networks by universities and corporations for the exchange of information led to the network idea spreading to the business sector, giving birth to the Internet. The Internet is a worldwide network of separate computers and computer networks connected together over national telecommunication systems so that information can be exchanged between them.

1.1.2 The World Wide Web

The World Wide Web (**WWW**) was created by Tim Berners-Lee. It is an application or tool that uses the infrastructure of the Internet to link together hypertext mark-up language (**HTML**) coded pages or sites. HTML is the language or code used to compose documents on the World Wide Web. It marks pieces of text and graphics in a document so that web browsers (software that allows you to see HTML documents across files and software on the web) know how to display them on the computer screen. HTML contains an interactive feature that allows the browser to respond to various actions of the user. Typically, clicking on the 'link' can open a new page, download a file, transfer the user to a new site and so on. The expansion of the simple text systems to incorporate sounds, images and video led to the invention of hypertext in 1965 by Ted Nelson. This meant that clicking on a word in a document on the screen would automatically connect to related documents on other computers.

Quite a number of abbreviations or acronyms are used when talking about the WWW. They are mainly associated with the different bits and pieces of procedures and programs that are needed to make the web work. They also relate to the various codes used, the places where information is stored and the conventions used by those who display material on the web in what is commonly referred to as hyperspace, i.e. the electronic world created with the WWW.

The World Wide Web is now an enormous library of information. The ease with which it can be used has led to the term the Information Superhighway.

HTTP	the protocol used to carry requests within the WWW
HTML	used to compose documents on the web and links

Abbreviation is the keyword when working on the Internet. The most commonly used abbreviations are explained below.

1.1.3 Website and Web Page

So what is a website? A website is simply a group of related HTML pages or documents that is made available to the WWW through an Internet service provider (ISP). Most websites have a home page that is very much like a welcome page with links to other pages or related sites. Links often look like a table of contents.

A web page may be defined as a document on the WWW. It is an HTML file that is located or identified by a unique URL or web address. Web pages normally contain links to other web pages or websites. Check out the site at **www.ecdlmanual.org/training** to further understand this concept.

1.1.4 Hypertext Transfer Protocol (HTTP)

As the Internet is made up of different networks, computers and operating systems, the WWW needs a common method for exchanging documents. The protocol – a set of rules – that allows text documents and files with built-in links (hypertext) to be transmitted across the WWW is known as the **Hypertext transfer protocol**, or HTTP. World Wide Web addresses typically begin with the letters http.

1.1.5 URL

A web address is written in lowercase (small letters) and is composed of a protocol abbreviation and a number of other parts separated by dots (full stops).

- http stands for hypertext transfer protocol.

- www shows that this is a world wide web address.

- The domain name is a principal part of the address. (A domain is a location or area where the pages are stored.)

- The top level domain often refers to a country or is one of a number of international domains such as .com (commercial), .net (network), .org (organisation) .gov (government) and so on.

1.1.6 Hyperlink

As you move the mouse over a web page, notice that the arrow pointer changes to the I-beam cursor. In some instances the mouse pointer changes to a hand with a pointing finger. This indicates that this particular piece of text or graphic is a **hyperlink**.

A hyperlink is a piece of text, an object or a graphic that acts like a button. Clicking a hyperlink performs an action such as moving to a different part of the same page, displaying a new page or moving you to another site altogether.

Anything that changes the mouse pointer to the hand as you move over it is normally is a hyperlink. Graphics that include a hyperlink will also change the mouse pointer to a hand.

1.1.7 Internet Service Provider (ISP)

An Internet service provider is a business that supplies Internet services to individuals, businesses and organisations. Typically, they host websites, provide connectivity services and offer worldwide delivery of e-mails and access to information on the Web.

E-mail messages can be prepared in advance before you connect to your ISP and then sent all together when you connect, thus saving on connection costs. When you are preparing mail without being connected, you are working **offline**. When you are connected, you are **online**.

E-mail is delivered immediately to the **recipient's ISP** to await collection. It does not go directly to the recipient's computer. E-mail that is addressed to you is received and stored by **your ISP**. In each case, the recipient has to check to see if there is any e-mail. Only then is it downloaded to the individual's computer. It works like the post office box system, where your mail is not sent to your home but placed in a box at the post office. You do not see your mail until you go to the post office to collect it.

E-mail is usually collected automatically when you first open the mail program but you can also dial up later at any time while you are using the program to check again for mail. You can also set the mail program to check for mail at regular intervals.

1.1.8 File Transfer Protocol (FTP)

File transfer protocol (FTP) is a program that allows you to transfer files between computers on the Internet as distinct from transferring files for immediate viewing. Transferring a file from a remote computer to your own computer is called **downloading** the file. Sending a file to a remote computer is called **uploading** the file.

1.1.9 Search Engine (7.1.1.5)

A **search engine** is a program that helps you to find information on the web. It stores listings of websites from all over the world and makes them easily available. Different search engines search in different ways, so you may find information using one that may be overlooked by another.

Search engines compile their listings either by using **human editors** (when resources are catalogued by a human editor and browsable by topic they are called web directories) or **automated crawlers** (a program that automatically fetches web pages. They can also be called spiders. A third kind of search engine – a **meta** search engine – uses other search engines to do the work. Some examples of different search engines are given here.

Human

LookSmart	www.looksmart.com	These search engines use **people** to classify websites into categories. They are good for finding information on general topics.
UK Plus	www.ukplus.co.uk	
Yahoo!	www.yahoo.com	

Automated

AltaVista	www.altavista.com	
Excite	www.excite.com	**Automated crawlers** read large numbers of web pages and store the text. They are good for finding very specific information.
Fast	www.alltheweb.com	
Google	www.google.com	
Lycos	www.lycos.com	
WebCrawler	www.webcrawler.com	

Create your Start Page!   Choose your favorite photo! »

New Members **Sign Up** · Excite Members **Sign In** · **Help** New!

Meta

AskJeeves	www.askjeeves.com	
Go2Net	www.go2net.com	
SavvySearch	www.savysearch.com	

> **Meta** search engines send your query to several other search engines and then list the results in one location.

Searching for information involves entering key words in a box or boxes on the search engine page.

A list of websites along with links which contain those key words is then displayed. The individual sites can then be accessed as required.

Many search engines have local versions for different areas. Check the main site for details. Yahoo!, for example, has a site for the UK and Ireland. Searching can be worldwide or concentrated on sites that are more local and possibly more relevant to your needs.

1.1.10 Cookie and Cache (7.1.1.6)

A **cookie** is a small identifier program. Cookies are placed on your hard disk by the server. When you return to the same site, the cookie notifies the server and often a customised version of the page is returned in response. For example, if you submit your name and request information from a web-based book vendor, it is not unusual to be greeted by your name and have information related to your last query updated and presented upon logging on to their website again.

Each time you visit a site, the browser saves the contents of the pages you view into a temporary storage area on the hard disk, usually a folder dedicated to temporary Internet file, called a **cache**. This speeds up the future downloading of these pages. It is possible to adjust the amount of space used to store these pages, as it can quickly gobble up space on your hard disk.

1.2   Security Considerations

1.2.1   Protected Websites (7.1.2.1)

Some websites, such as extranets, are protected to prevent unauthorised viewing. Others are protected so that only authorised people can download files. In order to access the full extent of these sites a username and password are requested. Upon inserting this information correctly, the user has access to authorised areas.

1.2.2   Digital Certificates (7.1.2.2)

If goods are to be purchased on the Internet the customer needs reassurance that the company they are dealing with is legitimate. This assurance is provided by digital certificates. These certificates provide information about the identity of the software authors, the date the software was registered with a certifying authority and some reference is also made to the software's security level.

Certification authorities usually provide software authors with a unique serial number, an expiration date and an encryption code for handling dealings that relate to their product across the web. Digital certificates identify authors and verify authenticity.

1.2.3 Encryption (7.1.2.3)

By encrypting files you are ensuring that they cannot be accessed or utilised except by the person for whom the communication is intended. If there is any attempt to intercept a file as it is being transferred across the Internet, the encryption offers a high level of security. Encryption is extensively used to protect information such as credit card numbers and sensitive information such as personal data or company secrets.

1.2.4 Credit Card Fraud (7.1.2.5)

Today, many online transactions are available on the Internet. These include online banking, shopping and services as diverse as gambling and speech writing. To pay for goods and services we are often required to surrender a credit card number. However, it is important to keep in mind that transactions of this nature require secure payment facilities. If you are asked to submit private details over the Internet, make sure that the digital certificate from the company you are dealing with is clearly displayed on the screen. This reassures you that the company is using a file encryption system. Should no certificate be displayed, you are effectively making the details you submit publicly available.

1.2.5 Infecting your computer (7.1.2.4)

With digital certificates and encryption there is also a level of protection against computer viruses. Viruses are unsolicited programmes that transfer themselves across the Internet and networks and install themselves on computers, causing considerable damage either to stored data or the computer's operation. They also have the capacity to regenerate themselves and pass themselves on to other unsuspecting users that are connected to the Internet. Invitations to download free software and applications need to be treated with caution. Downloading from a company with a digital certification is reasonably safe. Without such authentification, the safety of your computer cannot be guaranteed.

1.2.6 Firewalls (7.1.2.6)

A **hacker** is a person who breaks into computer systems with the intention of causing disruption or stealing data. To prevent unauthorised access to a network, IT managers use a piece of software, sometimes a combination of software and hardware, known as a firewall. This prevents unauthorised access.

1.3   First Steps with the Web Browser

1.3.1 Opening a Web Browsing Application (7.1.2.6)

The first step to accessing the Internet is to activate the browser. Make sure that you are located on the desktop of your computer and follow these steps to open Internet Explorer:

- Double click the Internet Explorer icon

OR

- Click once on the Internet Explorer icon on the taskbar.

Internet
Explorer

Alternatively, click the **Start** button and select **Internet Explorer** in the **Programs** menu or sub-menu.

If your computer is connected to the Internet over a network, it may make a connection immediately. If you are using a modem, the **Dial-up Connection** window appears.

The **Connect to** box displays the name of your ISP.

Your **user name** and **password** – received from the ISP – will be entered in the appropriate boxes.

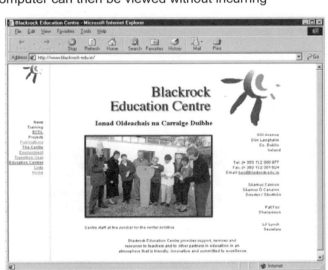

- Click the Save password box after you have typed your password so you don't have to enter the password every time you connect.

- To connect without showing this window in the future, click the Connect automatically box. (Do not click it for now.)

- Clicking the Connect button starts the connection process.

- Click the Settings button to display the various technical details required to make the connection. (You will not normally have to look at these and are advised *not* to alter any settings unless you know what you are doing.)

- Click the Work Offline button to start Internet Explorer without connecting to the Internet. Web pages that have been saved on your computer can then be viewed without incurring connection charges.

When you click the **Connect** button, the panel at the bottom of the window keeps you informed of progress. Various messages such as the following are displayed.

'Dialing...Connected to remote computer....'

'Verifying user name and password...Logging on...'

When the connection has been made, the Dial-up Connection window closes and a web page appears.

1.3.2 Connecting

Connecting to the Internet or to any other network is often referred to as **logging on**. When the Dial-up Connection window appears, do the following:

- Type your username in the **User name** box if it is not there already.

You may have to type your Password in the **Password** box (if the **Save password** box was not clicked).

- Click the Connect button.

The modem dials the ISP number and makes the connection. When the connection is successful, Internet Explorer opens a preset home page (or start page).

The home page that you see first is a web page that has been chosen by your computer. If a connection cannot be established, a message to that effect appears on the screen.

At the end of your browsing session when you want to close the browser use one of the following options:

- Open the File menu and select Close. This may not necessarily disconnect you from your Internet connection, but it closes the browser.

NOTE

If you are using your computer in the office, see your IT administrator for the correct instructions to disconnect.

Alternatively, if you work on a standalone PC and you are connected to the Internet via a modem, then you must select the Disconnect option. Right click on the **Modem Connection Icon** and select **Disconnect**.

1.3.3 Changing the Home Page (7.1.3.2)

The first page – the **home page** – that is displayed when you connect to the Internet will usually have been set by the browser vendor or the ISP.

You can set the page with which the browser opens to a web page of your choice. The easiest way to set a new start page is to first find and display the page you want to use.

- Open Internet Explorer if it is not already open.

- Find the page that you want to set as the start page, the Blackrock Education Centre page. Type http://www.blackrock-edu.ie/ into the address bar.

- Click Go.

- Select Internet Options in the Tools menu.

- The Internet Options window appears (see next page).

- Click the General tab at the top of the window if it is not already clicked.

- The address of the preset home page appears in the **Address** box in the **home page** section.

- Click the Use Current button.

- The address of the page currently displayed is inserted in the **Address** box.

- Click the Apply button to make your choice effective.

- Click OK.

MODULE 7

Now, when you next open Internet Explorer, your own choice of home page is the one that will be displayed.

Alternatively, type the address of your choice in the **Address** box. (The page does not have to be displayed first.) Then click **Apply** and **OK** as before.

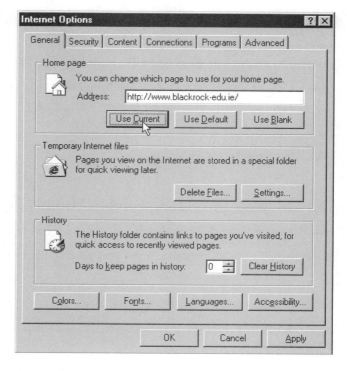

1.3.4 Displaying a Web Page in a New Window (7.1.3.3)

The new window option will be chosen if you want to hold the page you are browsing and display an independent page for further investigation. Just select **File New Window** option.

1.3.5 Stopping a Web Page from Downloading (7.1.3.4)

Web pages can be very big and slow when downloading. If you find yourself in a situation where you want to halt the pages being displayed, click on the **Stop** button on the Standard Buttons toolbar.

1.3.6 Refreshing a Web Page (7.1.3.5)

If the web page you want to view fails to load or if you want to view the up-to-date version, use the **Refresh** button on the Standard Buttons toolbar. Alternatively, select the **F5** key on your keyboard.

MODULE 7

1.3.7 Using Available Help Functions (7.1.3.6)

If you wish to find assistance with different aspects of the browsing application choose **Help**. This is available to you as you work with the Help function in one of two ways:

- Choose the Help menu on the Menu bar.
  Alternatively, use the **F1** key on your keyboard.

1.4 Adjusting Settings

1.4.1 Display and Hiding Built-In Toolbars (7.1.4.1)

Various toolbars are displayed at the top of the Explorer window, as in other applications.

The **Title bar** shows the name of the current website or page.

The **Menu bar** contains the usual menus as well as some specific to Internet Explorer.

The **Button bar** has a number of buttons that are used for various purposes.

The **Address bar** displays the address of the current website or page. It also has a Go button at the right-hand side.

If the current page extends below the viewing area, scroll bars enable the user to move over the page.

NOTE

> If you discover there is a toolbar missing click on the View menu, click **Toolbars,** then select the toolbar that you wish to make visible once again.

1.4.2 Displaying and Hiding Images on a Web Page (7.1.4.2)

When you turn off graphics, animations and so on, pages will download faster but then only the text is displayed. This may be preferable in some circumstances.

- Click the **Advanced** tab in the Internet Options window.

- Scroll to find the Multimedia section.

- Click to remove the tick from the Play animations, Play sounds, Play videos and Show pictures check boxes, as required.

- Click Apply to make your choices effective.

- Click OK.

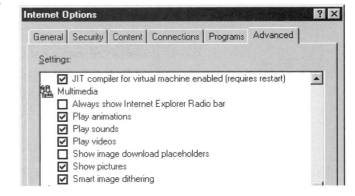

To display images, you must reverse the procedure.

NOTE

> Choose the **Refresh** button or the **F5** key if the pictures are still visible after you choose this option. It will reset the computer to your options.

1.4.3 Displaying Previously Visited URLs (7.1.4.3)

If you want to revisit sites, a quick way to do this is to use the Browser Address bar. This displays the addresses of any sites you have visited. If you select the address, it will appear in the address bar of your browsing application. Once reloaded you may use the Enter key of your keyboard or choose the Go button.

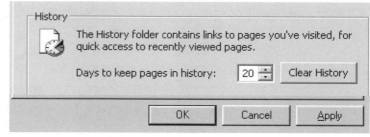

1.4.4 Delete Browsing History (7.1.4.4)

As you browse the Internet the website addresses are stored in a folder known as **History**. The storage of the addresses can be customised to suit your needs. In order to set the option to delete after 20 days, go into the View menu and select Internet Options… Make sure to select the **General** tab and view the History section. In the **Days to keep pages in history** select box, choose the number of days the history is to be kept for and then click on the **Apply** button followed by clicking on OK. If you want to delete outside the preset time, click on the **Clear History** button and then click **OK**.

1.5   Web Navigation

1.5.1   Accessing Web Pages

1.5.1.1 Go to a URL (7.2.1.1 and 7.1.1.4)

Every web page has its own unique address, known as a **URL** (uniform resource locator). See Section 1.1 of this module for more details.

When working with the Internet you will encounter two commonly used computer applications that assist you in navigating the Web – **Microsoft Internet Explorer** and **Netscape Navigator**. These are known as **browsers**. They allow people to access information, view images, hear sounds and watch video on the web. Other web browsers are available that work in a similar manner.

Many ISPs distribute software on CD-ROM that contains instructions for installing a browser on your computer. If the installation is successful, this will automatically configure your computer and establish a connection to the Web via the selected ISP. However, installing such software over a similar application that may already be present on your computer may cause problems. You should seek technical advice before using such CDs.

Once you have successfully connected to the Internet for the first time, be careful not to alter information in your settings as you may experience problems when you attempt to reconnect at a later stage. You should be advised that different ISPs require different information in the settings procedure. Expert advice is recommended.

To find and display a web page by typing an address, do the following:

- Click in the Address box. Your computer's home page address appears here.

  Alternatively, click again to the right of the current address in the address box. When the home page is downloaded, double click in the address box to select the address. Type over the old address with the new one you require. Use the backspace key to delete back to the dot after www to save typing the first part of the address again.

MODULE 7

395

- Type the new address.

- Press the Enter key or click the Go button at the end of the address box.

NOTE:

| You do not need to type **http://** when you are typing an address. Start with **www**. |

1.5.1.2 Activating a Hyperlink/Image Link (7.2.1.2)

As you move the mouse over text on the web page, notice that the arrow pointer changes to the I-beam cursor. However, for some of the text or images, the mouse pointer changes to a hand with a pointing finger. This indicates that the text or image is a **hyperlink**.

A hyperlink is a piece of text, an object or a graphic that acts like a button. Clicking a hyperlink performs a small action such as moving to a different part of the same page or displaying a new one.

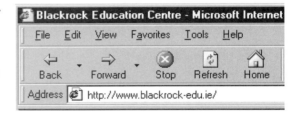

Pointer changes to a hand

1.5.1.3 Navigating between Previously Visited Web Pages (7.2.1.3)

As you click on links to go from page to page, you can use the browser buttons to assist you. Some of them are described here.

- **The Back** button returns to the previous page.

- The **Forward** button moves to the next page (but only if you have previously moved back).

- The **Stop** button stops the current action. Use this if the page is taking too long to appear or you change your mind about what you are doing.

- The **Refresh** button reloads the current page. Use this button if the page has not appeared properly or if you know it has changed since it first appeared.

- The **Home** button returns to the Home Page as set in the browser.

1.5.1.4 Web-based Forms (7.2.1.4)

Online shopping is a very popular form of using the Internet and many supermarkets provide an online shopping service to their customers. It is possible for a user to log on and choose from a stock list of groceries, and when the choices have been made, payment is made by credit card and the groceries are delivered at a prearranged time. In order to practise this part of the ECDL programme you must go to a practice site. Use the following procedure:

- Start your browser application by double clicking on the Internet Explorer shortcut key on the desktop or by using Start Menu, Programs, Internet Explorer.

- In the Address bar type in the address: **http://www.ecdlmanual.org/syllabus4**

  A **Login Box** will appear. This box has to be completed before you can enter the website.

- In lower case, type the word **blackrock** in the **User Name** box.

- Type in **ecdl** in the **Password** box.
  Remember that these words must be typed in lowercase.

- Click on the **OK** button to proceed.
  The support website window will open.

- Go to the **Complete a Form** link.

- Click with the left button of your mouse when the pointer changes to a hand while it is over this text.
  The form window will open.

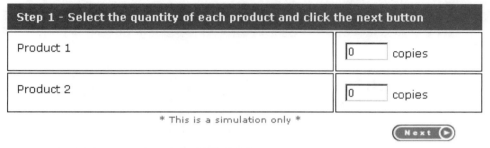

Step 1 - Select the quantity of each product and click the next button	
Product 1	0 copies
Product 2	0 copies

* This is a simulation only *

- Type the required information into the different boxes.

- Click on the **Next** button to proceed to the next step.
  A confirmation window will open when you have successfully completed the form or a transaction over the Internet.

NOTE

This is a simulation exercise. Information is not stored or retrieved from this exercise.

1.5.2   Using Bookmarks

1.5.2.1 Bookmarking a Web Page (7.2.2.1)

When you use the Internet on a frequent basis it is nice to be able to store your favourite addresses and site addresses so that you will not have to remember where the site is located on the Net. This facility is known as using **Favorites**. In order to store a website address in your browser, follow these steps:

- Go to a site with an address you want to store.

- Make sure that the web address is highlighted in the Address bar.

- Click the **Favorites** button in the Standard Buttons toolbar.
  The Favorites side panel opens in the browser page.

- Click on Add ...
  The Add Favorites window opens.

- In this window you can choose to add your web address to a predefined folder such as Links or Media.

- Click the **Create In** button if the full window is not displaying.

- The full window will then display all the folders available to you. The **New Folder...** button allows you to create a new folder if you select this button.

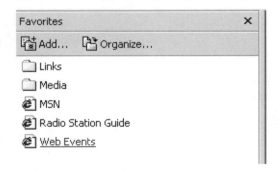

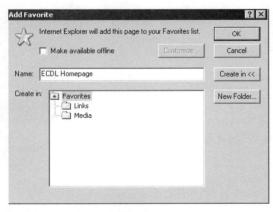

MODULE 7

- Type in the new folder name and click on the **OK** button to accept or click on **Cancel** to reject.

1.5.2.2 Displaying a Bookmarked Web Page (7.2.2.2)

If you want to display a bookmarked web page just follow the steps above and then select one of the saved web pages of your choice.

1.5.3   Organising Bookmarks

1.5.3.1 Creating a Bookmark Folder (7.2.3.1)

The Favorites folder can become quite clogged the more you add pages, so it is important to organise your web pages on a regular basis. Creating a folder for categories of pages is the best way of organising your Favorites folder and this can be done following these steps:

- Click on the **Organize**… button in the Favorites panel.
  The Organize Favorites window opens.

- In the Organize window select the **Create folder** option.

- Now type a relevant name for the folder.

- Click OK.

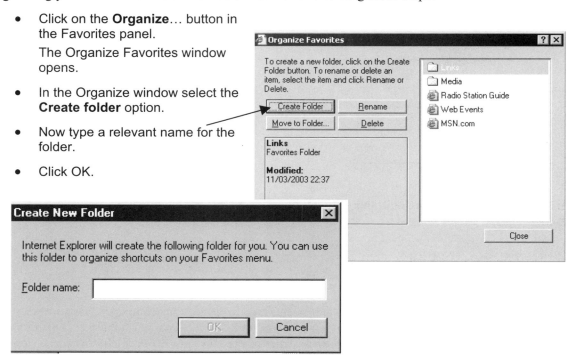

1.5.3.2 Adding Web Pages to a Bookmark Folder (7.2.3.2)

Make sure the Favorites panel is displayed on the left-hand side of your screen. Now click on the URL in the Address bar and drag and drop it in the folder you want to place it into.

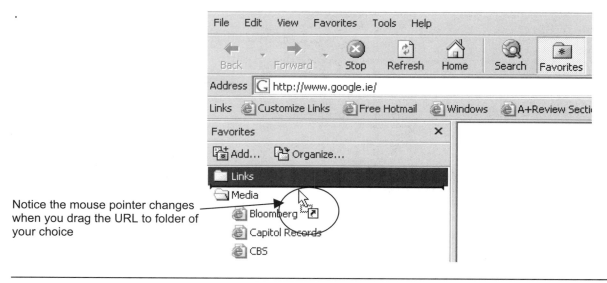

Notice the mouse pointer changes when you drag the URL to folder of your choice

MODULE 7

You can also move the URL to a folder by selecting the web address in the **Organize Favorites** window and then use the **Move to Folder...** option

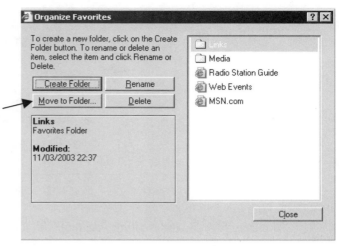

Click on URL and use the
Move to Folder button

1.5.3.3 Deleting a Bookmark (7.2.3.3)

Always make a conscious effort to delete unwanted bookmarks on a regular basis. This can be done easily by selecting the URL and clicking **Delete** in the Organize Favorites window.

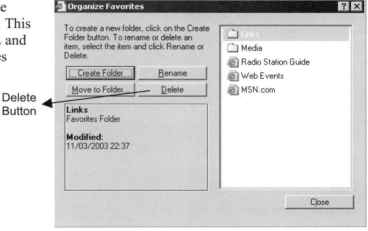

Delete
Button

1.6   Web Searching

1.6.1   Using a Search Engine

1.6.1.1 Selecting a Specific Search Engine (7.3.1.1)

A **search engine** is a program that helps you to find information on the Web. It stores listings of websites from all over the world and makes them easily available. There are many different search engines associated with the Internet, such as AltaVista, Yahoo, Google and Webcrawler to name just a few. In order to open the Google search engine follow these steps:

- Click on the Address bar with your mouse.

- Type http://www.google.ie.

- Click the Go button to right of the address bar.

- The web page for Google will be displayed.

1.6.1.2 Searching for Information Using Keywords and Phrases (7.3.1.2)

Searching often results in a very large number of pages being found, so do the following:

- Open Internet Explorer.

- Go to the Google site (www.google.ie).

- Type blackrock in the search box.

- Click on pages from the Ireland radio button.

- Click the Google Search button.

  The results page will show the number of web pages found containing the word 'blackrock' – in this case, 73 pages.

The results are listed in order, starting with those with the highest hits on their website.

10 or 20 sites are listed at the bottom of each page. The current page is emboldened.

Blackrock Education Centre
Blackrock Education Centre provides support, services and resources to teachers and to other partners in education in an atmosphere that is friendly ...
Description: Provides support for teachers in the south Dublin and Wicklow areas, and is financed by the Department...
Category: Regional > Europe > ... > Dublin > Localities > Blackrock > Education
www.blackrock-edu.ie/ - 2k - 17 Mar 2003 - Cached - Similar pages

To move through the pages you have three options:

- Click on the number 2 to see the next page.

- Click any page number to go to a particular page.

  Goooooooooogle ▶

  Result Page: 1 2 3 4 5 6 7 8 9 10   **Next**

- Click Next at the end of the list to go to the next set of pages, listing further sites.

1.6.1.3 Combining Selection Criteria in a Search (7.3.1.3)

Typing a word or two into a search engine usually brings up a wide range of results that can be confusing and unhelpful. Typing **blackrock** finds millions of matches. Such a list is of little use as it is far too extensive. The search needs to be refined or formed so it more specifically searches for the information you are looking for, such as if you are only interested in blackrock education in Dublin.

The more precise the key word or phrase you use, the more relevant the results will be. Some ways to narrow your search in order to find more relevant information are described here.

- Go to the Google site again.

- Click on pages from the Ireland radio button.

- Type blackrock + education in the search box.

- Typing **+** before a word means that the word must be included in the results.

- Typing **–** before a word means that the word must be excluded.

- Click the Google Search button. The number of pages found is now less.

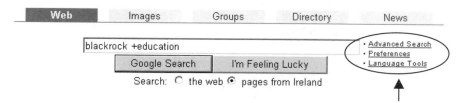

There is usually an **Advanced Search** button. Note the
links on the right to help you with advanced searches.

Here are some tips to help you use search engines effectively.

- Use the + and – symbols to include or exclude words, as described above.

- When you use uppercase letters (capitals), the search will find only capital letters. Lowercase finds both lower and upper case.

- To search for an exact word order, use quotation marks, e.g. **"Trinity College Dublin"**.

In Web Crawler, typing **trinity college dublin** without quotes finds over 100,000 pages. With quotes, the number of pages found is reduced to hundreds.

When you are not sure of the exact word or phrase to use, you can expand your search by using wildcard symbols. For example, program* finds programme, programming, programs and so on.

The websites of many large organisations can be accessed by typing in just a single word, e.g. yahoo, aerlingus, dogpile, eu, united nations and national geographic.

Meta search engines, such as **dogpile** and **askjeeves,** search all the regular search engines simultaneously and save you the bother of going to each one.

The **askjeeves** search engine allows you to type questions in normal English.

1.6.1.4 Duplicating from a Web Page to a Document (7.3.1.4)

All material that is accessible on the Internet is covered by international copyright, therefore, permission must be sought from the owners before any data can be used. A simple e-mail to the owners will usually get a positive response. In order to avoid problems at a later stage, copies of the responses should be kept in safe location. Go to **ww.ecdlmanual.org/syllabus4** to practise. Ordinarily, permission must be received from the site owners. Follow these steps after you have entered the website:

- Click on the Learn About Text link.

- Highlight the text by dragging the mouse over it.

- In the Edit menu, select copy.

- Now open a word processing document.

- Select Paste from the Edit menu in the word processing document.

To copy an image, follow these steps:

- Click the Download Media link.

- Click on the image with the right button of the mouse.

- A Shortcut menu appears.

- Choose the Copy command.

Shortcut Menu

MODULE 7

- Now open a word processing document.

- Select Paste from the Edit menu in the word processing document.

- If you save the file now the picture will be included within it.

When copying a URL to a Microsoft Word document, make sure you have selected the URL first and then use the Copy command in the File menu on the menu bar of the web window. Next, choose the Paste command in the Edit menu on the Menu bar of your word processing window.

1.6.1.5 Saving a Web Page to a Drive (7.3.1.5)

Web pages can be saved with or without graphics in order to minimise the amount of storage space on your computer. To save a web page, follow this procedure.

- On the Menu toolbar of an open web page choose File.

- Click Save As…
  The Save Web Page window opens.

Choose your location in the **Save in** box. Following this, give your file a name in the **File name** box. If you want to save with the graphics you can use the **web page complete (*.htm, *.html)** file type options. If you want to save the web page without the graphics you can choose to save it as a **Text file (*.txt)**.

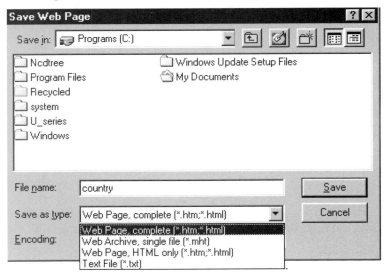

1.6.1.6 Downloading from a Web Page to a Drive (7.3.1.6)

Sometimes files are too large to be displayed in full on the Internet and are compressed in order to save space. When you go to open these, you are presented with a choice of either opening them while on the Internet (this could take some time if you are working from a modem) or you could select the option of saving them to a new location, e.g. the floppy disk or hard disk of your computer.

Files can have different formats and in order for you to work with them you may need to have a copy of the associated program which was used by the author to save them onto the Internet in the first place. Two popular formats are Pkzip and Acrobat, and evaluation copies of these can be downloaded from the Internet.

Image, sound and video files also have specific formats associated with them and here, too, you will need to have a copy of the particular software associated with their creation in order to run these afterwards.

To practise downloading a text file, image file, sound file and video file go the website **www.ecdlmanual.org/syllabus4**

1.6.2   Preparation

1.6.2.1 Web Page Formats (7.3.2.1, 7.3.2.2 and 7.3.2.3)

Before you print a web page it is useful to preview it and make sure that what you want printed is in view. There are a number of choices to be made in the pre-print choices.

- Go to **File** on the Menu toolbar.

- Select Print Preview…

The preview window has a specific toolbar which allows you to manipulate your web page in respect of its printing, page setup and navigating between each of the web pages if there is more than one.

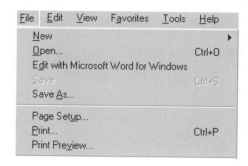

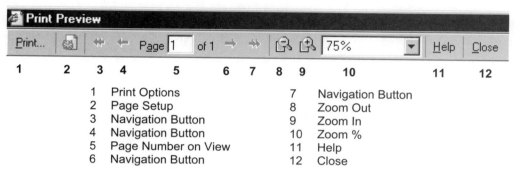

1 Print Options	7 Navigation Button
2 Page Setup	8 Zoom Out
3 Navigation Button	9 Zoom In
4 Navigation Button	10 Zoom %
5 Page Number on View	11 Help
6 Navigation Button	12 Close

To change the print options, paper size and so on do the following:

- Click the **Print…** button in the Preview window.

- Select the various items you require.

- Click **OK** when you have made your choices.

- If you click the **Print** button the choices you made will be carried out.

To alter the page orientation:

- Click the **Page Setup** button on the Preview window toolbar.

- Select either Portrait or Landscape.

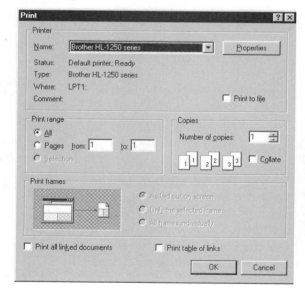

MODULE 7

In this window you can also adjust the measurements for each of the margins. A preview window is displayed showing the chosen adjustments.

If **OK** is chosen the new measurements will be reflected in the printed copy of the document. Clicking **Cancel** means you can rethink your requirements.

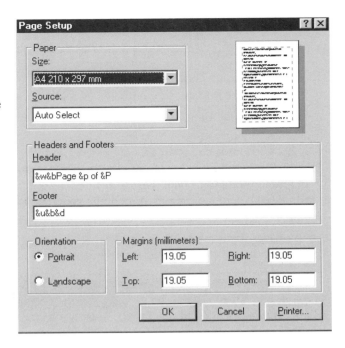

1.6.3 Printing

1.6.3.1 Web Page Print Options (7.3.3.1)

Remember when you want to print your web page that you will have to decide the print range – **All, Pages from** or **Selection** and the amount of copies of the pages. These options are clearly laid out in the Print window. First click on the File menu and select the **Print...** command. The Print window will open and now you can select one of the following options from the Print range.

All	This option prints the entire document.
Pages from	This option allows you to choose which pages to print.
Selection	This option allows you to select a specific part of the document to print.

In the **Copies** section you can decide how many copies of the document you want to print. If you choose more than one copy you can specify if you want them collated by selecting the **Collate** option.

When designing a web page it is possible for the designer to divide the page into a number of definite areas that can be scrolled up and down by the user. These divisions are referred to as **frames**. When the browser senses that frames have been used, the **Print frames** area becomes active. If frames have not been used, this area remains greyed out – this situation applies to most modern web pages. Check out the website at **www.ecdlmanual.org/syllabus4** for better understanding of these.

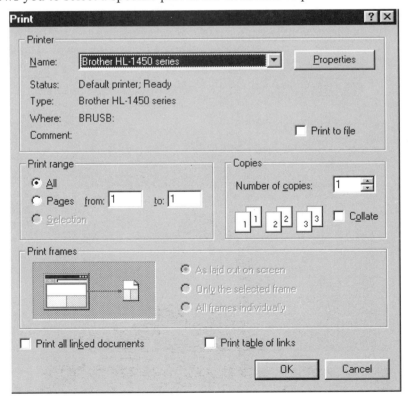

There are three print options available if your page contains frames. They are:

1 As laid out on screen – this prints the active page as you see it.

2 Only the selected frame – prints the section of the page that is active or that contains the cursor.

3 All frames individually – prints the page content one frame at a time.

Finally, having made all your choices, click OK to send your file to the printer.

NOTE

Before you start printing, make sure your printer is turned on and there is paper in it.

MODULE 7

Section 2   Communication

2.1   Electronic Mail

2.1.1 Concepts and Terms

In 1971, Ray Tomilinson sent the first e-mail. By 1998, some 14 million members of the ISPAmerica OnLine (AOL) sent 1 billion e-mail messages. It is estimated today that there are over 540 million Internet users.

2.1.1.1 Advantages of E-mail (7.4.1.2)

Electronic mail, or **e-mail** as it is commonly known, is the most widely used facility available on the Internet. Mail programs such as **Microsoft Outlook**, **Outlook Express**, **Netscape Mail**, **Eudora** and **Pegasus Mail** allow messages to be received locally or internationally for the price of a local telephone call.

E-mail is fast, cheap and convenient. You can send an e-mail to an individual or to a group of people at the same time. You can create mailing lists that send mail automatically to particular people. In addition, you can attach files such as spreadsheets, pictures and sounds to your e-mail messages.

E-mail messages can be prepared in advance before you connect to your ISP and then sent when you connect, which saves on telephone costs. When you are preparing mail without being connected, you are working **offline**. When you are connected, you are **online**.

E-mail is delivered immediately to the **recipient's ISP**, where it is stored and awaits collection. It does not go directly to the recipient's computer. Upon connecting to the ISP, the computer checks to see if there is any e-mail. Only then is it downloaded to the individual's computer. It works like the post office box system. The mail is not sent to your home but placed in a box at the post office. You do not see your mail until you go to the post office to collect it.

E-mail is collected automatically when you connect to the ISP and open the e-mail application. The e-mail application can be used to manage and compose e-mails without being connected. You can dial up your connection at any time while you are using the program to check for mail. The application can be set to check for mail at regular intervals.

Web-based e-mail refers to e-mail accounts whose functions are entirely located with an ISP. Unlike normal e-mail, which is opened from and downloaded to your home or office computer, Web-based mail is accessed on the ISP's computer. Your mail is stored remotely and when you open up your mail, it remains stored remotely and it is not downloaded to your computer. Web-based mail has the advantage of allowing you access to your mail wherever you are in the world. Normally, a username and a password along with the Web address of your ISP is sufficient to access your mail from any computer connected to the Internet.

It is possible to set up your normal e-mail account on another computer but this can be tricky, as there are a number of codes and settings to be remembered. Setting up someone else's computer to receive your mail is not always appropriate, as you can surrender your privacy in this manner and allow others to view your mail.

Web-based mail provides you with considerable flexibility in terms of access and also protects your privacy. You should note though that ISPs normally have limitations on the size and amount of e-mails you can store.

MODULE 7

Listed below are the basic hardware and software requirements you need to use e-mail.

1. A **modem** – this is an acronym for modulator demodulator. The modem changes the digital signal from your computer to the analogue signal of your telephone line. It can be located internally in your computer or linked externally.

2. A telephone line – this enables you to link to your ISP.

3. An account with an Internet service provider (**ISP**). With ISPs such as Hotmail or Yahoo, the account can be free of charge. Some ISPs require a fee for the service.

4. If you are already on a network in your place of work, a network Internet connector (**NIC**) will be required.

5. A browser is required. This is a piece of software that allows your computer to communicate across the Internet. The two most popular browsers are Internet Explorer and Netscape Navigator.

6. You will also need to have an e-mail client. This is a computer program on your machine that allows you to create, send, receive and manage your e-mail.

2.1.1.2 Make-up and Structure of an E-mail Address (7.4.1.1)

You need an e-mail address before you can send or receive e-mail on your computer. A unique e-mail address is allocated to you when you sign up with an ISP. The address is usually written in lowercase (small) letters and contains no spaces. A distinctive feature is the @ symbol which separates the person's name from the domain part of the address

In this example, Ethna Boland has an e-mail address in Ireland with Blackrock Education Centre. She has chosen **ethnab** as her username. Her address would be read aloud as "**Ethna B at blackrock hyphen edu dot ie**" but written as shown on the right.

Each e-mail address must be unique. The part after the @ symbol is usually the same for a particular ISP or company, so the person's actual name – before the @ symbol – cannot be duplicated. People often use a variation of their actual name to distinguish them from others with similar names. If Ethna Boland, for example, wanted to have the name **eboland**, she may discover that this particular name has already been taken. She would then have to choose another.

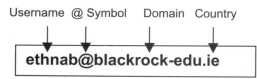

2.1.1.3 Network Etiquette (7.4.1.3)

The development of the Internet has created a true global village bringing together people with varying views, ideas and customs. In order that everyone can communicate without misunderstandings, a simple set of rules has emerged to form a convention for writing e-mails, known as **netiquette**. The netiquette protocol requires you to type a subject heading, to keep the message brief and ensure that your spellings are correct. The writing style is informal. E-mails are personal and the expectation is that they will be dealt with by the addressee. When you receive an e-mail you are expected either to respond or acknowledge its receipt.

2.2   Security Considerations

2.2.1   Unsolicited E-mail (7.4.2.1)

E-mail is a popular form of communication and is a powerful tool for placing messages right in front of the computer user. This facility is availed of by marketing and advertising companies as well as not-so-reputable businesses to advertise their services. Unwanted e-mail, known as **spam** or junk mail, has become an increasingly popular way for companies to reach people. A good way of preventing spam is to have a small number of e-mail addresses, one for business making sure you only give this address to those who are doing business with you and another for personal use. You must be careful when

MODULE 7

surrendering your e-mail address and personal details on Internet forms that you are not allowing them to be passed on to other vendors or inviting unsolicited mail.

2.2.2 E-mail Viruses (7.4.2.2)

A virus is a program that has been designed to interefere with the normal running of a computer. The Internet is a very convenient way of conveying viruses. E-mail attachments are notorious for carrying hidden viruses from computer to computer.

If you are unsure about the source of any e-mail message and if you were not expecting an e-mail with an attachment, consider deleting the message.

Be particularly wary of attachments with the extension **.exe**.

Note the check box at the bottom of the **Open Attachment Warning** window. Always check the box **Always ask before opening this type of file**. It is important to understand that this warning notice is not a virus checker, it is simply a warning notice. If you unclick this box, the warning will not be displayed in the future and the risk of virus infection is increased.

2.2.3 Digital Signature (7.4.2.3)

A digital signature is an electronic message or tag that may be used to validate the identity of the source of a message. It also certifies that the original matter of the message or document is intact. When working with e-mail over the Internet, security and privacy are particularly important. Digital signatures associated with reputable sources of information provide a level of guarantee in this regard.

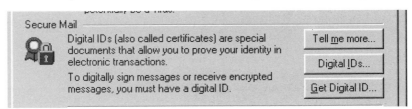

2.3   First Steps with E-mail

2.3.1 Opening and Closing an E-mail Application (7.4.3.1)

There are several mail programs available. The program used in this module, Outlook Express, is found on many Windows (95, 98, 2000, XP, ME) computers. You should be aware, though, that there are several different e-mail applications on the market.

To open Outlook Express, double click the icon on the desktop or click the icon on the taskbar.

Outlook Express

When Microsoft Outlook opens for the first time, it appears as in the illustration below.

To close the application, open the File menu and select Exit or click the Close button on the top right-hand corner of the window.

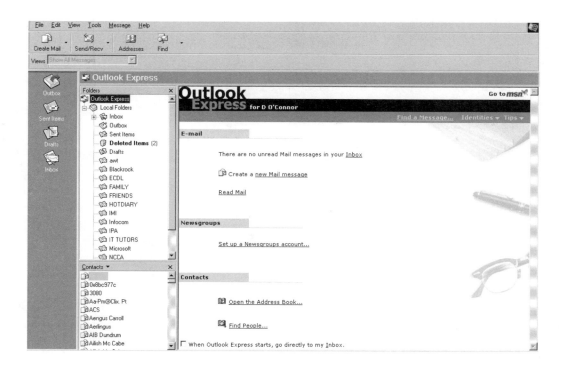

2.3.2   Opening a Mail Inbox for a Specified User (7.4.3.2)

Creating **users** (identity) within Outlook Express allows several people to share the same mailbox. For example, you and your work colleagues may share a computer. Each of you may become a user. When you log on under your **username** (identity), you can view your own e-mail. By using a unique password with your user (identity) name, your information can be kept private. Should your e-mails not be of a private nature, you can allow your mail to be opened along with other users' in the group.

Users are normally set up by the IT administrators in a company or organisation.

When you log in with your username to read your mail, the username itself will be displayed on the Outlook Express Title bar.

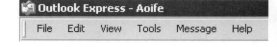

It is possible to switch from one user to another using these steps:

- Click on **Inbox** in the Folders panel displayed to the left-hand side of the application window.

- Open the **File** menu on the Menu bar.

- Select **Switch Identities**...

- Choose an alternative identity with mouse.

- Click **OK**.
  The new user's name will be displayed on the Title bar as Outlook Express presents the user's mail. Outlook Express may request a password before allowing access to the user's mail should the user's identity also include password protection.

MODULE 7

2.3.3   Opening E-mail Messages (7.4.3.3)

Outlook Express stores e-mail messages in different folders. Incoming messages are stored in a folder called the **inbox**. To view the e-mail in the inbox follow these steps:

- Click the **Inbox** if it has not already been clicked.

- A list of messages already received appears on the right panel. Each message is represented by an envelope icon.

- The sender, subject and other details are displayed for each message in columns beside the icon.

- Click on a message to display its contents in the **Preview** panel in the lower section of the window.

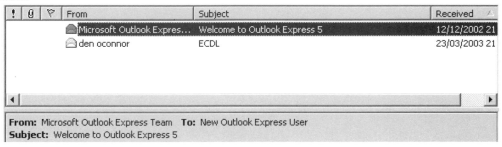

2.3.4   Switching between Open Messages (7.4.3.4)

In order to fully open an e-mail, simply double click on the icon with your mouse and a message window will open up on your screen. If there is more than one e-mail to be opened, hold down the **Ctrl** key while selecting the e-mails in turn. Right click the mouse and select **Open** from the shortcut menu. Each of the message windows will open in turn on screen. To navigate through the messages, use the **Previous** and **Next** buttons located on the toolbar.

Alternatively, you can use the **View** menu and select **Previous Message** or **Next**.

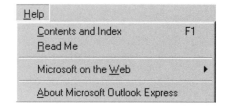

2.3.5   Closing E-mail Messages (7.4.3.5)

When you are finished with an opened message, you can close it by using the **Close** command in the File menu or by clicking the **Close** button on the e-mail's Title bar.

2.3.6   Using Help Functions (7.4.3.6)

From time to time you may need assistance with particular functions of Outlook Express. To gain assistance or additional information you can use the Help function for assistance you may require. Clicking the **F1** key brings up help from anywhere within the application. Refer to the Before You Begin module for a more detailed description of using the help function.

2.4   Adjusting Settings

2.4.1   Message Inbox Headings (7.4.4.1)

You can manage and arrange your inbox column preferences to suit your particular needs. The display can be customised using the available options as follows:

- Make sure you are in the **Inbox** folder.

- Click on the **View** menu.

- Select **Columns**.

- Select the column headings you want visible and then click the Show button. *Alternatively*, if you do not want a column displayed, select the column heading and click the Hide button.

- Click **OK**.

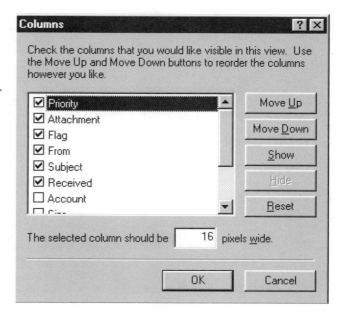

2.4.2 Displaying and Hiding Built-in Toolbars (7.4.4.2)

By default there is only one toolbar visible when you open Outlook Express. This view can be customised to show other toolbars that are available. If you open the **View** menu and select **Layout...** you will be presented with a window that enables you to select and deselect display options. When you are finished choosing your preferred options, click the **OK** button to accept the new view or **Cancel** to leave the view as it is.

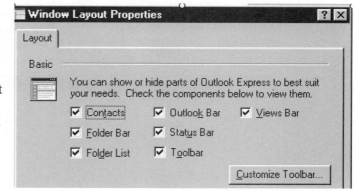

2.5   Messaging

2.5.1   Reading a Message

2.5.1.1 Flagging an E-mail Message (7.5.1.1)

Upon receiving an e-mail you may decide to attend to it later. By placing a flag beside the e-mail it is relatively easy to locate it again when you glance down your list of received mail. In order to do this, just follow one of these steps:

- Click to the left of a message to select it.

- From the **Message** menu select **Flag Message**.

2.5.1.2 Marking a Message as Unread or Read (7.5.1.2)

Messages displayed in the inbox are marked either as **read** or **unread**. There is a difference in appearance of the icons and the text associated with the read and unread mail. When an e-mail is unread, the icon is a closed envelope and the message text is **bold**. The ☑ **LiamCork** read message is indicated by an open envelope and the message text is normal.

Should the Preview window option be active, the icon and text message associated with the selected e-mail will take on the **read** status after a few seconds. The preview ✉ LiamCork option is available from the View menu and Layout options.

MODULE 7

Messages may also be manually marked as read or unread using the following procedures:

- Right click on any given message and select **Mark as Read** or **Mark as Unread** in the menu that appears.

  Alternatively, highlight the message and select **Mark as Read** or **Mark as Unread** in the **Edit** menu.

To mark all your messages as either read or unread do the following:

- In the **Edit** menu choose **Select All**.

- Return to the **Edit** menu and choose **Read** or **Unread** as appropriate.

2.5.1.3 Saving a File Attachment (7.5.1.3)

Practically any type of computer file can be added to an e-mail message as an **attachment**. Word documents, spreadsheets, pictures, sounds, etc. can all be sent to another person quickly and cheaply.

In order to open an attachment, you can follow one of these options:

- Open the e-mail and double click on the attachment icon.

  Alternatively, click on the Attachment icon in the inbox on the **Preview Header** pane.

When saving the file attachment you may use the following procedures:

- Right click the **Attachment icon** and choose **Save Attachment...** on the pop-up menu.

- Follow the normal procedure of saving from this point.

  Alternatively, right click the **Attachment icon** in the e-mail window to access the Saved Attachment option and the Save in box.

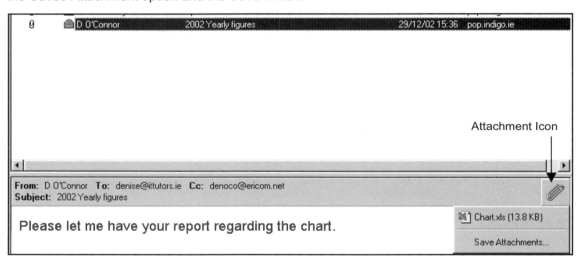

Attachment Icon

2.5.2   Replying to a Message

2.5.2.1 Reply Functions (7.5.2.1 and 7.5.2.2)

It is not necessary to click the **New Mail** button when you want to reply to a message. Two buttons on the toolbar help you to reply to messages that you have received.

The **Reply** button opens a new message window with the address of the sender in the **To** box.

The **Reply All** button opens a new message window addressed to all the recipients of the message if it was originally addressed to more than one person.

Follow these steps to use the reply options:

- Click the message in the inbox to which you want to reply.

- For this exercise, click the message that you have sent to yourself (and received).

- Click the Reply button to reply to the message. In this example, the reply goes back to yourself (again!). A new message window opens.

- Notice the following features of the new message window:

  The e-mail address for the reply is already inserted in the **To** box.

  The **Subject** box contains the word **Re:** and the subject of the original message.

The message panel displays the text of the e-mail with the heading **--- Original Message ---**. This particular option is activated by default in Outlook Express. To deactivate this display option unclick the **'Include message in reply'** in the **Tools** menu under **Options** and click the **Send** tab.

- Click in the message area of the window and type the reply. It is customary to type the reply above the original message.

- Click the Send button to send the message.

2.5.3 Sending a Message

2.5.3.1 Creating a New Message (7.5.3.1, 7.5.3.2, 7.5.3.3 and 7.5.3.4)

It is important to note that the procedure for setting up an e-mail account is not part of your studies for ECDL. It is assumed here that your e-mail account has been set up with an authorised ISP and that you are using Outlook Express as your default mail application.

To create a new e-mail message, follow this procedure:

- Open Outlook Express.

- Click the Create Mail button on the toolbar or select New Message in the Message menu.

  The New Message window opens.

- In the **To** box, type in the recipient's e-mail address, e.g. ethnab@netlink.ie.

- In the Subject box, type a brief subject heading for the message.

- Typing a subject is a recognised protocol.

- Type the message in the main part of the window.

- Enter additional recipient e-mail addresses in the To box, separating the addresses with a semicolon should you require others to receive the message.

You can also use the Cc (carbon copy or courtesy copy) box to include additional recipient addresses. Cc is generally used when recipients are not required to act on the message.

The Bcc (blind carbon copy) is similar in use to the Cc function. It allows the user

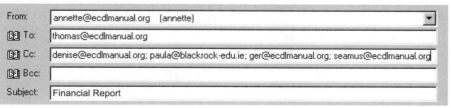

to send a copy of an e-mail to a recipient confidentially without the other addressees on the list being notified that this has been done.

Should the Bcc box not be displayed in the **New Message** window, go to the **New Message** window and select **All Headers** in the **View** menu.

To send an e-mail message you have just created, do the following:

- Click the **Send** button on the Message toolbar.

  The message is temporarily placed in the Outbox folder.

  Compose any further e-mails you require using the procedure above and use the Send button to place them in the Outbox folder.

- Click the **Send/Recv** button on the Outlook Express toolbar to post your mail.

- If you are working on a home computer, you may be prompted to connect to your telephone line. Should you be working on a network computer that is online at all times, there may be no connection requirements

2.5.3.2 Spell Check (7.5.3.5)

Make sure before sending your e-mail that the spellings are checked. This option can be easily set up so that the spellings can be checked automatically before the e-mail is sent using the following procedure:

- Select the **Tools** menu.

- Click on **Options**.

- Click on the **Spelling** tab in the window.

- Click on **Always check spelling before sending**.

- Now click the **Apply** button.

- Click **OK**.

  Should this option not be active you may manually check spelling errors when you have completed the e-mail by clicking the **Spelling** button on the toolbar.

  Alternatively, select **Spelling** in the **Tools** menu.

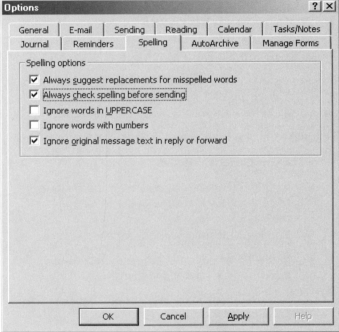

The spelling window will open and the in-built dictionary will suggest the correct spelling option for given words. Other minor corrections will also be suggested.

2.5.3.3 Forwarding a Message (7.5.3.9)

There may be occasions when you need to send a received e-mail on to someone else. You can do this using the **Forward** option that is available on the e-mail **Standard** toolbar. Use the following procedure:

- Open Outlook Express and go to the Inbox folder.

- Select a message in the inbox that you want to forward to another person.

- Click the **Forward** button on the Inbox toolbar.

  The **Fw:** message window will open.

- Enter the name of the intended recipient in the **To** box.

  The **Subject** box contains the **Fw:** prefix and the subject of the original message.

  The message section of the window contains the e-mail text with the heading

--- **Original Message** --- automatically inserted.
You may add additional text if you wish.

- Click the **Send** button to forward the message.

2.5.3.4 Sending a Message with an Attachment (7.5.3.6)

In this section you will need to either create or locate a document that you can use as an attachment. Additionally, you will need to create a new e-mail. This e-mail will be used to carry the document across the Internet.

Step 1 – Create a document using Notepad and name it Yearly Report.

- Save this document in the My Documents folder.

Step 2 – Open Outlook Express to create a new e-mail.

- Click the Create Mail button. The New Message window will open.

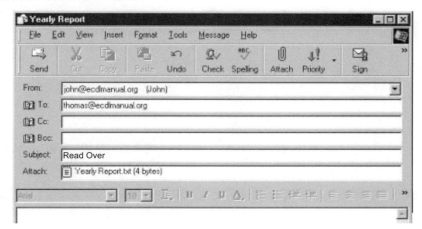

- Enter a destination address in the **To** box

- In the Subject box type the words Read Over.

- Click into the main message area of the e-mail window and type in a few chosen words.

Step 3 – Adding the attachment.

- Click the **Attach File to Message** button on the e-mail window toolbar.
  The Insert Attachment window opens.

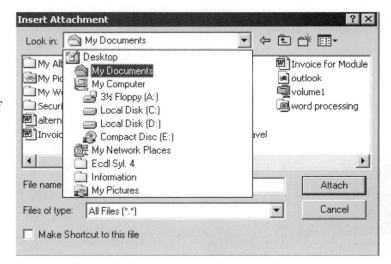

In the **Look in** box, find the location of the file you want to attach. For this example, locate the **Yearly Report** document you saved earlier in My Documents.

- Once you have found the file click to select it and then click the Attach button.

You will be returned to your e-mail window and within the **Attach bar**, an icon plus the file name will appear indicating that the file has been successfully linked with the message.

MODULE 7

2.5.3.5 Sending a Message with High or Low Priority (7.5.3.7)

Here we will give your message a **priority** level. Priority levels do not determine the speed at which the message is sent, it is simply a symbol indicating a level of importance of which you wish to notify your recipient.

There are three priority levels:

Normal (no symbol)

High (a red exclamation mark)

Low (a blue arrow)

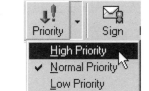

Messages are usually sent with normal priority. Assign a high level of priority using the following steps:

- Click the small arrow selector button to the right of the Priority button on the Standard toolbar to display the choices.
  Alternatively, select Set Priority in the Message menu.

- Select **High Priority.**
  A bar with the priority setting appears above the **To** box.

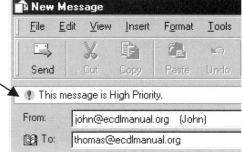

When the message is received, the recipient sees the priority mark to the left of the envelope icon in the received message list in the inbox.

2.5.4 Duplicating, Moving, Deleting

2.5.4.1 Duplicating and Moving Text (7.5.4.1)

Text in an e-mail can be manipulated in much the same manner as text in a word processing document. You can duplicate information within a message by using the Copy and Paste command. These buttons are located on the Standard toolbar of the e-mail window. Moving text within a message can also be done by using the Cut and Paste buttons on the Standard toolbar. *Alternatively*, you can avail of these commands in the Edit menu.

To duplicate or move information between active messages, make sure that both the source and the destination messages are open. Select the information from within the source message and then use either the Copy or Cut button as appropriate. Go to the destination e-mail, click in the message section of the window and click the Paste button. The text appears.

2.5.4.2 Duplicating Text from Another Source into a Message (7.5.4.2)

You can duplicate text from many open documents and place it into the message area of an e-mail. Follow these steps to copy information from a Word document into an e-mail message:

- Open any document where text can be located.

- Select a section of text and click the Copy button on the Standard toolbar.

- Open the e-mail program and click the Create Mail button.

- Click on the message area of the e-mail window and click the Paste button.
  The text appears.

- Complete the other sections of the e-mail before attempting to send it.

2.5.4.3 Deleting Text in a Message (7.5.4.3)

To delete information in an e-mail, select the appropriate text and then hit the **Delete** key on your keyboard. Should you delete text in error, click the Undo button to cancel the action. The text should then reappear.

2.5.4.4 Deleting a File Attachment from an Outgoing Message (7.5.4.4)

Should Outlook Express be set to store e-mails in the outbox before they are despatched, it is possible to delete attachments from messages you are forwarding, for example.

To remove an attachment from a message in the Outbox folders, do the following:

- Open the message in the normal manner.

- Right click the Attachment icon.

- Select **Remove** in the menu that appears beside the attachment.
  The attachment is deleted from the message.

- Send the message as normal.

2.6   Mail Management

2.6.1   Techniques

2.6.1.1 Efficient E-mail Management (7.6.1.1, 7.6.3.1 and 7.6.3.3)

As with other applications, you can set various e-mail options to suit your own way of working. These are available through the **Options** command in the Tools menu. To view the options do the following:

- Select **Options** in the Tools menu on the Standard toolbar.
  The Options window opens.

- Click the **Send** tab.

- In the lower part of the window, select or deselect the options you prefer by clicking in the check boxes.

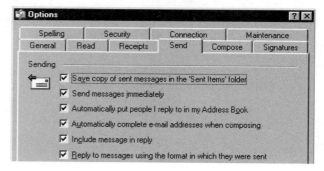

- To activate a choice, click an empty item check box. This will place a check mark in the box indicating that the option has been activated.
  Clicking a box that is already checked removes the check mark and deactivates the option.

Some of the options available are as follows:

Save copy... keeps a copy of all messages that you send.

Include message... inserts the original message when you use the Reply function.

Send messages... sends the message immediately when you click the **Send** button rather than placing them in the outbox.

2.6.1.2 Creating a New Message Folder

The Inbox and Sent Items folders become
cluttered very quickly. You may like to organise
the messages that you send and receive in a more
accessible manner using dedicated folders for
particular e-mails.

When you create a folder in Outlook Express, it
can be named appropriately to suit various
collections of e-mail such as family, friends,
work, club and so on.

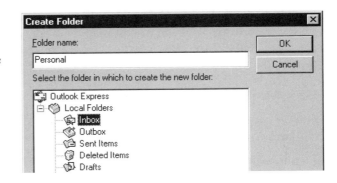

To create a new folder in the inbox, do the
following:

- Right click on the Inbox folder in the folder panel and select **New Folder**... from the menu that
  appears.

- Type **Personal** in the Folder Name box.

- Click OK.
  The new **Personal** folder is created as a sub-folder in the Inbox.

2.6.1.3 Moving and Copying Mail

Messages can be moved or copied from one folder to another. To move a message into the Personal
folder follow these steps:

- Select the message you want to move.

- Drag the message into the Folder List.

- Drop the message into the Personal
  folder.

- Do not release the mouse button until the
  Personal folder is highlighted.
  The message is then placed in the
  Personal folder.

- Click the Personal folder to view the
  messages inside.

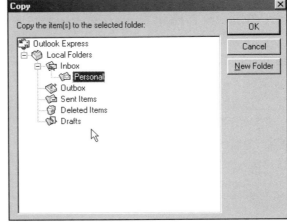

To place a copy of a message in another folder:

- Right click the message you want to copy.

- Select **Copy to Folder** in the menu that appears.

- *Alternatively*, select **Copy to Folder** in the **Edit** menu.

- In the Copy window, select the folder in which you want it to be placed.

- Click **OK**.

2.6.2 Using Address Books

2.6.2.1 Adding a Mail Address to an Address List (7.6.2.2)

The address book may be used to store e-mail addresses and other useful information about people
with whom you are in contact. You can then retrieve the information easily for use. Mailing groups,
often referred to as distribution lists, can be created should you need to send messages to a number of
recipients on a regular basis.

To add new contact details to the address book, do the following:

- Click the **Addresses** button on the toolbar.
  The Address Book window opens.

- Click the **New** button on the toolbar and select **New Contact** in the menu that appears.
  The **Properties** window opens.

- Type the first, middle and last name, the title and nickname in the appropriate boxes. Note that not all this information is required. Fill in as much as you need.

- Type the e-mail address in the **E-mail Addresses** box.

- Click the **Add** button.

The e-mail is set as the default address for that person.

If the person has more than one e-mail address, you can enter them all and then select the one you wish to set as the default by highlighting and clicking the **Set as Default** button.

To correct any mistakes you might have made in the entry, click the Edit button and retype.

To delete an address which may be one of many addresses for a contact, click to select it and then click the Remove button.

2.6.2.2 Deleting a Mail Address from an Address List (7.6.2.3)

Over time, contacts will change. To tidy up the address book, unused contacts can be deleted as follows:

- Open the Address Book.

- Right click the contact you wish to delete.

- Select **Delete** from the menu that appears.

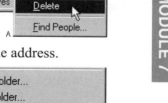

2.6.2.3 Updating an Address Book from Incoming Mail (7.6.2.4)

A sender's e-mail address can be sent directly to the address book from a received e-mail message. Using this procedure ensures accuracy in transferring the address.

- Right click on the message in the inbox or other folder.

- Select **Add Sender to Address Book** in the menu that appears.
  If the entry already exists, you will be prompted with a warning.

MODULE 7

- Open the address book to check the new entry.

- Double click on the address to add any additional information in the properties window that appears.

- Click the tabs at the top of the window for more detailed entries associated with the person you would like to record.

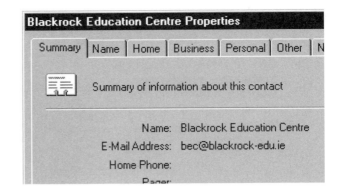

2.6.2.4 Previewing a Message (7.6.4.1)

There is a preview bar in Outlook Express and this allows you view the contents of an e-mail without opening it first. You can display this window either below the message list or beside it, or it can be hidden entirely if you wish. In the View menu click on Layout and in the Preview Pane section choose which options you want and then click the Apply button.

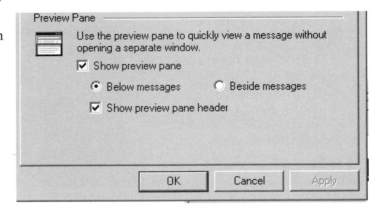

2.6.2.5 Distribution Lists (7.6.2.1 and 7.5.3.8)

To conveniently send an e-mail to several people at any one time, you can create what is known as a **group** or a distribution list. In this example, a group is created using the e-mail addresses of each member of a fictitious football team. The information will be stored in the **Contacts** folder of Outlook Express.

Enter the contact information into the **address book** using the following steps:

- Click the **Address Book** button in the Outlook Express program window. The Address Book window will open.

Addresses

- Click the New button and select New Contact. A New Contact window opens.

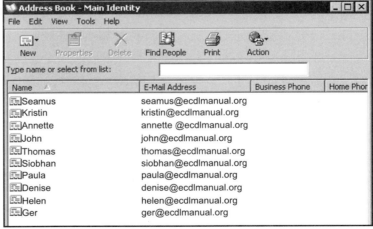

Address Book Window

MODULE 7

Now, include separate **contact** details for each member of the team.

- Type the name and e-mail address of the first team member into the appropriate boxes.

- Press the **Tab** key to go from one box to the next.

- Click the **Add** button to add the E-mail address to the box beneath.

- Click **OK**.

  Repeat this process for all the members of the team.

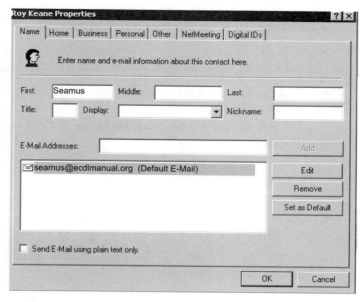

Name	E-mail Address	Name	E-mail Address
Seamus	seamus@ecdlmanual.org	Siobhan	siobhan@ecdlmanual.org
Kristin	kristin@ecdlmanual.org	Paula	paula@ecdlmanual.org
Annette	annette @ecdlmanual.org	Denise	denise@ecdlmanual.org
John	john@ecdlmanual.org	Helen	helen@ecdlmanual.org
Thomas	thomas@ecdlmanual.org	Ger	ger@ecdlmanual.org
Monica	monica@ecdlmanual.org		

Now bring together all the individual contact information under a single group name, in this instance, **Football Team.** Follow these steps:

- Click on the **Address Book** button to open the Address Book.

- In the Address Book window, click on the **New** button and select **New Group…**

- Type the name Football Team in the Group Name box.

- Click the **Select Members** button.
  The Select Group Members box appears.

- Click on each person and then the **Select** button adds the different e-mail addresses you have selected.

- Click **OK** when you are finished.
  The group name Football Team will be included on the mail identity list with other names in your address book.

To select the group from the address book as a target recipient of the new e-mail, use the following procedure to send the e-mail:

- Select the **Address** button on the Outlook Express toolbar.

- Right click the group name Football Team and choose **Action** from the menu.

- Select the **Send Mail** option.
  A New Message window opens with the group name included in the **To** bar.
  Complete the e-mail as you would normally do and follow the send procedure already described above.

MODULE 7

2.6.3   Organising Messages

2.6.3.1 Searching for a Message (7.6.3.1)

When you have many folders and large numbers of messages, you may need help to locate a particular one. You can search for messages with a number of criteria using the following procedure:

- Click the **Find a Message** button on the Standard toolbar in the Outlook Express window.
  Alternatively, select **Find** and **Message** in the **Edit** menu.

  The **Find Message** window opens.

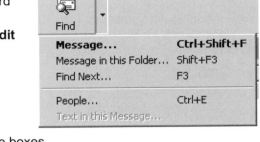

- Enter the required information in as many of the boxes as you can.

  The more information you can enter, the more detailed the search. You do not have to fill all the boxes.

- Select **Local Folders** to search all main folders and subfolders.

- Use the **Browse** button to select a particular folder to **Look in**.

- Make sure that you also select the dates in either the **Received before** or **Received after** boxes.

- Click **Find Now**.

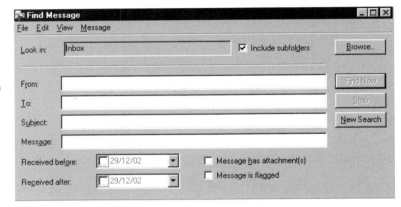

To begin a new search, click the **New Search** button.

2.6.3.2 Sorting Messages (7.6.3.4)

Messages in the **inbox** or other folders can be sorted according to the header labels subject, date and so on. To begin sorting a list of messages, do the following:

- Click the appropriate header bar at the top of the list to sort the messages.

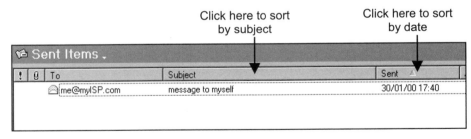

- Right click a header bar to select either Ascending or Descending for the sort.

(If there are no messages in the **inbox**, try the **Sent Items** folder in the left of the window. You will not be able to see the effect of sorting with only a single message.)

2.6.3.3 Deleting Messages

Mail is stored in the inbox and other folders until you decide to delete it. The first step in deleting an e-mail does not remove it altogether. It merely places the mail in a deleted items folder.

To delete mail, do the following:

- Click the message in the inbox (or other folder) that you want to delete.

- Click the **Delete** button on the toolbar.
  Alternatively, press the **Delete** key on the keyboard or select **Delete** in the **Edit** menu.
  The message is moved to the **Deleted Items** folder. (It is not actually deleted at this stage.)

Delete Button

2.6.3.4 Recovering a 'Deleted' Message

Double click the Deleted Items folder in the panel at the left of the Outlook Express window to open it.

Drag the message out of the folder and drop onto the inbox (or other folder).

If you deleted the sample message with the attachment, you should now move it back to the Inbox.

To permanently delete mail:

- Right click the Deleted Items folder.

- Select the Empty 'Deleted Items' Folder in the menu that appears.

Alternatively, select **Empty 'Deleted Items' Folder** in the **Edit** menu.

- The messages are now permanently deleted.

2.6.4   Preparing to Print

E-mail messages can be printed out as follows.

- Click the message you want to print to select it.

- Click the **Print** button on the toolbar.
  Alternatively, select **Print** in the **File** menu.

Print Button

- The Print window opens. It is similar to the Print window in other applications.

- In most circumstances, it is sufficient just to click **OK** to print the message.

2.6.4.1 Print Output Options (7.6.4.2)

When you decide you want to print an e-mail message you must ensure that the printer is turned on and that there is enough paper.

Now you must select the message you want printed. If you select the message in the Inbox you can print the entire message. Follow these steps:

- Click on the **Inbox** folder.

- Click on the e-mail message you wish to print.

Print Button

- Clink the **Print** button on the toolbar.

To print selected contents of a page you will need to open the e-mail first, then follow these steps:

- Click on the **Inbox** folder.

- Double click the e-mail whose contents you want printed. This will open the e-mail.

- Highlight the information to be printed.

- Click on the **File** menu on the menu bar.

- Select the **Print...** command. The Print window will open.

- Pick the **Selection** button in the Print Range section of the window.

- Click on **Print**.

To print more than one copy of an e-mail follow these steps:

- Click the Inbox folder.

- Double click to open the e-mail to be printed.

- Click on the File menu on the menu bar.
  In the number of copies area change the amount to the amount you require by either typing in the amount yourself or using the Selector buttons to the right of the number.

- Click on **Print** when you have made your choice.

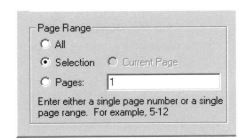

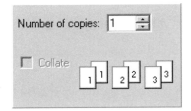

Index

Index

MODULE 7

MODULE 7

MODULE 7